A Different Order of Difficulty

D1548042

A Different Order of Difficulty
Literature after Wittgenstein

Karen Zumhagen-Yekplé

The University of Chicago Press :: Chicago and London

The University of Chicago Press, Chicago 60637
The University of Chicago Press, Ltd., London

Published 2020
Printed in the United States of America

29 28 27 26 25 24 23 22 21 20   1 2 3 4 5

ISBN-13: 978-0-226-67701-9 (cloth)
ISBN-13: 978-0-226-67715-6 (paper)
ISBN-13: 978-0-226-67729-3 (e-book)
DOI: https://doi.org/10.7208/chicago/9780226677293.001.0001

The University of Chicago Press gratefully acknowledges the generous
support of Tulane University toward the publication of this book.

Library of Congress Cataloging-in-Publication Data

Names: Zumhagen-Yekplé, Karen, author.
Title: A different order of difficulty : literature after Wittgenstein /
    Karen Zumhagen-Yekplé.
Description: Chicago : The University of Chicago Press, 2020. |
    Includes bibliographical references and index.
Identifiers: LCCN 2019032077 | ISBN 9780226677019 (cloth) |
    ISBN 9780226677156 (paperback) | ISBN 9780226677293 (ebook)
Subjects: LCSH: Wittgenstein, Ludwig, 1889–1951. Tractatus
    logico-philosophicus. | Modernism (Literature)—20th century—
    Philosophy. | Ethics in literature.
Classification: LCC B3376.W563 T7389 2020 | DDC 192—dc23
LC record available at https://lccn.loc.gov/2019032077

To you, the bold searchers and researchers, and whoever embarks with cunning sails on terrible seas—to you, drunk with riddles, glad of the twilight, whose soul flutes lure astray to every whirlpool, because you do not want to grope along a thread with cowardly hand; and where you can *guess*, you hate to *deduce*—to you alone I tell the riddle that I *saw*, the vision of the loneliest.

FRIEDRICH NIETZSCHE, "The Vision and the Riddle"

I have wandered to the limits of my understanding any number of times, out into that desolation, that Horeb, that Kansas, and I've scared myself, too, a good many times, leaving all landmarks behind me, or so it seemed. And it has been among the true pleasures of my life. Night and light, silence and difficulty, it seemed to me always rigorous and good.

MARILYNNE ROBINSON, *Gilead*

Getting hold of the difficulty *deep* down is what is hard.　　*like a plant*

　Because if it is grasped near the surface it simply remains the difficulty it was. It has to be pulled out by the roots; and that involves our beginning to think about these things in a new way. The change is as decisive as, for example, that from the alchemical to the chemical way of thinking. The new way of thinking is what is so hard to establish.

　Once the new way of thinking has been established, the old problems vanish; indeed they become hard to recapture. For they go with our way of expressing ourselves and, if we clothe ourselves in a new form of expression, the old problems are discarded along with the old garment.　　*yes*

LUDWIG WITTGENSTEIN, *Culture and Value*

Contents

Introduction: Difficulty, Ethical Teaching, and Yearning for Transformation in Wittgenstein's *Tractatus* and Modernist Literature

Did he find the problem . . . of . . . possible social and moral redemption . . . easier of solution?

Of a different order of difficulty.

—James Joyce[1]

We understand by immersing ourselves and our intelligence in complexity . . . the complexity of life.

—J. M. Coetzee[2]

Are you a bad philosopher then, if what you write is hard to understand? If you were better you would make what is difficult easy to understand.—But who says that's possible?!

—Ludwig Wittgenstein

People nowadays think that scientists exist to instruct them, poets, musicians, etc. to give them pleasure. The idea *that these have something to teach them*— that does not occur to them.

—Ludwig Wittgenstein[3]

Resolute Modernism

A Different Order of Difficulty argues that reading modernist literature after Wittgenstein—that is, in light of his contemporaneous writing, and in the wake of recent scholarly thinking about his philosophy—allows for a deeper understanding of the interwoven commitments related to the concerns with difficulty, oblique ethical

instruction, and a yearning for transformation that I argue lie at the core
of both Wittgenstein's philosophical method and literary modernism.
These three central preoccupations, I claim, also go on to shape modernism's afterlife in contemporary fiction.

Wittgenstein's declaration that his work was "strictly philosophical
and at the same time literary" has served as a generalized point of departure for a number of insightful and informative readings of his philosophy in a literary and cultural context since it first came to light.[4] And
yet, in our work as literary critics or philosophers or both, we have in
many ways only just begun to attend sufficiently to the rich relationship
between Wittgenstein's thought and the modernist literature that epitomizes his era's predominant cultural movement. The current moment is
a particularly exciting and timely one in which to engage in this ongoing
comparative, interdisciplinary work. The years leading up to the centenary of the completion of the *Tractatus* in 1918 saw an unprecedented
proliferation of new work on Wittgenstein and literature that builds on
earlier foundational scholarship spanning the fields of philosophy, intellectual history, art history, and literary criticism.[5]

A Different Order of Difficulty seeks to feed a growing critical interest in Wittgenstein and literature in a study that alternately engages, challenges, and complements existing treatments of the connections between
them. My intervention into the question of Wittgenstein's importance for
literary studies here strives to overcome the disciplinary divides between
philosophy and literature that often inhibit our grasp of this relationship
and thus our understanding of the various ways in which Wittgenstein's
philosophy is part of a larger intellectual and cultural movement.

In this book, I explore the relationship between Wittgenstein and
modernist literature by focusing attentively on a set of intersecting and
mutually illuminating formal, linguistic, ethical, and spiritual or existential concerns that Wittgenstein's philosophy shares with the modernist monuments of his literary contemporaries and the works of their
late-century heirs. These concerns coalesce around the three salient
modes of engagement I designated above—difficulty, ethical teaching,
and transformative yearning. Attending closely to these three core commitments affords us new ways of understanding the reciprocal relevance
of Wittgenstein's early philosophy and twentieth-century literature. I
work to make these new ways of understanding available in this book
through critical readings focused primarily on a set of key texts and fragments of literary high modernism and its afterlife—Franz Kafka's parable "Von den Gleichnissen" ("On Parables"), Virginia Woolf's *To the*

Lighthouse, James Joyce's *Ulysses,* and J. M. Coetzee's *The Childhood* *modernism*
of Jesus—each examined within the interpretive framework of a study
of Wittgenstein's *Tractatus Logico-Philosophicus.*

My reading of the *Tractatus* in this book is itself informed by the expanding so-called resolute program of Wittgenstein interpretation elaborated by philosophers James Conant and Cora Diamond, who remain
its leading proponents.[6] My aim is to make a literary-critical contribution to this interpretive program, one that sheds light on the relationship
between Wittgenstein's philosophy and modernist literature by attending closely to Wittgenstein's own (decidedly modernist) commitments
to difficulty, teaching, and transformation. These early commitments of
Wittgenstein's are largely obscured in more traditional literary-critical
and intellectual-historical treatments of his thinking, and thus too often
ignored in comparative literary-critical studies of Wittgenstein based on
these conventional accounts of his philosophy.

Finding new uses for Wittgenstein's thought in literary studies is this *project*
book's point of departure and the main focus of each of its five chapters.
A Different Order of Difficulty examines the *Tractatus* along resolute
lines in a series of sustained critical readings, each dedicated to a different writer, and all attentive to the points of philosophical and aesthetic kinship with each other and with Wittgenstein.[7] One of my central
claims here is that understanding Wittgenstein's philosophical project in
this way enables us to see how his philosophy, and recent scholarly work
in ordinary language philosophy and ethics conducted in a Wittgensteinian spirit, has an unprecedented power to awaken literary critics and philosophers alike to the ways in which the literature and philosophy of the
twentieth century and beyond are enlivened by the shared interrelated
commitments at the center of this study.

Conventional interpretations of the *Tractatus,* or what Conant and
Diamond refer to as "standard sorts of readings," broadly sketched, regard Wittgenstein's early book as one concerned with setting forth a series of substantive philosophical doctrines, each contributing to a metaphysical account of the relation between the form of language and the ✓
form of the world.[8] Such interpretations characteristically take at face
value the constitutive propositions of the philosophical theory they sup-
pose Wittgenstein to be advancing in the work. But readers who take
the aphoristic propositions of the *Tractatus* at face value must confront
a problem, namely that to do so is to fly in the face of Wittgenstein's
abrupt assertion at the book's conclusion that these same sentences are
in fact *einfach Unsinn,* simply nonsense.

Proponents of standard readings customarily try to handle this problem by claiming that readers of the book need not take its author's bizarre late-breaking declaration entirely literally. By pronouncing the sentences of the *Tractatus* nonsensical, they argue, Wittgenstein doesn't really mean that they are only truly meaningless strings of gibberish. Rather, they claim, these sentences are nonsensical only in a technical sense, or that they embody a more elevated sort of nonsense, able to convey to readers significant insights that will help them to grasp important aspects of the relationship between language and world that, in their view, Wittgenstein is keen to theorize in the *Tractatus*.

Resolute interpreters, on the other hand, reject this portrayal of Wittgenstein's project in the *Tractatus*. The text that standard readers endorse as a work of metaphysical doctrine resolute readers depict instead as a complex work composed in the service of its author's unswerving antitheoretical, antimetaphysical enterprise and dedication to disabusing readers of what he saw as their misdirected attraction to the kind of metaphysical thinking he enacts on the surface of the text. Firm in their convictions that Wittgenstein's shocking claim about his propositions' nonsensicality should be taken literally, resolute readers rebuff standard attempts to solve the difficulty of Wittgenstein's self-refuting announcement by inventing an illuminating, meaning-conveying sort of nonsense. They denounce the impulse to take such a logically specious step as indicative of a fundamental misunderstanding of the development of Wittgenstein's philosophical method and instructive aims.

My claim is that if we read the *Tractatus* resolutely, and against the background of the literature I examine here, Wittgenstein's early text emerges in singularly stark relief as a complex ethical-aesthetic puzzle of a distinctly modernist stripe. The book purports in name to be a logical-philosophical treatise—or so the title would seem to suggest. But as suitable as such a translation might seem, for Wittgenstein, it isn't an apt one at all. In the various exchanges that led to his settling on the current title, he ultimately rejected Russell's more modest alternative, "Philosophical Logic," in favor of the now familiar Latin title suggested by G. E. Moore, with its echo of Spinoza's *Tractatus Theologico-Politicus*. "For although 'Tractatus logico-philosophicus' isn't *ideal*," he wrote to the book's first translator, C. K. Ogden (who worried that title would hardly reassure readers of the book's accessibility), "still it has something like the right meaning, whereas 'Philosophic logic' is wrong. In fact I don't know what it means! There is no such thing as philosophic logic. (Unless one says that as the whole book is nonsense the title might as well be nonsense too.)"[9]

Wittgenstein's comments to Ogden rule out our describing the *Tractatus* as a treatise on philosophical logic. They also speak to his understanding of his book as nonsensical, something he affirms officially in the second-to-last of its austere numbered entries. There he tells us that all the propositions that make up the book's content are simply nonsense. Understanding *him*, he says, means recognizing this. The *Tractatus* turns out not to be a straightforward theoretical tract after all, but a pseudodoctrine meant to be cast aside once it has served what its author claims is its "elucidatory" purpose: getting its readers to "see the world in the right way."[10]

What's more, Wittgenstein maintained that his *Tractatus Logico-Philosophicus* was really a book about *ethics*. To complicate things further, he insisted that although the *aim* of the *Tractatus* is an ethical one, the ethical "part" of the book—the only part he says truly matters—is the part that appears nowhere among its spare aphorisms but is instead something its author chose to remain silent about. Over the course of the book, Wittgenstein explicitly takes up "the mystical," value, and transcendence. He engages in brief first-person confessional disclosure; makes oracular-sounding pronouncements; describes sudden epiphanic insight; and addresses the "riddle of life" before culminating in the religious figure of a ladder in a gesture toward closure that remains as open-ended and mysterious as it is revelatory (TLP 6.4312, 6.52, 6.521).

Wittgenstein's own concession that the *Tractatus* would appear "strange," then, hardly comes as a surprise.[11] What *is* surprising is the idiosyncratic authorial method he uses in the book, the combination of various modes of difficulty he deploys in it, and the disjuncture between the dense project he *appears* to be engaged in—developing a metaphysical theory about how language relates to the world—and what he posits as the book's overall ethical aim: to lead readers toward an enlightened kind of self-understanding gained through an improved relationship to language and life.

The *Tractatus* works toward realizing that ethical aim first by challenging readers to recognize that the consciously wrought faux argument Wittgenstein presents in the body of the text amounts to nothing more than the nonsense he says it is. Recognizing this, in turn, means coming to see that trying to make sense of the philosophical "theory" he has constructed (with an eye to seducing readers into grappling with the particular kind of cognitive and intellectual difficulty it poses on the surface) offers only the *illusion* of philosophical practice as he conceives it. As readers, we must learn to turn our attention away from the task of trying to understand the *Tractatus*'s nonsensical propositions (there is, ipso facto, no making sense of them) and focus instead on the question of how elaborating these propositions in the way he does serves the deeper and further-reaching philosophical and ethical aims of their wily author, utterer of nonsense and figurative language that he is. It is by responding to Wittgenstein's tacit call for readers to redirect our attention in this way that we can begin to discover on our own something he does not spell out for us straightforwardly in the body of the text: that his tactical move of setting up a mock doctrine with the nonsensical propositions of his "book of ethics" functions as a part of the instructive strategy he uses to prompt readers to shrug off the allure of metaphysics and engage instead in the clarificatory activity of the mind and spirit that he sees as the authentic task of philosophy.

As Wittgenstein sees it, participation in this philosophical activity entails a deep kind of work on the self, work toward overcoming one's linguistic and personal confusions through a transformative process of making the radical shift in ethical perspective one must make in order to regard philosophy, language, and the world with the sort of clarity he prompts his readers to strive for. The philosophical and poetic power of Wittgenstein's peculiar brand of ethical teaching in his strange hermetic book thus depends on his tactical use of difficulty, and on his conception of the extended way it stands to work on committed readers by leading us to face up to the rather different order of difficulty at issue in the text as a whole.

Therapy, Tactic, and Transfiguration

By reading Wittgenstein's book in this way, and in the context of a study of the literature of his time with attention to the interaction between these strategic and aspirational aspects of Wittgenstein's ethical pedagogy, I bring to the fore in this book the salient philosophical and aesthetic affinities between Wittgenstein and the modernist literature of the (long) twentieth century. Paying attention to each of the distinguishing features of Wittgenstein's method in the *Tractatus* allows us to regard Wittgenstein's esoteric book as a complex modernist puzzle as revolutionary in its experimental form, transformative ambitions, and dedication to everyday language's myriad possibilities as many of the "big" (and small) works we have come to see as exemplary of the twentieth-century literary canon.

A Different Order of Difficulty first examines Wittgenstein's thought with an eye to the philosopher's own formative literary sensibilities and distinctive, formally inventive writing style, and with a consideration of how his deployment of the tactical pedagogical devices he uses in the *Tractatus* serves as a catalyst for the dialectical strategy (of a Kierkegaardian stripe) on which the method of his book turns, if understood resolutely.[12] In the chapters that follow, I examine the impact of each of these aesthetic concerns on Wittgenstein's philosophical thinking and on the development of the unusual mode of ethical instruction he adopts in his early work. I highlight the distinction between the alleged treatise and its author's conception of the book's overall ethical aim and transfigurative aspirations, accounting for the very different nature of the specific exertions required by each of these facets of the text. By paying attention to both, and to the complicated relationship between them, I work to bring to light features of the *Tractatus* that help us to recognize compelling connections between Wittgenstein's creative exploitation of the different orders of difficulty in that perplexing philosophical project, and his modernist literary contemporaries' own notorious experimentation with difficulties of various hues.

Reading a set of perplexing texts of literary modernism and its afterlife alongside Wittgenstein's early work compels us to return to an examination of modernism's trademark difficulty with attention to the nuanced complexity of that enticing, absorbing, and often formidably exigent standout feature of twentieth-century literature. The comparative investigation of Wittgenstein's philosophy and modernist and neo-modernist literature that I undertake here shows how the various texts I examine effectively thrust modernism's multivalent difficulty on us as a point of inquiry. The *Tractatus*, after all, is a difficult text. It looks difficult in the way we might imagine a logical-philosophical treatise should look. But the trick is that the real challenge of the book lies in the personally transformative work it demands of readers, work that begins only after we have figured out, with the help of Wittgenstein's carefully orchestrated authorial tactics, that the logical theory we first thought made the book hard going was really not its true difficulty at all. The work of self-transformation that the *Tractatus* demands of its readers poses a deeper and more indefinite sort of difficulty, and with far higher ethical stakes, than the more (apparently) straightforward intellectual challenge posed by his (apparent) logico-philosophical treatise.

In the excerpt from *Ulysses* that inspires the title of this book, Joyce's fictional hero, Leopold Bloom, draws an implicit distinction between the two broad classes of difficulty exemplified in these alternate aspects of the *Tractatus*. Within the first category fall the largely resolvable, contingent problems of scientific fact, which test our discernment at a cognitive or intellectual level. At issue in the second are the significant moral,

spiritual, and existential preoccupations whose quality of difficulty exceeds the intellectual challenges and calls for erudition associated with
the first. In the passage, Bloom pointedly links concerns of this second
type to a contemplation of the possibilities of "social and moral redemption," to the labor of coping with the nagging, unanswerable questions
of meaning and being, and to a sustaining devotion to quests for solutions to such riddles of life that perseveres even in the recognition of their
representative insolubility. The commitment to the thoughtful activity
of questing that Joyce exemplifies in the meandering character of Bloom
himself is one that remains steadfast in the face of a prevailing modern
worry, even conviction, that such pursuits are but otiose exercises, the
toil they require but a vanity of vanities. The conundrums that arise in the
second category that Bloom delineates in the novel, he thinks, pose problems "of a different order of difficulty" (U, 699).

This different order of difficulty operates at the center of each of the
texts I examine in this book. My claim here is that the project of bringing
to literary studies the understanding of Wittgenstein made available by
resolute readings, while simultaneously exploring the resonance of Wittgenstein's ideas and writing style with twentieth-century letters, puts
us in a position to see how the *Tractatus* functions as a formally innovative aesthetic medium for its author's communication of his unorthodox brand of ethical teaching. Wittgenstein's idiosyncratic pedagogical
approach involves conscripting readers into a course of indirect interpretive training designed to prime us to respond more fully to the demands of the "different order of difficulty" at stake in his book, a genre
of difficulty that is also a central fixation of a body of twentieth-century
literature rooted in high modernist modes of technical and philosophical
experimentalism.

In the *Tractatus*, Wittgenstein doesn't move to resolve his readers'
problems by giving us direct answers to our philosophical or moral questions. He imparts no definitive, decipherable lesson or message. He lays
out no designated path toward the redemptive enlightenment coincident
with "seeing the world in the right way," nor does he give us a specific
picture of what things will look like from such a perspective. Wittgenstein offers no explanations of how to read his book, nor does he sup-
ply readers with a systematic theoretical program to follow in the quest
for clarity he seeks to put in motion with it. What he does instead is to
call on attentive readers to put our own moral imagination to the task of
figuring out how to respond to the text's initial provocation by setting
ourselves to the work of trying to rise to its strenuous demand that we
go on to transform our ways of seeing, living, and using language. It is by

taking up this personal work at the book's prompting that readers come to engage with the ethical dimension Wittgenstein ascribes to it. We are to recognize, in the course of our efforts to grapple with the book's compressed nonsensical sentences, the need to throw them away when they have served their salutary purpose of prodding us toward the activity of achieving the kind of ethical clarity that will help us in our struggles with linguistic confusion, life's most perplexing questions, the search for elusive answers, and the longing for transformative understanding.

Wittgenstein's early pedagogical method depends on his use of a deliberate authorial strategy. He artfully deploys a provocative, tactical kind of difficulty at a formal level, demanding that readers first confront that difficulty if we are ultimately to rise to the occasion of the different order of difficulty at issue in the text. This significant difficulty resides in the challenge Wittgenstein levels at his readers to undertake the hard work of effecting a radical change in the attitude or spirit with which we look on the world, use language, and live our everyday lives. Soliciting readers' engagement in this difficult, transformative work with the aim of getting us to "see the world in the right way" is his ultimate ethical aim in his book. The *Tractatus* is thus a text whose instructive force lies in the formidable exegetical gauntlet it throws down for readers with the aim of engaging us in the therapeutic activity of clarification Wittgenstein saw as the true work of philosophy.

Reading the *Tractatus* this way, I argue here, not only changes our perception of the therapeutic method Wittgenstein uses even in this early formulation of an ongoing philosophical project; it opens up a new dimension for studies in Wittgenstein and literature. Taking this approach to Wittgenstein also helps to reshape our conception of the decisive creative forces that propelled the cultural spirit of his particular time and milieu, the same zeitgeist that animated the high-modernist literary texts it engendered. Reading the *Tractatus* along these lines provides compelling new understandings of its author, who famously remarked that "philosophy ought to be written as one would *write a poem*," by emphasizing the importance of the literary to his early formulation of a lifelong philosophical project and fostering a renewed appreciation of Wittgenstein as a decidedly modernist writer (CV, 24). Looking at Wittgenstein's first work from this perspective also helps us to recognize in the *Tractatus* a very different set of distinguishing features than the ones that become apparent when the book is scrutinized according to a more traditional construal of that spare text as a work of theory, untouched by authorial guile. By the lights of antimetaphysical readings of the *Tractatus*, a set of unanticipated (and underexamined) traits emerge to attest to the thematic, formal, and tactical complexity of Wittgenstein's first work, guaranteeing its high-modernist bona fides.

Readers are first struck in this regard not only by Wittgenstein's treatment in the book of the problems of language and meaning that gripped the minds of so many early twentieth-century thinkers and writers, but also by the unusual experimental form in which he composes his puzzling book of ethics. Further experience of the text alerts us to an evident, though unaccustomed, brand of authorial cunning. Indeed, the task of finding our way to a better understanding of how the book works, and how it is meant to work on us, begins with a recognition of a principal tactical component of Wittgenstein's instructive method—the stunning disjuncture he strategically posits between the (nonsensical) logical-philosophical content he lays out explicitly for readers in the body of the text, and the transformative ethical ambition he envisions for the work as a whole.

Wittgenstein's way of communicating this ambition to his readers turns on his use of the Socratic-Kierkegaardian brand of irony that fuels his final self-destructive gesture vis-à-vis his own nonsensical propositions. These propositions serve as a kind of structural facade for the quest for clarity and authenticity he urges readers to take up on their own at his book's oblique behest. The solemnity with which Wittgenstein conveys his maieutical aspirations acts as an equipoise to the purposive authorial irony he employs as a catalyst to his reader's engagement with the text and the work toward radical change it solicits.

Further, Wittgenstein's concerted efforts simultaneously to employ and break with past conventions of philosophical thinking and writing, along with his manner of questioning the limitations of traditional genres of philosophical composition, show his work to be consistent with two of the basic features of modernism that Cavell points to in his discussion of the *Philosophical Investigations* as a modernist work.[13] The combined presence of these textual attributes, among others established consistently in dedicated studies of literary modernism, strengthens the case for regarding the *Tractatus* as a high-modernist work in its own right. Conversely, reading Wittgenstein resolutely also offers us new ways of understanding literary modernism and its legacy in contemporary fiction, for it calls on us to reexamine the mutually enlightening ways in which both twentieth-century literature and philosophy are enlivened by modernism's trademark affinity for textual difficulty, as well as by a less explored set of interrelated aspects I see as equally definitive: a fixation on existential questions and quests for significance; an attraction to varieties of spiritual and transcendent experience; and a yearning for profound transfigurative change.

Cavell was among the first to regard Wittgenstein as a modernist philosopher, focusing on the *Investigations*, rather than the *Tractatus*. If modernism is characterized by the stress put on the interpenetration of form and content, he argues, then the *Investigations*, whose form is internal to its instruction, should be considered a modernist work. The modernist text Cavell sees in the *Investigations* is a humanist one, generally forthright in its inquiry, dialogic and therapeutic in its communication, catholic in its ethos, its questions grounded in an everyday marked by a return to a post-Romantic investment in nature that informs his investigations of the complicated relations between grammar and the world, natural history, and forms of life.

The *Tractatus*, meanwhile, is a trickier text. It is an artfully orchestrated puzzle, one available only to readers attentive to its author's use of Socratic-Kierkegaardian irony. It is also a darker text, more informed by an acute cultural pessimism representative of what Charles Taylor points to as a resolutely Augustinian "world is fallen" movement characteristic of the avant-garde works of the early twentieth century.[14] Language itself comes into focus for the Wittgenstein of the *Tractatus* as an object of inquiry because (to allude to Heidegger's 1927 *Being and Time*) the world and nature have nothing to offer. The world has no value. Human nature is not the source of anything particularly good. Logic must take care of itself (TLP 5.473). The *Tractatus* is thus a text that holds to the fallenness and the mystery of the world. The transformative teaching Wittgenstein offers in the book announces itself in the quiet bombast of its magisterial prophetic tone. Wittgenstein's complex textual puzzle is one that works strategically to perplex readers in order ultimately to deliver us from the thrall of metaphysical confusion and nonsense (while simultaneously nurturing our experience of wonder and bewilderment in the face of mystery and upholding the significance of our nonsensical attempts to give expression to that experience). Evident in the *Tractatus* is Wittgenstein's Nietzschean investment in redemptive creative inspiration, and a dedication to careful aesthetic craft—put to the service of the book's ethical aim. In it, Wittgenstein also faces the pessimism of his age with a measure of hope that shows forth in his solemn commitment to the promise of its ultimate goal. In consideration of these combined defining aspects, I argue, the *Tractatus* is in general closer in its ethos to the works of Kafka, Woolf, and Coetzee than the *Investigations* is.

Wittgenstein shares with his literary modernist contemporaries a fixation on the problems of language that merges with a commitment to unconventional methods of ethical instruction and an enticement to the work of self-improvement. This commitment is rooted in a modernist investment in a striving for a secular-spiritual kind of transformation. The preoccupation with transfigurative change that becomes such a pressing concern of aesthetic modernism shows forth in a number of ways in the works I examine here. Common to each is the close attention they pay to the power of human longing for creative moral, spiritual, and existential enlightenment. Each of these diverse texts offers its own unique treatment of the dual sense of bewilderment and possibility that drives their respective internal characters' or targeted readers' varied modes of engagement in quests for the kind of clarity and authenticity that can be achieved only through a radical shift in worldview. The change in ethically imaginative ways of seeing and being that is the goal of the quests these writers explore promises to bring a new quality and depth to our understanding of human experience, our existence as selves among others, and our attitude toward ordinary language and life.

As I have noted above, Wittgenstein saw philosophy not as a body of theory, but as an activity, one whose aim is to clarify. The work of clarification that he takes to be philosophy's main concern contrasts markedly with scientific pursuits of certainty that involve making new discoveries. For Wittgenstein, the aim of philosophy is not to *discover* anything at all. Its task instead is to get us to see clearly the world we already inhabit, the language we already master, and to reveal to us who we are and the possible shape of our continued authentic development. While the natural sciences are underwritten by a dedication to providing explanations of the physical world, the work of philosophy as Wittgenstein understands it doesn't consist in seeking out explanations or in mounting theories. The clarity that Wittgenstein asks us to strive for, and which is a driving concern for his literary contemporaries and their successors, is clarity that is shaped by its complex relationship with opacity and open-ended questions.

Each of the authors I examine here treats clarity not as something that comes to us completely, all at once as in a moment of conversion, but as something achievable only through an ongoing process of working through the confusions and difficulties of language and life. As these writers construe it, the improved understanding that clarity brings is something we stand to gain through the experience of reading challenging texts like theirs, deliberately written to be as opaque as life can sometimes be. And yet the clarity they are after is not a clarity that, once attained, will succeed in doing away with all forms of obscurity. Rather, it brings with it the recognition that some aspects of life—those that give rise to our most persistent existential questions—will remain as mysterious and unresolved as the questions themselves.

commitment to mystery

In their different explorations of the labor of working through confusion and obscurity in search of such clarity, the texts I deal with in this book are also willfully invested in effecting a kind of parallel shift in the outlook of their most dedicated and perceptive readers. By way of their internal portrayals of a yearning for improved clarity of vision, then, they also seek to perform the accompanying task of refining our interpretive capabilities to help us to become more attentive and perspicuous thinkers and readers.

Yearning for clarity and personally transformative change runs through each of my central texts. Whether (and how) we, as readers with our own parallel senses of longing, are able fully to respond to the communicative gestures of these texts in a way that truly allows them actively to hone our capacities to read well and live well (in order, that is, to bring their ethical aims to fruition in our own lives and the other lives we touch), however, is not something they can ensure in and of themselves. Written into each of these texts is the idea that reading them with the kind of moral attention that can make us "finely aware and richly responsible," in Nussbaum's words—attention that will help us to recognize what the work they want us to do might entail, and imagine what that work will look like on the landscape of our individual lives—is something that each of us must do for ourselves.[15]

The Tractatus, *Common Experience, and Moral Perfectionism*

Wittgenstein's own understanding of the transformative ethical aim in the *Tractatus* merits some further consideration here.[16] In that book, Wittgenstein seeks to engage readers in a philosophical activity of clarification that is centrally focused on an ongoing work on the self (and one's attitude toward language and life). Just above, I described this activity as "the work of self-improvement," to which Wittgenstein was dedicated, along with a number of other modernist writers. To be sure, such a description might well suggest that Wittgenstein's approach to this kind of work bears (unfortunate) similarities to current neoliberal ideas about the ethics of entrepreneurial self, or to commercialized notions of "self-actualization" and "self-care." That Wittgenstein's moral perfectionism in the *Tractatus* does not serve such consumerist ends, however, should already be rather obvious (Beth Blum's persuasive recent accounts of the relationship between modernism's fixation on self-improvement and the concomitant rise of the popular self-help narrative and success manual notwithstanding).[17]

Less obvious, perhaps, is the fact that for Wittgenstein, work on the self is not the work of self-absorption. First, Wittgenstein's chosen method of ethical teaching, therapeutic even in his early text, demonstrates that his conception of the work on the self that goes hand in hand with achieving the transformation toward which his book tends is not an exclusively individual concern. Wittgenstein's instructive effort to guide readers in making a change in outlook that will bring clarity to our lives and use of language demands the concerted ethical work of striving to understand the linguistic and personal struggles of *others*. And, to make a point to which I will return in subsequent chapters, the work of understanding another person entails a Cavellian form of acknowledgment and a responsiveness to her particular confusions. This, in turn, depends on what Diamond describes as the activity of imaginatively "entering in" to the other person's way of seeing things.[18] Wittgenstein's way of acknowledging his readers and treating their attraction to nonsense with understanding is to enter imaginatively into their illusion and then respond to it by adopting his own kind of self-aware nonsense and then communicating it back to them. In order to understand the *Tractatus*, then, readers must responsively try to understand its author, as he says at proposition 6.45, by entering imaginatively into his own (purposefully employed) nonsensical expression. Despite its alienating esotericism, then, the *Tractatus* does foster in its community of readers a form of communicative exchange and desire to work toward mutual understanding.

Whether the work on the self that the *Tractatus* demands will have the valuable consequence of generating a wider common experience of clarity and the well-lived life is another story. To begin with, as I said just above, the *Tractatus* is a deliberately arcane work. As such, if it solicits the understanding of its readers (as it quite explicitly does), it also manages to push some away and to isolate others. And in the way that difficult parables do, the *Tractatus* makes its most robust, overt, and arguably even elitist appeal to the "one person" who will read it with understanding. The common experience of the *Tractatus*, considered at the most mundane, workaday level, is the contingent common experience created by its arduous interpretive demands. And given its difficulty, if the book has been the occasion of a gathering together of a community of ambitious (or exhausted) scholars, it has surely sequestered and defeated far more.

I would argue that Wittgenstein shares Cavell's basic commitment to seeing the work of self-transformation and self-realization as a pursuit that is not intrinsically individualist or elitist. That said, and as I show in chapters 2 and 5, the deliberately puzzling, sometimes alienating, parabolic mode of instruction Wittgenstein uses in the *Tractatus* nonetheless prompts us, by its very form and method, to question whether this early text really functions to elicit transformative engagement from *all* readers, or whether a sort of elitism subsists at its core.

To speak on a more serious level to the question whether the work on the self with which the *Tractatus* is concerned can have an extended effect on common experience, I would first say this: The *Tractatus* is not only an arcane book, it is also an idiosyncratic one. And the work on the self (of "seeing the world in the right way") that Wittgenstein leaves his community of readers to continue beyond the final pages of his book will undoubtedly take equally idiosyncratic shapes, to equally idiosyncratic effects. One consequence of Wittgenstein's abiding distrust of theory and eschewal of explanations and easy answers is that the *Tractatus* does not give us a rigidly ordered body of rules, nor a template to which our work on the self must conform. It offers us no set of directives we must follow to the letter. Nor does it give us a recipe for how to "see the world in the right way." He doesn't even tell us what the right way to see the world *is*. He tells us only that if we work to understand *him* (and what he is trying to get us to recognize with the help of his strange book), we will. What Wittgenstein gives us in the *Tractatus*, as he says, is a method. The ongoing ethically imaginative work of figuring out what seeing the world in the right way might possibly come to, might eventually be, is something he leaves up to us.

Seeing the work on the self that Wittgenstein demands in the *Tractatus* in this way, it becomes easier to understand how the transformative activity at stake in the book is unlikely to rouse legions to cohere in a common experience of (working together toward achieving) ethical transfiguration. Wittgenstein's philosophy is certainly revolutionary; but the radically new ways of thinking he puts forward in his work do not foment communal revolution conceived along familiar lines. The work of self-transformation so central to Wittgenstein's first book is neither automatically nor easily enacted on a grand scale.[19]

It's not that Wittgenstein doesn't feel the attraction of such a communal outlook. Important aspects of his thinking about the transformative ethical work at the heart of the *Tractatus*, after all, evolved under the influence of figures like Tolstoy, whose own transformative quest for the meaning of life and the best way to live it led him finally to find, in his embrace of Christianity, acetic morality, and the Russian peasant community, the attitude of ethical clarity that resolved his questions and granted him peace. There is nothing in Wittgenstein's early thinking that would rule out, a priori, then, the possibility that leading his readers to make a radical change in outlook might have extended effects on their wider social community. Wittgenstein's project in the *Investigations* lends itself more readily to a more grounded, democratic goal of achieving social justice. But that effect is not his primary aim in the *Tractatus*.

In many ways, Wittgenstein's ethical work of "self-improvement" is best understood as exemplifying a method engaged with a dimension of moral life and thought (rather than any competing ethical theory) that Cavell calls "moral perfectionism." Cavell describes perfectionism's concerns variously across his writing, and especially in his most comprehensive treatment of the issue in his 1988 Carus Lectures. Cavell's own brand of moral perfectionism (informed by the later Wittgenstein, Nietzsche, Emerson, Thoreau, and others) entails facing with courage the struggle to "come to see [oneself] and hence the possibilities of [our] world, in a transformed light," to work toward "self-knowledge," "becoming intelligible to oneself," "being true to oneself," "being lost to oneself," and "finding one's way" in the course of becoming the person one is. His moral perfectionism is concerned with the enduring reverberations of the fundamental Socratic question of how one should live, and with "what used to be called the state of one's soul, a dimension that places tremendous burdens on personal relationships and on the possibility or necessity of transforming oneself and of one's society." For Cavell, as for Wittgenstein, there is no reaching a perfect state of the soul, only endless steps toward reaching what Emerson calls an "unattained but attainable self."[20] Wittgenstein's moral perfectionism in the *Tractatus*, like Cavell's, works toward achieving self-understanding and the realization of inherent potential of the self through education and transformative work whose aim is not the perfected state of the self, but the journey toward a more authentic self.

Moral Perfectionism and Unbearable Conflict

On the subject of Wittgenstein's own engagement with the continuing need for change and readjustment in the ongoing ethical work of striving for authenticity, it is worth pausing briefly to consider the shift in method and conception of the workings of ordinary language that marks the evolution of his thinking from the *Tractatus* to the *Investigations*, something I will return to in chapter 4.

In pursuit of improved clarity and authenticity in his own thinking and writing as his philosophical work developed, Wittgenstein continued to struggle to be "true to himself" by working to overcome the grip of his own attraction to (and self-imposition of) illusory metaphysical ideals, and to fine-tune his views about how philosophy works to clear up our confusions about language and the myriad ways in which it enables us to express our experience of life in the world.

He completed his ambitious *Tractatus* with the conviction that it was, as Diamond describes it, a work "marvelously . . . fully achieved."[21] For in it he had reached, or so he thought at the time, a satisfactory resolution of the philosophical problems he was confronting. And yet the criticism of his early thought that he offers in the metaphilosophical passages of the *Investigations* (PI §§ 89–133) shows that he had gradually come to see his first work as deeply flawed, marked by what he called an "unbearable conflict" at its core (PI § 107).[22] Wittgenstein was to remain throughout his lifetime committed to his early conception of philosophy as an activity of elucidation, rather than as a theoretical tool for making new discoveries. But the remarks Wittgenstein makes in those sections of the *Investigations* speak to his recognition over time that his most entrenched view in the *Tractatus*—that there is an essential logical order that lies hidden beneath the surface of the varied expressions of our actual ordinary language—had been for him something akin to what Heinrich Hertz describes in his *Principles of Mechanics* (a book that he first read as a teenager and that would continue to influence him throughout his career) as a "confused wish" that gives rise to confused questions and what Hertz calls "painful contradictions."[23] Diamond figures Wittgenstein's confused wish in terms of its development into a *"shaping timeless principle*, a kind of injunction for his thinking . . . *unopposed* and indeed, in his thought, *unopposable*."[24] But the notion that there is a crystalline ideal order to language that we can *discover* with the help of philosophical analysis is an idea that is fatally at odds with the contrast Wittgenstein insisted on between the activities of philosophy and science, and his commitment to the idea that the practice of philosophy entails work of clarification of our existing language and life, rather than that of imposing requirements, summing up, or uncovering.

If we follow Diamond's recent suggestions about Wittgenstein's own dawning sense of the intolerable contradiction at the heart of the *Tractatus*, the result of what she describes as "his own imposition of a kind of myth on his thinking," we see that the moral perfectionism at issue in his early work is something that also extends to its author's own process of "coming to self-conscious awareness of the unconscious structuring of [his] life" in a way that accounts for the radical changes he made in his therapeutic philosophical method over time.[25]

Wittgenstein's self-conscious realization that a *"false necessity . . .* had shaped his thought" was an ethically transformative one, in a Tractarian sense.[26] It offers us a single concrete philosophical example of the kind of step the *Tractatus* suggests a person can take in order to revise his way of thinking in his ongoing quest to see things "in the right way" in Wittgenstein's sense. For he recognized that in his philosophical thinking at the time he wrote the *Tractatus*, he had been—in the language of the *Investigations*—bewitched, held captive by a picture of his own making (PI §115). To appeal to one of the phrases Cavell uses to describe moral perfectionism as he understands it, Wittgenstein came eventually to see that he had been, in a way, "lost to himself," needing to find a new approach in his pursuit of greater authenticity. Finally, in the psychoanalytic terms Jonathan Lear uses to describe a case that provides Diamond with an illuminating comparison, Wittgenstein recognized a need to work through and resist his own attractions to dogmatism and to reshape his life going forward in an effort to bring about a radical psychic change that would yield a clearer understanding of language and world that would translate into his philosophical work.[27] In the ongoing development of his thinking, as Diamond describes it, Wittgenstein strives consciously to "*own* [his] past philosophy in a new way."[28] Indeed, attending consistently to the voices of temptation that he works to overcome and that harken back to his earlier ways of thinking is part of the characteristic form of his later philosophy.[29]

Secular, Spiritual, Surface, and Depth

The overarching attraction to spiritual or transcendent experience in the work of the authors I examine in the following chapters makes it clear that even in the literature or philosophy of each of these avowedly agnostic or atheistic writers, secular modernity does not correlate to wholesale Weberian disenchantment.[30] The philosophical and literary projects of this book's central authors are all, to cite Joyce's portmanteau, "theologicophilolological" (U, 205). Their respective works feature a distinctive combination of the theological with the philosophical and the logical in their treatment of the struggles associated with a human striving to inhabit the space between the extremes of a concrete everyday on the one hand and a yearning for transcendence on the other.

Against the background of Wittgenstein's engagement with difficulty and complex ethical pedagogy in the *Tractatus*, I explore in the first chapters of this book writing by Kafka, Woolf, and Joyce, three chief figures of the high-modernist canon. In the final chapter, I turn to recent fiction by Coetzee, a living author writing in current dialogue both with Wittgenstein and with his modernist literary precursors. Thus, although

A Different Order of Difficulty is focused primarily on recasting the significance of Wittgenstein's *Tractatus* for studies in literary modernism (and vice versa), and thus on expanding the New Modernist canon horizontally from within by means of the comparatist interdisciplinarity of this study, its reach nonetheless extends beyond those parameters in two ways.[31]

First of all, I conduct my discussion of Wittgenstein's deployment of difficulty and commitment to an ethically instructive aim in the *Tractatus* with an eye to the continuity of these concerns in his later writing, despite the shift in philosophical and pedagogical method that distinguishes his posthumously published *Philosophical Investigations* from his early work. Second, by addressing Coetzee's work in the concluding chapter, my study moves beyond the temporal limits of literary modernism, traditionally construed, to touch on important ways in which Wittgenstein's thinking also sheds light on works of transnational contemporary fiction that represent what David James has called "modernist futures" because of their continued efforts to grapple stylistically, intertextually, and philosophically with the crises of language, identity, and faith so characteristic of the realistic spirit of the novels of thinking of the long twentieth century.[32]

A Different Order of Difficulty also departs substantially from two dominant trends in modernist studies today, namely (1) cultural studies and (2) the demand for formalism that underpins readings of modernist texts from New Criticism through deconstruction and other forms of poststructuralism. With his strident antitheoretical position and commitment to *looking* and *seeing*, Wittgenstein, is quite organically "postcritical," in the sense articulated by Rita Felski and others in recent influential work.[33] My own examination of twentieth-century literature in terms of Wittgenstein's focus on everyday language and life, and on the therapeutic and transformative ethical instruction that characterizes his philosophy, is thus framed by the ideas of a foundational figure of a tradition of ordinary language philosophy that naturally circumvents the logic of demystifying critique. In that regard, *A Different Order of Difficulty* implicitly coincides with an emerging body of scholarship dedicated to finding and developing compelling alternatives to modes of critique driven by a prevailing poststructural commitment to the hermeneutics of suspicion.[34]

I should add, however, that the ideas of the same framing figure I have just cast as a kind of postcritical philosopher *avant la lettre* also inform my departure in this book from certain postcritical approaches—those that advocate "surface reading," and others whose efforts to render the valuable service of freeing literary studies from the prolonged dominance of suspicious or symptomatic reading entail a suppression, if you will, of the critical impulse to attend to a text's depth, as well as its surface (not to mention the vital interaction between them that is so crucial to puzzle texts like the *Tractatus*).[35] The past decade or so has seen the long-overdue flourishing of postcritical thinking that has evolved since the 1960s in a series of attempts by literary critics to cure critique of the obsession, nurtured under the sway of suspicious hermeneutics, with plumbing the depths of the textual unconscious to expose the hidden, deep-seated agendas lurking there. But such curative challenges to the limits of critique prove misdirected and overzealous as long the remedy they prescribe derives solely from an overly reductive, critically limiting conception of what depth can *be* (i.e., other than a mere site for hermeneutic excavation and unveiling), or how its underlying presence in a text can *function* (i.e., by contributing complexity and significance to the experience of reading, rather than just raising our interpretive hackles and soliciting our participation in an enterprise of shrewd interrogation). Postcritical approaches that call, in one way or another, for relegating to the critical scrapheap *all* types of textual depth and *all* modes of interpretive engagement, it seems to me, risk throwing the baby out with the proverbial bathwater.[36]

Wittgenstein would later reject the idea he shared with Russell in his early philosophy—that the underlying realities of language are not visible on the surface, and that it is up to us to plumb the depths of what lies beneath actual language to get to its hidden logical essence. But as he makes clear in the 1946 remark that serves as the third of the three epigraphs with which this book begins, he is a philosopher given to expressing his ideas about the difficulty of life, philosophy, and the search for new ways of thinking and seeing in terms of both surface and depth. Wittgenstein of course famously remarks in the *Philosophical Investigations* that "everything is open to view," and that "what is hidden . . . is of no interest to us" (PI §126). Toril Moi makes Wittgenstein's claim that "nothing is hidden" a ready motto for her own postcritical work of bringing ordinary language philosophy to bear on literary studies. But for the purposes of my own project of bringing Wittgenstein to the study of twentieth-century literature here, it is also important to note that in his philosophical thinking and teaching, he was equally invested in significant kinds of depth (and its textual uses).[37]

I would argue further here that Wittgenstein's conception of the *Tractatus*, and of how it functions at the different levels of instruction he puts into play within it, does not stand in the sort of truly stark conflict with his later claim about everything being open to view that would suggest that we should neglect his consistent attentiveness to depth in favor of his commitment to openness and clarity. Wittgenstein composed the *Tractatus* to lead readers to clarity through obscurity, and his teaching in it depends on both. He saw the ethical aim of his early book not so much as *hidden* in it as something that becomes available only to those readers who, recognizing the text as a deliberately layered one, turn their attention to what lies beneath its surface.

In remarks Wittgenstein makes over the course of his lifelong philosophical investigations about the issues that most occupied him—logic, grammar, thoughts, questions, the "problems of life," "problems arising through a misinterpretation of our forms of language," as well as religious ritual, humor, and literary form—he frequently refers to these important concerns as being rooted in, or having the character of, *depth* (CV, 42, 62, 53; PI, §111).[38] Wittgenstein contrasts surface difficulty with the difficulty that requires us to dive deep down in order to get hold of them (CV, 48). He distinguishes "depth grammar" from that of a "surface" variety (PI, § 644), He claims that "the problems of life are insoluble on the surface and can only be solved in depth" (CV, 74).

I have argued here that the *Tractatus* can be read as a consciously crafted puzzle. As such, I have been concerned to show, it operates, quite by design (as puzzles do, and must), both on a surface dimension (on which we find the apparent metaphysical theory), and on a dimension of depth (in which resides in the book's unspoken ethical aim of leading readers to the clarity with which to overcome our reliance on such theories and see the world in the right way). To read only the surface of the text, ignoring completely its unspoken ethical "point," and deeper enigmatic aspects (aspects we intuit only through attention to Wittgenstein's ironic stance regarding his pseudopropositions) is to miss out on the transformative illumination the book promises (because we have neglected the tactical interplay between surface and depth on which the author depends in his aim of bringing this illumination about). Taken only at face value, the *Tractatus* does not reveal itself to be a book with very different stakes than we first thought it had and thus does not become for us the wholly different book than we first thought we were reading.[39]

On a superficial reading, the *Tractatus* is legible not as a book with an "ethical" pursuit, but as the presentation of a metaphysical doctrine. But the metaphysical doctrine that represents the book's content is precisely what Wittgenstein asks us to overcome, along with our need for the book's nonsensical propositions (expendable, we are told, once they have served their purpose of elucidating something to us readers).

Wittgenstein does not spell out for us overtly just how the disposable nonsensical theory that unfolds on the text's surface could ever manage to shed light on what he is trying to do (or make us do) with the text as a whole. To figure that out, readers must look at how Wittgenstein's "treatise" works at deeper level. Doing so, we gain a very different and richer experience of the text. Wittgenstein's method in the *Tractatus*, in its trickiest strategic aspects, relies on surface appearance and deeper complexity alike. This method depends on readers' ability not only to recognize both of the book's dimensions as distinct, but also to grasp the relationship between them. Unless readers come to appreciate the vital interaction of the different demands of the book—superficial *and* deep—Wittgenstein's Tractarian method will not work on readers in the way he designed it to do.

Acknowledging Wittgenstein's embrace of both depth and surface helps us to see that the (proto-)postcritical work in which his philosophy engages us does more than represent a satisfying alternative to the hermeneutics of suspicion. Wittgenstein's balanced attention to both dimensions also serves to temper some of the manifesto fervor that drives some proponents of postcritical work to cast depth itself into suspicion. As Moi shows in her recent work, drawing on Wittgenstein's philosophy in the study of literature has the potential to expand, rather than contract, the limits of interpretive possibility. But he also reminds us by his own example that the work of postcriticism, construed broadly enough to include him, need not be conducted at the expense of depth.

A Study of Coincidence

To be clear, *A Different Order of Difficulty* does not posit a direct intellectual-historical link between Wittgenstein and the literary writers that I explore here. My treatment of the relationship between Wittgenstein and twentieth-century literature in this book does not represent what one might call a "study of influence." As I show in chapter 2, Wittgenstein had only the briefest taste of Kafka's writing and found it not to his liking.[40] The only connection between Wittgenstein and Joyce was their mutual admiration for Tolstoy's "How Much Land Does a Man Need?," which Wittgenstein declared his favorite, and Joyce pronounced "the greatest story that the literature of the world knows."[41] To be sure, Woolf did occasionally cross paths with Wittgenstein in Cambridge and Bloomsbury circles and knew of his reputation from common acquaintances like Russell, Keynes, and others. But, as I show in chapter 3, although Ann Banfield and Jaakko Hintikka are both correct to argue that the impact of the *Tractatus* in Cambridge philosophy also reverberated in Bloomsbury, where it surely transformed the discourse of Woolf's cultural milieu, her links to Wittgenstein remained ever remote, and their mutual regard one of benign indifference.[42]

Rejecting the designation of "influence study" is thus hardly a feat, given the absence of any thriving personal or intellectual exchange between Wittgenstein and the literary figures I examine in this book. The living exception to this rule is of course Coetzee, whose fiction I discuss in the concluding chapter 5. Coetzee is uniquely positioned among the writers whose work I explore "after Wittgenstein," as the subtitle of this book indicates, to regard, from a late twentieth- and early twenty-first-century standpoint, the philosopher whom Coetzee's eponymous character Elizabeth Costello calls the "Viennese Destroyer."[43] Coetzee, whose fiction I read here, as I do that of Kafka, Woolf, and Joyce, in relation to Wittgenstein's thinking, is thus unique among the four fiction writers I deal with here in being historically situated quite literally, "after Wittgenstein." Coetzee came of age in a generation in which Wittgenstein was no longer the emblem of a new philosophical epoch, ushering in the "linguistic turn" that his works helped to set in motion, but an established entity of twentieth-century philosophy, whose body of work has long been the subject of research, scholarly debate, and controversy.

Coetzee himself undoubtedly gained familiarity with Wittgenstein's philosophy in his capacity as a linguist and academic. And although he remained on the whole quiet about Wittgensteinian themes in his writing before 2003, in his later fiction, especially in his 2013 novel *The Childhood of Jesus*, Coetzee takes a more discernible Wittgensteinian turn. The etiology of this shift can be attributed in part to Coetzee's collaborative involvement with philosophers Jonathan Lear, Robert Pippin, and Raimond Gaita. But Coetzee's more overt interest in Wittgenstein in recent years is most productively understood in relation to the work of a number of resolute Wittgensteinian philosophers (and others largely sympathetic with the moral thinking developed within that program) who have responded to the strong attraction Coetzee's later fiction has exerted on their own thinking in a set of publications that not only have gone on to exert their own influence on subsequent philosophical work in literature and moral thought, but have, arguably, helped to make the shape of Wittgenstein's thinking more visible on Coetzee's radar. Most influential of these publications is Cora Diamond's essay "The Difficulty of Reality and the Difficulty of Philosophy," to which I turn in my discussion of Virginia Woolf in chapter 3.[44]

Wittgenstein has also proved a figure of persisting fascination for a range of musicians, poets, playwrights, and fiction writers who draw on his thinking in their own work. Coetzee's later work secures him a prominent place in this last group, among such writers as Ingeborg Bachmann, Thomas Bernhard, Peter Handke, W. G. Sebald, Ricardo Piglia, and David Foster Wallace. The collective work of these authors attests to the varied ways in which Wittgenstein's thinking and writing has informed their own.[45]

As I have said, my decision to examine the work of my chosen constellation of fiction writers together in relation to Wittgenstein is not based on any sustained interaction they had with the philosopher or his ideas, nor certainly he with theirs. The conventional designation for the opposite of an influence study, while it might seem a bit too predictable to serve as a worthy alternative, and a bit too imprecise to be entirely apposite, does nonetheless offer a useful way to begin to describe the nature of the comparative project in which I am engaged in this book. For in a most general, primary sense, A Different Order of Difficulty does indeed entail a study of coincidence. In it, I attend to the remarkable points of concurrence of Wittgensteinian thinking and the thematic motifs and formal concerns of literary modernism exemplified in my central authors' diverse treatments of them. Rather than account for this concurrence by positing any strictly causal relation between these entities, or by grounding my analysis primarily in biography or intellectual history, I explore a representative set of the shared philosophical and literary affinities that make this concurrence show forth. I show that recognizing the connections among the philosophical, formal, and pedagogical investments common to Wittgenstein and his literary contemporaries and their inheritors allows us to see their respective works as pointedly devoted to modes of ethical instruction that seeks, through the deployment of various, mutually dependent orders of difficulty, to bring about a kind of transfigurative change in their readers. Attending to the transformative pedagogical aspects of these works generates a wealth of interpretive possibilities for comparative studies in Wittgenstein and literature, however contingent the word "coincidence" might also suggest the connections between them to be.

Works by Kafka, Woolf, and Joyce, the first three literary figures I focus on here, have of course long been recognized as definitive of the high-modernist cultural moment they inhabited along with Wittgenstein. The works by Coetzee that I examine here exemplify the millennial "novels of thinking," shaped by the continuing influence of the narrative themes, allusive intertextuality, ethical concerns, and formal techniques endemic to a philosophical and literary modernism it continues to elaborate and transform in its wake.[46] My justification for making these disparate figures cohere by reading them in conjunction with one another, and each in relation to Wittgenstein, does not derive from the uncontroversial fact of their shared canonicity. Looking comparatively at this particular set of representative modernist figures is instructive, for the relative absence of any other productive links between them induces us to focus our attention on their different modes of experimenting with form and idea, authorial aim and readerly engagement, and thus on the significant points of convergence of their commitments to difficulty, teaching, and transformation. This, in turn, leads us toward a new conception of these three commitments as the crucial driving concerns of modernism viewed in its broader interdisciplinary and temporal context.

special? (handwritten margin note)

Modernism and Its Difficulties

I begin my exploration of the three concerns of difficulty, oblique ethical instruction, and a yearning for transformation that Wittgenstein shares with the literary writers I examine here with a focus on the difficulty in which I take each of these other common concerns to be rooted. Looking at the different uses of difficulty at play in the *Tractatus* leads us to attend in more perspicuous ways to the notorious obsession with (and strategic deployment of) different modes of textual and existential difficulty that took hold of the cultural productions of the age in which Wittgenstein wrote.

T. S. Eliot, William Empson, and George Steiner all sang the praises of modernist difficulty. Laura Riding and Robert Graves, I. A. Richards, F. R. Leavis, and Helen Gardner all offer comprehensive analyses of modern poetry in terms of its complexity.[47] The proliferation of critical writing attesting to early scholarly excitement about the difficulty endemic to modernism would generate so much discussion in modernist studies that it ultimately had the loosely paradoxical effect of making talk about the difficulty of modernist texts into something simplistic, even trite—the stuff of entries in glossaries of modernist topics and keywords. Indeed, as Leonard Diepeveen notes, to say that modernism is commonly seen as difficult seems almost "beyond argument" to anyone "with some knowledge of twentieth-century high culture."[48]

Nonetheless, a handful of critics, Diepeveen among them, have in recent years turned their attention toward a reconsideration of difficulty as a powerful social and aesthetic force in the formation of modernism. In *The Difficulties of Modernism*, Diepeveen looks at how modernism first began to solidify as a recognized object of academic study around the pronouncement of difficulty as modern poetry's central characteristic. It was by means of the reception and assertion of the distinguishing difficulty of modernist literature that modernism was first "accomplished," brought to "completion" as an artistic happening that was no longer in flux, but was established as a matter of record.[49]

As Michael Levenson notes, the difficulty of modernist texts created a need for a rhetorically effective doctrine of structure, order, and form that critics could use to explain and justify a growing body of work.[50] Difficulty conferred legitimacy on a set of texts thus deemed "great art" by thinkers like Theodor Adorno. Adorno argued that art that challenges us to really look and see the world around us *must be difficult*. Art that is too familiar or accessible is too easily consumed. Because it does not make us uncomfortable, it does not make us think about the complexity and ambiguity that characterizes real life.[51]

Another critic who famously declared that modern poetry had to be difficult in order to respond adequately to the complexity of the modern world is, of course, T. S. Eliot. In his frequently quoted comment on difficulty in twentieth-century Anglo-American literary culture, Eliot epigrammatically observes:

> We can only say that it appears likely that poets in our civilization, as it exists at present, must be *difficult.* Our civilization comprehends great variety and complexity, and this variety and complexity, playing upon a refined sensibility, must produce various and complex results. The poet must become more and more comprehensive, more allusive, more indirect, in order to force, to dislocate if necessary, language to his meaning.[52]

As John Guillory and Craig S. Abbott have each argued, Eliot, Cleanth Brooks, and the New Critics not only recognized the strain of difficulty that characterized so many modern works; they valorized it as an integral part of a formalist agenda of revaluing literature and poetry.[53] Under the New Critics, modernist difficulty was made into a pedagogical concept to be deployed in the creation of a twentieth-century canon that would insure the cultural capital of modernist works. Guillory writes:

> Let us first of all acknowledge that for the New Critics the language of poetry, and of literature in general, was intrinsically *difficult*. This was not a difficulty which could be removed by

the glossing of sources, or by recourse to information about the author's life or beliefs, it was a difficulty which did not disappear in the process of interpretation so much as it was confirmed. One may go further than this and say that difficulty itself was positively valued in New Critical practice, that it was a form of cultural capital, just by virtue of imparting to cultural objects a certain kind of *rarity*, the very difficulty of apprehending them.[54]

The New Critics made difficulty into a benchmark of literary value, sophistication, and erudition to which they could appeal in their appraisal of the select set of literary and poetic works on which they sought to confer canonical status. Challenging poetic works by figures like Eliot, Pound, and Stevens, for example, were distinguished not so much from poetry dedicated to the simplicity that would seem to represent difficulty's more obvious opposite, but from "popular" verse deemed more accessible to mass audiences, and thus a less worthy object of academic study. From the very inception of critical studies in literary modernism, then, the New Critics' mandarin esteem for difficulty made it all too easy to equate scholarly efforts to pay attention to this salient, multifarious feature of modernist texts with an outlook of reactionary elitism. Their zeal in designating the highly variable quality of "difficulty" as an emblematic feature of literary modernism has made touting difficulty's importance into something of a critical truism at best, and tantamount to defending an outmoded highbrow polemic at worst.

But what Guillory says about what the New Critics originally recognized about the difficulty of high-modernist texts still certainly holds true for any reader who finds herself wrestling with the most perplexing examples of modernist poetry or fiction. For such works *do* often resist our attempts to resolve our confusion in the face of their difficulty by appeal to the glossing of sources, or through recourse to information available to us about a given author's life or beliefs. In *Ulysses*, Joyce self-reflexively calls attention to the plight of the reader who tries to resolve the "difficult problems in imaginary or real life" by appeal to "the literature of instruction" in just this way. In the novel, Bloom (himself a character whose wanderings are charted in a notoriously, self-consciously challenging modernist tome), searches for solutions to difficult problems posed in difficult literature only to find that certain strains of difficulty are impervious to resolution by such means. What Bloom discovers is something that readers of difficult modernist works know all too well. For "in spite of careful and repeated reading of certain . . . passages, aided by a glossary," Bloom derives only "imperfect conviction from the text, the answers not bearing on all points" (U, 677). What's more, among the many "difficult problems in imaginary or real life" that we encounter in our reading, there are some that seem to elude answers on *all* points. Such difficulties seem simply unresolvable (or, at the very least, to defy immediate solution). Alternately, as I show in an exploration of Wittgenstein's, Joyce's, and Diamond's various treatments of riddles in chapter 4, bringing such difficulties to resolution may ultimately depend on our ability as readers imaginatively to expand our notions of what can count as resolution in the first place, before we can recognize a solution when we see it, or invent a suitable one when we cannot.

Guillory's comment from that same passage above—that one of the aspects of modernist poetry that first caught the attention of the New Critics was that it entailed "a difficulty which did not disappear in the process of interpretation so much as it was confirmed"—also calls to mind the example of Kafka's writing, and Coetzee's (often Kafka-inflected) fiction. For as I show in my discussion of Kafka's parable in relation to Wittgenstein's *Tractatus* and "Lecture on Ethics" in chapter 2, and in my discussion of the difficulty of Kafka's parable in relation to Coetzee's enigmatic, parabolic *Childhood of Jesus* in chapter 5, the crux of Guillory's observation in that passage also serves as a point of departure for much early commentary on Kafka's work, Theodor Adorno's and Walter Benjamin's in particular.[55]

Both philosophers, among the earliest of Kafka's critical admirers, focus closely on how the peculiar difficulty of Kafka's writing pushes readers to the very limits of understanding while refusing us the comfort of explanation. Kafka solicits interpretation in every sentence, they each announce, while at the same time strenuously defying it. And even now, equipped with all the historicizing critical studies accumulated over the course of the past seventy-odd years, readers and critics continue to give voice to their sense that the difficulty at stake in Kafka's works remains ever intact, confirmed by our very failure to resolve it entirely with any combination of outside assistance and our own wits. But this same experience of struggle and failure that Kafka's difficult writing and active defiance of definitive interpretation gives rise to in readers also attests to the enduring power of the unique kind of teaching and interpretive training that Kafka has to offer. Equally inconclusive are the questions about the meaning of life that resound throughout Woolf's novels. Woolf's fascination with irresolvable, existential questions of what Bloom calls "a different order of difficulty" flourished in her writing under the influence of the same "Great Russians" who influenced Wittgenstein while he was writing the *Tractatus*.

Fourfold Difficulty

As George Steiner notes in his classic essay on the topic, "On Difficulty," when we describe a text as being difficult, we may mean a number of very different things.[56] Faced with trying to account for the functions and effects of the complex character of twentieth-century aesthetic forms, our critical practice requires some classification of different sorts of difficulty. Steiner offers a typology of four principal modes of difficulty that characterize modern poetry and literature: contingent, modal, tactical, and ontological. His taxonomy offers a helpful delineation of the different orders of difficulty at issue in the works of Wittgenstein, Kafka, Woolf, Joyce, and Coetzee that I examine in the chapters below.

Contingent difficulties are posed by the unfamiliar words and allusions readers encounter in modernist literature and poetics marked by a shift toward a new demand of literacy that requires the "archival gathering" necessary to understand the "museum-catalogue" of such works as Eliot's *Waste Land*, Pound's *Cantos*, or Joyce's encyclopedic *Ulysses* (OD, 26). Faced with unaccustomed vocabularies and obscure references, readers of such texts turn to dictionaries, concordances, or encyclopedias for clarification. We resolve these lexical forms of difficulty rather easily by looking them up.

As Joyce's Leopold Bloom attests, however, in his comment in "Ithaca" about appealing to "literature of instruction" to aid us in our task of reading difficult literature, the work of resolving contingent difficulty with the help of glossaries and compendiums can nonetheless leave readers with a lingering sense of having "derived imperfect conviction from the text" (U, 677) Modal difficulties occur when a text still seems opaque to us even after we have looked up all there is to look up and have rendered its lexical-grammatical components as clear as we can make them. We confront modal difficulties when the art work before us articulates a stance toward human conditions that we find somehow alien, or when we feel we are not a part of the audience for which it seems destined.

Of Steiner's four types of difficulty, it is the last two, tactical and ontological, that are my main concern in this study. Before moving on to an overview of the ontological difficulty that is closest to the "different order of difficulty" at the center of this book, I offer a preliminary account of tactical difficulty, in the various modes in which it manifests itself as a central component of the five primary texts that are my focus in the succeeding chapters.

Tactical Difficulty

Tactical difficulties are created by design; they result from an author's *deliberate* moves to deal in obscurity. Writers use difficulty strategically in a number of formal contexts in order to achieve various results. In the chapters below, I examine tactical difficulty in three main aspects. Most simply, such difficulty arises in the context of the formal and narrative experimentation characteristic of modernist innovation. Second, tactical uses of difficulty offer a means of baffling readers in instructive contexts—whether by endowing a set of works with cultural capital, and thereby luring readers to institutional academic study, or engaging readers instead in the creative interpretive work demanded by the kind of ethical teaching offered in parables and other extended parabolic works that operate in deliberate perplexity more generally. Third, this purposive use of obscurity serves to generate a more attentive and responsive communicative relationship between reader and text.

First of all, then, a text's difficulty can result, whether by accident or design, from a writer's calculated efforts to reinvigorate the language and form of his or her art, or to transform an existing instrument of thought or logical system through formal or linguistic experimentation directed at rising to a Poundian epochal challenge to "make it new." Think of the odyssey of different styles Joyce invites us to navigate anew in each of the episodes of *Ulysses*, for example (of which the alienating catechism of "Ithaca" is but one); or of the initially bewildering narrative compression of time and the syntactic innovation that characterize the overlapping fragments of free indirect discourse that Woolf uses so artfully in her novels to prompt readers to enter imaginatively and intimately into other minds; or, finally, of Wittgenstein's efforts in the *Tractatus* to lead readers to an authentic practice of philosophy (and way of living in the world) by acting as a kind of trickster or, in Steiner's words, "logical terrorist." With his aphoristic work of consciously deployed nonsensical propositions, Wittgenstein seeks to confer on his readers a new perspective of clarity by exploding from within the "soiled organon" of the illusory philosophical systems to which they are attracted (OD, 34).

In the second aspect with which I am concerned here, tactical difficulty functions to baffle the unsolicited reader, at least temporarily, and can also serve to beckon to a select coterie of elite readers—or indeed to the ordinary readers intent on accumulating the knowledge and sophistication required to attain the highbrow cultural literacy that will grant them entry into such an in-group. As Guillory and others have argued, the celebration of tactical forms of difficulty that function to exclude in this way has contributed to canon formation and justified the creation of attendant courses of academic study established to teach that canon to the uninitiated.

The tactical use of difficulty to bewilder the layperson while appealing to an elect readership is also a central feature of a very different mode of instruction that, as I have already indicated, is central to my study here: the parable. As I show in my discussion of Kafka and Wittgenstein in chapter 2, these miniature stories convey moral or spiritual teaching via simple illustrations, with the ostensible aim of making their point more readily understood by readers or hearers. But the simplicity of the genre is deceptive; parables function not to make interpretation easy for us, but often quite the contrary. To understand what a parable aims to teach us, we must perform the challenging creative work of bridging the gap between the figurative language of the telling and the view of reality it strives to illuminate through its teaching. Unlike some allegories can do, however, parables do not resolve into a single fixed message or clearly legible moral lesson applicable to corresponding real-life situations but can generate a proliferation of meanings. The point of parables is to engage readers in exegetical struggles that sharpen our critical faculties, making us more adept readers and thinkers, and possibly even fuller moral beings. For the ultimate aim of parabolic instruction is to get us to the point where we can go on to incorporate the imaginative skills acquired through our interpretive engagement with the parable form into the way we live our lives and communicate with others.

In *The Genesis of Secrecy*, Frank Kermode poses a crucial question about the availability to readers of the kind of moral instruction offered in parables. His question offers implicit guidance in my literary and philosophical investigations throughout *A Different Order of Difficulty*, and particularly in my reading of Kafka's, Wittgenstein's, and Coetzee's texts, each of which I argue works to challenge readers in a broadly parabolic way. The question is essentially this: do the Christian parables (and the wider genre of literary parables, Kafka's among them, for which Jesus's instructive mode in the Gospels serves as a model) strive to be accessible to all readers seeking a deeper understanding? Or, alternately, does their opacity function tactically to exclude all but an elect few among them?[57]

The question whether parabolic texts are destined for a select readership and work principally to impede the access of the unsolicited reader resonates in my reading of Kafka's inconclusive metaparable and in my discussion of Wittgenstein's and Coetzee's more extended parabolic works, and the method of ethical and religious instruction they epitomize.

In each of their instructively provocative works, these three writers share a particularly strong belief in the ethical and spiritual valence of literature and an equally strong commitment to the transformative possibilities of tactically difficult texts.

Wittgenstein's "book of ethics" functions parabolically in its own use of tactical difficulty to bring readers to the enlightenment of "seeing the world in the right way"—at least the readers who, as he says, will take "pleasure" in the book, and read it "with understanding" (TLP, p. 27). But are we then to attribute to Wittgenstein a spirit of pedagogical generosity, and ascribe to his text a potentially universal availability? Some things Wittgenstein says suggest that in spite of its daunting complexity, the *Tractatus* is a democratic book, written to appeal to the general reader's capacity of understanding. And yet, he opens his preface with the proviso that the book "will perhaps only be understood by those who have themselves already thought the thoughts which are expressed in it—or similar thoughts," thereby leaving open the possibility that the book's difficulty serves to draw insiders still further in, while restricting the access of the uninitiated (TLP, p. 27).

Wittgenstein's opening gambit in the *Tractatus* thus reaffirms the ambiguity Kermode identifies in his question about the general accessibility of the scriptural parables he considers, along with Kafka's latter-day riffs on parables uttered within that biblical tradition. The question also lingers in my treatment of the parabolic teaching at issue in Coetzee's enigmatic *Childhood of Jesus*. I return to this guiding question in my discussion of Coetzee's fiction at the end of chapter 5 (and the book itself), where I consider whether we should understand challenging parabolic works like these as composed with the aim of reaching *anyone* truly committed to seeking understanding (or the saving Word, literary or religious), or whether the teaching they have to offer stems instead from a commitment to remaining exclusive of all but the few already endowed with a certain baseline receptiveness to it.

In the third aspect I explore in this book, tactical difficulty operates to block or delay the interpretive process in a way that can deepen and intensify the experience of reading. By maneuvering readers into a state of perplexity that slows our apprehension, authors who deliberately deploy difficulty effectively compel committed readers to reflect more thoughtfully on the text at hand, and to pay meticulous attention to the particular textual features that give rise to our confusion. Attending to these features can offer guidance that galvanizes our resumed textual investigations. By imposing on readers both bewilderment and the delay in understanding needed properly to work through that bewilderment, writers who deploy difficulty in this way are better able to engage readers in the ongoing task of creatively grappling with our own sense of puzzlement with the aim of reaching the ultimate insights the text has to offer.

Wittgenstein's own tactical maneuvers in the *Tractatus* (his creation of a so-called treatise, made up of nonsense sentences that function ironically as a part of an instructive method meant to serve the consistently earnest ethical aim of promoting a radical change in his reader's outlook) are calculated, like the tactical difficulty my other central authors use in their own texts, to lead readers toward transformative understanding by imposing on us the delay in interpretation that gives us time to focus on the questions our perplexity gives rise to, and which go on to offer important guidance in our ongoing investigations.

The tactical use of difficulty that finds creative expression in Wittgenstein's self-proclaimed "strange" *Tractatus* is part of willed effort on his part to use a carefully wrought aesthetic work to reach his readers at a deep, ethical level. His method of doing so involves engaging us, step by step, up his proverbial ladder in a dialectical exchange in which he first uses Socratic-Kierkegaardian irony to subvert our misplaced allegiance to theory by tricking us into recognizing our confused attraction to nonsense. Once he has led his readers to such clarity, the text that got us there has served its purpose. Readers are to relinquish the book and set ourselves to the ongoing transformative work on the self only we can do. The difficult work toward which Wittgenstein seeks to guide us in the *Tractatus*, however, and which we must continue even once we have responded to the dialectical strategy he uses in the text, exceeds the merely tactical. It comes closer to the broad class of difficulty Steiner calls "ontological." The *Tractatus*, and each of the literary texts I examine alongside it in this book, are centrally occupied with this order of difficulty along with the others.

A Different Order of Difficulty

The three classes of difficulty I have examined so far are, ultimately, resolvable. But difficulties of the fourth category, ontological, cannot simply be looked up. They cannot be resolved by readjustment of sensibility, and do not result from intentional techniques of creative uncertainty. Ontological difficulty confronts us with unanswerable questions about the nature of human language, meaning, and significance, and the ultimate purpose of the being and the work of art. This category of difficulty becomes a desideratum in the turn to obscurity in the early twentieth century and continues to thrive at the center of contemporary literature like Coetzee's, elaborated in conscious relation to the ideas and formal concerns of his precursors.

Modernism's attraction to such difficulty arises in part from a cultural desire to break with the authority of traditionalism, and also from a sense of the inauthentic situation of humankind in a climate of an eroded relation to language. It manifests itself in the homeward turn to the oldest of questions and quests for answers featured so prominently in the Ithacan catechism at the heart of the *Nostos* of Joyce's modern Odyssey. It also shows forth in the questions of meaning and existence that plague Tolstoy during the life crisis he describes in his *Confession*, and in Wittgenstein's own meditations on these same questions under Tolstoy's and Dostoevsky's sway. Questions about the meaning of life also sound on relentlessly and inconclusively throughout Woolf's novelistic works, themselves written under what she calls "the Russian influence."[58] Questions of this sort also fuel the quest for self-transformation and a "new life" that both determines the form and propels the narrative of Coetzee's *Childhood of Jesus*. The formal inconclusiveness of Kafka's "On Parables" and its meditation on the meaning of poetics in everyday life emphatically performs the irresolvable nature of problems of ontological difficulty. In his concern in the *Tractatus* with the "problem of life" and the quest for its solution, Wittgenstein joins the literary writers I examine in this book in his engagement with this type of difficulty (TLP, 6.521).

Discussions of philosophical and literary struggles with questions of the meaning of life as a particularly twentieth-century fixation most readily calls to the popular imagination the later French existentialism of Sartre, Beauvoir, and Camus that emerged under the influence of Heidegger (whose thinking was informed by writing by Nietzsche, Kierkegaard, Tolstoy, and Dostoevsky).[59] By looking instead at Wittgenstein (whose early thinking, like Heidegger's, was differently shaped by these same figures), *A Different Order of Difficulty* offers an alternate approach to understanding modernism's peculiar attraction to these age-old concerns of existence. My attention to the fixation in the twentieth century and beyond on existential questions and quests for meaningful answers speaks to the extent to which both Wittgenstein's philosophy and the work of my central literary authors are rooted in existential ideas that are deeply related to, yet elaborated outside of, an established existentialist tradition.

Modernism's attraction to this class of difficulty emerges in a discursive convergence of early twentieth-century philosophers and writers

responding to the fragility and complexity of modern life and the cata-
clysm of war with an urgent attention to obscurity that brings them back
to the very oldest of riddles and questions of existence. This attraction
to difficulty shows forth as an obsession with the transformative power
of puzzles and enigmas, and the hard work of figuring out meaningful
solutions. The problems that Leopold Bloom designates as posing "a
different order of difficulty," as I have shown, exceed the multiple intellectual challenges or calls for erudition the self-consciously crafted "Big
Works" of high modernism also notoriously entail. At stake within them
is a search for answers to the elusive problems of existence: the meaning of life (and the quest for how best to live it), as we have seen, but
also the problems of the self and other minds; the possibility of redemptive change; the contrast between how things are in the world and their
significance from the point of view of the "higher," for example. Enduring existential problems like these, which have driven humanistic inquiry since the Enlightenment, become an especially pressing concern in
the fiction and philosophy of the early twentieth century. Exploring the
ways in which these difficulties are handled in the work of Wittgenstein,
Kafka, Woolf, and Joyce is my task in chapters 1–4 of this book.

In chapter 1, "Wittgenstein's Puzzle: The Transformative Ethics of
the *Tractatus*," I offer an account of to the key aspects of the "resolute"
program of Wittgenstein interpretation I have adumbrated in this introduction. I also examine Wittgenstein's 1921–22 work in relation to the
different philosophical and cultural contexts out of which it arose. I turn
in the chapter to Wittgenstein's claim in the *Tractatus* that "ethics and
aesthetics are one" (TLP, 6.421), relating that claim to his more general
views about the ethically instructive capacity of certain works of literature. I account for the impact of these views on the unique aesthetic form
of the book, and the relationship of Wittgenstein's stylistic craft to his
teaching method in the book and conception of its transformative ethical aim. I go on to consider the literary character of Wittgenstein's philosophical writing, returning to a remark of his that I cited briefly at the
beginning of this introduction: that "philosophy ought really to be written only as one would *write a poem*" (or perhaps rather that "philosophy should really only be *poeted [Philosophie dürfte man eigentlich nur
dichten]*"). Wittgenstein makes it clear that his commitment to this view
was hardly a weak one, for as he avers, it effectively "[sums] up [his] attitude to philosophy" (CV, 24). At the end of the chapter, I take up the
question of how Wittgenstein's aesthetic commitments and ethical aspirations in the *Tractatus* contribute to the book's engagement (and ours)
with the different orders of difficulty at issue within it. I explore how

these commitments inform Wittgenstein's reliance on number of different orders of difficulty in his chosen way of leading his readers to clarity
by way of obscurity. Wittgenstein's embrace of opacity and obscurity in
the *Tractatus*, I suggest, speaks to the connection between his work and
Kafka's.

In my second chapter, "The Everyday's Fabulous Beyond: Nonsense,
Parable, and the Ethics of the Literary in Kafka and Wittgenstein," I
continue my exploration of the uses of obscurity in the oblique modes of
teaching offered in Wittgenstein's and Kafka's different modernist texts,
turning to a discussion of the resonances between Kafka's brand of parabolic teaching (exemplified in his metaparable "On Parables") and the
parabolic aspects of Wittgenstein's own method of ethical instruction in
the *Tractatus*. The chapter addresses the rigorous exegetical demands of
Kafka's and Wittgenstein's respective texts. Both require readers to take
up the combined cognitive and affective work necessary (though not
sufficient) to the task of trying to figure out what they would have us recognize and come to understand about (modern) life via our engagement
with the indirect teaching and training conveyed in their philosophical-
poetic texts. The point of these works is not to deliver knowledge or certainty. In their authors' attempts to lead readers to change their ways of
seeing, speaking, both texts remain deliberately open-ended, unresolved,
and fraught with ambiguity.

In the context of a reading of Kafka's parable, I examine Wittgenstein's commitment in the *Tractatus* and informal 1929 "Lecture on Ethics" to the view that "ethics and aesthetics are one" (TLP, 6.421), and
that ethics includes "the most essential part of what is generally called
Aesthetics."[60] I explore that commitment in terms of its connection with
another view Wittgenstein held in these early texts: that ethical sentences
are nonsensical by their very nature, and that all our attempts to give
expression to our ethical or religious experience of the world will necessarily result in nonsense (LE, 36–44). Like the "ethical" sentences we
use to give voice to our experience of the joy and difficulty of life, metaphorical figures, seen from a Tractarian perspective, amount to expressions of nonsense. Yet Wittgenstein's desire to disabuse his readers of an
attachment to metaphysical nonsense does not keep him from valuing
figurative language any more than he does the human tendency to come
out with nonsense when it comes to expressing our ethical experience
of life. I argue in the chapter for the potential significance and literary-
critical uses of these facets of Wittgenstein's ethical teaching for literary
studies. Reading the *Tractatus* and "On Parables" together sheds important light on the intimate relationship among both authors' various

uses of nonsense, obscurity, and figurative language. It works to clarify how Kafka's and Wittgenstein's different ways of embracing obscurity, nonsense, and their textually instructive uses hang together with their keen shared interest in the communicative power of poetic and figurative language—the kind we find not just in "high literature," but in the figurations that animate jokes, parables, stories, and ordinary turns of phrase. If these are sometimes dark, they are no less illuminating for it.

In one way or another, each of the succeeding chapters of *A Different Order of Difficulty* continues the work of grappling with the central question Kafka puts before us in his short, late work: how do literature and the humanities guide us in the perplexity of existence and the struggles of life in the face of the apparent gap between the everyday real and the always unattainable yet still longed-for "higher"?

Chapter 3, "Woolf, Diamond, and the Difficulty of Reality," attends to the abiding modernist obsession with the question of life's meaning that shows forth especially vividly in Woolf's writing in the expressions of a longing for painfully out-of-reach answers to the perennial existential questions "why?" that pervade the godless ordinary world of her novels. The chapter focuses specifically on Woolf's *To the Lighthouse*, for it is in that elegiac novel that these preoccupations arise with greatest urgency. Woolf's fixation on question, quest, and the yearning for a revised understanding of life in the novel offers a way of coping with the specific category of "different-order" difficulty that Diamond calls "the difficulty of reality" and describes as the experience of an ordinary sublime so astonishing that it resists our very cognitive powers.[61] Diamond's account of this weighty order of difficulty creates a new philosophical context in which also to understand Woolf's treatment of the difficulties of life in her writing. Reading Woolf with reference to Diamond shows us how matters that lie at the heart of Woolf's novelistic form intersect with the Wittgensteinian and Cavellian preoccupations that inform Diamond's own thinking about literature and moral philosophy. Making connections among Wittgenstein's, Diamond's, and Woolf's different treatments of these issues brings into clearer focus the philosophical sympathies that attest to the mutual significance of each of their particular brands of modernism.

In chapter 4, "Wittgenstein, Joyce, and the Vanishing Problem of Life," I examine how Wittgenstein's *Tractatus* and the "Ithaca" episode of Joyce's *Ulysses* both explore problems of "a different order of difficulty" through the guise of the more routinely difficult "propositions of natural science" (TLP, 6.53). Both texts are structured in a catalogue of questions and ordered assertions that gives the appearance of progressing toward a conclusion that the author ultimately withholds. Both rely on pseudoscientific precision in their treatments of moral and existential matters; make similarly performative use of dogmatic, didactic tones; and echo the language of scripture alongside that of science and logic. Joyce and Wittgenstein challenge readers to work to understand their respective authorial (and deauthorizing) strategies and the relationship of their distinct faux doctrines to the literary, ethical, and philosophical aims of their works. Significantly, both the *Tractatus* and "Ithaca" gesture at a grounded, secular kind of transfiguration, characterized by what Wittgenstein describes as the "vanishing" of one's problems that goes along with "seeing the world in the right way" (6.521, 6.54). I argue in the chapter that in Leopold Bloom, Joyce creates a modern literary exemplar of a person who has come to see the world rightly in just this way. He adopts a creatively willed attitude of reflective peace and resolution that grants him temporary rest from the onslaught of questions with which he is confronted in the "impersonal catechism" that provides "Ithaca" with its form. Bloom's ethical perspective is one I liken to the outlook Wittgenstein calls "happy," and which he says makes the world "become quite another" (TLP, 6.43). In the *Tractatus*, I argue, Wittgenstein aims to steer his readers toward a sort of secular-spiritual transfiguration similar to the one Bloom achieves in "Ithaca." The transformative impulse of Wittgenstein's early work is in many ways galvanized by his reading of Tolstoy, but it also coincides with Nietzsche's conception of authentic redemption as a secular, post-Christian form of transfiguration.

Joyce's move away from an interest in epiphany in his early work to a depiction of Bloom's protracted, counter-epiphanic transfiguration by the end of *Ulysses* runs parallel to the transition that occurs between Wittgenstein's early and later work in the philosophical method with which he approaches the search for clarity. Looking at these two works together gives us new purchase for understanding both the continuity of Wittgenstein's philosophy (from early to late) and also the change he makes from the method of the *Tractatus* to that of the *Investigations*.

My discussion of Wittgenstein's conception of a "happy" attitude toward the world and of the transfigurative, yet inconclusive, end to Bloom's meandering quest and Wittgenstein's clarificatory philosophical activity anticipates my discussion in chapter 5, "A New Life Is a New Life: Teaching and Transformation in Coetzee's *Childhood of Jesus*." That chapter deals with Coetzee's depiction in his enigmatic, highly intertextual novel of a very different (and equally inconclusive) quest for a "new life," and critical assessment of the "happy" as an ideal goal for the work of ethical self-transformation. This concluding chapter, a point of synthesis of many of the book's overarching concerns, examines Coetzee's treatment of an unrelenting longing for new ways of seeing, and living, and being at home in language and the world. In it, I argue that in *The Childhood of Jesus*, Coetzee draws on the form of the parable, and also on Wittgenstein's thought and instructive method, in his own attempt to use his own suggestive parabolic text to train us therapeutically to be more attentive readers and ethical thinkers.

1   Wittgenstein's Puzzle: The Transformative Ethics of the *Tractatus*

Anything your reader can do for himself, leave to him.
—**Ludwig Wittgenstein**[1]

All I give you is a method. I cannot teach you any new truths.
—**Ludwig Wittgenstein**[2]

You Must Change Your Life

The work of coming to understand Wittgenstein's philosophical, ethical, and aesthetic pursuits in the *Tractatus* in light of the attraction to difficulty, transformation, and oblique instruction that establishes a such a vital connection between his thinking and writing and that of his modernist literary contemporaries, I think, really must begin with an overview of the book's rootedness in the broader early twentieth-century cultural context in which it first appeared. Wittgenstein completed the *Tractatus* while a prisoner of war in Italy in the summer of 1918, after having served as a soldier during the Great War. The *Tractatus*, the only major work Wittgenstein would publish in his lifetime, first materialized as the "Logisch-Philosophische Abhandlung," in *Annalen der Philosophie* in 1921. It would later emerge in its authorized book version, with an introduction by Bertrand Russell and under its familiar Latin title, in C. K. Ogden's English translation in 1922. The book we now know as Wittgenstein's *Tractatus* is thus a work that came into being in its final form during the First World War. It is also a work that ultimately emerged, along with the works by Woolf, Joyce, and Kafka that I examine here, into the world of that war's aftermath—an era of sweeping historic and cultural change and unprecedented artistic creativity and productivity.

In *Wittgenstein's Ladder*, Marjorie Perloff takes both source contexts (the war and the world of its aftermath) to be definitive, reading the *Tractatus* as a "war book and also as an avant-garde one." Begun in 1915 under the principal influence of Frege and Russell, the *Tractatus* would be transformed by Wittgenstein's war experience from the more straightforward, scientifically minded logical treatise of the dictated "Notes on Logic" into a text that, as Perloff points out, also bears resemblance to the avant-garde poetics of the 1910s and 1920s.[3]

In his own account of Wittgenstein's life and its relevance to our understanding of the philosophical stakes of his work, Ray Monk emphasizes the shift in the *Tractatus*'s development during the war. "The remarks in it about ethics, aesthetics, the soul and the meaning of life," he observes, "have their origin in . . . an impulse that has as its stimulus a knowledge of death, suffering and misery."[4] Monk also credits Wittgenstein's fervent reading of Tolstoy (whose treatment of the soul and the question of the meaning of life offered Wittgenstein a salve in this time of crisis during the war) with contributing to a "kind of personal transformation" and "religious conversion" in the man, which also brought a new spirit to his work, transforming the *Tractatus* from "an analysis of logical symbolism in the spirit of Frege and Russell into the curiously hybrid work which we know today, combining as it does logical theory with religious mysticism" (DG, 116).

Monk affirms that Wittgenstein's motives for enlisting in the Austrian army were more complex than just a desire to defend country or empire. His move to join up in the first place was something his sister, Hermine, attributed to what she called "an intense desire to take something difficult upon himself and to do something other than purely intellectual work." She saw his choice to enlist as linked to his desire to "turn into a different person" (DG, 111).[5]

Hermine Wittgenstein's reflection calls our attention to the yearning for radical change that drove Wittgenstein to face warfare and expose himself to potentially harrowing circumstances in a dramatic attempt to satisfy it. It was this same kind of yearning that led Wittgenstein to seek out what he would later call the "saving" word in Tolstoy's *Gospel in Brief*, the book he claimed "virtually kept him alive" during his time at the front (DG, 132). As Perloff argues throughout her writing on Wittgenstein and the bearing of his personal life on his philosophy, an ardent spiritual longing for self-transformation—a longing to become a different person—was a desire he would nurture throughout his life.[6] That the persistent longing for change Wittgenstein felt in his life also informed his philosophical thinking is made especially evident in the transformative aspirations of the *Tractatus*.

Wittgenstein was deeply and consistently interested in modes of self-reflection and first-person confessional expression, which he saw as a means of warding off self-deception and evasion by undertaking the hard work of grappling with confusion, complexity and opacity with the aim of achieving the clarity, acceptance, and courage so important to his philosophical thinking. His view that confession can play an important role in a person's efforts to take her life in new directions has a great deal to tell us about the kind of ethical teaching he sought to impart to his readers in his philosophical work. As I indicated in the introduction, the transformative aim of the *Tractatus* is inseparable from the activity of elucidation and of overcoming confusion (both personal and philosophical) in which the book's author takes himself to be engaged, and in which he asks that his reader take part. The nonsensical propositions that Wittgenstein uses to guide our imagination across the arc of the book's pseudoargument, in effect, represent a selection of the very kinds of pseudopropositions that he himself finds attractive. These pseudopropositions function as a part of Wittgenstein's complex therapeutic method of being responsive to the metaphysical impulse of his readers, an impulse he has felt himself, and which he recognizes as part of the human condition. Wittgenstein performs in the *Tractatus* a thoughtful consideration or interrogation of the things he is "tempted to say"—to use a phrase that (as Cavell often emphasizes) frequently frames his remarks in the *Investigations*. With this in mind, I want to suggest here that if we aim to read the book with the kind of understanding its author seeks for his reader, we would do well to view it against the background of his commitment to rituals of confession (including literary accounts of the experience of such rituals by Augustine, Tolstoy, and others) in his philosophical practice as well as in his life. For we can begin to see the shape of the ethical transformation Wittgenstein seeks for his readers by seeing it as analogous to the kind of personal renewal one might seek through an honest confession of one's "sins." The difficult process of self-assessment that confession and other forms of first-personal disclosure entail bears a deep resemblance to the process of overcoming illusion toward which Wittgenstein aims to lead his readers in the *Tractatus*.

In a conversation with Friedrich Waismann of the Vienna Circle in the years following the publication of the *Tractatus*, Wittgenstein emphasized the importance of his use of the first person, describing it as "something very essential." When there is nothing more to be stated, he says, "all I can do is step forth and speak in the first person."[7] The claim I want to make here is not that the *Tractatus* itself is exactly a confessional work. Among the book's numbered propositions, we find neither the author's personal musings nor any hint of the factual account of his life or chronicling of his moral failings that we might expect a strictly confessional narrative to contain. Wittgenstein expresses himself in the first person only occasionally; at the very beginning and the very end of the book, and at 5.63 and 5.631, and then in only a quite abbreviated fashion. And yet it is important to recognize that this is no mere passing rhetorical move. Rather, it is an important ethical and aesthetic aspect of his early authorship, one whose contribution to the overall method of the *Tractatus* should not be underestimated.

Attention to Wittgenstein's view of the importance of first-person expression also serves to remind us that while the *Tractatus* hardly qualifies as a characteristic example of confessional writing, it is nonetheless a book written from the "religious point of view" of an author who, although he declared himself "not a religious man," was deeply drawn to Augustine's and Tolstoy's different confessional works, and who himself saw confession as a valuable move toward combating illusion to attain the kind of clarity in life that he hoped would also carry over into an improved understanding of language, and the practice of philosophy.[8] I want to suggest here that we can begin to understand Wittgenstein's remark at the end of the *Tractatus*—that it is only by overcoming illusion that gives rise to nonsense that we can come to "see the world in the right way"—by viewing it in light of his later claim that "confession has to be part of your new life" (CV, 18).[9]

The fixation on self-transformation that led Wittgenstein to engage in practical rituals of confession and attentive reading of the narratives of mystical experience and conversion offered by Augustine, Schopenhauer, Tolstoy, and William James also underwrites his philosophical pedagogy from the *Tractatus* onward. It is visible in the aim of his first book, where it finds expression in the promise he holds out in the penultimate proposition: that by surmounting (*überwinden*) the sentences of the book (or, more aptly, *overcoming* them, as an illness or a confusion), attentive readers will have undergone a vital change in outlook that will allow us to "see the world in the right way."[10] The metaphor Wittgenstein later uses to express his conception of the work of the philosopher (as that of offering therapeutic treatment to the sicknesses of the under-standing and the will) speaks to the continuity of his commitment to a therapeutic method from his earliest work to his latest.[11] In the *Philo-sophical Investigations*, Wittgenstein famously views philosophy as a therapy used to deliver readers from the pictures that hold us captive, thus helping us to find our way about by teaching us to look with greater clar-ity on the problems of philosophy, language, and life (PI, §123, §115).

Wittgenstein's consistent engagement with a desire for self-transformation arises repeatedly throughout his writing in echoes of the calls for transfiguration that resound in the modernist literature of his time. Such calls are exemplified in Rainer Maria Rilke's famous com-mand at the end of his 1908 poem "Archaïscher Torso Apollos": "Du mußt dein Leben ändern," "you must change your life."[12] Expressing his antitheoretical views in a 1946 notebook, for example, Wittgen-stein proclaims that "sound doctrines are all useless." He then concludes abruptly and succinctly: "you have to change your *life*" (CV, 61). His talk of "seeing the world in the right way" in the *Tractatus* also coin-cides with Robert Musil's narration in *Der Mann ohne Eigenschaften* of a quest for "the right way of living [*das Rechte Leben*]."[13]

The Tractatus *and the Modernist Milieu*

Wittgenstein's thinking thus clearly has resonances with the literature of his modernist milieu. And yet, while certain elements of his philoso-phy speak to his sympathy with the spirit of modernism, he was often quite unsympathetic with the artistic developments and technological climate of his age. Kevin Cahill argues that "one can read the *Tractatus* as containing a critique of metaphysics-*cum*-critique of culture," and in-deed that there is a spiritually-charged cultural critique running through all of Wittgenstein's philosophy.[14] His own modern (and modernist) cul-tural critique—internal to what he declared was the ethical point of the *Tractatus*—is rooted in related complaints he issues throughout his man-uscripts that what he describes in the *Tractatus* as "the whole modern conception of the world" (TLP, 6.371) is driven by a misplaced faith in the power of causal-scientific explanation that numbs the sense of the "wonder" for the deeply mysterious place of human life in the world that he would have us reawaken in ourselves. In an early draft of the foreword for *Philosophical Remarks*, Wittgenstein writes that the spirit of his age, characterized by an idolatry of progress, the pursuit of sci-entific advancement, and scientistic explanation, is "alien" and "uncon-genial" to his own ways of thinking (CV, 8). He has no sympathy for the prevailing current of European civilization, he writes, and does not understand its goals. "My type of thinking is not wanted in this present age," he once said to his friend Maurice Drury. "I have to swim so strongly against the tide. Perhaps in a hundred years people will really want what I am writing."[15] In the intervening decades since he made that remark, a diverse set of philosophers, intellectual historians, and literary critics have attended to Wittgenstein's aversion to the spirit of his times and ambivalence about the modern while offering a variety of compelling accounts of his works that place them firmly in the canon of modernist cultural productions that exemplify the predominant aesthetic movement of the twentieth century.[16]

Appearing in its most influential book form in 1922, the *Tractatus* emerged squarely within modernism's much-touted annus mirabilis, which also saw the publication of Joyce's *Ulysses*, Woolf's *Jacob's Room*, and T. S. Eliot's *The Waste Land*. As Michael North points out in his *Reading 1922*, the "miracle year" that, with the appearance of the *Tractatus*, ushered in the "linguistic turn" and produced some of the chief works of Anglophone high-modernist experimentation, was also declared in the *Daily Mail* as the first truly postwar year in England. It was likewise the first year of the new, post-Christian era announced by Ezra Pound, the year F. Scott Fitzgerald pronounced the definitive moment of the Jazz Age (and the year in which he set *The Great Gatsby*). That year, which has also aptly been called the annus mirabilis of the Harlem Renaissance, *Shuffle Along* took the stage, and Claude McKay's *Harlem Shadows* was published in tandem with such works as James Weldon Johnson's *Book of American Negro Poetry*, and Carter Woodson's *The Negro in Our History*. During the course of that same year, F. W. Murnau released his war-inspired *Nosferatu*; Rilke wrote his *Sonnette an Orpheus* and finished his *Duineser Elegien*; and Kafka began work on *Das Schloss*, published "Ein Hungerkünstler," and wrote many more short parables and aphorisms. In "Mr. Bennett and Mrs. Brown," Woolf famously dates the year that "everything changed" at 1910, but as North observes, "it is worth mentioning . . . that she first started writing about this break in 1922."[17]

Wittgenstein's Habsburg Vienna origins provide another context in which to view the source of the characteristics that he shares with a broader cultural modernism. In their *Wittgenstein's Vienna*, first published nearly fifty years ago, philosophers Allan Janik and Stephen Toulmin brought to Wittgenstein studies a radical reinterpretation of the bearing of the philosopher's life on his work.[18] With their pivotal study, Janik and Toulmin offered an important supplemental alternative to existing intellectual histories that examined Wittgenstein almost exclusively in terms of his connection to the analytic philosophical tradition of Frege, Russell, and Cambridge philosophy, thereby obscuring his rich formative relationship with the late Habsburg Viennese culture in which he came of age. Their point of departure is the question "What philosophical problems did Wittgenstein himself already have in mind, before he ever got in touch with Frege and Russell?" (WV, 28).

Arguing that Wittgenstein's thought is only fully intelligible when considered in relation to the "historical and cultural background which formed integral parts of [his] original *Problemstellung*," Janik and Toulmin situate their reading of his work in the intellectual and cultural context of fin-de-siècle Vienna in the final years of the "*Kaiserlich und Königlich*" empire that Musil satirically called "Kakania" (WV, 32, 13). As they point out, the milieu in which Wittgenstein grew up "was one of the "most fertile, original and creative periods in art and architecture, music, literature and psychology, as well as in philosophy." As a member of a particularly well-connected family, growing up in "a house that formed one of the cultural foci of Viennese life in the years between 1895 and 1914," Wittgenstein had unparalleled personal exposure to the work of preeminent artists, composers, and scientific thinkers of his time and place—among them Ludwig Boltzmann, Sigmund Freud, Heinrich Hertz, Theodor Herzl, Gustave Klimt, Adolf Loos, Karl Kraus, Ernst Mach, Fritz Mauthner, Arnold Schönberg, Robert Musil, Otto Weininger, and Stefan Zweig (WV, 9).

Wittgenstein's writing became increasingly legible in a modernist context not only in the wake of Janik and Toulmin's book, but also as a result of the publication that soon followed of the collections Cahill has called "extratextual" sources—the various volumes of diaries, students' lecture notes, personal recollections, and recorded conversations, especially those of Maurice Drury and Rush Rhees—and the appearance in 1977 of *Vermischte Bemerkungen* (known to the English-speaking world in Peter Winch's translation as *Culture and Value*), a volume of remarks selected from Wittgenstein's *Nachlass* that covers a range of questions associated with religion, ethics, and the arts.[19] In his writing on Wittgenstein's later work, Stanley Cavell has been equally instrumental in articulating the relationship between Wittgenstein and cultural modernism.[20]

The ongoing relevance of Janik and Toulmin's study attests to its lasting impact on the field. Indeed, the work of expanding understandings of the cultural roots of Wittgenstein's thinking that they began in the early 1970s has since provided an important, enduring resource for philosophers, critics, and intellectual historians writing in the wake of their seminal (and now updated) study. *Wittgenstein's Vienna*, and the varied scholarship it has gone on to inspire, continues to loom large as the background of even the most recent work in Wittgenstein and modernism as a topic of inquiry.

Scholarship that has contributed to our understanding of Wittgenstein's relation to the culture of his time nonetheless has not ignored his rather prickly and ambivalent attitude toward modernism and modernity, one that was informed by the influence on his thinking and cultural perspective of figures as diverse as Kraus and Oswald Spengler.[21] As Perloff, Charles Altieri, and others have correctly characterized him, Wittgenstein simultaneously appears to be what Michael LeMahieu has summed up as "an unacknowledged modernist, an avowed anti-modernist, and then again a modernist *malgré lui*."[22] That Wittgenstein's identity as a twentieth-century thinker should involve such a composite of conflict, however, arguably does as much to lend support to seeing Wittgenstein as a creature of modernism as it does to undermine it.[23]

Resolute Tractatus *and Literary Modernism*

The affinities between Wittgenstein and literary modernism around which *A Different Order of Difficulty* coheres are made especially visible by the expanding program of Wittgenstein interpretation that has unfolded under the aegis of the groundbreaking line of interpretation now best known as the "resolute" program, which I adumbrated in the introduction. Most generally construed, readings that contribute to this program account for the ways in which the peculiar method and structure of the *Tractatus* serve an abiding therapeutic aim. Read in a resolute vein, Wittgenstein's early text is thus one in which he is already engaged in an overall therapeutic philosophical activity previously most commonly associated with his later work in the *Investigations*. The therapeutic aim of Wittgenstein's gnomic early book underwrites his method of using an indirect, curative pedagogy geared ultimately (if stealthily) toward bringing about radical change in its reader's ethical outlook and practice of philosophy. Resolute readers locate Wittgenstein's commitment to instruction in the book not in his attempt to put forth metaphysical doctrines or theories about the way language relates to the world, but in his ethical aim of bringing about this dramatic shift in its readers' worldview. Barring local disagreements, adherents to a general resolute program agree in insisting that we take Wittgenstein at his word when he says at the end of the book that the compressed numbered propositions that make up the body of the text we had heretofore taken to advance a logical, metaphysical theory are, in fact, simply nonsense. We are to throw these propositions away, as he says, once they have served what he claims is their clarifying purpose (TLP, 6.54).

In an attempt to find a suitable publisher for his newly completed book, Wittgenstein wrote to Ludwig von Ficker, publisher of the Austrian journal *Der Brenner*. Since it first came to light, Wittgenstein's letter to von Ficker has provided Wittgenstein scholars with invaluable insights into his own conception of the aim of his notoriously difficult book. It is worth reiterating here that Wittgenstein generally eschewed explanation of his work during his lifetime, doing remarkably little to decompress or explain that work to others, even when their misunderstanding of the work was most evident to him.[24] Thus, the letter to von Ficker stands out as Wittgenstein's most patient and personalized attempt on record to offer a reader salient clues to guide him in understanding how to go about reading the *Tractatus*. The content of this letter reveals a great deal about Wittgenstein's philosophical concerns, both ethical and stylistic, and can thus provide us with valuable assistance in understanding the kind of puzzle the *Tractatus* represents.[25]

Wittgenstein tells the publisher: "you won't—I really believe—get too much out of reading it. Because you won't understand it; the content will be strange to you." He continues:

> In reality, it isn't strange to you, for the point of the book is ethical. I once wanted to give a few words in the preface which are actually not in it, but which I'll write to you now because they might be a key for you: I wanted to write that my work consists of two parts: of the one presented here, plus all that I have *not* written. And it is precisely this second part that is the important one. My book draws limits to this sphere of the ethical only from within, as it were, and I am convinced that, this is the ONLY *rigorous* way of drawing those limits. In short, I believe that where *many* others today are just *babbling* [*schwefeln*], I have managed in my book to put everything into place by being silent about it. Therefore, the book will, unless I'm quite wrong, have much to say that you want to say yourself, but perhaps you won't notice that it is said in it. For the time being, I'd recommend that you read the *preface* and the *conclusion* since these express the point most directly.[26]

Wittgenstein's attempt to offer a "key" to understanding the form, content, and method of his "strange" text in his letter provides readers of the *Tractatus* with a number of insights about the book and about its author's general ethical aims. Conant and Diamond have both taken these clues to heart in positing an instructive *frame* that provides structure to Wittgenstein's teaching in the *Tractatus*.[27] It is in this letter that Wittgenstein openly declares the aim of his book to be an *ethical* one.

Because Diamond's designation of the frame of the *Tractatus* has been a point of some controversy, resulting in further elaboration of the idea among resolute readers, it merits further brief attention here. Diamond initially launched the idea of the frame in the geographic terms suggested by Wittgenstein's letter to von Ficker, in which he says it is to be found in the preface and concluding remarks (the body of the text comprising all the other propositions). Following Diamond's lead, Conant also emphasizes the instructive value of the *Tractatus*'s framing propositions. In the wake of Diamond and Conant's early treatment of the issue, questions arose among commentators about whether even resolute readers could make their interpretation plausible without appeal to the guidance of any of the remarks from the body of the text. Critics have also posed questions about whether there can be any independent criterion for judging which propositions should be understood as belonging to the body of the text, and which to the frame.[28] Their questions generally look something like this: "if there are sentences in the *Tractatus* that readers are supposedly allowed to take as meant literally, and as belonging to the 'frame,' then there must be some way of determining which sentences these are. So, for example, if Diamond or Conant or another resolute reader should draw on proposition 4.112, saying that 'Wittgenstein holds that philosophy is an activity,' then surely they must be taking 4.112 to also part of the 'frame.' So what else are these resolute readers counting as 'frame,' and what is the justification for this?"

In response, Conant argues that the frame of the *Tractatus* does not conform to spatial restrictions; whether a proposition is part of the frame is a function a question not only of *where* it occurs in the text, but of *how* it occurs. He broadens the notion of the book's frame to include those sentences in the body of the text that comment on the overall elucidatory strategy of the work, namely those that articulate Frege's context principle (around 3.32), the austere conception of nonsense (around 5.73), and those that discuss the nature of philosophy, situated at the middle of the book, around TLP, 4.112.[29] In a further elaboration of Conant's claims, Michael Kremer argues that the propositions of the frame are the ones that do not succumb to the disintegration of the "theory" developed in the *Tractatus*, which is wrought by the corrosive effect of the book's self-refuting process of clarification. The propositions of the frame are the ones that survive the disintegration of the illusion of sense with recognizable determinate sense still intact.[30]

In the guidance he offers to von Ficker, Wittgenstein goes further than pointing him to the "frame" of his book. He also tells him that the *Tractatus* consists of two parts. The first, he says, is presented in the sentences that make up the body of the book's propositional content. The second part, the truly "important" one, he says, is the one he has not written down, but has instead remained silent about. In the letter, Wittgenstein assures von Ficker that the book has much "in" it that a philosophical layperson would want to say himself, if only he could recognize it within the form of the "strange" or foreign-seeming [*fremd*] text. This statement has led Diamond to attend to the question of what something's being "in" a nonsensical text like the *Tractatus* might amount to, and also to suggest that Wittgenstein meant to address his "strange" book to the ordinary person's understanding rather than to her ignorance ("Ethics and Imagination," 149).

I will return to both of these concerns in the chapters that follow, where I examine them in the context of my discussions of "writing absences" into texts, and the availability of the kinds of oblique ethical teaching aimed at leading readers through obscurity toward clarity that we find not only in Wittgenstein's *Tractatus*, but also in parables like Kafka's, and in extended parabolic writing like Coetzee's.[31] Wittgenstein's efforts to make the teaching he offers "in" his complicated book accessible to his readers, I argue here, hinge on the work he does to draw our attention not only to the differences between the intellectual and cognitive challenges the book initially poses and the tactical and "different" orders of difficulty at issue in it, but also to the complicated interaction between them. For each of these orders of difficulty plays a role in the peculiar method of ethical instruction he employs in the *Tractatus*.

Understanding Wittgenstein's method means first following the advice he offers to von Ficker by looking to the "frame" of the book in its most explicitly established narrower form: its preface and conclusion. In the preface, Wittgenstein tells us that the *Tractatus* is "kein Lehrbuch"—not a textbook (TLP, p. 3). It is thus not a book dedicated to imparting or explaining philosophical doctrine. We will not find any arguments in it to which we can appeal for assistance in finding solutions to the problems of logic, language, or life. The work of philosophy, for Wittgenstein, is an activity of clarification (TLP, 4.112). As such, it does not consist in the construction and deployment of new theories or doctrines destined to solve fundamental dilemmas about how we ought to live and think, but in the work of striving to gain clarity about our relationship to the life we already lead and the language we have already mastered. In the preface, Wittgenstein tells us that the book deals with the problems of philosophy. He aims to show us that having such problems in the first place arises from our tendency to misunderstand the logic of our language. Here Wittgenstein also offers us what he takes to be a summary of the book: "what can be said at all must be said clearly, and what we cannot talk about we must remain silent about" (TLP, p. 3).[32]

This claim would seem to suggest that the early Wittgenstein held that there are two categories: things that can be spoken about, and things that cannot. His next remarks seem to suggest that one of his primary aims in the book is to draw a clear line between these two separate categories. But what he goes on to say in the following paragraph also seems as if it were meant to prompt readers to question the intelligibility of just such a picture. Wittgenstein's initial account of the aim of the book, "to set a limit to thought," is immediately withdrawn as confused. According to the revised account he offers, the book's aim is to set a limit not to thought but to the *expression* of thoughts, a limit that can be drawn only in language.

We cannot set a limit to thought in thought, Wittgenstein explains, for in order to do this, we would have to be able to distinguish what can be thought from what cannot. And to draw such a distinction, we should have to *specify* what cannot be thought. And this in turn would require that we be able to do something impossible, namely to grasp in thought that which cannot be thought. For Wittgenstein, the idea that we can form thoughts about the limits of thought, then, is a nonsensical one.

As Diamond points out, it is important that we pay close attention to Wittgenstein's initial false start in his statement of his book's intent in the opening paragraphs of the preface, for his momentary vacillation there contains an implicit warning. As David Cerbone points out, "Wittgenstein's point here, and throughout the *Tractatus*, is that the idea of a limit to thought is self-undermining in the sense that there is no *intelligible* way in which one can be drawn. Doing so, Wittgenstein is saying here in the Preface, would require having some grasp of what lies beyond such a limit. Indeed, the very suggestion of a *limit* implies that there is *something* which is being excluded, which lies outside of the range of thought and so cannot be reached."[33] We should remain attentive to the kinds of philosophical enterprises we engage in, Wittgenstein's false start indicates, for certain kinds of philosophical endeavors (attempting to draw a limit to thought, or to posit a philosophical self, for example) will only inevitably yield nonsense. What Wittgenstein goes on to tell us in his revised discussion of limits is that while we cannot coherently draw a limit to thought, we *can* draw a limit to the *expression* of thoughts in language. Once such a limit is drawn, what we have within the boundaries of language are straightforwardly intelligible sentences. What lies on the other side of this limit is for Wittgenstein "einfach Unsinn": simply nonsense (TLP 6.54).

The limit Wittgenstein speaks of in the preface cannot be drawn from a perspective somewhere *outside* thought and language from which we can judge the nature of language and its ability to represent reality. Part of what Wittgenstein aims to show us by drawing a limit to language from the *inside* is that such a "sideways-on" perspective does not exist.[34] To attempt to take such a position beyond the limits of language is only to succumb to exactly the kind of metaphysical delusion he wants us to overcome. We can occupy a position only *within* language and the world, and therefore the limits of language can be set only from inside language. We can draw the limits of language from within by specifying all that can be said meaningfully in straightforwardly intelligible sentences. Doing this will show us what is sayable. And once we specify all that can be said meaningfully, we will also be able to see that anything that does not fall within the "limits" of intelligible language (anything other than the straightforwardly intelligible sentences we have specified) will be simply nonsense.

Wittgenstein holds in the *Tractatus* that we can only delineate what *can* be said clearly (and thereby distinguish it from what *cannot* be said) by gaining clarity about the logical structure of our language. For once we are clear about the logic that is internal to our language, he believes, we will gain clarity about what our temptation to pose nonsensical philosophical problems comes to. It is this task of elucidating the structure of language that is the overt primary concern of the *Tractatus*.

Wittgenstein reports further in the preface that the book's purpose would be met if it gave pleasure to the person who read it "mit Verständnis," with understanding. Later, he declares "the *truth* of the thoughts communicated in the book" to be "unassailable and definitive." He believes himself to have found "the final solution of the problems." Shortly after, however, he adds that if he is not mistaken in this belief, "then the second thing in which the value of this work consists is it shows how little has been done when these problems are solved" (TLP, pp. 29–30).

If we follow Wittgenstein's instructions and look to the conclusion of the book for further clarification, what we find there is Wittgenstein's quite elusive claim that all the propositions of his purported treatise are "simply nonsense." He also indicates that it is by understanding *him*, the author—and the philosophical labor in which he is engaged (and in which he seeks to engage readers)—that we will come to recognize this.[35]

In his concluding remarks, Wittgenstein writes,

> 6.53 The correct method in philosophy would really be the follow-
> ing: to say nothing except what can be said, i.e. propositions
> of natural science—i.e. something that has nothing to do with
> philosophy—and then, whenever someone else wanted to say
> something metaphysical, to demonstrate to him that he had
> failed to give meaning to certain signs in his propositions.
>
> 6.54 My propositions serve as elucidations in this way: anyone
> who understands me eventually recognizes them as nonsen-
> sical, when he has climbed out through them, on them, over
> them. (He must, so to speak, throw away the ladder once he
> has climbed up it.) He must overcome [*überwinden*] these
> propositions, and then he will see the world in the right way.
>
> 7. What we cannot speak about we must be silent about.[36]

Wittgenstein describes the book's nonsensical propositions as "eluci-dations." We are to throw them away, along with the proverbial ladder he famously invokes, once they have served their pedagogical purpose of helping us to attain the clarity the book aspires to bestow on us. We can understand how Wittgenstein takes such nonsensical propositions to serve an *elucidatory* purpose only if we follow his advice and direct our attention toward trying to understand *him*, the author who penned such nonsense, rather than his propositions. Understanding *him* means understanding the kind of clarificatory activity he takes himself to be en-gaged in, and the role he takes nonsense to play in this activity.

To understand the author is to see that the *Tractatus* cancels itself out once it has done the job it set out to do. The reader who approaches the book with the understanding Wittgenstein solicits at the outset is asked ultimately to overcome its propositions, along with her attachment to the problems they are concerned with, in order to see the world in the "right way" whereby these problems "vanish" because they have ceased to be problems (6.521).

From the start, then, the *Tractatus* sets readers up for at least two starkly contrasting experiences of the text. Prior to hitting on Wittgen-stein's declaration of the nonsensicality of the book's sentences in its penultimate proposition, we are invited to engage in a straightforward reading of an (apparently) sound, logical and metaphysical theory. That theory unfolds in a series of (ostensibly) well-founded assertions that develop in a linear (or, alternately, a nonsequential, relational, tree-structured) argument, presented in the seeming absence of any proximate authorship. As Ben Ware has observed, at the initial stages of reading, what is most immediately striking about the propositions of the *Tractatus* is their tone of authoritative pronouncement, one that issues forth in a paradoxically "authorless style." The central ideas of the text, he writes, "are presented not as an option to the reader . . . which can be argued for or against, but rather as a set of (deceptively) unquestionable statements."[37] These statements are themselves interspersed throughout the text with substatements, numbering 1–7: "1. The world is all that is the case"; "1.1 The world is the totality of facts, not of things"; "1.11 The world is determined by the facts, and by these things being *all* the facts"; and so on to the silence of the book's famous concluding dictum: "wovon man nicht sprechen kann, darüber muss man schweigen."

The book's final tautological maxim that we should be quiet about what we can't talk about is directly preceded by the penultimate proposition 6.54, in which Wittgenstein declares his own sentences to be "simply nonsense." He pulls the rug out from under our feet in that proposition with the stunning news that the theoretical system we have just taken ourselves to have worked through is ultimately meaningless. Ware compares the reader's astonished response at the book's declarative self-annulment to the shock-experiences of modern metropolitan life that Walter Benjamin famously describes in his essay on Baudelaire, and to which he returns in his *Passagen-Werk*.[38] Although the shock-experience Benjamin identifies arises from a sense of alienation, it nonetheless functions dialectically in a "technique of awakening" (*Teknik des Erwachens*), in which we must come to recognize the crucial distinction between dream and wakefulness.[39] Wittgenstein's own parallel technique of awakening in the *Tractatus* is one he employs to get his readers to see the difference between living, speaking, and philosophizing in a state of confusion and (self) deception, on the one hand, and coming to clarity, on the other.

The sense of puzzlement with which most readers first receive the *Tractatus* can be attributed in part to the fact that Wittgenstein's unusual authorial strategies cause the book to clash with our preconceptions about what a logical-philosophical text should look like. Although the text might in certain aspects bear a resemblance to the treatment we might expect would be given a logical-philosophical subject matter, it also differs in decisive ways. After all, when we pick up a book entitled *Tractatus Logico-Philosophicus*, we generally assume that it will contain a treatment of logical problems and their solutions. What we generally do *not* expect to find in it are discussions of mysticism, value, and transcendence, and talk of "seeing the world in the right way." We may indeed await a treatment of problems of philosophy, logic, and language, but most likely not talk about the problem of the meaning of life (TLP, 5.621, 6.4311, 6.4312, 6.52, 6.521). Issues like these may well strike us as being out of place in a so-called logical-philosophical text. Such issues, we might think, should really be discussed and dealt with in the field of ethics and moral philosophy.

Conversely, if we are already acquainted with Wittgenstein's letter to Ficker, and thus also with his claim that the book has an ethical intent, we might even wonder why Wittgenstein spends so much time and energy going on about logic. Although the stated purpose of the book is to clarify the logical structure of language, remarks about what are typically viewed as ethical, existential problems and their solutions also surface in the text alongside the author's discussion of logical and linguistic problems and their solutions. But in the end, even Wittgenstein's most well-intentioned and supposedly helpful claims to von Ficker cause us further perplexity. For the letter does more than clue us in to the idea that the most important part of the book lies in its ethical aim; it also gives us access to Wittgenstein's still more mysterious claim that this same "most important part" is not to be found anywhere among the propositions that make up the written text. He also tells von Ficker that the ethical is delimited from "within" by the book, delimited in the only way that it can be: by its author's silence about it. When we look to the propositions of the *Tractatus*, however, what we find is Wittgenstein's inscrutable claim that ethics is by its very nature inexpressible, and that thus it is impossible for there to be propositions of ethics (TLP, 6.421). In the next entry, he continues:

> It is clear that ethics cannot be put into words.
> Ethics is transcendental.
> (Ethics and aesthetics are one.)

To his spare, perplexing assertions that ethics is inexpressible, and that ethics and aesthetics are one, Wittgenstein adds the puzzling remark that ethical problems cannot be resolved in the way that the problems of natural science can be resolved (TLP, 6.4312). There can be no solution to a problem like that of the meaning of life, he tells us. For solutions to ethical problems can be found only in the *disappearance* of such problems. Wittgenstein writes in proposition 6.52:

> We feel that even when *all possible* scientific questions have been answered, the problems of life remain completely untouched. Of course there are then no questions left, and this itself is the answer.

In the next proposition, 6.521, he continues with the following statement:

> The solution of the problem of life is seen in the vanishing of the problem. (Is not this the reason why those who have found after a long period of doubt that the sense of life became clear to them have then been unable to say what constituted that sense?)

As I remarked briefly in the introduction, Wittgenstein drew on a lifetime of thinking about Hertz's writing, and his diagnosis and dissolution of the problem of the nature of force. As Michael Kremer points out, Wittgenstein had, at one point, chosen a line from Hertz's *Principles of Mechanics* as a motto for the *Philosophical Investigations*: "When these painful contradictions are removed," Hertz writes, "the question as to essence will not have been answered; but our minds, no longer vexed, will cease to ask illegitimate questions."[40]

Elizabeth Anscombe has suggested that Wittgenstein "probably had Tolstoy in mind" when he wrote proposition 6.521.[41] There is little doubt that it was his reading of Tolstoy that led Wittgenstein to incorporate into his own work the notion that the solution of the problem of life can be found only in the vanishing of the problem.[42]

Readers have been understandably baffled and disquieted by these aspects of the *Tractatus*, especially Wittgenstein's declaration of the nonsensicality of his book. After all, how could he possibly take himself to convey important truths in a text that declares that "propositions cannot express anything higher" and whose own propositions are said to amount only to patent nonsense (TLP, 6.421)?[43]

Some commentators, Elizabeth Anscombe and P. M. S. Hacker most prominent among them, have tried to deal with the question of the role that nonsense plays in the *Tractatus* by drawing distinctions within the idea of nonsense itself.[44] Relying on a particular reading of Wittgenstein's distinction between saying and showing elaborated in the remarks

between propositions 4.12 and 4.124 of the *Tractatus* (a distinction resolute readers see as just one of the rungs on the ladder Wittgenstein
would have us throw away), they divide the category of nonsense into
two parts, positing a second sophisticated species of nonsense that they
distinguish from the utter meaninglessness of gibberish.[45] Such readers, whom Conant has deemed "irresolute" because of their "ineffabilist" views regarding nonsense, attribute to this extra kind of nonsense
a special feature that enables it to convey ineffable truths, and to guide
readers in apprehending these truths through the putative "theory" they
ascribe to the *Tractatus*. For Anscombe, Hacker, and others, the nonsensical propositions of the *Tractatus* help to articulate and communicate to us a special kind of theory that cannot be said but only shown.
Anscombe writes that "an important part is played in the *Tractatus* by
the things which, though they cannot be 'said,' are yet 'shown' or 'dis-
played.' That is to say: it would be all right to call them 'true' if, *per im-
possibile*, they could be said: in fact they cannot be called true, since they
cannot be said, but 'can be shewn,' or 'are exhibited,' in the propositions
saying the various things that can be said."[46]

The reach of ineffabilist conceptions of the nonsense of the *Tractatus*
can be seen in the appeal it has had in a number of critical treatments of
the book in literary studies. Perloff, to cite just one example, embraces
the sort of interpretation of Tractarian nonsense advanced by Anscombe
and Hacker, arguing that Wittgenstein's mystical pronouncements in the
Tractatus aim to show important ineffable truths.[47] Interpretations like
these rest on the belief that Wittgenstein could not possibly have been
entirely serious about renouncing his nonsensical propositions at the end
of the *Tractatus*.[48] Commentators who hold on to such beliefs endeavor
to explain away the challenge posed by Wittgenstein's assertion of the
nonsensicality of his propositions with suggestions that there are, as Anscombe claims, "things that would be true if they could be said" but
which are nonetheless unsayable, or that "what Wittgenstein means by
these remarks . . . is, in his view, quite correct, only it cannot be said."[49]
Resolute readings dismiss such accounts of Wittgenstein's treatment of
nonsense in the book as incoherent, the result of their proponents' misguided desire to cling to the very rungs of the proverbial ladder Wittgenstein would have us throw away, and to hold on steadfastly to the very
nonsensical propositions their author tells us we are to overcome if we
understand him. Such "irresolute" conceptions of nonsense amount to
what Diamond calls "chickening out."[50]

Conant and Diamond outline two interrelated general features that
suffice to make a reading program "resolute." The first involves what

Diamond has dubbed an "austere" view of nonsense.[51] In the *Tractatus*, Wittgenstein deals with only two categories: sense, and nonsense.[52] There are no logically distinct kinds of nonsense, but only one kind—the kind we find in strings of signs that fail to express anything (owing to our own failure to assign a determinate meaning to them). Conant and Diamond both argue that when Wittgenstein refers to his sentences as nonsense, he does not mean that despite their being improperly formed, we can still make out the gist of what they are trying to say. Nor does he indicate that those nonsensical sentences are somehow mysteriously endowed with the capacity to gesture at and grant us illuminating-yet-ineffable ethical insights about what lies beyond the limits of language. Rather, when he says his sentences are "simply nonsense," what he means is that they really are just bits of gibberish, logically indistinguishable from a phrase like "piggly wiggle tiggle"—and that we really should give up the idea that they are trying to say anything at all ("Ethics and Imagination," 151). Thus, when Wittgenstein surprises readers at the end of the book with the unexpected revelation that its constituent propositions are nonsensical, what he means is that they are just straight-up, garden-variety nonsense. What he does not mean is that they represent a comfortingly special kind of ethically illuminating, truth-gesturing sort of alternative or supplement to that regular old nonsense. Taking seriously Wittgenstein's claim that the *Tractatus* is made up of nonsense propositions means also facing up to the fact that no body of nonsense sentences could ever make coherent sense. The nonsense sentences of the book cannot, therefore, succeed in spite of this fact at gesturing effectively at a corresponding body of ineffable truths.

The second general defining feature of readings consistent with a resolute program is the rejection of the idea that recognizing these propositions as nonsensical depends on any application of a theory (whether of meaning, logic, ethics, etc.) that has been advanced in the body of the work (a theory, that is, that could specify the conditions under which a sentence makes sense and the conditions under which it does not).

The body of the *Tractatus*, made up as it is of sentences of sheer nonsense, does not, indeed cannot, represent a metaphysical theory of logic or language (whether ineffable or effable). For if we take seriously the logical nonsensicality of the book's propositions (as resolute readers would have us do), we must then face up to the fact that they do not amount to any theory of anything at all. Although together the propositions of the *Tractatus* may seem to take the shape of a full-blown philosophical argument, they are in fact nothing more than meaningless strings of words that express no coherent thoughts.

In his practice of philosophy, Wittgenstein was, throughout his lifetime, staunchly antitheoretical. He distinguishes the notion of the ethical aim he pursues in the *Tractatus* from the conception of ethics as a theoretical subject area to be dealt with (or as he was fond of putting it, "babbled" or "gassed" about) in philosophy departments. Wittgenstein was concerned actively and specifically to set himself against philosophical practice built around claims of the kind G. E. Moore makes in *Principia Ethica*—that the direct object of ethics is knowledge, and that ethics (as Moore engages in it) is a scientific study.[53]

Wittgenstein went on the record to clarify to members of the Vienna Circle that just as his thinking did not arise from any theory, neither did it seek to advance any theory. Nor, *pace* Moritz Schlick, should it be put into the service of one.[54] As he remarked to Friedrich Waismann in 1929, "I think it is definitely important to put an end to all the claptrap about ethics—whether intuitive knowledge exists, whether values exist, whether the good is definable."[55] The authenticity of Wittgenstein's commitment to this view is shown in the fact that nowhere in his thought does he adhere to theories of ethics or meaning. Nor does he insert himself into the metaethical or metaphysical debates going on in what Cavell calls the philosophical "profession of expertise."[56]

To get a clear view of the kind of ethical teaching Wittgenstein means to impart to his readers, we must recall that in his view, neither ethics nor logic constitutes a branch of knowledge with its own particular subject matter or set of truths. For Wittgenstein, neither ethics nor philosophy generally is a science or limited sphere of philosophical discourse among others (TLP, 6.4312, 6.52). In the *Tractatus*, he tells us that philosophy is neither a natural science nor an academic discipline advancing a body of doctrine, but an *activity* aimed at clarifying our thoughts and propositions (TLP, 4.112).[57] In his view, in order for there to be a branch of thought we could properly call "ethics" or "moral philosophy," there would have to be a body of ethical propositions for moral philosophy to clarify, a certain set of problems to set about solving. But as we have seen, it is precisely the existence of such a body of ethical propositions that Wittgenstein explicitly denies in the *Tractatus*. At proposition 6.42, he makes the notorious remark that ethics is inexpressible. What he tells us is that "it is impossible for there to be propositions of ethics. . . . Ethics cannot be put into words." Since ethics cannot be expressed in words, then neither can ethical questions or problems be expressed in words. Nor can we talk meaningfully of answers or solutions to such problems, for according to Wittgenstein, an answer can exist "only where something *can be said*" (TLP, 6.51).

In the place of any doctrine or theory, what Wittgenstein offers read-ers in the *Tractatus* is thus a tactically arranged, complex *mock* doctrine about language, logic, and their relation to reality.[58] This self-undermining pseudoargument is one that Wittgenstein elaborates self-consciously with the aim of disabusing his readers of our confused tendency to succumb to the thrall of metaphysical systems that lead us to mistake nonsense for sense, or to see the labor of philosophy as an absorption in doctrine, rather than as participation in the activity of clarification in which he seeks to engage us.[59] Wittgenstein's strategy in the *Tractatus*, as Conant sees it, is to lead readers to clarity via deception. In the book, Wittgen-stein offers up an apparent metaphysical theory in order to display to readers our tendency to succumb to an attraction to the nonsense from which he aims to deliver us. As Alice Crary explains:

> These sentences serve as a sort of metaphysical lure—first en-couraging the reader to envision herself occupying an external standpoint and then, by inviting her fully to articulate the things she imagines she can say once she has occupied it, placing her in a position in which she can recognize that she is putting incon-sistent pressures on her words and that *no* rendering of them will satisfy her. Thus the *Tractatus* delivers us from the illusion that we can do philosophy in a traditional vein through its presenta-tion of nonsensical sentences that, to the extent that they seduce us, equip us to lead ourselves out of our state of illusion.[60]

Wittgenstein thus contrives a work of logical-philosophical nonsense and uses it to draw readers temporarily into taking seriously the illusion that what he is saying makes sense, only then to explode this illusion from within by showing us that the sentences that have seduced us into the illusion that they make sense are simply meaningless.[61] By tempting readers to engage in the mock doctrine he constructs in the *Tractatus*, Wittgenstein sets up a philosophical mirror in which we can recognize our attraction to metaphysics as confused. Rather than set about directly confronting his reader's nonsense, or the illusion from which it arises, Wittgenstein uses nonsense to participate performatively in precisely the kind of confusion he seeks to cure in his reader. Wittgenstein's method in the book relies on the use of an indirect dialectical kind of therapeu-tic instruction that Conant likens to Kierkegaard's in his pseudonymous works, particularly his *Concluding Unscientific Postscript*.[62]

Readers of the *Tractatus* begin by facing the difficulty apparent at the bottom rung of his figurative ladder (from which point the book appears to be advancing a set of theories about logical form and the relationship between language and world). We start off worrying about the challenge of figuring out the apparent theses of the *Tractatus*, and how they hang together logically. But the more arduous challenge the *Tractatus* levels at readers has to do with getting us first to overcome our confused attraction to the metaphysical nonsense expressed in the book's propositions. This misdirected attraction leads us to try to make sense of these propositions and what they have to tell us. Succumbing to their allure in this way diverts our attention from a focus on how these propositions *function* within the text as a whole, and what the overall text urges us to *do*. Our responsiveness to the instructive method Wittgenstein employs in the book is shown in our ability to recognize that the sentences of the book—and the faux doctrine they amount to—are nothing more than the nonsense he says they are, and thus no more worth clinging to than the propositional ladder he famously tells us to throw away once we have mounted its elucidating rungs.

Thus, at some point in the philosophical development Wittgenstein induces us to undertake, readers must relinquish the call of the first-order difficulty at play on the surface of his book in favor of seeing it as a component part of the complex method of philosophical instruction he offers in the text in pursuit of the overarching ethical aim of the project as a whole. Once we have realized, with the help of Wittgenstein's indirect teaching and tactical cunning, that we have been laboring under illusions that impede our clear understanding of philosophy and how it should be practiced, we can begin the process of overcoming these illusions by taking up the hard work on the self that is needed if we are to make the radical change in worldview the text demands.[63] We must, then, redirect our attentions and energies from this first-order difficulty if we are ever successfully to climb (and, ideally, ultimately surmount) Wittgenstein's ladder to face the deeper order of difficulty (of coming to see things with a certain clarity of vision) that will allow us to throw that ladder, now a superannuated crutch, away. What we are left with once we have outgrown our reliance on Wittgenstein's self-consciously elaborated nonsense sentences is just ordinary language. We reach the end of the book not by getting to the last page, but by arriving at a point in Wittgenstein's philosophical activity at which the elucidation has served its purpose.[64]

An important distinguishing feature of Wittgenstein's method is to be found in the demand he places on readers to perform the difficult task of trying to understand an author who talks nonsense. Meeting such a demand requires that we learn to look at language, world, self, and other from new and unaccustomed perspectives. It also requires of us a certain amount of creativity and what Diamond calls "a very particular use of the imagination." According to Diamond, it is important to view Wittgenstein's attempt to draw readers into the imaginative understanding of a person who utters nonsense as a central part of the clarificatory activity in which he takes himself to be engaged in the *Tractatus*. Wittgenstein's book, she says,

> in its understanding of itself as addressed to those who are in the grip of philosophical nonsense, and in its understanding of the kind of demands it makes on its readers, supposes a kind of imaginative activity, an exercise of the capacity to enter into the taking of nonsense for sense, of the capacity to share imaginatively the inclination to think that one is thinking something in it. ("Ethics and Imagination," 157)

In order to understand the utterer of nonsense, then, we must ourselves enter imaginatively into the illusion that what he says makes sense. As Diamond puts it, "if I could not as it were see your nonsense as sense, imaginatively let myself feel its attractiveness, I could not understand you" ("Ethics and Imagination," 157). As she points out, understanding another person involves performing an activity of acknowledgment, in which we imagine ourselves into the other person's way of seeing things (while simultaneously holding on to our understanding that such a way of seeing things is nonetheless illusory). It is precisely this kind of imaginative activity in which Wittgenstein takes himself to be engaged in the *Tractatus*. He utters nonsense about philosophy in an attempt to treat with understanding the person held in thrall to illusion, self-deception, and complacency. Wittgenstein uses his own self-aware nonsense as a way of entering into the nonsense that springs from his readers' confusion with the aim of getting us to recognize our nonsense for what it is, and find a way out of it. Wittgenstein's purposeful use of nonsense in his book also carries with it the demand for a reciprocal kind of receptive, imaginative understanding from his readers. For in order to benefit from the method of the *Tractatus*, we too must engage in a kind of imaginative understanding of its author's use of nonsense.

As Diamond reminds us, however, it is important to be aware of the decisive difference between the nonsensical sentences he writes in the *Tractatus* and the nonsense of which the *Tractatus* aims to cure its readers. The important difference between these two instances of nonsense is not one of category but of use; it is a difference that lies in the distinct external circumstances in which the nonsensical propositions of the *Tractatus* and the nonsensical propositions of the metaphysician are uttered. "The former," Diamond explains, "are recognized by their author to be plain nonsense, the latter are not; the former are in the service of an imaginative understanding of persons, the latter are the result of a sort of disease of the imagination, and the philosopher who comes out with them lacks that understanding of himself which the *Tractatus* aims to secure for us" ("Ethics and Imagination," 160).

Wittgenstein hopes that readers will take from the *Tractatus* a clearer understanding of our own tendency to utter nonsense. But recognizing this tendency does not mean, in his view, that we must give up coming out with nonsense in all situations. Wittgenstein does not ask us to give up the nonsensical talk that allows us to give expression to our ethical experiences, for example. Nor does he want us to give up self-aware nonsensical talk like his own in the *Tractatus*, uttered with the aim of entering imaginatively into an understanding of other people.

Wittgenstein's notion of the inexpressibility of ethics, and the essential nonsensicality of the sentences we use to give expression to our ethical or religious experience, is another complicated issue to which I will return in chapter 2. There, in relation to Kafka's investigations into the creative power of literary and religious language in daily life, I look at what Wittgenstein says in his "Lecture on Ethics" about the nonsense of sentences that are expressive of wonder and "absolute value" (as opposed to the nonsensical utterances about metaphysics of which he aims to cure us, for example) and how their figurative function differs from that of metaphor.[65]

As I said above, the early Wittgenstein holds that ethics is unsayable, since ethical propositions have no sense. As we will see in chapter 2, the sentences we come out with when we feel compelled to give expression to experiences of life we take to be ethically and existentially charged are by their very nature nonsensical. This is a condition they share (since Wittgenstein holds that there is only *one* category of nonsense) with both the self-consciously employed sentences of the *Tractatus*, and the sentences his therapy aims to disabuse us of. Wittgenstein's logical analysis in the *Tractatus* of the general form of proposition gives us a view of all senseful language. In doing so, it thereby also shows us that any sentence that does *not* conform to the general form of a proposition—the sentences we confusedly fall for, and those we go on to utter unreflectively when we talk theoretically or metaphysically, come to nothing more than nonsense arising from misunderstanding and misuse. But it also shows us something important about nonsense in its varied uses. Nonsense can

be used creatively, with the aim of expressing ourselves ethically or poetically (and this includes putting deliberate nonsense to work as an an-
tidote to hapless nonsense, at Wittgenstein does in the *Tractatus*). Creative uses of nonsense or secondary sense (creative secondary uses of
language) uttered with these ethical or aesthetic goals in mind thus expand and enhance our communicative capabilities. As such, Wittgenstein wants to keep them in play in our lives with language.

Wittgenstein explains in the "Lecture on Ethics" that he does not
want to condemn or even discourage our tendency to try to speak ethically about such things as the meaning of life. And although he consistently expresses a mistrust of ethical *theories*, he nonetheless composed the *Tractatus* with the overall *aim* of leading his readers to face the
world and the tasks life presents them in the right kind of ethical *spirit*.
Wittgenstein thought of the spirit of the ethical not as something that
is revealed in any desire to issue ethical theories but as something that
shows forth in the attitude with which we face life and the world as a
whole. Rather than being a subject that can be straightforwardly taught,
then, ethics for Wittgenstein, like logic, penetrates the world and all our
thought and talk. It appears in our sense of humor, and in stories we tell,
in our poetry and music, and also in the ordinary talk of our daily lives.
Such forms of personal expression provide us not only with an outlet
for our creativity, but also with imaginative ways of giving voice to our
views of the world. Certain jokes, gestures, or works of literature, even
though they offer no explicit moral teaching, do have the capacity to reveal to us things about life and the world that help us to think better and
more clearly and to approach life in an ethical spirit.[66] The *Tractatus*
marks Wittgenstein's attempt to show us that even certain philosophical works can succeed in engaging their readers ethically in just this way.

Poeted Philosophy and Twentieth-Century Literature

Wittgenstein himself once remarked that he had "summed up [his] attitude to philosophy" when he said that "philosophy ought really to be
written only as one would *write a poem*," or that "philosophy should
really only be *poeted* [*Philosophie dürfte man eigentlich nur* dichten]"
(CV, 24).[67] This remark is indicative of Wittgenstein's attitude toward
philosophy and philosophical writing, and also about his views about
the important bearing that the aesthetic character of a philosophical
work can have on the ideas its author aims to express. As Conant points
out, the remark also serves to emphasize the importance of viewing the
Tractatus as a piece of meticulously composed and polished philosophi-

cal *writing*, crafted in a unique manner by an author with a certain overall purpose in mind.[68]

Wittgenstein speaks to the relationship between the philosophical sea change he seeks to effect and of the literary character of his chosen form of expression, in an unpublished remark he made in 1938. "If I do not want to teach a more *correct* way of thinking," he writes, "but rather a movement of thought [*eine Gedankenbewegung*], then my aim is a 'transvaluation of values' [*Umwertung von Werten*] and I think of Nietzsche, also in so far as in my opinion, the philosopher should be a poet."[69]

The nod he gives to Nietzsche in that passage from the *Nachlass* attests to Wittgenstein's appreciation of his philosophical precursor's subversive, counterphilosophical mode of engagement, his inimitable writing style, and his commitment to willed, creative acts of transformation. The passage also makes it evident that Wittgenstein viewed Nietzsche's aesthetic commitments as a writer in relation to his own repeated insistence that the work of the philosopher should be understood as intimately related to that of the poet. His philosophical project in the *Tractatus* is one he saw as bound up with an aesthetic commitment to a mode of stylistic presentation whose poetic reach extends to encompass the ethically imaginative "movement of thought" and "transvaluation of values" necessary for readers to achieve the kind of transformation toward which he seeks to lead them. His investment in the aesthetics of philosophical writing, and his view that "ethics and aesthetics are one," is evident in the *Tractatus* at all levels (TLP, 6.421). It can be seen in the peculiar instructive method Wittgenstein conceives as most conducive to the task of engaging his readers tactically in the creative work of transformation. It can also be seen in the difficult and inspired ethical labor that such work entails, the precise nature of which Wittgenstein leaves pointedly unspecified, something the reader must navigate on her own. Finally, it is also visible in the stylistic choices he makes by crafting the formal medium for that method, assembled in the text itself, in the way that he does.

I argue in this book that resolute readings of the *Tractatus* offer us important ways of seeing the correspondence between Wittgenstein's thinking and some of the central concerns of modernist literature that might be otherwise lost on us were we to pursue the more traditional readings of that book. As I have shown, reading the *Tractatus* resolutely keeps us attuned to the different orders of difficulty at issue in a book whose constructed pseudotheory of philosophy and logic is *intellectually* taxing in and of itself. Resolute readings also prompt us to consider the paramount importance of paying attention to the *ethical* dimension of the book, and to the demanding challenge Wittgenstein levels at readers in his call for us to take up the difficult work of self-transformation that is required if we want to respond with understanding to what he aims to teach us.

Wittgenstein's notion of the revolutionary change he sought to bring about in his readers' ethical worldview with the help of his instructive method is bound up with his views about the intimate relationship between poetry and the art and craft of philosophical writing to which he aspired. Speaking of the *Investigations*, Cavell draws our attention to the importance of taking Wittgenstein's chosen writing style as essential to his way of philosophizing, "the manner to the method." Wittgenstein's reconception of philosophy and of the form of philosophical problems, Cavell argues, gives rise to Wittgenstein's use, from the *Tractatus* on, of the aphorism as his primary mode of expression. Wittgenstein endeavors, early and late, to free his readers, and the words we use, from metaphysical capture and to return us to the appeal of the everyday. He taps into the power of the aphorism to exhibit both the allure of metaphysical claims, and the clarity toward which he is trying to lead us. The form of the aphorism functions to display that clarity to us together with "a satisfaction or acknowledgement of the obscurity from which clarity comes."[70] Cavell's observations about Wittgenstein's use of the aphorism in his later work also serve to remind us of the need to acknowledge and find satisfaction in the modes of difficulty and mystery that Wittgenstein deploys in his acutely puzzling early work, where they are enmeshed with his commitment to the pursuit of clarity and with getting readers to follow his guidance without appeal to explicit theoretical directions for doing so.

Resolute approaches also attend to these stylistic concerns of Wittgenstein's and bring to light the literary character of the book and the aesthetic challenges that are so intimately involved in his formally tactical delivery of the ethical one. For if readers are to understand the nature of the transformative ethical work in which Wittgenstein would sincerely have us engage, we must first see it as at one with aesthetics, as Wittgenstein suggests at 6.421. We must come to recognize that the authorial stance he takes with regard to the book's content as one of a kind of Socratic ironic distance that contributes to the dialectical strategy so central to his overall authorial method, and which Conant suggests he formulates in the manner of Kierkegaard.[71] Recognizing Wittgenstein's ironic authorial engagement with the propositions of his text (which he carefully elaborates and then reveals as nonsensical, to be thrown away once we have overcome them) means also seeing that the highly aestheticized self-immolating gesture on which Wittgenstein's pedagogical method turns is itself expressive of a solemn and quite unironic commitment to getting his readers to see the stark difference between working to understand the author who utters nonsense on the one hand, and trying to understand the propositions that make up his pseudodoctrine on the other.

The Obscurity from Which Clarity Comes

I conclude here by returning to a subject I first discussed in the introduction: the tactical deployment of difficulty on which Wittgenstein's overall method of leading readers to clarity turns in the *Tractatus*. A central feature of the tactical difficulty Wittgenstein uses in his construction of his aesthetic puzzle of language, logic, and ethics is his deliberate use of obscurity in his effort to lead his readers toward clarity through his teaching. This feature of Wittgenstein's method also characterizes the parabolic teaching that Kafka and Coetzee use in the works that I explore in the next and concluding chapters, respectively. That I should claim that obscurity is an active agent in a putative treatise so often understood as definitively dedicated to its precise opposite, and whose author declared it "crystal clear," might seem surprising. And yet, I maintain that examining Wittgenstein's tactical engagement in opacity and ambiguity in his "book of ethics" adds depth and complexity to our understanding of his use of difficulty in the *Tractatus* more broadly.

George Steiner's claim in his essay on difficulty that the poet's strategic use of difficulty in his efforts to experiment with (and thereby transform) the language that is the medium of his craft is not meant to "forge a new tongue," but to "revitalize, to cleanse 'the words of the tribe,'" calls to mind Wittgenstein, who sought not to create a new logical language in the manner of Frege or Russell (as Russell first mistakenly thought, and claimed in his introduction to the *Tractatus*), nor even a supreme symphonic language of perfect expressiveness in the spirit of Mallarmé.[72] What Wittgenstein sought to do instead was to change his readers' confused relationship to ordinary language, which he saw as "part of the human organism and no less complicated than it," and as "in perfect logical order" just as it is (TLP, 4.001, 5.5563). Wittgenstein expresses this view of ordinary language again in the *Investigations*:

> It is clear that every sentence in our language "is in order as it is." That is to say, we are not *striving after* an ideal, as if our ordinary vague sentences had not yet got a quite unexceptional

sense, and a perfect language awaited construction by us.—On the other hand it seems clear that where there is sense there must be perfect order.—So there must be perfect order even in the vaguest sentence (PI, §98).

In her *Modernist Fiction and Vagueness*, Megan Quigley observes that "in contrast to Russell's and Frege's 'perfect language,' Wittgenstein shows that truth can be found even in, and precisely in, the vaguest sentence."[73] Quigley argues that worries about the vagueness resulting from language's unavoidable imprecision, and the correlative efforts to create a *Begriffschrift* for a language of perfect precision, lie at the heart of the innovations in fiction and philosophy in the early twentieth century. She demonstrates that vagueness, far from being a linguistic or aesthetic deficiency, is in fact a defining attribute of modernist fiction. In her discussion of Wittgenstein and Joyce, Quigley examines the accord between Joyce's early interest in creating a logical and systematic approach to language and Wittgenstein's (apparent) attempt to set out what Russell describes in his introduction as "the conditions for a logically perfect language."[74] Both Joyce and Wittgenstein ultimately turn away from their visions of a logically perfect language and from movements of linguistic perfectionism aimed at stamping out the problem of imprecision, Quigley argues, in favor of grappling with "the puzzle of language's vagueness."[75]

Wittgenstein candidly acknowledges in the *Investigations* that imprecision and vague sentences are part of our everyday language.[76] The view of vagueness he expresses in that later work represents no dramatic departure from the view about language he held when he wrote the *Tractatus*. That said, in that earlier book, Wittgenstein is not so much concerned with the prevalence of vagueness and (ordered) imprecision in ordinary language. Such vagueness is mild; it is not what really troubles him. In the *Tractatus*, Wittgenstein is intent on mounting a strategy of clarification aimed at combating the confusion that gives rise to patent nonsense. This is something he does by appeal to vagueness' bolder, more formidable twin, obscurity. Indeed, Wittgenstein's tactical use of difficulty in the *Tractatus* entails an engagement with obscurity that plays an important role in the dialectical, parabolic mode of ethical instruction at the heart of the method he employs in his textual puzzle.

In his calculated effort to lead his readers toward a radical change in outlook, it is not resolution in perfect linguistic precision Wittgenstein is looking for, but resolution in total clarity. In order to get his readers to make the shift in attitude needed to see the world more clearly, he shows himself willing to embrace opacity and ambiguity (and to thrust his readers into it as well), risking paradox by making attention to the obscure an important part of a philosophical activity he saw as dedicated to clarification. Wittgenstein's commitment to an aesthetics of obscurity, ambiguity, and indirection is evident in the fact that he thought plunging even his most prepared and committed readers into utter bewilderment to be an integral part of his ethical pedagogy. Unless we attribute to Wittgenstein a conscious commitment to obscurity, after all, it is hard to see why he would knowingly write a book so unusual in its form, logic, and instructive aim, and do so in spite of his awareness that even the readers most poised to understand it would be extremely hard-pressed to make sense of it.

Wittgenstein recognized from the outset that the book would be opaque to most readers. In a letter he wrote to Russell months after the *Tractatus*'s completion, he told Russell that, however arrogant it might sound, he believed he had solved all the problems they had discussed in the years before the war. Of course, he went on, "*nobody* will understand it; although I believe it's all as clear as crystal."[77] To the philosopher C. K. Ogden, who with the help of Frank Ramsey was busily translating the "Abhändlung" into English, Wittgenstein wrote, perhaps only half-jokingly, "rather than print the Ergänzungen [clarifying supplements Ogden considered adding to the text] to make the book fatter leave a dozen white sheets for the reader to swear into when he has purchased the book and can't understand it."[78] Wittgenstein's friend Engelmann, with whom he had spent much of his time during the war discussing ethical expression in literature and poetry, wrote Wittgenstein upon receipt of the book to tell him that with each reading the book gives him "more and more joy," a joy that increases the more he "understands it." Engelmann's experience as an unassisted early reader of the text proved to be unique (DG, 157). This is perhaps because Engelmann's long conversations with Wittgenstein as he was working to complete the *Tractatus* granted him insights into the evolution of the author's conception of the book that others were not party to.

Engelmann's positive response also proved unique among the three people Wittgenstein most hoped and expected to understand the work. The first of the remaining two is Frege, the logician to whom Wittgenstein acknowledged his greatest debt. Frege famously wrote to Wittgenstein that he found the book "difficult to understand" and was unable to make "proper headway." He was concerned about the imprecision of Wittgenstein's language, which left him "tangled in doubt" about what Wittgenstein wanted to say. The sparse form of the book got in the way of Frege's ability to pin down its meaning. "For the most part," he tells Wittgenstein, "you put your sentences down one beside the other without sufficiently detailed justification. I thus often do not know whether I ought to agree, for their sense is not clear to me."[79]

The third person was of course Russell. The introduction to the *Tractatus* that Russell would write (in large part to assuage the worries of reluctant publishers with the guarantee of a market for the book if it appeared under his imprimatur) only proved to Wittgenstein that his Cambridge mentor had not understood the work either. After receiving the German translation of the introduction, Wittgenstein tells Russell: "I couldn't bring myself to have it printed with my work after all. For all the refinement of your English style was, obviously, lost in the translation and what was left was superficiality and misunderstanding."[80]

Another way that the *Tractatus* demonstrates Wittgenstein's will to trade in the difficulty of obscurity is the fact that a decisive aspect of the challenge he mounts in the *Tractatus* is his authorial use of a tactically indirect pedagogy, one that depends on the effect of leaving readers in the dark in a number of ways. First of all, nowhere in the book does he *explain* how his pedagogical method works. The "key" insights into how to read it that he gives in his letter to von Ficker derive in part from guidance he "once wanted to give" in "a few words in the preface," but then decided to leave out. These missing directions do of course linger in the sparse, diminished form in which they appear in the preface and conclusion of the book, to which he draws von Ficker's attention. But by actively removing the "few words" that are now not in the preface, but are rather "in" the second, unspoken "part" of the book, Wittgenstein also relegates them—to put things in his own figurative (as well as logically nonsensical, by his lights) spatial terms—to a "place" somewhere "between the lines" of the text. "There" they linger, as they do in the instructions of the preface. But the key insight Wittgenstein offers to von Ficker also haunts his project of ethical instruction in a rather different way, since it remains shrouded, as it were, in the obscurity that encompasses his conception of the work of the text as a whole.

The important "part" of the *Tractatus*, we will recall, is not the one presented in the book's content. It lies instead in all that he has "*not* written."[81] Thus, if readers are to respond to Wittgenstein's reticent teaching in the book in the way he hoped we would (while, as his comments in the letters to Russell and Ogden attest, knowing in advance that we most likely would *not*), we must somehow learn to navigate the obscurity generated by Wittgenstein's move to opt for silence, and his eschewal of the kind of explanatory "babbling" he sees as the inevitable result of treating ethics as an area of theoretical study rather than as an activity that brings clarity to our experience of the world and to our expression of that experience in language. Since he doesn't tell us straight out, we must work to figure out for ourselves just what he is trying to get us to see about language, life, and the practice of philosophy by juxtaposing the two "parts." Wittgenstein describes the bipartite arrangement of the *Tractatus* explicitly only in his letter to von Ficker. He does not mention it outright anywhere in the book, leaving it so barely implicit as to be almost entirely imperceptible to anyone reading it without the guidance he provides in that letter, or the commentary that has emerged in its wake.

Looking at Wittgenstein's investment in the difficulty of obscurity in this way reveals two important things about his "strictly philosophical and, at the same time, literary" project in the *Tractatus*.[82] First, that Wittgenstein's chosen mode of teaching, dedicated as it is to the "ethical" task of vaulting readers to a "higher," or more evolved point from which to speak and see the world more clearly, is bound up with an attention to (and concerted use of) figurative language. Wittgenstein's use of tactical difficulty as a part of his instructive method thus turns on his use of metaphor. The relationship of figurative language to Wittgenstein's philosophical writing becomes evident even in our efforts to describe the gist of what he is saying to von Ficker, as I just did above, without appeal to the kind of figurations and distancing scare quotes that characterize my attempt. Second, the choice bit of information that Wittgenstein leaks to von Ficker also attests to the fact that the alternately obscurantist and revelatory tactics he uses in his difficult book with the goal of leading his readers from obscurity to clarity are tactics he uses quite deliberately. As he tells the publisher, he removes clarifying phrases from his preface, guards his silence about all that matters, and talks nonsense about the rest.

In the tip he gives to von Ficker, Wittgenstein also reveals his appreciation for the aesthetic form of his overall project in the *Tractatus*. For by offering the publisher the clues he does, Wittgenstein demonstrates his commitment to safeguarding his book's ability to function as a puzzle. For if readers are to engage in the dialectical, parabolic process of instructive therapy through which he seeks to lead them, they must experience the text at a series of stages, moving from obscurity to clarity as they rise to the different challenges attendant to each rung of Wittgenstein's propositional ladder. If he is to maintain the mock-doctrinal conceit that acts as a lynchpin for his strategic method in the *Tractatus*, he must keep the unsuspecting reader in the dark. Keeping the more straightforward directions he gives von Ficker under wraps in the book itself serves Wittgenstein's aim of getting readers to figure out for themselves how to respond to his unusual brand of teaching and go on to work toward the enlightenment the book promises by working through the obscurity in which he first plunges them. This is a question to which I will attend closely in the succeeding chapters of this book.

Thus, Wittgenstein's way of "delineating the sphere of the ethical" in the book—by keeping *silent* about it—may be "rigorous," as he says, but it hardly seems driven by a search for precision in the manner of Russell, Frege, and others. The method and goal of Wittgenstein's teaching depend too centrally on remaining implicit, undefined and open-ended to conform to the demands of the precision sought by his mentors. In his chosen mode of instruction, Wittgenstein places far more faith in his reader, and far more trust in his reader's linguistic, ethical, and imaginative capabilities (and indeed human fallibility) than is allowed in the kind of corrective programs of reform elaborated in so many early twentieth-century attempts to formulate languages of perfect precision. And these imaginative capabilities, which Wittgenstein implicitly solicits by calling on readers to change their ways of seeing the world, thrive in the face of the possibilities made available by the embrace of opacity at the heart of teaching in the *Tractatus*. The experience of clarity that results from creative attention to the sense of possibility that attends interpretive confrontations with obscurity is a far richer one than any that could be achieved through an imposed precision that may prove ultimately more imaginatively restrictive than it is salutary. Some of the richly imaginative uses of language in which Wittgenstein expresses a special interest would be curtailed or ruled out entirely if they were made to conform to systematic linguistic precision—the complex linguistic intention he calls "secondary sense," for example, or the nonsense that results from our attempts to give expression to our religious or ethical experience, to which I turn in the next chapter.

Wittgenstein's engagement in modernist uses of obscurity also shows forth in the fact that the indirection and lack of specificity that characterize his method extends to his treatment of the kind of transformative change toward which he aims to lead his reader. The path he lays for readers who want to follow him toward achieving the kind of clarity that would allow them to "see the world in the right way" is not immediately clear, for all the importance that signposts would have in his later writing. What he gives us in its place is the literary, scriptural figuration of a ladder, a tool for climbing to an uncertain height, which is then thrown away. Wittgenstein's therapeutic method in the *Tractatus* unfolds from his foregone diagnosis of his reader's confusion. But it does not involve giving us a prescription we can follow to the letter in our efforts to overcome what ails us. Figuring out how to go on in our long-term work of overcoming is something he leaves up to us.

2

The Everyday's Fabulous Beyond: Nonsense, Parable, and the Ethics of the Literary in Kafka and Wittgenstein

66. He is a free and secure citizen of the world for he is attached to a chain long enough to allow him all of earthly space, and yet only so long that nothing can drag him beyond the earth's limits. At the same time he is also a free and secure citizen of heaven, for he is also attached to a heavenly chain with similar dimensions. If he wants to reach earth, the heavenly collar chokes him. If he wants to reach Heaven, he is choked by the earthly collar. And in spite of this, he has all the possibilities, and feels that it is so; indeed, he even refuses to attribute the whole thing to a mistake in the original chaining.
—Franz Kafka[1]

A Great Deal of Trouble Not Writing about One's Trouble

This chapter takes up the question of the significance of Wittgenstein's philosophy for literary studies through a comparative reading of the stakes and aims of Kafka's and Wittgenstein's circa 1922 puzzle texts "Von den Gleichnissen" ("On Parables") and the *Tractatus Logico-Philosophicus*. I examine the ethical weight of these two writers' shared investment in the philosophical depth of riddles, irony, and parabolic and nonsensical expression as unusual modes of indirect instruction about our ordinary language and world, the yearning for transcendence, and the failure to achieve it. My central aim in discussing Wittgenstein's *Tractatus* and "Lecture on Ethics" alongside Kafka's parable here is to examine some of the ways in which Wittgenstein's philosophical outlook, writing, and method are deeply relevant to literary studies, and particularly to our understanding of literary modernism.[2]

But aside from Kafka's established position as an exemplary figure in the European modernist canon, why bring him into an effort to say something new about Wittgenstein and the relationship of his thought to literary modernism? Kafka is not known to have read Wittgenstein, nor was he one of the modernist figures Wittgenstein was known to have enjoyed, or with whom he had some connection, however tenuous. In fact, Wittgenstein's acquaintance with Kafka's writing was, at best, extremely limited. The more than twenty thousand pages of Wittgenstein's unpublished writings contain no mention of Kafka. The only recorded testimony of his having read Kafka at all survives in the form of a humorous anecdote related by the philosopher Elizabeth Anscombe. As Ray Monk tells it, while a student of Wittgenstein's, she lent him some of Kafka's novels in an effort to share with him her enthusiasm about Kafka's writing. Upon returning the books to her in rather short order, Wittgenstein quipped: "This man gives himself a great deal of trouble not writing about his trouble." He recommended instead that she read Otto Weininger, a man who, he assured her, really *did* write about his trouble.[3]

A thorough unpacking of the implications of Wittgenstein's loaded yet rather inscrutable comment, so as to understand more fully the relationship of his thought to Weininger's writing (and indeed, troubles), would call for a different discussion entirely.[4] My choice to invoke Wittgenstein's reported remark at the outset of this chapter is inspired not so much by its undeniable epigrammatic qualities as by a relevance to the current discussion that exceeds the merely ornamental. After all, if Kafka is a man who gives himself troubles not writing about his troubles, what of Wittgenstein, the man who troubles to confront the "problems of philosophy" and to disabuse his readers of their philosophical and personal confusions by simultaneously mesmerizing and perplexing them with an enigmatic book the constituent propositions of which he declares at the end to be "simply nonsense" and which opens and closes with the famous oracular dictum "Wovon man nicht sprechen kann, darüber muß man schweigen" (what we cannot speak about we must be silent about)?[5]

With the exception of their personal diaries and letters, both Wittgenstein and Kafka are men who go to quite a lot of trouble not writing (at least not directly) about their troubles—the problems they struggle with and prompt their readers to struggle with in turn. Indeed, the poetic and philosophical force of the two texts I examine here ironically *depends* on the very method of willed opacity that Wittgenstein curmudgeonly criticizes in Kafka's work. Goading readers toward clarity in challenges that turn, paradoxically, on a provocative brand of obscurantism is an important aspect of the instructive methods at the heart of both Wittgenstein's and Kafka's creative philosophical and literary endeavors.

Part of what makes "On Parables" and the *Tractatus* so challenging to readers is that both rely on parabolic modes of instruction aimed not at the didactic communication of a complicated lesson in an apparently simple form, but at leading readers to take up the hard work (of both the intellect and the spirit) of engaging in literary and philosophical activities that seek to change our ways of seeing things. Both Kafka's and Wittgenstein's texts are works whose philosophical or ethical "points," are made through what is *not* in them, rather than through anything they say explicitly. In Cora Diamond's terms, both texts are marked by absence. Both leave it up to their readers to figure out how to learn something from that absence (of answers, explanations, resolutions, or straightforward teaching) by turning this absence into something that transforms our understanding of the problems and mysteries of language and life.[6] What Eli Friedlander says of Wittgenstein's *Tractatus* also provides us with an apt description of Kafka's parable, since each of these works "perspicuously represents an empty place" of nonmeaning we must come to recognize in the midst of our search for interpretive clarity and understanding. Each performs the intrinsically contradictory task of succeeding in its aim "only by bringing us close to the failure or disintegration of language in such a way as to illuminate or provide an elucidation."[7]

On Parables

Kafka's late short work "On Parables" goes like this:

> Many complain that the words of the wise, time and again, are only parables [*Gleichnisse*], but inapplicable to daily life, which is all we have. When the wise man says, "Cross over," he does not mean that one should cross over to the other side, which one could still manage, after all, if the result of going that way made it worth it; he means some sort of fabulous Beyond [*sagenhaftes Drüben*], something we do not know, which he cannot designate more precisely either, and which therefore cannot help us here at all. All these parables really intend to say is only that the incomprehensible is incomprehensible, and that we knew

already. But all that we have to struggle with everyday: that is a different matter.

Thereupon someone said: Why all this resistance? If you followed parables, you would become parables yourselves and with that free of your daily cares.

Another said: "I bet that is also a parable."

The first said: "You have won."

The second said: "But unfortunately only in parable."

The first said: "No, in reality; in parable you have lost."[8]

Kafka's compressed piece on parables is perhaps among the most difficult of his works. His metaparable deals almost entirely with the abstract themes of storytelling, joke telling, hermeneutical understanding, and the instructive value of tales, which, by their very nature, demand interpretation. The parable thus supplies the reader with far fewer of the more tangible themes (the Unreal city, bureaucracy, authority, melancholy, uncanny guilt, the absurdity of the human condition, and the defeat of the individual living under the sway of the coldly mechanical twentieth century, to name just a few) to which readers of his more extended parabolic novels can at least point, and cling.

Kafka's philosophically challenging little tale depicts an exchange between a set of interlocutors who vocalize (in a manner reminiscent of the conversations and simple language games of the *Philosophical Investigations*) conflicting viewpoints about figurative language and its bearing—or failure to bear—on the realities of everyday life. It is a parable with two parts. The first uses aphoristic expression to set out the problem in question: the apparent incommensurability between the mystical "words of the wise" and the unknown "fabulous Beyond" they profess to address, on the one hand, and the concrete language and "things we struggle with every day," on the other. The second part is dedicated to a jousting interpersonal exchange that serves as a Kafkan exegesis (depending in part on the *parody* of exegesis) of the problem outlined in the first. The parable as a whole delivers no clearly stated lesson or particular message. There is nothing given in the parable that spells out for us the moral we are designed to take from it.

The parabolic form is of course most famously used in the Gospels, where it figures as Jesus's chosen teaching method for leading his followers toward redemption and salvation. As Joshua Landy points out, if the Gospel of Mark is to be believed, Jesus is a figure of enigma, secrecy, and deliberate obscurity who never made a speech without using a parable,

a form developed from the *mashal* of Talmudic and midrashic hermeneutics to become the core of his pedagogical practice of honing his followers' aptitude with figurative language and therefore with a certain
mode of thinking.[9] In *The Genesis of Secrecy*, his groundbreaking study
of enigmatic passages and episodes in the Gospels in relation to the narrative opacity of a set of twentieth-century works by Kafka and others,
Frank Kermode points to ways in which Kafka, in his unique modern
parables, expands on the model established by Jesus's obscure instructive tales in the Gospels, especially those of Mark and Matthew.

Both Landy and Kermode emphasize the ways in which parables seek
to challenge us obliquely to become more adept thinkers and readers
through an engagement with a literary form characterized by concision,
obscurity, and a rejection of the literal in favor of the figurative, and of
immanence in favor of transcendence. Parables do not transmit information or clearly legible moral lessons to be applied to corresponding
real-life situations. They don't teach by way of their propositional content; they offer us training by means of their form. Seen in this way,
with attention to their best-known scriptural point of origin, parables
(religious and secular alike) seek to transform their readers' or hearers'
modes of thinking and living by granting them figurative access to a kind
of higher plane.[10]

By sharpening our interpretive skills in the way they do, parables can
also train us as moral beings by requiring of us a complicated kind of
interpretive philosophical and imaginative work that we must also incorporate into the way we think, live, and communicate with others.[11]
What Diamond says, in a similar vein, about Wittgenstein's *Tractatus*
also applies to Kafka's "On Parables": "The book doesn't 'teach' one
philosophy, in the sense that it has no teachings on offer; and as long as
one restricts oneself to looking for teachings, one will be unable to learn
anything philosophical from it."[12] Neither text functions (as the simplest
of allegories can do) by pointing us to a concrete event, object, or narrative outside of it that will provide a key to unlock its preestablished,
transparent message.

"On Parables" opens up a space for readers to continue the exegetical work performed within it by adding further interpretations to the debate. The impulse to add to the parable's last line our own "I bet that is
also a parable" signals the bewildering and possibly unending interpretive task that this layered piece demands of its readers. This same inclination to redeploy that riposte with greater imaginative insight on a critical
meta level in order thereby to rise to the parable's challenge (by rising
above the failure of its internal voices to identify and put to rest the ques-

tions it raises with anything wiser than a wisecrack) also speaks to the important way the parable plays on the hubris and performance anxiety of readers who long to be "in on" the joke and are eager to follow its parabolic movement toward a deeper understanding we worry may entirely elude us. James Conant and Michael Kremer emphasize an oscillation between arrogance and a fear of failure that readers of the *Tractatus* can be said to share with the readers of Kafka's parable.[13] Eager to become part of the apparently select readership that will "find pleasure" in the *Tractatus* by approaching it, as Wittgenstein says in the preface "with understanding," we wonder whether we are up to the challenge of reading the book in such a way as to successfully understand its author and the transformative experience of elucidation that his work as a whole aspires to bestow on us.

Seeing Kafka's parable as a two-part piece also helps us to recognize something crucial about the interpretive demands it makes of its readers. Understanding what the parable has to convey to us depends on our ability to pay careful attention to the ways in which the "point" of the parable emerges, unstated, amid a cacophony of voices, from a gap between the two extremes of experience it depicts: everyday facticity (our predicament in the "daily life," which is "all we have") on the one hand, and a fantastic pure transcendence (represented by the calls to "cross over" to the fabulous beyond and to "become parables"), on the other. In part, Kafka negotiates the tension between these two extremes by playing on the linguistic and generic conventions of parable, prophetic pronouncement, joke, and witty gaming repartee, blurring the modes of communication appropriate to each and exploiting our expectations about tone, timing, delivery, and conclusion. The parable, which culminates in a dual gesture of interpretive fallibility and transformative promise, represents the kind of disquieting "grammatical joke" that Wittgenstein describes as having the character of significance that gets at the very depth of philosophy.[14]

Two-Part Ethical Puzzle

Wittgenstein's *Tractatus*, for its part, is also (as Wittgenstein tells von Ficker) a complex instructive puzzle text that "consists of two parts": the one he presents in the book, and all that he has *not* written. The transformative pedagogy and distinguishing formal features of the *Tractatus* (e.g., the unique aphoristic form of the book's numbered propositions; its ladder structure; Wittgenstein's authorial voice, framing remarks, ironic strategy of conscious use of nonsense, and final self-refuting gesture) all play a role in the book's transformative pedagogy and ethical aim. This aim involves leading us out of our philosophical complacency and delivering us from the confusions in which we become ensnared while philosophizing (confusions such as the idea that there are limits of language and thought to which we can restrict ourselves or go beyond, the idea that there is such a thing as an external point of view from which to survey language and thought, and so on) by engaging us in a process that culminates (at least ideally) in an enlightened understanding and clear vision of the world, life, philosophy, and language (all of which Wittgenstein sees as interdependent parts of the same endeavor).

As we have seen, a central aim of the *Tractatus* (one Wittgenstein casts as ethical) is to deliver us from our tendency to utter nonsense born of metaphysical confusion. In his "Lecture on Ethics," however, Wittgenstein explores the nonsense that results from our attempts to give linguistic expression to our moral or spiritual experience of the world and sense of the meaning of life.[15] In the lecture, Wittgenstein says of all such expressions that "nonsensicality [is] their very essence" (LE, 44). They are the product of a yearning to "go beyond the world and . . . significant language" by giving in to the "tendency to . . . write or talk Ethics or Religion" (LE, 44). Yet the tendency to utter nonsense in such cases is not something we should work to *overcome* (as we are to do with our tendency to come out with metaphysical propositions according to the "correct" method in philosophy he outlines in *Tractatus* 6.53). Wittgenstein emphasizes instead that there is something deeply important about this tendency and its role in our ordinary language and life; he would not ridicule it for the life of him. While Moore describes ethics in *Principia Ethica* as "the general inquiry into what is good," for Wittgenstein, "ethics so far as it springs from the desire to say something about the ultimate meaning of life, the absolute good, the absolute valuable," can be no science and "does not add to our knowledge in any sense." Although the tendency (his own included) to write or talk about ethics will only ever result in nonsensical expressions, this particular use of nonsense nonetheless provides us all with what he calls "a document of a tendency in the human mind" that he "cannot help respecting deeply" (LE, 44).

In a conversation with members of the Vienna Circle recorded by Friedrich Waismann, Wittgenstein brings both Heideggerian dread and Kierkegaardian paradox to bear on his discussion of the anxiety that attends our attempts to talk about ethical experience, talk that is characterized by an abiding failure to signify. In the conversational fragment, Wittgenstein repeatedly and metaphorically describes all efforts to express such experience as reflective of the "impulse to run up against the limits of language":

> I can readily think what Heidegger means by Being and Dread. Man has the impulse to run up against the limits of language. Think, for example, of the astonishment that anything exists. The astonishment cannot be expressed in the form of a question, and there is no answer to it. Everything which we feel like saying can, a priori, only be nonsense. Nevertheless, we do run up against the limits of language. This running-up-against Kierkegaard also recognized and even designated it in a quite similar way (as running-up-against Paradox). This running-up against the limits of language is *Ethics*. I hold that it is truly important that one put an end to all the idle talk about Ethics—whether there be knowledge, whether there be values, whether the Good can be defined, etc. In Ethics one is always making the attempt to say something that does not concern the essence of the matter and Never can concern it. It is a priori certain that whatever one might offer as a definition of the Good, it is always simply a misunderstanding to think that it corresponds in expression to the authentic matter one actually means (Moore). Yet the tendency represented by the running up-against *points to something*. St. Augustine already knew this when he said: What, you wretch, so you want to avoid talking nonsense? Talk some nonsense, it makes no difference![16]

One important starting point for an account of Wittgenstein's relevance to literary studies (in the absence of any clearly stated Wittgensteinian literary program) is to be found in his claims that our attempts to give voice to the experience of astonishment at what we take to be ethically or spiritually significant about ordinary life (a category of expressions that would seem to include most, if not all, figurative language, and by extension, all literary endeavors) will necessarily result in nonsense that arises from a human tendency that Wittgenstein says *points to something* and a tendency for which he declares his deepest respect.

What Wittgenstein says in the "Lecture on Ethics" and in his conversation with Waismann about the importance of nonsense as a kind of expressive form or conduit for the ethical experience that shapes our lives shows that Wittgenstein's philosophical interest in nonsense is not limited to the cases in which metaphysical confusion is the source of our tendency to misuse language and come out with sentences that fail to make logical sense. For he attends not only to the stultifying effects of nonsense when it is uttered by someone in the grip of logical confusion; his treatment of it also extends to a focus on the *generative* features of language to which it also gives rise when used in ethical and aesthetic contexts. And while Wittgenstein speaks quite pejoratively of the nonsense that arises from our misunderstanding of language in the first context—from a tendency he seeks to correct—it is important to note that in the "Lecture on Ethics," he is keen to express his esteem for creative expressions that defy strict logical sense in the second context, in "a desire to say something about the ultimate meaning of life, the absolute good, the absolute[ly] valuable" (LE 44).

It is also worth noting in this regard that Wittgenstein's concerns in the *Tractatus* with the "misunderstanding of the logic of our language" that lies at the root of our philosophical problems, and in his later writing with the "entire mythology" that is stored within our language, are intertwined from the very start with his concerns with literary tales as a formative medium for our ethical thinking (TLP, p. 3; 4.003).[17] Both of these phrases have their source in Wittgenstein's reading of the afterword to a German edition of the Grimms' *Kinder- und Hausmärchen*, written by the Austrian writer and critic Paul Ernst. According to Rush Rhees, Wittgenstein repeatedly claimed that he ought to have acknowledged Ernst as the originator of these notions when the *Tractatus* was first printed.[18] In his afterword, Ernst talks of confusion springing from an "interpretation of a misunderstood tendency of our language" (*Deutung einer mißverstandenen Tendenz der Sprache*), and of the cultural pervasiveness of the ethical themes of fairy tales. Such tales, Ernst writes, "contain our ethics; they represent our poetic understanding."[19]

Another useful point of departure for any attempt to account for the bearing of Wittgenstein's philosophy on literary studies is to be found in the relationship between Wittgenstein's early position regarding the inherent nonsense of "ethical" sentences and his tendency (deliberately demonstrative of its coincidence with our own) to turn repeatedly to figurative language and literary example in his effort to articulate this view. Wittgenstein calls our attention to the potential for creative expression when nonsense arises in the context of communicative attempts to attest to experiences of life that we take to be ethically or spiritually charged.

Wittgenstein's use of figurative language in his discussion of nonsense and ethics in his "Lecture" is complicated, however, by his claim that, although ethical and religious language (always nonsensical by its very essence) tends inherently toward paradox, metaphor, and simile, these are but empty figures that necessarily miss the mark when it comes to making full logical sense. What we attempt to say when we use such language (e.g., when we describe our ethical experience as "wonder at the existence of the world" or as a sense of feeling "safe in the hands of God," to cite Wittgenstein's examples in the "Lecture," what we are trying to say escapes straightforward sense because such attempts endeavor, in Friedlander's words, to "present the transcendence of absolute value by means of something that can be said, a fact"[20] As Wittgenstein puts it:

> in ethical and religious language we seem constantly to be using similes. But a simile must be the simile for *something*. And if I can describe a fact by means of a simile I must also be able to drop the simile and to describe the facts without it. Now in our case as soon as we try to drop the simile and simply to state the facts which stand behind it, we find that there are no such facts. And so, what at first appeared to be a simile now seems to be mere nonsense. (LE, 42–43)

The normal tropological movement between what is said and what is meant does not apply in such cases because there is no literal meaning to which ethical language can correspond. Our sentences about ethics (sentences like "I wonder at the existence of the world" or "I feel absolutely safe") represent a desire to signify that is necessarily bound up with a *failure* to signify. Saying what we mean to say when we talk about significant experience, then, necessarily depends on saying things that, strictly speaking, make no sense at all.

Diamond and Friedlander both take up the question of the literary dimension of Wittgenstein's philosophy by focusing on Wittgenstein's investment in the book as entity in his early writing. Wittgenstein mentions two books in the *Tractatus*: the work itself and the imagined *The World as I Found It* he talks about within it (TLP, 5.631). In the "Lecture on Ethics," Wittgenstein imagines two more books. First is the fantastical "big book," which contains "the whole description of the world" written by an "omniscient person," and which presents readers with the sum total of "facts, facts and facts but no Ethics" (LE, 39). Such a "world-book" "would contain nothing that we would call an *ethical* judgment or anything that would logically imply such a judgment. For Wittgenstein, ethics can be concerned only with absolute judgments, which cannot describe any state of affairs. The book of facts he imagines "would contain all relative judgments of value and all true scientific propositions and in fact all true propositions that can be made." But the facts described in such a book, Wittgenstein tells us, are in no ethical sense good or bad, for "there are no propositions," he says, "which, in any absolute sense, are sublime, important, or trivial." Instead, each of these facts would all stand on the same level. Even a description of a murder would be on exactly the same level as the falling of a stone (LE, 39).

The second imagined book in the "Lecture," the apocalyptic book of pure transcendence, is the opposite of the first imagined book of facts:

> if I contemplate what Ethics really would have to be if there were such a science, this result seems to me quite obvious. It seems to me obvious that nothing we could ever think or say would be *the* thing. That we cannot write a scientific book, the subject matter of which could be intrinsically sublime and above all other subject matters. I can only describe my feeling by the metaphor, that, if a man could write a book on Ethics which really was a book on Ethics, this book would, with an explosion, destroy all the other books in the world. (LE, 40)

The *Tractatus*, as Friedlander sees it, is stretched between the opposing temptations the thought experiments presented in these two "impossible" books exemplify: that of pure fact and that of pure transcendence.[21] Giving into the first temptation leads us to see the book as concerned essentially with the possibility of language to picture facts. Giving in to the second is to see the whole point of the book as an effort to gain a mystical grasp of a transcendent source of value outside the world. The *Tractatus* occupies the gap between both extremes. Its primary aim is to open us to our own experience—as revealed through everyday language—by leading us beyond the dichotomy of facticity and transcendence, away from the urge to transcend the limits of language and toward a recognition that our ordinary dealing with things has a significance that is at once linguistically meaningful and ethically valuable.[22]

Wittgenstein's complex project in the *Tractatus* can thus give us a new critical language for articulating the literary and philosophical stakes of Kafka's parable (in which obscure teaching about the dichotomy between facticity and transcendence, struggles with mythical limits of language, and the yearning to find meaning beyond them are also central). Reading "On Parables" in light of Wittgenstein's mock-doctrinal early work, which strives to work ethically on readers by ensnaring us in a puzzle with a therapeutic aim, also prompts us to recognize the mock-parabolic and diagnostic (though never wholly curative) aspects of Kafka's short piece. Likewise, looking at the *Tractatus* with Kafka's parable in mind leads to new ways of understanding the role that Wittgenstein's interest in figurative language plays in his early thinking and teaching about ethics.

More broadly, all this suggests that looking at these two works in relation to each other calls on us to account for their shared and respective contributions to what I described at the outset of this book as an overriding compulsion among early twentieth-century writers to respond to the unfathomable trauma of war and the unprecedented complexity of modern life with the creation of works whose preoccupation with difficulty leads them back to struggles with the oldest and most fundamental existential riddles.

Kafka and Wittgenstein are exemplary in this regard, since both speak in their works to what I take to be definitive aspects of secular modernism: an attraction to mystery and transcendent experience that is manifested in an obsession with the transformative power of puzzles, riddles, and insoluble questions. Both Kafka and Wittgenstein make use of irony in their different treatments of a human devotion to searches for solutions to life's philosophical problems, something both of them also regard quite sincerely as a matter of deep significance. Wittgenstein's and Kafka's explorations of language, text, and meaning are marked by a distinctly modernist fascination with difficulty that brings about the potent intermixture of obscurity, clarity, and revelation; hope and pessimism; and possibility and failure that lies at the heart of their work. They are rooted in the concrete world, trying to make sense of it through literature with a philosophical bent (Kafka) and philosophy (which Wittgenstein claimed really ought to be "poeted") that depicts a deep-seated human urge to strain in our ordinary language and lives toward an ineffable, extraordinary Beyond.[23]

Gleichnis *and Likeness*

The "Gleichnis" of Kafka's title not only connotes "parable" and "similarity" but also points to figurative and poetic language in general. Wittgenstein was almost certainly thinking of the broader meaning of "Gleichnis" when he used the English word "simile" in his discussion of ethical expressions in the "Lecture on Ethics." Given the importance of "Gleichnis" to the thought of both of these writers, it is helpful to examine some further salient likenesses between Wittgenstein's and Kafka's works.

Kafka's depiction of different levels of mundane, spiritual, and literary understanding offers us valuable insights into the kind of interpretive engagement that a text like the *Tractatus* demands, since the parable (like Wittgenstein's aphoristic "treatise") deals internally with the decisive difference between a reader's imaginatively "getting" the philosophical import of a story (or riddle, or joke) and *not* getting it, between a reader's ability to engage imaginatively and ethically with a text—to make of it something from which philosophy can be learned—or not.[24]

It also points to the difference between the person who tries to see from the perspective of the utterer of nonsense or the teller of parables and the person who sees such a worldview as utterly foreign. Kafka's delineation of this difference, like Wittgenstein's, turns on an examination of the relationship (or lack thereof) between the activities and difficulties of everyday life on the one hand and those of literary expression and oblique spiritual or philosophical teaching on the other. The *Tractatus* and "On Parables" both implicitly critique doctrines that would posit an unbridgeable divide between ordinary language and world and what lies beyond their mythical limits. One of Wittgenstein's aims in the *Tractatus* is to get readers to acknowledge our tendency to create metaphysical systems, to rely on pictures and language that disguise our thought. Such pictures lead us to posit things like "the limits of language," which we then find ourselves bumping up against.

Wittgenstein's and Kafka's puzzles entail an interpretive challenge that is coincident with the aim Wittgenstein saw as ethical. Each of them draws on the power of literature and philosophy in order to lead readers to transform our way of looking at everyday language and the world and also to make a shift in our views about the kind of work that literature and philosophy can do to contribute to that change. Although both of their respective texts call for making a change in the ethical attitude that will allow us to see our problems with language and life more clearly, they are each designed to call into question the status, value, and even hope that one can ever arrive at uncomplicated solutions to those problems. Both Kafka's and Wittgenstein's texts tend toward a satisfying resolution (coming to see the world clearly, and to understand the relationship between literature and everyday life). But they also work strenuously to defy their readers' attempts to sum up their lessons neatly; neither text offers up the final answer they so relentlessly strive after, and which we crave.[25]

Furthermore, each of these works is dedicated to disabusing us of the misconception that there is any such thing as a single method for attaining philosophical, personal, or linguistic clarity, just as there is no particular ethical "part" of the *Tractatus*, or special place located beyond the world and sensible language toward which philosophy and literature can gesture without appeal to nonsensical language or the figurations of metaphor and fantasy.[26] Both Wittgenstein and Kafka repudiate explanation, doctrine, and dogmatic thinking while simultaneously drawing upon traditional narratives of spiritual instruction and conversion. They riff on the form of the parable and appeal to the formal structure and solemn voice of religious scripture, gesturing at the opaque aspects of its mode of instruction as well as its redemptive promise. These moves to resist the lure of doctrine and dogma provide Kafka and Wittgenstein with a compelling way of exploring a human yearning for truth and clarity and the thirst for what Wittgenstein calls "wonder" in the face of mystery and uncertainty. But this same yearning, they caution, can also give way to efforts to confront mystery with the construction of doctrines whose work to resolve mystery (by explaining it away or containing it within an ordered system) effectively extinguishes astonishment.

In the antidogmatic spirit that fuels their indirect teaching, both authors work artfully to set up in their texts a disjuncture between what we might first have thought they were getting at and what they end up leaving us with. Wittgenstein claimed he sought not to teach us new truths but to give us a method for seeing more clearly our ordinary language and world.[27] Kafka turned to the form and genre of the parable not to clarify any particular truth, but to explore different ways in which the difficult realities to which modern humanity must submit—authority, mortality, dread, radical uncertainty, and the absence of God—can be weighed and faced creatively in works of art that demand enduring interpretative commitment.

Nonsense and Ethical Experience in Wittgenstein's "Lecture on Ethics"

In "On Parables," Kafka offers readers his own brand of literary-philosophical puzzle that turns on nonsense, tautology, and transformative interpretation. In the first part of the piece, Kafka's speaker gestures at (and holds at a narrative distance in a ventriloquizing frame) a vague, complaining "many," who deem the parables of the wise inapplicable to the realities of daily life. On the view attributed to this vague, anonymous group, the wise man's command that we "cross over" to an elusive "fabulous Beyond" is an unhelpful directive since it fails to designate any (literal) place to which we (literally) should *go*. Although its lofty poetic tone or promise of deliverance may hold an attraction for some,

the command hardly amounts to a practical prescription for the problems that plague us "here" in our grounded everyday lives. What's more,
strictly speaking, such parabolic commands make no *sense* at all. All that
parables do, according to the point of view Kafka's speaker vocalizes,
is resort to (logically nonsensical) figurative language. If the wise man's
command could be paraphrased, the plaintive many invoked by Kafka's
speaker seems to indicate, its meaning might be transmissible to them
in the form of a helpful message or piece of advice. But the parabolic
form in which the wise man expresses his command is a form that actively *resists* paraphrase. By its parabolic nature, the command defies the
kind of reductive reading that one (or at least one of the "many") might
hope would render it "applicable to daily life." Attempts to unpack the
meaning of his parabolic command of to "designate it more precisely,"
Kafka's speaker indicates, only result in tautologies like "the incomprehensible is incomprehensible," the very sort of senseless expression Wittgenstein uses in the *Tractatus*. Thus, from the point of view of the complaining "many," the words of the wise do nothing to explain, let alone
offer us salvation from, the difficulties of the human condition.

The wise man's parabolic "directive" to "cross over" resonates in
powerful ways with what Wittgenstein says in his "Lecture on Ethics"
about the intrinsic nonsensicality of ethical or religious statements. In
the "Lecture," Wittgenstein distinguishes between absolute and relative
judgments of value. Words that are commonly understood to have an
ethical import ("good," "right," "valuable"), he tells us there, can be used
in a "relative" sense, in which we assign to the object they modify value
that is always *relative* to some preestablished standard or purpose. For
example, in a statement like "This is the right road to Grantchester," we
can explain the use of the word "right" by describing the state of affairs
that led us to make this judgment—stating, perhaps, that a certain route
is "the right road" to Grantchester because it is the road that gets us there
most directly and efficiently (LE, 39).

But such value words can also be used very differently in sentences
that make no reference whatsoever to any fixed purpose or standard.
When such words are used in an "absolute" (or "ethical") sense, that is,
when they are used—as Kafka's sage uses them—in parabolic religious
statements and imperatives to (i.e., to "cross over" to "the right road"),
they are used in a context in which they have no predetermined logico-
linguistic role.

In Wittgenstein's view, when we say that someone ought to take "the
right road," or "the better path," we cannot explain what it is we want
to say by an appeal to facts, since to speak of an "absolute good" is to

stretch language beyond its relative uses by depriving words like "good" of any relation to a predetermined standard. "Our words used as we use them in science," he states, "are vessels capable only of containing and conveying meaning and sense, *natural* meaning and sense. Ethics, if it is anything, is supernatural and our words will only express facts; as a teacup will only hold a teacup full of water even if I were to pour out a gallon over it" (LE, 40). All our efforts to put ethics into words, he says, appealing to metaphor, will in the end represent only vain attempts to "*go beyond* the world and . . . run against the boundaries of language." Wittgenstein insists in the lecture that nothing that makes sense could ever express what he wants to say when he tries to give voice to the experience he takes to be ethical. He attempts to clarify his position by entertaining counterarguments that seek to resolve the paradox "that an experience, a fact, should seem to have supernatural value" by suggesting that "what we mean by saying that an experience has absolute value is just a fact like other facts and that all it comes to is that we have not yet succeeded in finding the correct logical analysis of what we mean by our ethical and religious expressions," he concludes: "Now when this is urged against me I at once see clearly, as it were in a flash of light, not only that no description that I can think of would do to describe what I mean by absolute value, but that I would reject every significant description that anybody could possibly suggest, ab initio, on the ground of its significance" (LE, 44).

For Wittgenstein, expressions of ethical experience are nonsensical not because we have not yet found the correct ways of articulating them, but because their nonsensicality is their very essence. Ethically significant experience, which Wittgenstein sees as something of absolute value, defies all senseful description. Our efforts to speak about it will invariably yield nonsense.

I return here to a point of clarification I touched on above: The *Tractatus* represents Wittgenstein's attempt to free readers from the thrall of metaphysics and to overcome their tendency to utter nonsense. But in his view, there is a decisive difference (not of *category* but of *use*) between the *unexamined* metaphysical nonsense that he wants to get us to overcome and the *self-conscious* nonsense he uses in the *Tractatus* to get us to do so. "Don't *for heaven's* sake be afraid of talking nonsense," he would write in a notebook from the 1946, "but you must pay attention to your nonsense" (CV 56). Wittgenstein's position that ethical sentences are nonsensical by their nature is not such that he wants us to curtail our urges to give expression to our significant ethical or spiritual experience as he does our urges to come out with metaphysical nonsense.

Whereas the tendency to utter metaphysical nonsense speaks only to a deep-seated philosophical and personal confusion, the nonsensical utterances we use to describe our ethical experience provide us with a vital means of creatively communicating our experience of being. This point lies at the heart of Wittgenstein's view that "ethics and aesthetics are one" (TLP, 6.421; cf. LE, 38).

In order to grasp the import of Wittgenstein's views about the role of nonsense in an ethical context and its connection to aesthetics, it is helpful to reconsider the stunningly creative move Wittgenstein makes in pursuit of the ethical aim he ascribes to his book of nonsense. He performatively engages readers in the elaborate mock doctrine he imaginatively conceives as an apt therapeutic response to our confused investment in metaphysics. Attending to this creative impulse, which gives rise to the *Tractatus* as the full work of ethical depth and tactical complexity it becomes when understood as a whole, reminds us that nonsense employed self-consciously to serve an ethical aim (i.e., of leading another person to clarity), like nonsense expressive of a person's ethical outlook, can offer us thoughtful and morally imaginative ways of working toward a better understanding of our own lives and the lives of others. Broadly construed, nonsense is not only the essence of expressions of ethical and religious experience. Wittgenstein's thinking about nonsense is relevant to our studies of literature because in its wider reach, it is also a communicative mode for the variety of aesthetic forms and genres (literature included) in which we attest to our experience the pain and wonder of being in our various quests for clarity.

Wonder at the Existence of the World and the Existence of Language Itself

In the "Lecture on Ethics," Wittgenstein offers several paradigmatic examples of the kind of experience we feel inclined to describe as having ethical significance. His example par excellence is that of "*wonder at the existence of the world*," an experience that gives rise to sentences like "how extraordinary that anything should exist" (LE, 41). Wittgenstein tells us that the verbal expression of such an experience is only nonsense. In the ordinary sense of the word, wondering is directed at a particular state of affairs within the world that we can marvel at. But as Michael Kremer puts it, to speak of wonder *at the existence of the world*, is to stretch the verb into a kind of abstraction, depriving it of its habitual kind of object. What's more, expressing wonder at the existence of the world is like saying "how wonderful that the world is the world" or—to

return to Kafka's parable for a moment—expressing wonder at a tautology like "the incomprehensible is incomprehensible." But to express
wonder at a tautology is simply nonsense (LE, 42). As Kremer points
out, the experience of such wonder seems closely related to what Wittgenstein calls "the mystical" at *Tractatus* 6.44: "not *how* the world is
but *that* it is." It is also related to the experience of what the *Tractatus*
conceives of as the presuppositions of logic, the experience which is "no
experience," and which at *Tractatus* 5.552 he says "we need [in order]
to understand logic": not that such and such is the case, but that something *is*."[28]

Expressions of wonder at the world, Wittgenstein tells us, are not expressions of a desire to know the scientific explanations for the world's
existence. We say such things not when we are looking at the world or
at the sky as we might look scientifically at an explainable fact. We say
them when we want to express our astonishment at the world's or the
sky's being "*whatever it is*" (LE, 42). We are given to saying such things
like, "how wonderful the world!," he says, when the world strikes us as
somehow strangely miraculous. In contrast, "the scientific way of looking at a fact is not the way to look at it as a miracle" (LE, 43). To regard the experience of wonder at the existence of the world as we would
a scientific fact would be to fail to grasp the ethical import of such an
experience. ("Man must awaken to wonder," Wittgenstein wrote in a
1930 notebook entry. "Science is a way of putting him back to sleep")
(CV, 5). Inseparable from our experience of the world as miraculous is
the recognition that there can be no explanation for such a miracle; indeed, that a miracle cannot be explained is part of what makes it a miracle. And once a miracle has been scientifically explained, Wittgenstein
asks, "where would the miracle have got to?" (LE, 43).

Wittgenstein goes on to report that he is "tempted to say" that the
right expression in language for the miracle of the existence of the world,
though it is not any proposition *in* language, is the existence of language
itself. The presentation of all senseful language that he offers in the *Tractatus* (with the general form of proposition at TLP, 6) is meant to draw
our attention to *the* language, "language itself," and thus to let us see
the world from a different perspective. Wittgenstein's claim about "language itself" is thus related to what he says at *Tractatus* 6.44 that the
mystical is "not *how* the world is, but *that* it is."

Conant argues that the idea of a philosophical perspective on the logical structure of the world is but the illusion of a perspective, an illusion
of a view from sideways on from which the *Tractatus* aims to free us.
Kremer affirms this view, pointing out that the idea that we can achieve

a perspective on the world "as a limited whole," "*sub specie aeterni*," as he says, is an idea the *Tractatus* invites us to throw away (TLP, 6.45).[29] But as Diamond points out, *pace* Kremer, to speak of the philosophical activity of achieving clarity about language as "changing one's perspective on the world," as Wittgenstein does, is to use words in a decidedly, deliberately *figurative* way, taking words out of their everyday use. Diamond sees the figurative use of the idea of a "perspective on the world" as something that plays an important role in Wittgenstein's conception of ethics and the way he thought his method could lead readers toward a decisive change in outlook. "It is as if by presenting the general form of proposition, Wittgenstein had drawn a circle around the totality of language and made its 'thereness' for us open to view," Diamond writes. "Its 'thereness' stands for the 'thereness' of the world." The upshot of this account is not a rejection of *Tractatus* 6.41, with its talk of value lying "outside the world." Instead, it offers a different way of understanding what Wittgenstein is saying there. We may initially take him to suggest in that proposition that value is something we cannot reach with words. But by seeing his language of "outside" as figurative, Diamond suggests, "the world as something 'seeable' is part of a perspective that we can come to occupy" imaginatively, through a responsiveness to metaphor. And we can occupy this perspective without adopting the illusory conception of a sideways-on perspective that Conant criticizes.[30]

Nonsense and Secondary Sense

Attempts to give verbal expression to experiences that have ethical or religious value for us give rise to what Wittgenstein refers to here again in the "Lecture" as a "characteristic misuse of our language" (LE, 41). As is the case when he speaks of the nonsense of "ethical" sentences, Wittgenstein is concerned to emphasize their generative potential in this context, and his talk of "misuse" is not pejorative. What he is talking about is the unusual linguistic intention that gives rise to nonsense, or to what he later describes as "secondary sense."

When we make ethical or religious use of phrases (like Kafka's "cross over," for example), he tells us, we might be tempted to think that we are using them as similes (or *Gleichnisse*), figurative stand-ins, that is, for some particular something we want to talk about. Like parables, however, ethical expressions as Wittgenstein understands them prove resistant to paraphrase. Because there are no worldly facts standing behind them, the ethical use of these words, in his view, is not *metaphorical* (or it ceases to serve that purpose). Rather, it is nonsense that emerges from wonder "at the existence of language itself," nonsense expressive of a yearning he takes quite seriously (LE, 43–44). Wittgenstein's discussion of the inexpressibility of ethics in the *Tractatus* and in the "Lecture on Ethics" is ultimately an attempt to show us something about the odd kind of linguistic intention we have when we feel moved, as he says (once again using nonsense as figurative language), to "go beyond the world" and utter ethical sentences (LE, 44). Our desire to say what we want to say when we feel so moved would only be thwarted if, in an attempt to refrain from uttering nonsense, we tried to limit all our talk to empirical descriptions. As I said above, although such ethical talk is nonsensical, it nevertheless plays an important role in our lives, allowing us to express ourselves in ways that that no empirically meaningful sentence could allow.[31]

Wittgenstein explores this kind of complex linguistic intention in his remarks on what he calls "secondary sense" in "Philosophy of Psychology—a Fragment" (formerly part 2 of the *Philosophical Investigations*).[32] There, Wittgenstein discusses the inclination to describe peculiar experiences by saying things like "for me the vowel *e* is yellow" or "Wednesday is fat and Tuesday lean" (PPF, §§ 202, 216). When a person utters a sentence like "the vowel *e* is yellow," although she may call attention to the oddity of her sentence by setting it apart with the help of qualifying framing remarks (such as, "I am tempted to say," for example), this person is not, according to Wittgenstein, using the word "yellow" in a nonliteral or extended sense. "The secondary sense is not a 'metaphorical' sense," he writes. "If I say, 'For me the vowel *e* is yellow,' I don't mean: 'yellow' in a metaphorical sense—for I could not express what I want to say in any other way than by means of the idea 'yellow'" (PPF, §216). The sentence in question could of course be made into a logically meaningful one if we gave a new meaning to "yellow" for all occurrences of the word as an adjective applied to vowels or sounds. But when we want to express something about ourselves and our peculiar way of seeing the world by saying things like "*e* is yellow," giving the word "yellow" a new meaning is precisely what we do *not* want to do: "I want to use *these* words (with their familiar meanings) *here*," says Wittgenstein (PPF, §216). There are times when we do *not* want to give meaning to a sign or signs in some proposition if the proposition would make clear sense as a result. In cases like these, saying just what we want to say to describe our personal experience demands using words like "yellow" outside the contexts in which they have a fixed meaning. Were we to try to rectify the situation by turning a sentence involving ethical nonsense or secondary sense into a determinate meaningful proposition, that sentence would, by virtue of its very meaningfulness, fail to match the kind of complex linguistic intention it expresses.

Diamond invites us to imagine that the desire to express a feeling of wonder *that* the world exists might give rise to questions like, "Why is there anything?" Such an interrogatory utterance is modeled on the form of questions that look to the world (to all that is the case) for answers. And yet, as Wittgenstein indicates, an utterance like this one, although it may make psychological or emotional sense, and although it may represent the best way we can find of expressing our mystification in the face of our lived existence in the world (an impulse that Wittgenstein sees as ethical), it doesn't make *logical* sense. An utterance like this one, though it looks like a question, is not in fact a question at all. Likewise, there is no answer that can satisfy what it reaches for in its apparent interrogation. Our astonishment that anything should exist, he says in the 1929 conversation with Waismann, cannot be expressed as a question.[33] The kind of answer a "question" like "Why is there anything?" anticipates is not an answer that addresses how things stand, or what is the case. No senseful proposition designated by the general form of proposition Wittgenstein elaborates in the *Tractatus* (that is, no straightforward sentence of fact, natural science, logical necessity, the laws of physics, etc.) would provide us with an acceptable answer to this "question" that isn't one. At 6.52, Wittgenstein writes that we feel that "even if *all possible* scientific questions were answered, the problems of life still have not been touched at all." There are no senseful logical sentences that will provide us with the answer we are looking for when we ask a "question" like "why is there anything?"

Wittgenstein writes in the *Tractacus* that if an answer cannot be put into words, the corresponding "question" (i.e., the utterance that seemed to want such an answer) also cannot be put into words. The riddle does not exist. If a question can be asked at all, then it can also be answered (TLP, 6.5). Diamond points out that the reader Wittgenstein has in mind in proposition 6.5 is working under the presumption that the question she is asking calls for an answer that is *inexpressible* (that is, one that somehow emanates from an imagined realm of value that lies *beyond* language). Wittgenstein wants to go on to transform that understanding. The method of philosophy he outlines at 6.53 helps him to do so. There, he tells readers that the correct method of philosophy would be to say nothing except what can be said (i.e., the propositions of natural science, i.e., something that has nothing to do with philosophy). This method comes into play when our interlocutor says something metaphysical, and we are called on to demonstrate to him that he has given no meaning to his propositions. Diamond takes seriously that Wittgenstein sees talking sense a philosophical method in its own right, used to lead others to philosophical clarity. One can come to understand how talking sense could serve as a philosophical method if one sees such a method as directed toward helping another person to recognize that no talking sense would offer a solution to the problem she is concerned with when she asks an apparent question like "why is there anything?" ("Limits of Sense," 244). Diamond writes:

> Wittgenstein thinks that we can be helped philosophically by seeing that nothing in the realm of sense is what we are seeking, and that talking only sense, or imagining a huge amount of sense-talking, can itself help us to reach the point at which we can say: I see nothing that made sense would be what I want; I see that I could reject a priori anything you say in answer to my question if it made sense. Talking sense is a method of philosophy if talking sense is a way of enabling someone to see that anything like *any of this* (all this sense) would not be what she wants. ("Limits of Sense," 244)

Here Diamond draws a distinction between thinking of the inexpressibility of something as a matter of its lying *beyond* the expressible, beyond the limits of language, and thinking of it as *not within* the expressible, not within what can be said. She argues that the activity of philosophy, as Wittgenstein practices it, works to make us aware of two elements of our tendency to "go beyond significant language" with an eye to redirecting it. One facet of this tendency is seen in our inclination to reject ordinary propositions that describe how things are in the world (propositions that can neither satisfy our desire to talk about what is ethically valuable, nor answer our [non-]question "Why is there anything?"). Another is seen in our desire to go beyond ordinary descriptive language to talk about what is ethically valuable.

How philosophy can affect this tendency is by clarifying (from "within" language, rather than from some imagined external philosophical perspective) what belongs to ordinary senseful propositions. In giving us the general form of a proposition, Wittgenstein gives us a rule for the construction of all senseful language—all senseful propositions as well as all senseless tautologies and contradictions (TLP, 6). By giving us a way to see the language we can understand and use with this complete clarity, Wittgenstein also takes himself to be enabling us to see clearly that no proposition at all will ever be what we want when we want to talk about ethics (TLP, 6.42, 6.5; "Limits of Sense," 259–60). To talk about ethics, we must use language that is figurative.

Gleichnis *and Nonsense*

It bears repeating that if Wittgenstein composed the *Tractatus* in an effort to lead us toward recognizing our tendency to find confused metaphysical positions or sentences attractive, in the "Lecture on Ethics" he states that the impulse to utter patent nonsense to talk about the ethical significance of the world is something he does not want to criticize (LE, 44). In his view, our attraction to ethical sentences is not something that deeper self-understanding can or should make disappear. Nor, as we have seen, is ethics a limited sphere of philosophical discourse among others. Like logic, ethics for Wittgenstein penetrates all thought and language. It is not something that one can meaningfully describe, but something that shows forth in the spirit with which we face life and the world as a whole. For Wittgenstein, in the language of his contemporary Heidegger (invoking Hölderlin), it is in the poetic way in which we dwell on the earth that the ethical is revealed. The ethical, which for him is "the most essential part of what is generally called Aesthetics," shows forth in our imperfect, often confused or fragmented attempts to express experiences they take to be ethically significant. It shows itself in our humor, literature, music, art, and—not least of all—ordinary language. For Wittgenstein, certain jokes, gestures, tones of voice, or works of literature, even though they offer no explicit or coherent story or clear moral teaching, even when they do not entirely succeed at the difficult or even impossible task of expressing what we take to be sacred or painful, do nonetheless have the capacity to reveal to us things about life and the wonder and horror of the world and human experience. Indeed, the *Tractatus* is Wittgenstein's attempt to show that philosophical works also have the capacity to express ethical experience in this way, even though he claims that there is nothing said, strictly speaking, within the body of the text. We will not find an ethical theory in the nonsensical sentences of the *Tractatus*. Its ethics resides in the clarifying activity in which it is engaged and toward which he hopes to point his readers

Up to a point, Kafka's parable shares this aim, since it also seeks to engage its readers in the work of adopting different ways of seeing the world through a participation in riddling and an attention to language that Wittgenstein describes in the "Lecture on Ethics" as nonsensical. As I have argued above, Kafka's and Wittgenstein's works span the tension between the pure facticity and pure transcendence represented by the opposing impossible books of Wittgenstein's thought experiments in his lecture. But while both authors make it their business to call our attention to the pitfalls of inclining toward either extreme, each nonetheless betrays his investment in the power of figurative expressions of our longing for transcendence to give voice to our experience of the extraordinary within the ordinary.

I take the thrust of Kafka's "On Parables" to be that parables and literary or otherwise figurative uses of language *are* relevant to daily life (not that their lessons are easily understood) and that "crossing over" (by adopting an attitude that allows us to enter imaginatively) into a "realm" where literary or religious language might enliven our daily lives is indeed worth it. As Kafka attests over and over again in his diaries and letters, he saw work in such figurative language as *vital* to his own life. But "On Parables" also complicates this picture, calling into question the effectiveness of this aim (of eliciting understanding in others through exceedingly obscure parabolic teaching), and the promise of the process it seeks to set in motion as well as our ability actually to take it up. The parable thus offers a critique of the implicit call for transformation that resounds in Kafka's own work, as well as Wittgenstein's.[34]

When Kafka's wise man says, "cross over," he is making use of the kind of ethical or religious expressions Wittgenstein discusses in the "Lecture on Ethics" in order to direct his listeners to the "right" road toward an enriched poetic and spiritual worldview. As Kafka's speaker says, the sage certainly doesn't mean that we should cross over to some actual place that we can designate ostensively. The "location" he is gesturing at is a place beyond the world and senseful language, as it were. Kafka's framing of the discussion that unfolds through the voices of the speaker from the first part of the parable, his sage, and two interlocutors from the second part allows him to explore not only the different planes of understanding (and the gulfs between them) that are the parable's most obvious issue, but also the subtler questions about levels of engagement with the unconscious, self-conscious, and "ethical" nonsense Wittgenstein would have us recognize.[35] The spiritual command of Kafka's sage—that we "cross over"—is nonsense in just the way that Wittgenstein sees all ethical, religious (and by extension, I argue, poetic and literary) language to be nonsense.

What Kafka's sage wants to convey with his talk of crossing over to "some sort of fabulous beyond," his speaker recognizes, can be expressed in the way he wants it to be only if the sage eschews attempts to speak with straightforward meaning in order to "designate more precisely" what he has in mind. As in the case of sentences Wittgenstein describes as having "secondary sense," utterances like the sage's reveal a complex linguistic intention that cannot be fulfilled by employing a more "precise" sentence that would make full logical sense. The sage is saying just what he wants to say when he urges his interlocutor to "cross over." Those given to expressing themselves in this way (whether for religious or poetical reasons) will not be cured of their desire to do so by a teaching method like the "correct" one Wittgenstein describes at *Tractatus* 6.53. What Kafka's sage is saying renders strange the relationship between the literal and figurative and proves resistant to interpretations that seek to reformulate his command in straightforwardly factual, senseful terms. What he says is equally resistant to methods of instruction that would seek to disabuse him of his nonsense or to curb his desire to say what he says in just the way he says it. What Kafka's sage (and in turn the speaker who quotes him to his own purposes) is saying about everyday reality thus *depends* on literary language—a language that paradoxically gestures not at that reality, but at a fabulous space beyond ordinary language and world.

But the sage's gesture within the parable is one that folds over on itself. For by pointing to a realm beyond language and the world, the wise man also manages to speak from within Kafka's fictive frame to a conception of reality capacious enough to encompass a real human yearning for an imaginative elsewhere attainable through religious and fictive modes of language. Landy claims that the literary mode of instruction presented in parables, "does the work of gradually shifting the listener to a higher plane" from which figuratively to see "the world *sub specie ae-ternitatis*, as though with the eyes of God."[36] Within Kafka's parable, the sage thus speaks to the power of this instructive mode to expand our notion not only of literary and poetic form and ethical and spiritual teaching, but of the shape of real life. He also elicits our astonishment at the miracle of the existence of language itself that Wittgenstein talks about in the "Lecture on Ethics" and the *Tractatus*.

As Diamond shows us in her work on Wittgenstein, in order to understand teaching imparted through nonsense sentences that speak to ethical significance, readers or listeners must try to understand the person uttering the nonsense. We must try to enter imaginatively into the speaker's particular kind of nonsense.[37] And this is precisely what the complaining "many" of Kafka's parable do not do. They represent a remote collective entity existing within Kafka's minifiction, and yet beyond the reach of the appeal of figurative language. Unreceptive to tautology and complex linguistic intention, they cannot (or will not) entertain what the "words of the wise" have to teach about the incomprehensible because they do not (or cannot) adopt the imaginative perspective that a deep understanding of their gist would require.

Becoming Parables

The way parables work on the receptive insider, on the other hand, Landy suggests, is that they "help those who can appreciate the power of figurative discourse to become people who can *follow* it and help those who can follow it to become people who can coin fresh metaphors of their own."[38] The ideal recipients of Jesus's parabolic teaching, in Landy's analysis, are those who can model their imaginative responsiveness to that figurative mode of teaching on that of the Syrophoenician woman whose story appears in the book of Mark. The Syrophoenician woman's inspired response to one of Jesus's parabolic remarks (in this case uttered with the aim of rebuffing her and putting her in her place) is to produce her own figurative language and deliver it back to her interlocutor in a reply that establishes a communicative exchange between them. By responding to Jesus's parable with her own use of metaphor, the Syrophoenician woman thus adds a new dimension to Jesus's original metaphor before volleying it back to him under this new communicative application.[39]

The Syrophoenician woman's move to respond to Jesus's figurative language with a parabolic display of her own mental acuity, proficiency with words, and skillful manipulation of the power of metaphor in her exchange with the master of parables himself sets the stage for Kafka's own take on the form in "On Parables." The gap Kafka posits between everyday life and a "great beyond," bridgeable only through the kind of parabolic and poetic figuration his metatext, at once represents and holds up for examination as the object of a formally unending discussion about the value of parables in everyday life. Kafka invokes the Syrophoenician woman's figurative cunning and ease with a parabolic comeback in the back-and-forth banter of his own parable's closing dialogue.

The debate Kafka sets up performatively displays the power of parabolic instruction simultaneously to confuse, exclude, entice to exegesis, and elicit in its participants a false sense of mastery. Kafka's closing exchange also performs the interpretive failure to resolve the riddle at the parable's core, a failure on which the very form depends, for reasons experiential, existential, and instrumental.

On an experiential front, by featuring the failure of the figures speaking within the text to come up with a stable, satisfying final interpretation that will resolve their debate (and put an end to the reader's puzzlement), the parable is able to address the perplexed reader's acute experience of the insoluble difficulty of the text. But the parable also has an existential reach, since its treatment of the failure to resolve the problems of meaning at issue in it also speaks authentically to the fallible human predicament more broadly. Parables are thus forms in which the layered types of difficulty Steiner describes as "tactical" intersect with those of an unresolvable sort that he calls "ontological." Finally, on an instrumental level, by portraying the interpretive failure to resolve the problems at stake in it, the parable also underscores the importance to the form of the ongoing heuristic participation in the critical training it has to offer.

In the exchange that takes place in the second (exegetical) part of "On Parables," Kafka further develops his characterization of a reader or listener oblivious to the complexities of the indirect moral lessons conveyed by parables, on the one hand, and, on the other, a "someone" (*Einer*), the first intervening figure in the final dialogue, who at least tries straightforwardly—rather than through instructive indirection—to tell others that they should give themselves over to their instructive sway. The exchange between the two interlocutors is initiated by this first figure, who, making a sage pronouncement (or perhaps *mocking* such a pronouncement, or perhaps offering only the mere appearance of wisdom in an ultimately hollow bit of advice), intones: "If you followed parables, you would become parables yourselves and with that free of your daily cares."

This injunction to follow, and thus "become" parables represents either a literary platitude (perhaps a nicety meant to put an end to an unproductive debate), a call for radical escapism, or yet another example of a nonsensical sentence expressive of a strange linguistic intention conveyed through the use of the secondary sense of a word or phrase, in this case "to become parables." The first of the figures to intervene in the second part of Kafka's parable within a parable is eager to indulge, or to encourage others to indulge (in a tongue-in-cheek manner at the very least), the imaginary possibility of giving oneself over, so to speak, to a life led parabolically, to taking a figurative perspective on the world. But the meaning of such a suggestion remains unclear. For in what would "becoming parables" consist?

Should we interpret the call to become parables as an enticement to inhabit a figurative state of mind, to dwell poetically on the earth, in Hölderlin's sense (and Heidegger's after him)? Or dwell in possibility and metaphor, in Emily Dickinson's sense?[40] Or to live in such a way as to be receptive to the strange kind of instruction parables have to offer?

Is the call to follow parables meant for everyone, or does its implicit challenge effectively divide its audience into two camps (an elect group of insiders somehow already predisposed toward inscrutable tales, on the one hand, and others excluded by their impenetrability, on the other)? In any case, what the first man in Kafka's parable is calling for involves his hearers' engagement in a kind of *becoming*. He calls on his interlocutors within the text (and the readers outside the text) to begin a transformative process that will allow them to occupy a different interpretive reality that promises a sort of redemption. Unless, of course, what he is calling on us to do is to give up on reality altogether, opting instead for a life lived in a strange realm of fantasy or scriptural hermeneutics.[41]

A person open to parabolic modes of instruction and imaginatively inclined toward literary, fictive, and figurative modes of describing the world might take the call of the first man for such a metaphorical transformation in stride, but such a pronouncement may leave others unsatisfied. Thus, this first man's approach will likely fail as a therapeutic curative aimed at getting his hearers and readers to overcome their resistance to seeing the importance of parables to ordinary life. Like the sage in the first part of the parable, whose ethical nonsense is not used in such a way that the complaining "many" can understand him (in the way Wittgenstein the utterer of nonsense asks us to understand *him*, rather than his sentences, in the *Tractatus*), the spokesman for parabolic conversion in the second part also fails to elicit with his ethical nonsense the understanding of his interlocutors or the readers of the parable he inhabits, or to awaken in them a desire for change (TLP, 6.54). The first man, who suggests that were we to follow parables we would ourselves become parables and be rid of our daily cares either sets up a relation between parable and reality that demands a literal interpretation that leads to paradox (once *Gleichnis* becomes reality, where will the *Gleichnis* have got to?) or urges us parabolically either toward a life of escape, or to death (literal or figurative) that will free us from our daily cares. Neither of these possibilities succeeds in bridging the gap between concrete world and figurative word in order to fulfill the redemptive yearning to bring the extraordinary to bear on the ordinary that underlies Kafka's parable as a whole.

The parable's concluding dialogue unfolds across a cluster of different genres. It is at once an exegetical dispute, a contest in competitive philology, a slapstick Vaudevillian squabble, a shrewd game of the Dozens, and a joke steeped in a long diasporic cultural tradition of Jewish humor.[42] The first man's interlocutor ("another," "the second") responds to his suggestion with a gesture of one-upmanship: "I bet that's also a parable," he parries. To this claim, the first figure concedes, "You have won." "But unfortunately only in parable," the second retorts. The second figure's responses to the words of his interlocutor (and opponent, in what has now become a game of the Dozens) demonstrate both the competitive nature of his particular A-HA *Erlebnis* and his expertise in designating only the outward linguistic and generic form of the first figure's utterance. In parable he has lost.

It is worth noting that the second figure in the debate does not even go so far as to offer a reductive paraphrase of the parable's lesson (something that would of course also represent losing at parable, but at least having put some interpretive *effort* into the process, however flatfooted). If what the second man says represents a momentary interpretive victory in this game, then, it also demonstrates a far deeper failure to grasp the interpretive value of the method of working toward understanding that Kafka's parable affords us. The second figure shows himself to be unable to respond to the parable, in the creative, communicative manner in which the Syrophoenician woman does to Jesus's parable. He is unable to shift his stance toward language and existence in such a way as to dwell in the possibility of metaphor, or in the sage's "great beyond."

It could also be said that the first figure loses in parable too. For he has failed to help the second to see things in a way that would lead him to "win" by grasping the full value of what the parable has the potential to show him—although in the context of Kafka's metaparable, the first man's lack of explanation does not represent a failure to acknowledge the confusion of the other and attempt to provide him with elucidation with the words he does utter.

That said, it is of course important to remember that these are two figures conversing within the fictive frame of a parable on parables. In that sense, the only way they can win or lose in their game of hermeneutics is, quite literally, *in* the parable that is their only reality. To really "win" or "lose" in parable or in reality (to speak coyly of parables as if the interpretive work they demanded only amounted to participation in a zero-sum game) is ultimately to engage in work that we as readers must do for ourselves.

It may be easier to conceive of how a person could "lose" in parable, especially a parable like Kafka's, than it is to really get a handle on what "winning" would entail. We can see how a person might be poised to "lose" at parable, after all, by being too stubbornly obtuse, unimaginative, uninspired, or simply too cynical about the question of how literature can shape our lives to follow the spirit of the form's characteristically oblique guidance in such a way as to ever have a chance of really "getting" it. What may be harder to grasp—and for some readers more than others—is the idea that "winning" in parable (at least "winning" conceived as something that happens in the flash of some victorious coup), is not the endgame of the form. Thought of in this way, it is certainly not the goal of puzzling parabolic texts like Kafka's and Wittgenstein's.

As readers, we might stand humbled before Kafka's challenging parable and still consider ourselves more aesthetically perceptive and intuitive than Kafka's second man, the prosaic runner-up, fated to win only in reality. Yet knowing how (and when) we have reached a satisfactory resolution to the problems it charges us to untangle is a rather different ball of wax. Like the figurative steps that readers of the *Tractatus* must take to reach the figurative vantage point from which figuratively to "see the world in the right way," the path toward the ideal solution we might imagine will assure us of such an interpretive triumph is one denied us in (and by) the text.

The work of understanding that parables demand, as I have suggested above, does not entail efforts to reduce them to "applicable" legible messages by means of paraphrase that renders the fictive literal and the opaque transparent. What readers are asked to do in response to the cognitive and ethical challenge Kafka's parable throws down is to take up the gradual work of making ourselves receptive to the puzzles of metaphor, and engaging in our own productive modes of interpretation and use of figurative language.

In spite of the fact that the first man gets the last word with his apparently climactic punch line, however, "On Parables" ultimately takes its place in a long history of Old and New Testament parables, conundrums, and jokes without a clearly delivered moral or solution.[43] Indeed, the seductive appeal of Kafka's text lies in the way it provokes our engagement in interpretation while at the same time thwarting it. As Walter Sokel has pointed out, Kafka's works "lure us toward metaphysics and theology, but frustrate and mock anyone who allows her- or himself to be swept beyond their appearance of a call for meaning to the attempt to find one."[44] Similarly, in the *Tractatus*, Wittgenstein makes use of a Kierkegaardian mirroring strategy by contriving a mock-doctrinal work of nonsense that lures readers into taking seriously the illusion that what he is saying makes sense only to explode that illusion from within.[45] Like Kafka, then, he entices us with metaphysics and theology as a way of showing us how attractive such illusions can be, how strong our tendency is to defer to the (illusory) authority of what we take to be meaningful philosophical positions, and, finally, how to avoid their sway. In the manner of the parable, Wittgenstein's *Tractatus* is a text of oblique instruction dedicated to offering readers training in thinking and reading that will help us to see the world more clearly.

Rootedness and Reaching

The complexity of the word "Gleichnis" in Kafka's title thus carries over into the treatment of the different problems of outlook and confusions about language (poetic and ordinary) that Kafka offers in his "On Parables." Kafka's play with and within the parable form with the range of figurative, literal, instrumental, and spiritual understandings and misunderstandings of his inscrutable cast of characters allows him to present readers not just with a single mirror in which to see ourselves and our linguistic and spiritual confusion but with a number of mirrors.[46] The ending with which he leaves us is frayed, inconclusive, and open to continued debate and commentary in spite of its snappy punch line. Part of the joke is, of course, that no one really has the last word here. The parable's final line ("I bet that is also a parable") sets it up for the reader to continue the work of interpretation indefinitely.

Both Wittgenstein and Kafka use nonsense (which, for Wittgenstein, is not *Gleichnis*—not likeness, not simile) and *Gleichnis* (which, as Kafka uses it, resembles Wittgenstein's nonsense put to literary use) in their efforts to offer a picture of our everyday struggles with the mysteries of life and language and to depict a modern human condition characterized by deep and inherently frustrated yearning for truth, redemption, and ever-elusive answers.

In a letter to his friend Max Brod, Kafka describes himself as a man whose feet are rooted in the world (and Word) of an infertile and conservative religious past from which he yearns to be free. His forelimbs, however, *are* free to reach into the heights above him. Although they find nothing firm to grasp, in their desperate waving about, he finds what he calls "inspiration."[47] Kafka's description of his simultaneous rootedness in the world and yearning for a fabulous Beyond points not only to the rooted "stuckness" that is the cause of his despair, but also to the literary creativity that his despair awakens—the inspiration to create something new to tell us, something "modern" perhaps, in strange stories that convey the pain and beauty of this world and the longing to be free of it. This is the longing to give oneself over to another realm in the way one can only give oneself over to literature or to death. Kafka finds transformative creative expression in his very pessimism about the possibility of transformation. Against such pessimism (a measure of which he nonetheless shares with Kafka), Wittgenstein—who in the *Tractatus* still holds out a sincere hope for the redemptive possibilities of personal changes (whether they be the momentary epiphanic revelations he points to when he talks of seeing the world *sub specie aeternitatis* or a more enduring conversion to "seeing the world in the right way")—claims that the coincidence of ethics and aesthetics occasions the transformative value of literature, for it is in literature that the experience of the ethical is expressed most compellingly as narrative enlivened by nonsense (CV, 5).

3

Woolf, Diamond, and the Difficulty of Reality

For loudly though we talk of the advance of realism and boldly though we assert
that life finds its mirror in fiction, the material of life is so difficult to handle
and has to be limited and abstracted . . . before it can be dealt with by words.
—Virginia Woolf[1]

There is nothing . . . that answers, or bears on, the problems of life. But the very
fact that in these books, as we may imagine them, there are answers to every
imaginable question can help us to transform our own desire for an answer to
the problem of life.
—Cora Diamond[2]

Woolf and Wittgenstein. And Diamond

In her "Woolf and Wittgenstein," Pamela Caughie broaches
the question of the relationship between these two figures
by calling into question the status of the "and" that joins
them in her title. "Typically, she says, "the grammar of
coordination would suggest one of two kinds of relation:
influence, reinforced by the biographical connections between the two writers, or shared sensibility." The first option that Caughie presents seems the less persuasive of the
two. For while Woolf and Wittgenstein surely came into
contact during Wittgenstein's time at Cambridge, and
while Woolf "certainly knew of him," we have no evidence that Woolf ever actually read his work or was in any
way knowledgeable about his philosophy.[3] There are no

references to Wittgenstein in Virginia Woolf's diaries, and only a few incidental mentions of him in her letters. Leonard Woolf confirms in a letter that he and Virginia "knew Wittgenstein," but not well, though they did see "a certain amount of him."[4] It is likely, Ray Monk conjectures, that Woolf and Wittgenstein would have met socially at one of John Maynard Keynes's parties. "If so," he concludes, "neither seems to have made much impression on the other."[5] Gaile Pohlhaus Jr. and Madelyn Detloff have likened Wittgenstein's presence in Bloomsbury circles as that of "something of a Mordred figure who barges into Camelot and causes the philosophical Round Table to splinter."[6]

Meanwhile, Woolf's Bloomsbury life and connections certainly brought her into what Ann Banfield describes as a "continuous discussion" with the Cambridge philosophers in her midst. Banfield points out that "the participants in the endless Bloomsbury talk included the eminent figures of British philosophy" who, like Russell, Moore, Whitehead, Keynes, Ramsey, and others, were also Woolf's friends and acquaintances, people with whom she met, as Wittgenstein did, as colleagues and intellectual peers.[7] Jaakko Hintikka writes that Woolf could easily have acquired knowledge of the philosophical ideas of the time, including Wittgenstein's, "through the almost subconscious osmotic processes of conversation and listening."[8] Some of the "aural knowledge" Woolf acquired of their thinking came in the guise of formal lectures. Woolf is known to have attended talks by Russell, Moore, and Keynes, for example.[9] But Leonard Woolf avers of Wittgenstein that he and Virginia "did not go to his lectures."[10] For Wittgenstein's part, he was known to speak of Woolf only briefly after her death, to Rush Rhees.[11] As Monk points out, Wittgenstein's comments to Rhees about Woolf's family background and its effect on her literary and critical ambitions could have been based on personal acquaintance, or equally well only on hearsay, gleaned from things said by their mutual friends (DG, 256). In any case, given the rather insubstantial connection between Woolf and Wittgenstein forged by any clear and direct mutual influence, we are left to trace the relationship between these two thinkers and writers as one rooted in the more promising second option that Caughie presents: shared sensibility.

In her groundbreaking book *The Phantom Table*, Banfield examines Virginia Woolf's preoccupation—and that of Bloomsbury more generally—with the epistemological questions raised in Cambridge philosophy during the first quarter of the twentieth century. The era that provides the context for her inquiry is one Banfield places "squarely within the period of Russell, which ends with Wittgenstein's ascendancy."

And yet, she continues, "this does not prevent the *Tractatus* from playing a role in our reconstruction of Bloomsbury's intellectual world," since "its conceptions, language and dominant metaphors find their counterparts in Woolf, not because she came under its influence, but because she shared its ways of thinking."[12]

Banfield astutely posits these shared ways of thinking (the result of fortuitous, perhaps *zeitgeistig* philosophical kinship rather than any direct mutual influence) and then lets them rest without pursuing them much further. Such concerns, after all, fall outside the purview of her work on Woolf's engagement with Russell, Moore, and Fry, and the philosophical background of Bloomsbury. But accounting for salient affinities between the author of the *Tractatus* and his high-modernist literary contemporaries, Woolf among them, figures centrally in my effort to reframe understandings of the significance of Wittgenstein's philosophy for studies in modernism more generally in this book.

Woolf writes in "The Leaning Tower" that "books descend from books as families descend from families."[13] Caughie points to the striking connection between Woolf's description of intertextual kinship in that essay and the analogy of family resemblance for language games that Wittgenstein outlines in the *Philosophical Investigations*.[14] At §66, Wittgenstein describes a "complicated network of similarities overlapping and criss-crossing" that he characterizes in §67 as "family resemblances." "In language and literature as in families," Caughie writes, "there is continuity without a common core of shared features." "What matters," she goes on to say, "is what our comparison enables us to do."[15]

In this chapter, my comparative endeavors to bring out the shared ways of thinking Banfield points to do not derive from biographical and historical connections between the two writers. Nor are they based on direct parallel readings of Wittgenstein's and Woolf's respective works. Nor indeed are they based on any full reading of the *Tractatus* in relation to Woolf's novels. Instead, my account of the impact of resolute interpretations of Wittgenstein on studies in modernism turns its focus in this chapter to the work of one of the program's primary proponents, Cora Diamond. Here I offer a reading of Woolf's *To the Lighthouse* together with Diamond's writing on literature and moral life (writing that is, as we have seen, deeply marked by her inheritance from Wittgenstein).[16] Diamond's attention to riddle and difficulty in her general body of work extends beyond her focus on Wittgenstein's peculiar use of difficulty in the *Tractatus*. For it also informs her moral thinking about how literature like Woolf's deals in unexpected and indirect ways with challenging ethical questions, asking readers to deal with them in turn.

The difficult work of striving to gain clarity about oneself (and of coming to understand others and what they say, even when what they say makes no sense to us) is, for Diamond, something that the *Tractatus*'s overall transformative challenge requires. And as we have seen, this kind of work involves a different order of difficulty than the more straightforward intellectual challenge Wittgenstein's logico-philosophical treatise poses on the surface.

I first attend here to Woolf's commitment (one I argue she coincidentally shares with Wittgenstein) to grappling with some of the signature issues of modernism: question, quest, and a longing for vision or a revised understanding of the world and of our place in it as a way of confronting and coping with the realities of human hope and suffering. I then probe Woolf's engagement with these issues by reading her novel *To the Lighthouse* in light of Diamond's essay "The Difficulty of Reality and the Difficulty of Philosophy."[17] Diamond's keen insights in that essay about literature's capacity for ethical instruction, and her discussion of the experience of an ordinary sublime so painful or astonishing that it resists our understanding and categories of thought, present for this study an experience of different-order difficulty we have yet to consider. The experience Diamond explores in her essay, and which (taking a phrase from John Updike) she calls the "difficulty of reality," thus adds to the typography of modernist complexity that I adumbrated in the introduction. Diamond's discussion of the sort of difficulty she points to illuminates a new philosophical context in which to understand more clearly and profoundly the stakes and aims of Woolf's novel, and the particular way Woolf addresses in it the difficulties of modern life.[18]

One important subsidiary effect of looking at Woolf and Diamond together here is that doing so also allows us to make significant connections between Woolf's thinking and Wittgenstein's, connections that continue to bring into focus the philosophical sympathies that attest to the mutual relevance of their idiosyncratic brands of modernism. Reading Woolf alongside Diamond also prompts us to recognize important ways in which the central issues of Woolf's novel intersect with the Wittgensteinian (and in the case of the "Difficulty of Reality" essay, also Cavellian) preoccupations that inform Diamond's own thinking.

These shared preoccupations include concerns about the role different orders of difficulty play in ethical instruction imparted in works whose quest for clarity is bound up with a purposive obscurity. With his *Tractatus*, Wittgenstein certainly gives us a book we can describe in these terms. Woolf's own engagement in obscurity is somewhat more attenuated. The difficulty of Wittgenstein's text is apparent first in its austere aphoristic form—the medium for the unorthodox mode of therapeutic ethical instruction it seeks to impart to the ready reader (in defiance of any prior expectations she may have harbored about just what she stood to learn about philosophy from the logical-philosophical treatise).[19] The *Tractatus*'s challenge ultimately lies in its call for the reader's commitment to the transformative work required to "see the world in the right way." What Woolf has to show us about how to see the world in her novel comes to us not with the mystifying bravado of Wittgenstein's enigmatic final pronouncements in the *Tractatus*. Nor is *To the Lighthouse* animated by the difference between readerly expectation and authorial aim that Wittgenstein sets up in his book. Yet the challenge of Woolf's novel is also bound up with experiments in narrative form (elegiac rather than aphoristic), crafted with the aim of redirecting her readers' attention to her sentences and thus enhancing their view of life.[20] Woolf's intersubjective mode of free indirect style allows her masterfully to enter imaginatively (as Diamond puts it) into the conflicting, overlapping thoughts of her cast of characters, a party that dances up and down in Lily Briscoe's imagination as a "company of gnats, each separate, but all marvellously controlled in an invisible elastic net," as it does under the guidance of Woolf's stream-of-consciousness narrative strategy (TL, 28). Woolf's free indirect style allows her to stand at a distance from the narrative while enabling her readers to observe her characters—participants in that narrative—by presenting us with fragments of their private musings, their communicative interactions, and a sense of the ambivalence with which they regard the conflict between the pain of separateness and the need for solitude. Woolf traces the pattern of her characters' shifting moments of intimacy and detachment, perceptiveness and prejudice, expansiveness and impenetrability that give shape to their thinking lives.[21]

The obscurity of Woolf's novel—its darkness as well as its difficulty—I argue here, is something that also arises from her attunement to the kind of "difficulty of reality" that Diamond describes. Speaking specifically of Cavell's orienting assumption that obscurities, paradoxes, mysteries, and ambiguities are internal to the philosophical insights we get from literature and film (i.e., rather than something that simply impedes our transparent understanding of those phenomena), Stephen Mulhall addresses the more general task faced by all readers and viewers who seek, beyond their initial bewilderment or failure of understanding, the potential new perspectives that such challenging texts can afford. We must not only strive to attain clarity about obscure works of art, but also find our way toward such clarity by working through their difficulty to reach an understanding that casts light on our predicament in the world. We come to see our forms of life more clearly by following the guidance such texts offer, paradoxically, by way of their own obscurity. The point is not to avoid the achievement of clarity, Mulhall writes, "but to recognize that such clarity that can be achieved must be clarity about just these obscurities, hence clarity that must be the result of working through those obscurities rather than banishing them, and so may result only in making it clearer to both author and reader that obscurity is internal to" the phenomena of literature, photography, and film.[22] Speaking about the effort of working hard to rise to the occasion of the transformative challenge embodied in Rilke's poetry, Richard Eldridge follows John Gibson's suggestion that we should turn to difficult works of literature in order to "read the story of our shared form of life."[23] "This is the suggestion we must pursue," he says, "if we are to have any hope of unpacking the jointly cognitive and emotional work of acknowledging and working through" that reading difficult literature demands of us.[24]

Wittgenstein, Woolf, and Diamond all engage difficulty as a part of their explorations of human striving for communion and communication in this shared form of life. Wittgenstein and Woolf both also share concerns regarding the problem of skepticism about what other people think and feel. Ongoing struggles with problems of the self and other minds, and with subjective and objective reality, are of course a central difficulty of Woolf's novel, in which "subject, object and the nature of reality" is a central motif.[25] Wittgenstein, Woolf, and Diamond each deal with what Cavell sees as the tragic recognition of our own separateness from others, and our attempts to achieve a semblance of communicative and existential unity with them by trying imaginatively to consider life from their different embodied perspectives with empathic acknowledgment. Each writer also considers the capacity of literature and fairy tale to convey a sense of beauty or of the "terrible" in the world. They also tap into a human longing for the sense of wholeness, transformative understanding, wonder, safety, and peace to stave off illusion or despair.

Russophilia

I began above by locating the primary source of the connections among Woolf, Diamond, and Wittgenstein in their shared focus on question and quest and the cognitive and existential difficulty out of which such probing searches arise. This is because as I see it, if, as Banfield asserts, Wittgenstein's dominant philosophical conceptions and metaphors find counterparts in Woolf, it is due in no small part to the fact that both authors labored under the influence of Tolstoy, Dostoevsky, and (at least in Woolf's case) Chekhov in their attempts to grapple with what Wittgenstein calls "the problem of life" (TLP, 6.521).[26] What Woolf points to as Tolstoy's central question—"Why Live?"—lies at the heart of the insoluble problems that her characters and voices tackle explicitly, time and again, from the first novels and stories to the last.[27]

Woolf famously extols these Russian writers in "Mr. Bennett and Mrs. Brown," "Modern fiction," "The Russian Point of View," and other essays for their attention to the human soul and spirit, in all its sadness, suffering, and curiosity.[28] What she finds compelling about them is that in their depictions of the human world and the way life is, they "accumulate; they accept ugliness; they seek to understand; they penetrate further and further into the human soul with their terrible power of sustained insight and their undeviating reverence for truth."[29] Russian literature, Woolf writes, assumes that "in a world bursting with misery the chief call upon us is to understand our fellow sufferers." This understanding is gained not through the intellect alone, but with the heart, Woolf qualifies, quoting a passage from a short story by the lesser-known writer Elena Militsina. The passage sums up for Woolf the ethos of Russian literature generally: "Learn to make yourselves akin to people. I would even like to add: make yourself indispensable to them. But let this sympathy be not with the mind—for it is easy with the mind—but with the heart, with love towards them" (RPV, 183). Compared to this generation of Russian writers, who present "human life in all its width and depth," and attend to "every shade of feeling and subtlety of thought," Woolf finds that English Victorian and Edwardian novels come up short. The Russophilia that gripped British artists and critics in the early twentieth century played a formative role in Woolf's elaboration of her own methods as a modern writer. In 1919, in the early phases of her work as a novelist and essayist, and at the peak of her fascination with Russian literature, Woolf asserts that "the most inconclusive remarks upon modern English fiction can hardly avoid some mention of the Russian influence, and if they are mentioned one runs the risk of feeling that to write of any fiction save theirs is a waste of time."[30]

The thing that most captivates Woolf about the work of these Russian writers, and which would ultimately have a transformative effect on her own novels, is their commitment to inconclusiveness. Chekhov, Woolf writes, is "aware that modern life is full of a nondescript melancholy, of discomfort, of queer relationships which beget emotions that are half ludicrous and yet painful, and that an inconclusive ending for all these impulses and oddities is much more usual than anything extreme.

He knows all this as we know it, and at first sight he seems no more
ready than we are with a solution."[31] In Chekhov, "nothing is solved"
(RPV, 185). In Tolstoy, she says, "nothing is finished; nothing is tidied
up; life merely goes on."[32]

As Diamond reminds us, Wittgenstein's admiration of Tolstoy, and
the ways he draws on Tolstoy's methods in his own philosophy, owes in
large part to Wittgenstein's appreciation of the way Tolstoy deals with
the difficulty of "the character of the world" indirectly in his works,
giving "a sense of the mysteriousness of life, and the way life goes" in
the absence of explicitly ethical statements or arguments about how
we ought to reflect on these things.[33] In support of her claim, Diamond
points to Wittgenstein's preference for Tolstoy's novella *Hadji Murad*
over his novel *Resurrection* as a way of emphasizing his partiality to
works that "turn their back on the reader," as well as to his contrasting antipathy to works that strive more heavy-handedly to tell readers
straightforwardly what they ought to think or feel.

Wittgenstein's deep appreciation for Tolstoy's writing casts light on
his conception of how an ethical spirit is (and is not) communicated
through art and literature. His admiration for Tolstoy can be attributed
in part to his view that in certain of his works, unlike in others, Tolstoy
succeeds in communicating things about the ethical spirit of the world
without resorting to any overt theoretical preaching or moralizing talk.
Wittgenstein is harshly critical, however, of the novels that represent
more accurately a disguised attempt on Tolstoy's part to set forth moral
doctrine in prose. The contrast Wittgenstein draws between the works
he respects and those he does not is clear in his very different responses
to *Hadji Murad* and *Resurrection*. Wittgenstein sent a copy of the first to
Norman Malcolm and, in an accompanying letter, prompts Malcolm
to read it. "I hope you get a lot out of it, because there is a lot *in* it," he
tells him.

> You see, when Tolstoy tells a story he impresses me infinitely
> more than when he addresses the reader. When he turns his back
> to the reader then he seems to me *most* impressive. . . . It seems
> to me his philosophy is most true when it's latent in the story.[34]

Tolstoy's way of clarifying moral life in his stories, Wittgenstein argues,
works best when he "turns his back to the reader" rather than trying to
turn his literary texts into platforms for the delivery of moral lessons.
When he speaks in his letter to Malcolm of there being a lot "in" Tolstoy's *Hadji Murad*, it might look as if what Wittgenstein means is that

there is some specific, sharply delineated moral lesson to be found in the novella that one can easily point to. What I take him to mean, rather, is that the tale as a whole—through the descriptions it offers, and how they strike and move us—has the capacity to show us new ways of looking at our familiar world. In Wittgenstein's view, Tolstoy's story elicits in its readers an attentive imaginative and affective response to life that he, too, upholds as philosophically instructive.[35] *Hadji Murad* is thus exemplary for Wittgenstein of literature's capacity to enlighten our understanding and expand our moral thinking in ways that modes of philosophical practice—which privilege moral theorizing, and give precedence to facts, principles, and straightforward rational argument above other expressions of the creative imagination—cannot. It is in just this way that one can speak of there being ethical teaching *in* the *Tractatus*, active in the overall aim of the book, in spite of Wittgenstein's claim that it contains no ethical propositions. On Wittgenstein's view, a philosophical work (like the *Tractatus*) can change our perspective in a way a work of art can do. And just as Wittgenstein thinks the ethical significance of *Hadji Murad* is upheld in the way Tolstoy manages to keep comparatively silent about ethics in it, he thinks the ethical significance of the *Tractatus* hangs on his keeping silent about ethics too. As Wittgenstein's friend Paul Engelmann writes of his own experience with poetry generally, and with Uhland's poem *Graf Eberhards Weißdorn* in particular, "poetry can produce a profound artistic effect *beyond* (but never without) the immediate effect of its language. . . . The poem as a whole gives in 28 lines the picture of a life."[36]

When Engelmann passed Uhland's poem on to him, Wittgenstein responded with a letter in which he made an observation similar to the one he made about Tolstoy's writing in his letter to Malcolm: that the ethical force of the poem lies not in anything the poet says in its verses but in what he shows in language with the poem overall. Like certain of Tolstoy's stories, then, Wittgenstein admires Uhland's poem because of the picture of the shape of a life he offers us in it. What Wittgenstein finds remarkable about the poem is that by adhering only to what is sayable, Uhland succeeds in capturing in his poem not just the series of the words and lines it is composed of, but an entire world. To Engelmann, Wittgenstein writes:

> The poem by Uhland is really magnificent. And this is how it is: if only you do not try to utter what is unutterable then *nothing* gets lost. But the unutterable will be—un unutterably—*contained* in what has been uttered![37]

Argument and Attention

Woolf's admiration for the nineteenth-century Russian novel also inspired in her an attitude of resistance to novels intent on advancing systematic philosophical positions by literary means. While in her own essays and memoirs, Woolf figures her ideas about the emergent modern literature of her time as amounting to a kind of "theory" ("Modern Fiction") or "philosophy" (*A Sketch of the Past*), she was nonetheless suspicious of novels seeking to present overt or unnuanced applications of philosophical ideas. "When philosophy is not consumed in a novel," she writes, "when we can underline this phrase with a pencil, and cut out that exhortation with a pair of scissors and paste the whole into a system, it is safe to say that there is something wrong with the philosophy or with the novel or with both."[38]

Diamond has long been concerned with bringing the aspirations of moral philosophy into relation with the moral imagination exercised in certain works of literature. Her essay "Anything but Argument?," originally published in 1982, represents one of her earliest interventions into the "ancient quarrel" between the philosophers and the poets. The essay unfolds from Diamond's criticism of an assertion Onora O'Neill makes in a review of Stephen Clark's book *The Moral Status of Animals*. Clark's book engages critically with a long tradition of philosophy that dismisses modes of thinking that attend to rationality to the exclusion of a responsiveness to what he calls "the heart's affections and the plain evidence of sense."[39] The statement of O'Neill's that Diamond takes as the point of departure for her own essay is that "if the appeal on behalf of animals is to convince those whose hearts do not already so incline them, it must . . . reach beyond assertion to argument."[40] Diamond counters that by placing argument at the crux of her conception of moral philosophy, O'Neill forecloses the possibility of accounting for the moral force of certain works of literature and its relevance to ethical thinking and teaching. In her criticism of O'Neill, Diamond demonstrates her affinity for Iris Murdoch's view that "the most essential and fundamental aspect of culture is the study of literature," since literary forms (the novel in particular) offer readers an "education in how to picture and understand human situations."[41] For Murdoch, good works of literature thus do a better job of fostering our imaginative capacity to inhabit the perspectives of others than any analytical treatise can. And as Diamond points out, O'Neill's position cannot account for the transformative capacity of the imaginative exercise of literature to change readers' prevailing inclinations, redirect their attention, and alter their affections.

In "The Difficulty of Reality and the Difficulty of Philosophy," as we shall see, Diamond is as deeply critical as Wittgenstein and Woolf are of the authorial move of "presenting arguments within the frame of fiction," and of the interpretive move of reducing literary prose to *therefore* arguments or "pulling out ideas and arguments as if they had been simply clothed in fictional form as a way of putting them before us" (DR, 48, 53).[42] In her "Difficulty" essay, Diamond criticizes what she takes to be the impoverished approach of philosophical thinking about literature adopted by the philosophers and critics who served as respondents to J. M. Coetzee's 1997–98 Tanner Lectures on Human Values. As she sees it, the responders' accounts of the moral power of those lectures (later published along with Amy Gutmann's introduction and responses by Marjorie Garber, Peter Singer, Wendy Doniger, and Barbara Smuts as *The Lives of Animals*) are collectively misguided. They tend all too often to train their critical focus on the structure of the (often failed) philosophical arguments about human treatment of nonhuman animals, which they take Coetzee himself to be concerned to advance indirectly through the voice of his fictional character, Elizabeth Costello. But, as Diamond writes, "for none of the commentators does the title of the story have any significance in how we might understand the story in relation to our lives, the lives of the animals we are" (DR, 48). The commentators overlook the fictive status of the woman novelist at the center of the novel—a self-described "wounded animal" trying to "save her soul." They also fail to attend to the nuance of what she says about Kafka and literary realism, and what they have to teach us about the "complexity of life," or how humanistic explorations of love, good, and evil can satisfy our human longing for a "guidance in perplexity" that responds to a craving that Costello tells her sister, Blanche, is in the end a "quest for salvation."[43]

I will return to Coetzee's own investment in teaching through obscurity, and quests for guidance in perplexity and salvation, with regard to Wittgenstein and his commentators, in the context of a more in-depth discussion of Coetzee's *The Childhood of Jesus* in chapter 5. For the moment, however, I want to direct Diamond's thinking back to Wittgenstein, Woolf, and their Russians.

In her introduction to "Having a Rough Story about What Moral Philosophy Is," Diamond returns to the issue of argument in moral philosophy in a discussion that is relevant to the question of how Woolf's writing, and *To the Lighthouse* in particular, works to "enlarge the moral imagination" in the way Diamond thinks good literature can, by reorienting our attention toward aspects of life that we must look on not only with the mind but, as both Clark and Militsina say, "with the heart." "Wittgenstein's own 'habit of reading,'" Diamond writes, "has little to do with seeking out strains of philosophical arguments to be found in literary texts. Instead, his practice entails "a reading for absences." So too, Diamond suggests, "he writes absences."[44] Though I will not be directly concerned here with Woolf's "Great Russians," I am concerned with looking more closely at her own particular investment in writing absences, in keeping alive in her novelistic works the "inconclusiveness of the Russian mind" and what she describes as "the sense that there is no answer, that if honestly examined, life presents question after question which must be left to sound on and on after the story is over in hopeless interrogation that fills us with a deep, and finally it may be with a resentful, despair" (MF, 163).

Religious Points of View and the Work of Secular Transformation

As I have argued so far in this book, Diamond's approach to Wittgenstein allows us to see the *Tractatus* as a modernist puzzle text, one whose author uses a challenging parabolic mode of instruction in order to prompt his readers to take up the ethical and philosophical work that will (ultimately, ideally) lead them to make a change in worldview that will enable them to handle the most difficult problems of life. The book's exegetical challenge plays a central role in Wittgenstein's ethical project of engaging readers in the therapeutic activity of clarification he saw as philosophy's true task.

Building on Diamond's approach to Wittgenstein within studies of Woolf allows us to attend to the mutually enlightening ways in which the work of both writers is enlivened by an investment in the modes of the difficulty that has itself become such a definitive trait of modernism. Also visible in their works is the more spectral and less explored aspect of modernism I have argued is equally definitive: an attraction to varieties of spiritual and transcendent experience, manifested in an obsession with the transfigurative power of philosophical and existential conundrums. The difficulty both Wittgenstein and Woolf deal with in their respective works is expressive of a yearning for solutions to problems related to the vast irresolvable questions of life's meaning that Wittgenstein explores in the *Tractatus* (6.4312–6.521) and which, for Lily Briscoe in Woolf's *To the Lighthouse*, "traverse the sky of the soul perpetually." For Lily, the question "What is the meaning of life?" is a simple one, "one that tended to close in on one with years," but which remains unanswered. "The great revelation had never come. The great revelation perhaps never did come. Instead there were little daily miracles, illuminations, matches struck unexpectedly in the dark" (TL, 164–65).

Woolf's and Wittgenstein's different deployments of difficulty bear on the ethical weight of their shared engagement with the existential questions and crises presented by ordinary language and life. The human longing for answers to these questions or for satisfactory solutions to these problems that Woolf and Wittgenstein both tap into in their different works is further complicated by their common tendency to "see every problem from a religious point of view," as Wittgenstein once put it, in spite of their committed agnosticism or atheism.[45]

In his *Religious Experience and the Modernist Novel*, Pericles Lewis asserts that in spite of her animus toward that "old savage," God, Woolf, the daughter of committed agnostics, was nevertheless receptive to mystical experience and sought to embrace in her writing a generalized spirituality, independent of the authority of a Judeo-Christian God and able to accommodate the pluralism of modern life.[46] If Woolf rejected the dogmatic and intolerant aspects of religion, she nonetheless understood the uses of enchantment and sought though her literary experiments to effect a reenchantment of the modern world via its Weberian disenchantment. Woolf's novels frequently envision a classical, pagan alternative to Judeo-Christian monotheism. Her engagement in a search for new models of sacred community is especially evident in her distinctive formal method of gathering together multiple intertwining streams of consciousness that allow her to explore varied intimate experiences and "the multiple spiritual perspectives that contend in a disenchanted world where unitary models of truth have dissolved."[47] Woolf's exploration of alternative forms of spirituality is also evident in her efforts to describe the raptures, ecstasies, and "moments of being"—her term for a modern sublime experience that features so prominently in many of her works, and especially in *To the Lighthouse*.[48]

One important thing that Woolf inherited from the agnosticism of her parents, paired with an ancestral Protestant tradition of combined Clapham Sect evangelism, Calvinism, and Quakerism, was a sense of work as moral duty. Lewis points to Woolf's own intense productivity and the reading and writing schedule she maintained throughout her life. Woolf's commitment to her work has a fictional counterpart in *To the Lighthouse*, where Mr. Ramsay, Charles Tansley, and Lily Briscoe all look to their artistic and intellectual labor as the source of meaning that Mrs. Ramsay seeks in her work toward social reform.[49]

Woolf's moral commitment to work is something I want to relate here to the kind of arduous labor that the modernist texts at issue in this book demand of their readers. As we have seen, Wittgenstein thought of work in philosophy as a kind of "work on oneself. On one's own conception. On the way one sees things (And what one demands of them)." At the heading of that remark, he says this: "DIFFICULTY OF PHILOSO-PHY NOT THE INTELLECTUAL DIFFICULTY OF THE SCIENCES, BUT THE DIFFICULTY OF A CHANGE OF ATTITUDE, RESISTANCES OF THE WILL MUST BE OVERCOME."[50] Wittgenstein's philosophy and the texts of literary modernism I explore here demand of their readers an engagement in a philosophical and interpretive activity that requires a deep commitment to a kind of work he takes to be ethical in spirit. The kind of work such texts demand, as Wittgenstein sees it, surpasses the exertions of rational intelligence required to resolve hard scientific problems. Readers of differently difficult texts like Wittgenstein's and Woolf's are asked to overcome their "resistances," adopt new ethical attitudes toward the world. And as Woolf remarks, changing "an 'attitude' is not simple; it is highly complex" (RPV, 183).

Taking up the difficult work of overcoming resistances and shifting worldviews in a way that makes us at home in our lives and language is somewhat analogous to the task Woolf says English readers must do if they are to understand the writing of Tolstoy, Dostoevsky, and Chekhov. For the fact that in the works of these writers, she says, "nobody thinks of explaining" things creates a sense of "bewilderment" in unaccustomed British readers (RPV, 186, 183). Finding themselves without a "code of manners which writers and readers accept as a prelude to the more exciting intercourse of friendship," English readers find that they "do not know which to use, a fork or their fingers" (CF, 434). Work to understand these "alien, difficult" texts, to overcome a sense of their foreignness, and gain an "intimacy" marked by the "give and take of familiar intercourse" depends on their trying hard not to "impute, distort, to read into them an emphasis which is false" (RPV, 187, 182). Readers of texts they find unfamiliar or in some way obscure must likewise set themselves to the task of grappling with the thought-provoking and sometimes puzzling new forms of writing such works present to them. This initial task is bound up with the work of engaging with the difficult existential and spiritual questions at issue within them. That steady kind of work, further, is to be conducted by readers who are already sufficiently insightful and committed to allow the text to work on them in such a way that they would bother trying to make the shift in attention required for them to begin to see things differently at the text's formal and affective nudging. Reading difficult texts that bewilder us with their unorthodox style means trying to rise to their challenges by being more attentive to how and what they can teach us through their difficulty. By "teach" here, I do not mean that difficult texts instruct us because they have something in particular to *tell* us, for it is not that there is a single describable lesson we are to extract from them. I mean, rather, that they are designed to train us by cultivating our mental and affective capacities through the practice of reading them and struggling with their difficulty. The work ethic that difficult texts demand of their readers, then, entails an openness to complexity and a willed striving for a change in outlook, mode of expression, and way of living. A tall order indeed. And, as Richard Eldridge writes, "no recipe for how one is to change one's life so as to achieve expressive power is on offer." The better ways of seeing and leading our lives that these literary and philosophical works urge us to strive for, even seek to convert us to, is a something "we know not what."[51]

Existential Questions and the Quest for "It"

In their different ways, Woolf and Wittgenstein both deal with life as something fraught with inconclusive or illusory searches for meaning, fueled by the desire to contemplate the world *sub specie aeternitatis* (TLP, 6.45), and the drive to "see the world in the right way" (TLP, 6.54), in Wittgenstein's terms, and to grasp the vague and elusive "it" that is the deictic object of so much contemplation and search in Woolf. Woolf leaves the "it" she refers to so often in her writing essentially, even necessarily, vague and mysterious, as tantalizing as any unsolved riddle.

On February 27, 1926, for example—around the time she was composing the scene of Mrs. Ramsay's solitary meditation in the section "The Window" of *To the Lighthouse*—Woolf offers in a diary entry her own first-person expression of her attraction to the fundamental questions about the human predicament, to quests for the peace of discovery and resolution, and her interest in examining a longing for what Wittgenstein calls the "mystical feeling . . . of the world as a limited whole" (TLP, 6.45):

> I have some restless searcher in me. Why is there not a discovery in life? Something one can lay hands on and say "This is it"? My depression is a harassed feeling. I'm looking; but that's not it— that's not it. What is it? And shall I die before I find it? . . . Then (as I was walking through Russell Square last night) I see the mountains in the sky: the great clouds and the moon which is

risen over Persia; I have a great and astonishing sense of something there, which is "it." It is not exactly beauty that I mean. It
is that the thing is in itself enough: satisfactory; achieved. A sense
of my own strangeness, walking on the earth is there too: of the
infinite oddity of the human position; trotting along Russell
Square with the moon up there and those mountain clouds. Who
am I, what am I, and so on: these questions are always floating
about in me: and then I bump against some exact fact—a letter,
a person, and come to them again with a great sense of freshness.
And so it goes on. But on this showing, which is true, I think,
I do fairly frequently come upon this "it"; and then feel quite
at rest.[52]

The restlessness of the ongoing search for a "discovery" that Woolf
describes at the beginning of this fragment is one we might compare to
the years-long work of composition and revision that lays the ground-
work for the vision that marks Lily Briscoe's decisive completion of her
painting at the end of *To the Lighthouse*. In her diary entry, Woolf describes her own pursuit of the vague and elusive "it" as something motivated by an undefined sense of astonishment and awe related to what
Wittgenstein speaks of in his 1929 "Lecture on Ethics" and in interviews with Friedrich Waismann of the Vienna Circle as the wonder one
might feel that anything (the world, language itself) exists.[53] It is "not
exactly beauty" that Woolf means when she tries to sum up the experience of chasing a sublime "it," but a kind of enough-ness. This sense of
fulfillment at least temporarily achieved is combined in Woolf's experience with an uncanny sense of her own strangeness and the strangeness
of the human condition generally. As I will show later in this chapter,
the experience Woolf depicts in her diary entry is something akin to the
encounter with beauty, goodness, or mystery that Diamond includes in
the range of phenomena she cites as cases of the difficulty of reality. In
Woolf, the experience gives rise to the same kind of existential questions
and quest for meaning that are Lily Briscoe's obsession in the novel:
Who am I? What am I?

As I have said, much of the combined secular spirituality and commitment to existential questioning in Woolf's writing comes by way of
her interest in nineteenth-century Russian novelists and short story writers, most notably Tolstoy, Dostoevsky, and Chekhov. Her attraction
to the work of those authors, I argue, is the source of the brand of existentialism that characterizes her writing. Critics have long recognized
Woolf's fascination with existential questioning, and the connections

between her writing and the theme of existential crisis that first makes its appearance in English letters around the time of Pater, gaining urgency in modernist art and literature at a time when "the possibility of the utter contingency of everything . . . became a major preoccupation of imaginative writing."[54] But only a few critics, most notably Lucio Ruotolo and Douglas Mao, have devoted any sustained attention to the connection between Woolf and existential thought (*Solid Objects*, 44).[55]

Ruotolo argues that Woolf's evolving ethics encompass "both existentialist and anarchic presumptions."[56] He calls on Heidegger's existential analysis of *Dasein* to illuminate Clarissa Dalloway's complex interaction with being and nothingness.[57] Mao explores "the striking similarity between the questions asked by Anglo-American writers in the early twentieth century and those posed, roughly contemporaneously, by Continental philosophers of existence" and suggests that Woolf's modes of existential inquiry exercised a "small but significant" influence on the work of Jean-Paul Sartre (*Solid Objects*, 17, 20). Where Sartre's approach is "a shade technological," however, "Woolf's is a shade theological."

Sartre and Woolf are linked first in the way they both raise the questions of why anything at all should exist. Existential questions like these are of course intimately related to the exemplary (non)question that, as we saw in chapter 2, Diamond poses in her examination of Wittgenstein's notion of the nonsensicality of the utterances we come out with in our attempts to express the existential experience he sees as ethical—"Why is there anything?" Second, Sartre and Woolf are linked by their shared struggle with the problem of every subjectivity's isolation from all others. Third, they are connected by the naked clarity with which they both render these anxieties in their fictions (*Solid Objects*, 44). Given Woolf's relationship on the one hand to Cambridge philosophy via the thought of other members of her Bloomsbury circle (the existential cast of which can be attributed in part to G. E. Moore's emphasis on the brute facticity of existence), and to Sartre on the other, Mao suggests that "it would be fair to say that . . . Woolf's writing constitutes one of the direct links between Anglo-American philosophy of the early part of the century (after William James and before the ascent of ordinary language analysis), and Continental philosophies of existence, between the deployment of solid objects against idealism and the Heideggerian-Sartrean campaign to restore to philosophy the primacy of Being" (*Solid Objects*, 53).

For Mao, Woolf's very Bloomsbury answer to the existential questions that resound in her novels—Lily's "what is the meaning of life?,"

Rachel's "What does one do? Why is one sitting here, after all?" in *The Voyage Out*—goes something like this: What one does, what one must do, is make art:[58]

> The coincidence of the closing of the novel with Lily's completed work suggests that in painting Lily addresses not only Mrs. Ramsay's haunting, but also a more general crisis of meaning: both are resolved, if only temporarily, by the fashioning of art, that intervention in the material that sustains the miracle and ecstasy of the human dead and the object world, and yet also brings them into ordinary experience, relieving the one of its capacity to torment and the other of its power to frighten. In making, one finds both purpose and peace, and in Lily's painting the existential question and the imperative of production meet . . . though in this case Woolf seems more concerned with the process and difficulty of making them than with the destiny of the made. (*Solid Objects*, 63)

Woolf's investment in the existential question and the unresolved—or unresolvable—quest is evident even in the most rigorously analytical searches conducted in her novels (think, for example, of Mr. Ramsay's pursuit of privacy and quest for successful logical-philosophical and professional progression from A to Z, or—failing Z, to R [TL, 37–38]). Most notable in *To the Lighthouse* is Lily Briscoe's quest for meaning and for fulfilling (and, in the face of claims that "women can't paint, women can't write" also vindicating) creative vision and the longing for access to the mysterious private buzzing "hive," the sealed mind of the other, that she shares with the rest of the novel's main characters vis-à-vis each other (TL, 51, 55). Also guiding the novel's treatment of the human struggle with the "perplexity of life" is Mrs. Ramsay's "effort of merging and flowing and creating," and longing to suspend the moment and to achieve peace, hope, and unity in a "summoning together" on a "platform of stability" on which "there was no future to worry about" (TL, 95). The searches that wend their way through the novel are each fueled by an inchoate underlying desire to get at the hazy object Woolf calls "it" in her diary entry. In *Orlando*, Woolf figures the search for "it" as an attempt at "netting the wild goose," the "fin in a waste of waters"; and as an effort to make some kind of leap of faith or transformative shift able to bring about an enhanced clarity of outlook and relief from pain, loss, and isolation (O, 10–11). This (sometimes active, sometimes latent) yearning for "it" persists in Woolf's writing even in the presence of a more despairing intellectual recognition that no such transformative solutions to what Wittgenstein describes in the *Tractatus* as the "riddle of life" are surely, entirely, permanently achievable (TLP, 6.4312, 6.5).

Just as Woolf's own avowed lack of religious belief does not preclude her tendency to see problems from the "religious point of view" shown in the way she represents yearning for a certain ethico-spiritual engagement with the world, her doubt that the answers to life's most nagging existential questions are attainable likewise does not prevent her from giving in to the temptation to pose these questions in a variety of possible formulations over and over again in her writing. The doubtful sense *Jacob's Room*'s narrator voices in the pronouncement that "the problem is insoluble," a sentiment Woolf echoes in both *To the Lighthouse* and *The Waves*, exposes the tension between hopeful longing and sense of futility and despair that characterizes the kind of questioning her works explore.[59]

This tension is also evident in Woolf's interludes about the sleepwalkers and visionaries in the apocalyptic "Time Passes" section of *To the Lighthouse*, in which she compresses time and dissolves the human ego into the sleep and dream of an historicized postlapsarian night of the chaos of the Great War. In that interchapter, Woolf simultaneously evokes, in a Wittgensteinian vein, the romantic transcendental visions of wholeness and mystical labor and deflates them as mere illusion:

> It seemed now as if, touched by human penitence and all its toil, divine goodness had parted the curtain and displayed behind it, single, distinct, the hare erect; the wave falling; the boat rocking, which, did we deserve them, should be ours always. But alas, divine goodness, twitching the cord, draws the curtain; it does not please him; he covers his treasures in a drench of hail, and so breaks them, so confuses them that it seems impossible that their calm should ever return or that we should ever compose from their fragments a perfect whole or read in the littered pieces the clear words of truth. For our penitence deserves a glimpse only; our toil respite only. (TL, 131–32)

At privileged epiphanic moments, the curtain of appearances is parted to reveal to humankind a fleeting sense of yearned-for peace, resolution, harmony, and completeness (as recompense for our penitent toil). But divine providence imparts only brief, intermittent flashes of the mystical wholeness sought. The existential and metaphysical questions posed by the figure of the visionary seekers of "Time Passes" remain indeterminate and unanswered. The many fragmented questions that accumulate in Woolf's oeuvre—here from *The Years*, for example: "Why— why—why?"; "Where did thought begin?"; "Am I that, or am I this?"; "Are we one, or are we separate?"—are presented "as if a puzzle were solved, and then broken."[60] Questions "as to what and why and wherefore," "where to begin?," "where are we going?," "how do you explain it all?," and "What does it mean then, what can it all mean?" proliferate throughout *To the Lighthouse* (TL, 132, 161, 169, 182, 149).

The elusiveness of the answers sought in the reiterated questions of "Time Passes" is something Woolf goes on to detail with wry humor in *Orlando*:

> Having asked then of man and of bird and the insects, for fish, men tell us, who have lived in green caves, solitary for years to hear them speak, never, never say, and so perhaps know what life is having asked them all and grown no wiser, but only older and colder (for did we not pray once in a way to wrap up in a book something so hard, so rare, one could swear it was life's meaning?) back we must go and say straight out to the reader who waits a tiptoe to hear what life is—Alas, we don't know. (O, 271)

And as *Orlando* draws to a close, having reached "the present moment," the wild goose still flies overhead, still sought, still unreachable. Woolf's narrative thus works to keep its central enigmas intact. To questions such as "of what nature is death, and what nature life?" the narrative offers us answers like this: "Having waited well over half an hour for an answer to these questions, and none coming, let us get on with the story" (O, 68).

It Should Not Exist, Yet Undoubtedly, It Is

According to Diamond's reading of the *Tractatus*, as I have described it, the book aims to lead readers out of philosophical and personal confusion and complacency and through a transformative process that would culminate (at least ideally) in an enlightened understanding and clearer vision of the world, life, philosophy, and language. As I will emphasize shortly with reference to Diamond's "The Difficulty of Reality and the Difficulty of Philosophy," however, certain ideas that stem from Wittgenstein's (and Cavell's) thinking also point us toward instances in our experience of reality—the everyday reality that the *Tractatus* would have us see more clearly—when reality is such that it becomes somehow strangely resistant to our comprehension. And that this experience of nonclarity, indeed of unintelligibility, is (if paradoxically) a significant part of the everyday we struggle, as per Wittgenstein's instruction, to see clearly.

As I will show, Woolf's *To the Lighthouse* explores ways in which individual experience of an overwhelming difficulty of reality heightens people's sense of isolation from each other. But her novel also gestures at ways in which the common experience of such unresolvable difficulty can foster a recognition of other people (and their otherness itself), as well as a responsiveness to them that can draw people together in an attitude of mutual acknowledgment.

Woolf's (and Wittgenstein's) attraction to riddle, enigma, and unanswered questions flourished under the influence of the work of writers like Tolstoy and Dostoevsky that took hold during the years of the Great War, modernism's cataclysmic epochal event. We will recall that in her *Wittgenstein's Ladder*, Marjorie Perloff reads the *Tractatus* as an avantgarde text, and as a "war book," the product of the specific, historical circumstances into which it emerged.[61] Indeed, the book was finished while Wittgenstein was fighting on the Eastern Front and as a prisoner of war in Casino, Italy. During that time, Wittgenstein turned for solace to Tolstoy's *Confession* and *Gospel in Brief* and was an avid reader of Dostoyevsky's *Brothers Karamazov*. His habit of carrying *The Gospel in Brief* with him at all times earned him the moniker "the man with the Gospels" among his fellow soldiers. The kind of personal transformation Wittgenstein strove to attain during the war (for a time in daily confrontation with death) and long after its end (indeed, throughout his life) also surfaces as a strong theme in his philosophy. Ray Monk suggests that if Wittgenstein had spent the entire war behind the lines, the *Tractatus* would likely have remained what it was at its first inception of 1915: a treatise on the nature of logic (DG, 137). Remarks that show the ways of thinking Wittgenstein shares with Woolf, remarks having to do with grappling with the meaning of life—and with transcendence, epiphanic insight, "the mystical," the will, about fate, riddles and searches for solutions—first begin to appear in Wittgenstein's notebooks (many of which are to be found in the final version of the *Tractatus*) only after he arrived at the front in 1916, taking Tolstoy and Dostoevsky along with him.

The First World War and its aftermath is also, of course, a central theme in Woolf's three major novels of the 1920s: *Jacob's Room*, *Mrs. Dalloway*, and *To the Lighthouse*. The devastating losses wrought by war and the everyday ravages of time's passing haunt *To the Light-house* as a whole (Andrew, the oldest son of the Ramsay's eight children, whose promise Mrs. Ramsay so anxiously strives to safeguard, is, we are told, "killed by the splinter of a shell instantly" (TL, 159).[62] This news is delivered in the well-known brackets Woolf uses to report all the devastation that befalls the family during the ten intervening years as time passes between the novel's first part, "The Window," and its last, "The Lighthouse." In another bracketed report, the Ramsay's oldest daughter, Prue, dies in childbirth. But in spite of Mrs. Ramsay's repeated exhortations to her "old antagonist, life" to "stand still here" in an impossible suspension of coherence and still-life plenitude, each of the children whose innocence and promise Mrs. Ramsay so longs to protect must in the end (whether literally or figuratively) "grow up and lose it all" (TL, 63, 62). Mrs. Ramsay's almost uncanny preoccupation with this eventuality exceeds a simpler sense of a mother's worry or anticipatory nostalgia, something that any form of consolation or "realistic" rational perspective could stave off. Hers is a prescient apprehension of the truth of life as offering no such longed-for safety, no salvation, as something "terrible, hostile, and quick to pounce on you if you gave it a chance" (TL, 63). As Mrs. Ramsay perceives it,

> the monotonous fall of the waves on the beach, which for the most part beat a measured and soothing tattoo to her thoughts and seemed to repeat . . . I am guarding you—I am your support . . . at other times suddenly and unexpectedly . . . had no such kindly meaning, but like a ghostly roll of drums remorselessly beat the measure of life, made one think of the destruction of the island and its engulfment in the sea, and warned her . . . that it was all as ephemeral as a rainbow—this sound which had been obscured and concealed under the other sounds suddenly thundered hollow in her ears and made her look up with an impulse of terror. (TL, 19–20)

In *To the Lighthouse*, Mrs. Ramsay is characterized by a yearning for a joint experience of wonder and security in the face of anxieties about the hazards of the world and the remorseless beat of the measure of life. Her longing is worth considering here against the backdrop of the two representative examples of the experience of "absolute value" that, as we saw in chapter 2, Wittgenstein offers in his "Lecture on Ethics": the feeling of "*wonder at the existence of the world*," and "experience of feeling absolutely safe." Both sentences are nonsense, representative of the sincere and deliberate "characteristic misuse of our language [that] runs through *all* ethical and religious expressions."[63]

A craving for such wonder simmers beneath the surface of *To the Lighthouse,* a novel that begins with the announcement of the "extraordinary joy" that Mrs. Ramsay's opening phrase of qualified promise ("Yes, of course, if it's fine tomorrow) convey to her six-year-old son, James. Her words endow "with heavenly bliss" even the most run-of-the-mill stuff of life, seen in the pictures of the everyday objects he cuts from the illustrated catalogue of the Army and Navy stores in the novel's first pages. At Mrs. Ramsay's words, a refrigerator becomes something "fringed with joy." A long-dreamed-of expedition seems to James finally within reach (TL, 7–8). Mrs. Ramsay, too, expresses her wonder at the world by leaning to inanimate things, feeling that at times "they expressed one . . . became one . . . knew one, in a sense were one" (TL, 66).

Mrs. Ramsay also marvels at her children and their creations: James's sensitivity, Prue's beauty, Andrew's gift for mathematics, Nancy's and Roger's wildness, Rose's "wonderful gift with her hands" and fruit-bowl creation ("How odd that one's child should do that!"). A ten-penny tea set made Cam happy for days (TL, 61–62). In the sense in which Wittgenstein describes it in the "Lecture on Ethics," this kind of wonderment has sense. One can, after all, imagine one's children might have turned out otherwise, can imagine that the things and happenings in one's life in the world might be different than they are. "But it is nonsense to say that I wonder at the existence of the world, because I cannot imagine it not existing" (LE, 41–42). Logically speaking, these rules of sense would certainly hold even with Woolf's fictive Mrs. Ramsay. But though she cannot, strictly speaking, imagine the world's not existing, in the moments in which her "pessimism" and uncanny sense of doom intrudes on her thinking about the future, she comes as close as one can.

In her "Difficulty" essay, Diamond points to Miłosz's poem "One More Day," and what he writes there about his amazement in the face of a beauty that, as he says, "should not exist." "There is not only no reason for it," he continues, "but an argument against. Yet undoubtedly it is."[64] Mrs. Ramsay's wonder at her children, and at the world they inhabit and which she longs to hold in suspension, is likewise haunted by a sensitivity to the paradox at the back of Miłosz's sense of awe in his poem. Her recognition of the fragility and impossibility of the beauty that "should not exist," but which currently stands before her, is definitive of the maternal character Woolf places at the center of her novel. Indeed, Mrs. Ramsay, placing her shawl over the pig's skull in the nursery, thus striking a compromise that resolves at once the conflicting desires of her two youngest children and lulls them to sleep, becomes the very figure of "security and warmth, in night fears when we are small, in dread of the beast's fangs and in the terror of dark rooms" that Miłosz evokes in that poem. Equally definitive is Mrs. Ramsay's preoccupation with the impossibility of all the unfathomable beauty in her midst. This is the sublime awareness that astounds Miłosz in his poem, and which gives rise in Woolf's novel to Mrs. Ramsay's desire to perform the equally impossible feat of holding the ongoing existence of all this beauty at a still point in time.

The second main example of the experience of absolute value Wittgenstein offers in the "Lecture on Ethics" is a sense he says one might call "feeling *absolutely* safe." He describes this feeling as "the state of mind in which one is inclined to say, 'I am safe, nothing can injure me whatever happens" (LE, 42). "We all know what it is in ordinary life to be safe," he continues: "I am safe in my room, when I cannot be run over by an omnibus. I am safe if I have had whooping cough and cannot therefore get it again. To be safe essentially means it is physically impossible that certain things should happen to me and therefore it's nonsense to say that I am safe *whatever happens*" (LE, 42). To articulate a craving for absolute safety, however, we must stretch language beyond the word's ordinary uses in a way that allows us to express an existential experience of desire for salvation that is unmoored from the narrowly circumscribed relative safety that refers to some particular danger or other that has been avoided.

Longing and "That Lie"

Wittgenstein's notion of absolute safety in the "Lecture on Ethics" is especially relevant to the way Woolf represents the longing, threaded with irony and a sense of skeptical unease, for divine safety and the solace of religious belief that Mrs. Ramsay expresses during a rare moment of solitary contemplation in the section of *To the Lighthouse* "The Window," after her children have gone to bed. I quote the passage at length:

> For now she need not think about anybody. She could be herself, by herself . . . to think; well not even to think. To be silent; to be alone. All the being and the doing, expansive, glittering, vocal, evaporated; and one shrunk, with a sense of solemnity, to being oneself, a wedge-shaped core of darkness, something invisible to others. . . . It was thus that she felt herself; and this self having shed its attachments was free for the strangest adventures.

When life sank down for a moment, the range of experience seemed limitless. . . . Beneath it is all dark, it is all spreading, it is unfathomably deep; but now and again we rise to the surface and that is what you see us by. Her horizon seemed to her limitless. . . . This core of darkness could go anywhere, for no one saw it. They could not stop it, she thought, exulting. There was freedom, there was peace, there was, most welcome of all, a summoning together, a resting on a platform of stability. Not as oneself did one find rest ever, in her experience . . . but as a wedge of darkness. Losing personality, one lost the fret, the hurry, the stir; and there rose to her lips always some exclamation of triumph over life when things come together in this peace, this rest, this eternity; and pausing there she looked out to meet that stroke of the Lighthouse, the long steady stroke, the last of the three, which was her stroke. . . . Often she found herself sitting and looking, sitting and looking with her work in her hands until she became the thing she looked at—that light, for example. And it would lift up on it some little phrase or other which had been lying in her mind like that—"Children don't forget, children don't forget"—which she would repeat and begin adding to it, It will end, it will end, she said. It will come, it will come, when suddenly she added, We are in the hands of the Lord.

But instantly she was annoyed with herself for saying that. Who had said it? Not she; she had been trapped into saying something she did not mean. She . . . met the third stroke and it seemed to her like her own eyes meeting her own eyes, searching as she alone could search into her mind and her heart, purifying out of existence that lie, any lie. She praised herself in praising the light, without vanity, for she was stern, she was searching, she was beautiful like that light. . . .

What had brought her to say that; "We are in the hands of the Lord?" she wondered. The insincerity slipping in among the truths roused her, annoyed her. (TL, 65–56)

Here, Woolf offers a picture of a solemn moment of impersonality, undifferentiated self, and mystical fusing with the world and the eternal passage of time. Mrs. Ramsay's apophatic meditation is marked by her identification with an object—the lighthouse, and the cyclical temporal movement of its searching beams alternating with wedges of a darkness that spread into limitless invisibility and unfathomable depths. Released from the pressure of activity, Mrs. Ramsay experiences a fleeting sense of peace and transcendental stability. Yet, her "exclamations of triumph over life" emerge in an incantatory series of repeated phrases ("Children don't forget, children don't forget. . . . It will end, it will end. . . . It will come, it will come") that seem as much about an awareness of life's poignancy and the proximity of death as about peace, plenitude, and possibility. Mrs. Ramsay's repeated mantras finally culminate in an automatic utterance that surprises and dismays her: "We are in the hands of the Lord" (TL, 66).

This phrase is one she disavows instantly, expressing annoyance at having let slip "that lie": "Who had said it? Not she; she had been trapped into saying something she did not mean" (TL, 66). She retracts the statement just as quickly, dismissing it as a bit of what she habitually calls (in her motherly English usage rather than in Wittgenstein's logical sense) "nonsense," or at the very least an "insincerity slipping in among the truths" (TL, 67). Her gesture of denial conveys an anxiety Woolf shares about the temptation to translate momentary experiences of mystical, existential engagement with life and death or a longing for peace and safety into the language of religious belief. Woolf underscores both the tendency toward such slippage and the anxiety and lack of true conviction that accompanies it by having Mrs. Ramsay say what she says only then to deny it at once. Significantly, Woolf does not bracket the phrase by embedding it in a narrative frame suggestive of the self-conscious distance of inverted commas or an "as it were" (she does not, that is, write something like "And though she had long ago given up on a belief in God, at once Mrs. Ramsay felt she could imaginatively understand the desire of the faithful to say something like 'We are in the hands of the Lord' to describe her experience").

Mrs. Ramsay's startling religious ejaculation knocks her out of her mystical reverie and back into grounded, rational query. "How could any Lord have made this world?" she asks, when "there is no reason, order, justice: but suffering, death and the poor. There was no treachery too base for this world to commit; she knew that. No happiness lasted; she knew that" (TL, 67). What Mrs. Ramsay knows about the way the world works informs her decisive commitment to *not* meaning "We are in the hands of the Lord." Whatever the significance of her mystical experience, whatever truths she is communing with at the moment of rupture that utterance represents are not things that can be summed up in an easy theistic statement about divine providence. Such a phrase cannot be the bearer of meaning if uttered outside of the language game of religious belief, a language game Mrs. Ramsay does not play. She reverts to the use of religious language in absence of other vocabulary with which to describe her quite secular existential longing to do the impossible: to hold life still, to keep the world intact just as it is. And yet it is worth noting that the phrases that prove less jarring and objectionable to her, phrases that we are led to interpret as being in some sense more representative of her experience—"It will end, it will end," "It will come, it will come"—do not convey much meaning either. Without more clarity about what "it" amounts to, none of these propositions, strictly speaking, makes full sense. And yet, descriptions of moments like this, in phrases that express the emerging, becoming, unknown in the tense of the future, drive home to us that there is no other word more specifically suited to saying what Woolf or Mrs. Ramsay want to say; no word that would convey their experience of yearning more clearly or meaningfully. Again, "it" is the word they want, with all its inarticulate vagueness.

Still Life Just Now

The woeful yearning for safety and stillness that Mrs. Ramsay craves in her moment of depersonalized solitude before the long steady stroke of the lighthouse becomes a longing for unity and coherence that is briefly satisfied during the famous dinner of *Boeuf en Daube* that she carefully and anxiously orchestrates for her family and their invited guests toward the end of "The Window." Seated together around a table ornamented with her daughter Rose's inspired centerpiece creation, perplexing in its strange (and impermanent) beauty, the members of the dinner party are suspended in the moment, "held together" as a whole (TL, 108). Viewed against the backdrop of the window illuminated by candlelight, they are transformed under Mrs. Ramsay's gaze into a modernist still life that confers on their hostess a passing sense of comfort and serenity. At this moment, for Mrs. Ramsay,

> everything seemed possible. Everything seemed right. Just now (but this cannot last, she thought, dissociating herself from the moment while they were all talking about boots) just now she had reached security; she had hovered like a hawk suspended; like a flag floated in an element of joy which filled every nerve of her body fully and sweetly, not noisily, solemnly rather, for it arose, she thought, looking at them all eating there, from husband and children and friends; all of which rising in this profound stillness (she was helping William Bankes to one very small piece more, and peered into the depths of the earthenware pot) seemed now for no special reason to stay there like a smoke, like

> a fume rising upwards, holding them safe together. Nothing need
> be said; nothing could be said. There it was, all round them. It
> partook, she felt, carefully helping Mr. Bankes to a specially ten-
> der piece, of eternity; as she had already felt about something dif-
> ferent once before that afternoon; there is a coherence in things,
> a stability; something, she meant, is immune from change, and
> shines out (she glanced at the window with its ripple of reflected
> lights) in the face of the flowing, the fleeting, the spectral, like a
> ruby; so that again tonight she had the feeling she had had once
> today, already, of peace, of rest. Of such moments, she thought,
> the thing is made that endures. (TL, 107)

With the repeated use of the deictic "just now" at the beginning of
the passage, Woolf demonstrates Mrs. Ramsay's recognition that the
very stability and possibility over which she "hovers like a hawk suspended" during this present moment "immune from change" is already
shifting inexorably into a future context in which the "thing made that
endures" nonetheless "could not last." The sense of exalted wonderment that shines forth for Mrs. Ramsay "all lit up hanging, trembling,"
and which Woolf figures as a fume rising to eternity, is something Woolf
pulls back down to earth time and again in her free indirect narrative.
Mrs. Ramsay's sublime moment of being and satisfaction, in which
nothing need or indeed could be said, is something Woolf grounds in
the mortality and vulnerability of everyday human life, by attaching it
to Mrs. Ramsay's patterns of thought and intermittent turns to domesticity, talk of boots, the depth of an earthenware pot. As Louise Hornby
points out, the stillness Woolf explores in this passage is the stillness of
the inanimate world of objects that assert their permanence against the
fragility and expendability of the observer.[65] Indeed, at the end of the
chapter, Mrs. Ramsay considers the "chairs, tables maps" that would
"carry . . . on when she was dead" (TL, 116).

The still life of the Ramsay's dinner is soon shattered; a pear (its
shape reminiscent of Prue's own doomed fecundity) is grabbed and consumed (TL, 111). That the view of life Wittgenstein describes as *sub specie aeternitatis* in the *Notebooks* and *Tractatus*, as contemplation of the
world as a limited whole against the background of all eternity, is only
an illusion, however ardently longed for, is something Mrs. Ramsay already knows.

Reminded by Mr. Bankes of her youthful friendship with a couple
called the Mannings, and a cold day spent on the Thames with them
twenty years before, Mrs. Ramsay muses about the life of that now

remote couple with surprise that "it was still going on." "Now she went among them like a ghost; and it fascinated her, as if, while she had changed, that particular day, now become very still and beautiful, had remained there, all these years." "How strange," she repeats, "that they should be going on there still. For it was extraordinary to think that they had been capable of going on living all these years when she had not thought of them more than once all that time" (TL, 90). Likewise, and still more poignantly in the context of the "inexplicable and irremediable death of the mother" that is to come, conversations will still go on around a phantom table, her children will continue to laugh, even when she is no longer there to observe them (TL, 111).[66]

We Behold Them as They Are When We Are Not There

Earlier in "The Window," Lily Briscoe asks Andrew to explain to her what his father's philosophical work entails. "Think of a kitchen table . . . when you're not there," he instructs (TL, 26). Of this exchange, Banfield writes, "this is what the photograph, starting with the first photograph, Niépce's picture of the table set with no one visible, literally and uncannily does: in the look of that table which needs no observer to look at it in order to continue to look like a table and therefore to be sensibilia of a table, the viewer meets with a start his own absence. In her essay 'The Cinema,' Woolf herself observed just this of the appearances recorded on film: 'We behold them as they are when we are not there. We see life as it is when we have no part in it.'"[67]

In her essay "*L'Imparfait de l'Objectif*: The Imperfect of the Object Glass," Banfield analyzes the peculiar temporality and impersonal subjectivity of photographic moments like these in Woolf's work. Banfield examines this strange temporal perspective as it is expressed in the equally strange tense of the sentences used to depict the "camera consciousness" that guides Woolf's narrative form. It is this photographic consciousness at the end of *The Waves* that Woolf's storyteller, Bernard, describes as "the world seen without a self."[68]

I turn to Banfield's discussion of photography here first of all because it offers a clear articulation of Woolf's creation of such a narrative consciousness in *To the Lighthouse*. But I also highlight Banfield's essay at this point in anticipation of my discussion below of Diamond's reading of Ted Hughes's poem "Six Young Men," which relies centrally on an ekphrastic use of a photograph. My discussion of the role of Hughes's poem in Diamond's essay will benefit from Banfield's analysis of the photographic epistemology that Woolf explores in her novel, and which

Roland Barthes theorizes in his *Camera Lucida*. Some of the views on photography that Barthes considers in that essay dovetail with aspects of Cavell's thinking about still photography within his body of work on moving pictures. While Cavell's views on photography are not immediately relevant to the ideas about knowing and acknowledging others that Diamond engages with in her essay, the affinities between Barthes and Cavell are important to bear in mind in advance.

In her essay, Banfield focuses on Barthes's quest for the *noeme* of the photograph, "that thing," that "distinguishes it . . . from any other image."[69] What sets the photograph apart from all other forms of aesthetic representation is the mechanical objectivity that makes it not just a likeness of the object it represents, but an "authentication," a certificate of a past presence (CL, 91). For Barthes, what is particular to the photographic image is *reference*. The photograph is never without its referent, that is, whatever it is a photograph *of*. "It is as if the Photograph always carries its referent with itself," he writes. Image and referent are "glued together" (CL, 5–6).

Banfield identifies the photographic referent with Russellian sensibilia. These are sense data that are not necessarily sensed, the appearance of things in places where there are no minds to perceive them.[70] Think of a table, then, when you're not there. Produced by a mechanical process, the recorded image is no longer anyone's sensation. The referent of the photographic image is not something first seen by human observer, but something captured by the lens of the camera. By connecting the photographic referent with sensibilia, Banfield makes the photographic image into something that is not straightforwardly objective, but is instead characterized by what she describes as a neutral, impersonal kind of subjectivity. It is "subjective but subjectless," as she puts it (OI, 77). The subjective-objective dichotomy in Banfield's reading of Barthes is such that the photograph remains subjective by continuing to present the image from a perspective, even when that perspective is emptied of any embodied perceiver. The dualism does not resolve into objectivity over subjectivity, however. The lens captures the sense data of the world as they would be received if there were a subject to occupy the camera's position.

The particular referentiality of the photograph is deeply connected for Barthes in the referentiality of deictics and demonstratives, Woolf's beloved shifters, which are always referred to from the subjective perspective of the first person. They have to do with showing, particularly of a kind that implies exchanges with others: "Show your photographs to someone—he will immediately show you his: 'Look, this is my brother;

this is me as a child,' etc.," says Barthes. "The Photograph is never anything but the antiphon of 'Look,' 'See,' 'Here it is'; it points a finger at
certain *vis-à-vis* and cannot escape [the] pure deictic language" of a *this*,
a *that*, a *there*, a *here*, a *lo!* (CL, 4–5).

Deictic sentences reflect the speaker's point of view. They take the
form "here is the table I am sitting at now." In Barthes's attempt to name
the essence of photography via its deictic referentiality, however, he
runs up against "the resistance of ordinary language, which fails to offer
the appropriate tense to capture the photographic moment" (OI, 75).
Speaking of his experience looking at a photograph taken of a road near
Jerusalem in 1850, Barthes writes something that, as we shall see below,
resonates particularly with Hughes's reception of the photograph in his
poem. "Three tenses dizzy my consciousness," he writes: "my present,
the time of Jesus, and that of the photographer, all this under the instance of 'reality'" (CL, 97).

Barthes finds it impossible to describe his experience of the photo,
since doing so would mean bringing together three tenses that must remain distinct in spoken language. He finds an appropriate linguistic form
to capture his experience of the "strange pastness of being-here-now"
of that photograph not by combining tenses but by combining a past
tense with a present-time deictic (OI, 74–75). His solution is to assign to
the photograph a specifically narrative, literary tense: the aorist, preterit
tense, which designates an absolute, unqualified pastness of a completed
event. This tense is merged in the photographic moment with a present
deictic, a "now" of the first-person observer (OI, 75). But Barthes also
writes that the "strange stasis" that the photograph achieves is that of
a past event arrested in incompleteness and imperfection (CL, 91). The
tense of this stasis is for Banfield not the deictic present merging with the
aorist past, but with the imperfect. As Barthes writes, "the imperfect is
the tense of fascination: it seems to be alive and yet it doesn't move: imperfect presence, imperfect death; neither oblivion nor resurrection; simply the exhausting lure of memory."[71]

Banfield is thus moved to correct Barthes's account of the mingling of
tenses that characterizes the photographic moment, rewriting Barthes's
noeme of photography, *ça a été*, "that has been" with the peculiar phrase
"this was now here," or in the French that makes the imperfect tense
more immediately legible, "*ça était maintenant ici*" (OI, 76). Hornby
articulates the decisive difference made by seeing the photographic moment in terms of the imperfect tense rather than the aorist in this way:
"the time of the photograph deals with the loss and preservation of on-
goingness within a specific moment. Its paradox is that photography

preserves what is (suspended, interrupted, incomplete), rather than what was."[72] Photography, and literature like Woolf's, which adapt to narrative the strange temporality of the photographic moment, are thus able to hold together and at once imperfect presence and imperfect death.

In her correction of Barthes, Banfield assigns to the photographic moment an equally narrative and literary mixing of tenses, the combination of which meets resistance in ordinary usage but finds a home in the free indirect style prevalent in the nineteenth- and twentieth-century novel and so characteristic of Woolf's brand of represented speech and thought. "This oxymoronic combination of present and past, life and absence of life, movement and stasis," Banfield writes, "can be translated, not by the *imparfait* of the spoken language, but by a use of the *imparfait* restricted to written narrative and, specifically, the novel. This is the tense which, in French, marks the *style indirect libre*, that style for the representation of consciousness" (IO, 76).

Banfield offers several examples of the merging of deixis and the imperfect tense that marks a novelistic free indirect style. One of these is a passage from *Madame Bovary*: "*Quel bonheur dans ce temps-là! quelle liberté! quel espoir! quelle abondance d'illusions! Il n'en* restait *plus*, maintenant!" (OI, 76, Banfield's emphasis).[73] Alongside these lines from Flaubert, we might place a fragment from the passage about Mrs. Ramsay above: "*Now* she *went* among them like a ghost; and it fascinated her, as if, while she had changed, that particular day, now become very still and beautiful, had remained there, all these years" (TL, 90, my emphasis).

Toward the end of "The Window," Mrs. Ramsay pauses to look back over the threshold at the fading communal dinner scene and pronounces it "already the past" (TL, 114). "As Mrs. Ramsay hesitates on the threshold," Hornby writes, "she pauses the narrative that is contingent on her life and relegates it to the past, writing herself out of the world while at the same time assuring herself that the world will not, in fact, disappear without her, but instead remake itself anew." She continues:

> The unoccupied point of view that photography allows produces a temporal blankness or the empty temporality of delay or hesitation. This is the suspended time of the solar eclipse, the time of waiting for an inevitable darkness that itself has a prolonged duration in excess of instantaneity. The eclipse witnessed by Woolf in 1926 lasted twenty-four seconds. Twenty-four seconds, that is, of a rubbed-out world when time could not be controlled.[74]

The Fisherman and His Wife

Mrs. Ramsay's longed-for sense of safety, wholeness, stillness, and suspension of time is something she achieves in the novel only in the stark
tableau of death that Woolf gives us only pages after the *Boeuf-en-Daube*
dinner scene. In the characteristically compressed and abrupt fashion of
"Time Passes," we get this report: "[Mr. Ramsay, stumbling along a passage one dark morning stretched his arms out, but Mrs. Ramsay having
died rather suddenly the night before, his arms, though stretched out, remained empty]" (TL, 132).

This bracketed remark follows directly on the heels of one of the
main instantiations of the poignant disembodied narrative of "questioning and wondering" that becomes so pressing and prolific in "Time
Passes" (130). Here, the experience of a harrowing difficulty of life is
conveyed in an outpouring of fragmented questions whose answers are
always pending. As lights and lives are extinguished and the cyclical lap-
ping of sea waves inexorably erodes the sands on which the characters
once stood, a chorus of mystic visionary questioners paces the beach to
"ask of the sea and sky what message they reported or what vision they
affirmed" (TL, 137). They seek to assuage their solitude in a quest for
answers. Woolf writes:

> Should any sleeper fancying that he might find on the beach an
> answer to his doubts, a sharer of his solitude, throw off his bed-
> clothes and go down by himself to walk on the sand, no im-
> age with semblance of serving and divine promptitude comes
> ready to hand bringing the night to order and making the world
> reflect the compass of the soul. The hand dwindles in his hand;
> the voice bellows in his ear. Almost it would appear that it is
> useless in such confusion to ask the night those questions as to
> what, and why, and wherefore, which tempt the sleeper from his
> bed to seek an answer. (TL, 132)

Woolf's use of the qualifying "almost" in the passage above renders
the narrative's conviction of the futility of the visionaries' "questioning
and wondering" and longing for wholeness more tentative than at other
moments in "Time Passes" and the rest of her oeuvre. With her use of
"almost" here, Woolf reveals the persistence of hope even within the
"downpouring of immense darkness" (TL, 125).

The sleeper is given, if only for a brief moment, to succumb to the
temptation of believing in the remote possibility that an answer is within

her grasp, and this even within a narrative interlude in which all other images of grasping, reaching, or clutching attest only to the cosmic irony of such a belief by consistently coming up empty-handed—Mrs. Ramsay's death is announced, after all, in the bracketed remark immediately following the passage. Mr. Ramsay's arms, outstretched to hold her, remain empty. The only other grasping gesture portrayed in "Time Passes" works to underscore the peril and absurdity of human existence: "Sometimes a hand was raised as if to clutch something or ward off something, or somebody groaned, or somebody laughed aloud as if sharing a joke with nothingness" (TL, 126).

Later in the same interlude of "Time Passes," Woolf continues:

> That dream, of sharing, completing, of finding in solitude on the beach an answer, was then but a reflection in a mirror, and . . . to pace the beach was impossible; contemplation was unendurable; the mirror was broken. (TL, 138)

These passages call attention to what I have been describing as Woolf's treatment in *To the Lighthouse* of a general sense of yearning for (always elusive) consoling answers to the big enduring questions of life. The first passage also speaks to a desire—one related to Mrs. Ramsay's own—to fly in the face of the "terrible" in the world by exerting a certain control over how things happen in it. The second passage above speaks of an "unendurable contemplation," presenting a difficulty of understanding (and a loss of correspondence truth) in the figure of a broken mirror. These passages articulate problems related to the human will and to the self's unrecognizability to itself and to others. In doing so, they underline Woolf's narrative experiments with Russian-style questioning. They also speak to her engagement with what Martha Nussbaum describes in her discussion of *To the Lighthouse* in relation to Cavell's work as "our epistemological insufficiency toward one another and our unquenchable epistemological longing." For Woolf's novel is quietly obsessed throughout with the "venerable problem" of other minds (Nussbaum, 732). As Nussbaum points out, Woolf suggests that the problem of other minds is "not simply an epistemological problem, a problem of evidence and certainty, but above all an ethical problem, a problem produced by the motives and desires with which we approach beings who are both separate from us and vital to our projects" (Nussbaum, 732). In this sense, Woolf anticipates Cavell's arguments about the skeptic. For also central to Woolf's novel is the sense of metaphysical finitude, the tragic character of human separateness that preoccupies

Cavell, and which, as we shall see shortly, Diamond is concerned to respond to in her "Difficulty" essay.[75]

Mrs. Ramsay's outlook of joyful acceptance and coherence during the dinner scene, coupled with her desire to stop time and make the world reflect the "compass of the soul," is one we can view in terms of the Grimm tale "The Fisherman and His Wife," which Mrs. Ramsay reads distractedly and intermittently to her son James in the first part of the novel. The Grimm story offers us an important intertextual point of contact between Woolf and Diamond. For it is to this same story that Diamond turns in her "Ethics and Imagination and the Method of Wittgenstein's *Tractatus*" in order to explore the sense of the "terrible" and of terrible evil as it works on readers of the fairy tales that Wittgenstein found to be ethically powerful.[76] Her discussion of the ethical weight of that tale is also used to clarify Wittgenstein's sense of the attitude toward the world he describes as "happy" (or in terms of its "unhappy" opposite) in the *Tractatus* and the notebooks he kept as he was writing it.[77] In the Grimm story, a fisherman captures an enchanted flounder and spares its life. Upon his return home, his wife, Ilsibil, demands he return to the flounder to ask him to grant her what quickly becomes a long series of wishes. Her initial desire to trade in her filthy shack for a cozy cottage soon gives way to wishes for increasing material wealth and power; first she demands to be king, then emperor, then pope. On the morning that she wakes up unable to bear the fact that the rising and setting of the sun and the moon are beyond her control, she sends her reluctant husband back to the flounder with her final angry command that she "become like God." The command elicits a supernatural gale and the wife's abrupt return to her original squalor.[78]

For Diamond, the wife in the story, and what she goes on to want and to do, shows us the character of someone who takes an "unhappy" attitude toward life and the world as a whole that she argues is so central to Wittgenstein's conception of ethics. Wittgenstein's concept of this "happy" outlook, which I will examine more extensively in the context of a discussion of Joyce's Leopold Bloom in the next chapter, is an attitude Diamond describes as one marked by an "acceptance of the independence of the world from one's will . . . the acceptance of the fact that what happens, happens, that one's willing this rather than that is merely another thing that happens and that one is in a sense 'powerless'" ("Ethics and Imagination, 154). In Ilsibil, however, we get a figure filled with "a deep dissatisfaction with the world's not meeting the conditions she lays down" ("Ethics and Imagination," 166). Diamond goes on to articulate the sense of "something terrible and sinister" that arises

in her own reading of "The Fisherman and His Wife," starting from Ilsibil's very first wish. This sense of terrible evil has nothing to do with
that wish on the surface—there is nothing particularly terrible, after all,
about wanting to live in a tidy cottage rather than a stinking hovel. But
Diamond suggests that the Grimm story presents us with evil that functions on a variety of different levels.[79] In doing so, she draws on Wittgenstein's notes on anthropologist James Frazer's description of eighteenth-
century Scottish rituals of sacrifice, in which he too draws a distinction
between natural and supernatural evil. In his discussion of ritual and
religious practice there, he points to cases that might lead us to ask,
"whence the sense of something dark and terrible in what at one level
may seem entirely innocent?" He writes:

> I want to say: The deep, the sinister, do not depend on the his-
> tory of the practice having been like this, for perhaps it was not
> like this at all; nor on the fact that it was perhaps or probably
> like this. Indeed, how is it that in general human sacrifice is so
> deep and sinister? . . . No, the deep and the sinister do not be-
> come apparent merely by our coming to know the history of the
> external action, rather it is *we* who ascribe them from an inner
> experience. . . .
>
> When I see such a practice, or hear of it, it is like seeing a
> man speaking harshly to someone else over a trivial matter, and
> noticing from his tone of voice and facial expression that this
> man can on occasion be terrible. The impression that I receive
> here can be very deep and extraordinarily serious."[80]

In her essay, Diamond distinguishes evil of a more mundane, inconsequential stripe—the kind of evil that lies "close to home," something
one might even get used to, on the one hand, and a deeper sort of evil,
one that represents "something terrible, black and wholly alien that you
cannot even approach" on the other ("Ethics and Imagination," 166).
The sense of evil that the Grimms' story gives us seems "to be justified by
nothing that is as it were available on the surface of events. . . . We have a
sense of something dark and terrible 'within,' as we might say" ("Ethics
and Imagination," 167).

Mrs. Ramsay's benign will to control time and tide is, of course,
also to be contrasted with what Diamond depicts as the more malevo-
lent grabbiness of the fisherman's wife. What distinguishes Mrs. Ramsay from Ilsibil, the woman in the Grimm story, is her consistent recognition in Woolf's novel of the world's refusal to conform to the order

she could impose upon it. Mrs. Ramsay recognizes what Wittgenstein declares at *Tractatus* 6.373–74: that the world is independent of her will. That "even if everything we wished were to happen, this would only be, so to speak, a favour of fate." The difference between Mrs. Ramsay's ethical attitude and Ilsibil's lies in Mrs. Ramsay's acceptance of the difficult reality that the sun and the moon will go on rising and setting even without her say-so. Or even that the sun's rising tomorrow is a hypothesis, not an unassailable necessity (cf. TLP, 6.36311). Yet I would argue that Mrs. Ramsay's sense of fate is intimately connected to the fairy-tale ethics of the cosmic "terrible," magical sea-churning force that the Grimm story gives us, a sense of "something terrible, black and wholly alien" that Diamond is keen to call our attention to in her discussion of the moral weight and imaginative capacity of the story ("Ethics and Imagination," 166).[81]

The solemn attitude of possibility, acceptance, and peace that Mrs. Ramsay adopts in her moment of plenitude during the dinner scene in "The Window" is one of attachment and loyalty. In spite of her dread in the face of what she recognizes as a rubbed-out world of eclipse, she strives to inhabit a world of life. Her outlook represents a "happy" attitude toward the world as a whole, in Wittgenstein's sense. It goes without saying that Mrs. Ramsay does not represent the agent of terrible blackness that Ilsibil does in Diamond's reading of the Grimm story. But in giving us a character so attuned to an uncanny force of the terrible in the world, Woolf nevertheless presents us with a proximity to what Diamond calls "the difficulty of reality."

The Difficulty of Reality and the Difficulty of Philosophy

In "The Difficulty of Reality and the Difficulty of Philosophy," Diamond builds on Wittgenstein's and Cavell's ideas about the nonsense of expressions of ethical experience and the difficulty of understanding others to add another dimension of perplexity to the different orders of difficulty I outlined in this book's introduction. The difficulty Diamond describes entails what Stephen Mulhall characterizes as a "constitutively enigmatic" experience of ordinary human life.[82] Experience of such difficulty is received with a sense of bewilderment capable of stifling our hopeful or even our most "hopeless interrogation," replacing it with a stranger sense of woundedness, confoundedness and isolation (MF, 163). It is a difficulty that has to do, in Woolf's words, with an "unendurable contemplation" that stops us in our tracks with a complete inability to grasp reality at all. A "difficulty of reality," for Diamond,

is the experience in which we take something in reality to be resistant to our thinking it, or possibly to be painful in its inexplicability, difficult in that way, or perhaps awesome and astonishing in its inexplicability. *We take things so.* And the things we
take so may simply not, to others, present that kind of difficulty,
of being hard or impossible or agonizing to get one's head
around. (DR, 45–46)

As Diamond describes it, a difficulty of reality can arise from experience
of trauma or horror, but there is no necessary conjunction in her mind
between the difficulty of reality and evil, anguish and suffering. For, as
we have already seen in the fragment from Miłosz that Diamond takes
as an example of such a difficulty, it can also potentially arise from an
encounter with beauty, or (as in another case she points to, of the "in-
comparable and inexplicable" gesture of grace that saved a twelve-year-
old Ruth Klüger from a selection at Auschwitz) from a sense of awe at
an act of overwhelming goodness that shocks us with equal force, but
which we would not, as we would of a traumatic difficulty of reality,
"wish to wish away" (WA, 87–88).[83] Diamond points to philosopher
Roy Holland's description of one aspect of a miracle as a happening that
is at the same time both empirically certain and conceptually impossible.[84] An encounter with beauty or goodness can astonish us as a miracle
would. Like an experience of trauma, the experience of beauty or goodness can strike us as an impossible reality that nonetheless *is* (DR, 60).
Such an impossible reality can drive us to disturbance trying to encompass it within our usual ways of thinking and speaking.

Diamond's essay seeks primarily to engage philosophically with
Stanley Cavell's thinking about skepticism, and with J. M. Coetzee's
Tanner Lectures (which were later to form a part of his novel *Elizabeth
Costello*), including a set of philosophical responses to those lectures
now compiled in *The Lives of Animals*. Although she looks at Czesław
Miłosz, Ruth Klüger and Mary Mann to explore the range of phenom-
ena she is concerned with, Diamond's notion of the difficulty of reality is
rooted in a literary example associated with aspects of World War I that
also inform both Wittgenstein's and Woolf's work: Ted Hughes's poem
"Six Young Men," written in the late 1950s.

Exposure: This Was Here Now

At the heart of the poem is a 1914 photograph of six smiling men, friends
of Hughes's father, seated in a spot intimately familiar to the speaker

and eerily unchanged. All are profoundly alive; yet within six months of the snapshot, all are dead. Hughes's poem captures life and death simultaneously in the fading keepsake exposure superimposed on the "flash and rending" of war that falls onto these smiles now forty years "rotting into soil." The four decades that have faded and ochre-tinged the image have not wrinkled their faces or hands. Pictured here, their expressions "listen yet," though their faces are forty years underground. The celluloid of the photograph "holds them well," arrested and suspended in a confounding stasis of a past now, imperfect and incomplete (CL, 71). These six young men from a past captured and fixed on celluloid represent what Barthes speaks of as "that rather terrible thing which is there in every photograph: the return of the dead" (CL, 9).

Hughes brings out in the last stanza the horrible permanent contradiction that Diamond takes to the heart of her notion of a difficulty of reality:

> That man's not more alive whom you confront
> And shake by the hand, see hale, hear speak loud
> Than any of these six celluloid smiles are,
> Nor prehistoric or fabulous beast more dead;
> No thought so vivid as their smoking blood:
> To regard this photograph might well dement.
> Such contradictory permanent horrors here
> Smile from the single exposure and shoulder out
> One's own body from its instant and heat.[85]

The title of Diamond's essay is "The Difficulty of Reality and the Difficulty of Philosophy," yet she tells us that if she could add one word to the title, it would be "exposure." The word obviously speaks to Hughes's poem, which speaks of a "single exposure" of the photograph itself, determined by shutter speed, lens aperture, and scene luminescence. As Mulhall writes, "the difficulty of reality that Diamond is trying to locate here is . . . inseparable from the fact of photography: the instant and heat of the rending flash that shoulders out language and thought registers both the worst of war (the rifle-barrel and the bomb) and the camera's reliance upon the dazzling light of a flashbulb to take its single exposure" (WA, 91). Hughes's poem, with its connections to the senseless, discombobulating reality of war, which will bring death to the six lively faces captured in the still frame of the photograph, also recalls Wilfred Owen's war poem "Exposure."[86]

Owen's 1918 poem tells of soldiers trapped in a frigid no-man's-land between life and death, literally dying of exposure between trench and battlefield while "nothing happens." "Exposure" is a poem that brings a bodily sense of the sheer animal vulnerability of the human being together with the delirium, madness, and psychic affliction wrought by war from its very first line: "Our brains ache." Diamond's difficulty of reality is the experience of such an ache of the brain. Though unlike Owen's lament, expressed in a "we" that includes the others suffering in silence alongside him, the pain of the difficulty of reality that Diamond points to is compounded in its agony, since it is suffered by a subject who must also endure the isolation from others that is part and parcel of such an experience. The isolation suffered in the experience of a difficulty of reality is itself related to Cavell's use of the word "exposure" in *The Claim of Reason* to describe a human situation in which our knowledge of others, and of their suffering, may at any time be overthrown.[87]

If exposure haunts Diamond's conception of the difficulty of reality, Cavell's body of work on film and photography also looms in the background. Indeed, Cavell's reflections on the relationship between photographs and reality, his attention to the automatism of the camera itself, and his appreciation of the "aura or history of magic surrounding" photographs and the mystery surrounding what the image conveys to us are relevant to my concerns with both Diamond and Woolf here.[88] For Cavell, as for Barthes, the realism of photography is not a question of presenting viewers with a likeness of its object (as we are given to say a painting does). Rather, it presents us with some kind of sensed visual transcription of an object or a person, which somehow captures the thing itself (WV, 17). When we look at a photograph, at what Barthes calls its "emanation of past reality," Cavell says, "we see things that are not present" (CL, 88; WV, 18). Conversely, the camera makes a world present to us from which we are absent (WV, 18). "The reality in a photograph is present to me while I am not present to it; and a world I know, and see, but to which I am nevertheless not present (through no fault of my subjectivity), is a world past" (WV, 23).

The experience of a difficulty of reality that Diamond sees figured in the sense of the violent astonishment before the photograph that Hughes figures in his poem is one that shares negatively in the sublimity of the epiphanic ethical experience of wonder at the world that Wittgenstein puts forth as the example par excellence of his experience of absolute value in his "Lecture on Ethics," and which Woolf also thematizes throughout her novels as an effort to embrace "life." But in order to understand the kind of experience Diamond points to as exemplary of the difficulty of reality, it is important to appreciate the decisive difference between it and Wittgenstein's example of feeling wonder at the existence of the world, a feeling of wonder Woolf also explores in her writing. For the sense of wonder Wittgenstein describes suggests an openness to the world, a yearning to understand and articulate one's place in it, an acknowledgment of the others with whom we share this place, albeit in expressions that are, for him, inherently nonsensical. The experience of a difficulty of reality, on the other hand, is constituted by a radical failure to understand that is met with an utter lack of responsiveness from other people. The experience of sublime awe that Diamond is concerned with does not inspire the flight and freedom of wonderment. The blow it delivers is met instead with an ache of the brain, an enclosed, unacknowledged, and paralyzing stupefaction.

Blows, Shocks, and Moments of Being

Before returning to a discussion of the details of Diamond's notion of the difficulty of reality, I want to take a slight detour here, turning briefly to Woolf's own treatment of sublime experience in both the inspiring and paralyzing varieties figured respectively in Wittgenstein's sense of wonder and Diamond's difficulty of reality above. In her late memoir *A Sketch of the Past*, Woolf posits a relationship between both sorts of astonishment that will be helpful in our discussion in the conclusion of this chapter of Diamond's views about the ethical power of works of literature that represent difficulties of reality.

In *A Sketch of the Past*, Woolf isolates exceptional, ethically charged "moments of being," moments of vision or ecstasy, when life's significance emerges from behind the tissue of non-being that makes up the "cotton wool of daily life" (SP, 72). Moments of being, for Woolf, are first experienced as dreadful and disorienting "shocks" or "blows" (SP, 72). Then, with perspective gained over time, they become the object of belated self-conscious contemplation and authorship—sublime moments viewed, then, from the relative safety both Kant and Burke require of this aesthetic category, safety that becomes available only with the passage of time required to synthesize them, to preserve and transmit them through the techniques of her art of fiction and memoir (as each of the authors Diamond cites in her essay go on to do as well). The three examples Woolf provides of such moments, rooted in her earliest childhood memories, attest to her attunement to Wordsworthian "spots of time" elaborated in the *Prelude*.[89] The impressions of life and the violent shocks and despair it inevitably delivers leave a lasting mark on the writer's psyche that goes on to transform her art. The moments of being she describes also promise a "revelation of some order," "a token of some real thing behind appearances" that she makes real by putting into words. Woolf continues:

> From this I reach what I might call a philosophy; at any rate it is a constant idea of mine; that behind the cotton wool is hidden a pattern; that we—I mean all human beings—are connected with this: that the whole world is a work of art; that we are parts of the work of art. Hamlet or a Beethoven quartet is the truth about this vast mass that we call the world. But there is no Shakespeare; there is no Beethoven, certainly and emphatically there is no God; we are the words; we are the music; we are the thing in itself. (SP, 72)

Her first example of such a moment comes from a memory of a fight she had at a young age with her older brother, Thoby. The pummeling left her with a sense of "hopeless sadness," she remembers, an awareness of her own powerlessness, and a sense of "something terrible." The second example arises after she overhears her parents talk about a family friend, Mr. Valpy, who had killed himself. Walking on a path by the apple tree in the garden at St. Ives afterward, she connects the tree with Valpy's suicide and finds she cannot pass it. This childhood experience put her into a "trance of horror," she writes. "I seemed to be dragged down, hopelessly, into some pit of despair from which I could not escape. My body seemed paralysed" (SP, 71).

Both of these two moments of being end in horror, paralysis, and what she calls "a state of despair" (SP, 71). But a third memory gives way to a sense of plenitude and satisfaction that ultimately acts as a catalyst for her writing. Woolf recounts a moment evocative of Blake's "Auguries of Innocence" in which she experiences a sense of wholeness while contemplating a flower in the same St. Ives garden: "I was looking at a plant with a spread of leaves," she writes, "and it seemed suddenly plain that the flower itself was a part of the earth; that a ring enclosed what was the flower; and that was the real flower; part earth; part flower. It was a thought I put away as being likely to be very useful to me later" (SP, 71).[90] The flower comes to represent a conceptual shift in her life as a writer. It represents for her a breakthrough that brings with it insights

into the importance of these moments of being to her conscious authorial power to explain them. "When I said about the flower 'that is the
whole,' I felt that I had made a discovery. I felt that I had put away in my
mind something that I should go back to, turn over and explore," she
writes. "In the case of the flower I found a reason; and was thus able to
deal with the sensation. I was not powerless. I was conscious—if only at
a distance—that I should in time explain it" (SP, 72–73).

Woolf's moments of being have a source in a difficulty of reality,
in Diamond's sense. Upon their initial blows or shocks, they leave her
with an incomprehensible sense of pain, horror, or beauty that paralyzes
her. But they also represent experiences she is later able to contain to
the extent that she can encompass them in her writing life. She suggests
that perhaps "as one gets older one has a greater power through reason
to provide an explanation; and that this explanation blunts the sledge-
hammer force of the blow," making the shocks valuable, and thus welcome (SP, 72). What's more, Woolf claims, it is her capacity to receive
such shocks that makes her a writer:

> I hazard the explanation that a shock is at once in my case fol-
> lowed by the desire to explain it. I feel that I have had a blow;
> but it is not, as I thought as a child, simply a blow from an enemy
> hidden behind the cotton wool of daily life; it is or will become a
> revelation of some order; it is a token of some real thing behind
> appearances; and I make it real by putting it into words. It is
> only by putting it into words that I make it whole; this wholeness
> means that it has lost its power to hurt me; it gives me, perhaps
> because by doing so I take away the pain, a great delight to put
> the severed parts together. (SP, 72)

I spoke above of Diamond's views about the ethical power of works
of literature that turn on a central figure of a difficulty of reality. In her *A
Sketch of the Past*, Woolf points us to ways in which representations of
difficulties of reality in literature and memoir can be put to the ethically
instructive purpose of confronting the reader with stark depictions of reality that capture our minds and have the potential to make us see our
real world differently. I want to emphasize again here that what literary
representations of such difficulties have to reveal to us about life does not
come down to a specific moral lesson delivered directly in the text. What
such depictions do have to offer us, what they prompt us to see if we read
them with the kind of attention they call for, is not something that readers can settle on with a sense of ease or certainty by the end of the telling.

Shouldered Out

One of Diamond's examples of texts that present readers with a difficulty of reality is Mary Mann's short story "Little Brother." In the story, two poor children are witnessed playing with the corpse of their stillborn baby brother, the only doll they have ever had. Diamond says that the terribleness of what happens in the story, and the terribleness of the felt resistance of the narrated reality to our familiar modes of moral thought, are inseparable (DR, 64). "The telling, fully felt," she writes, ousts us "from a familiar sense of moral life, from a sense of being able to take in and think a moral world. Moral thought gets no grip here" (DR, 64). Another story that Diamond—appealing to the words A. S. Byatt uses to describe the Mann story—calls similarly "spiky with morals and the inadequacy of morals" is Leonard Woolf's "Pearls and Swine." On one level, it offers a critical look at racism and colonialism. But on another level, it speaks to a sense of the terrible in human life that exceeds the moral designation the first level of criticism affords.

Although the difficulties of reality presented in such stories defy our attempts to understand them by appeal to our familiar sense of moral life, they nonetheless have the potential to be deeply ethically instructive. By presenting readers with rare and astounding instances of a "coming apart of thought and reality" that Diamond insists are an uncanny part of ordinary life, such works of literature force us to gaze with an unaccustomed austerity at problems of human existence that diverge from what "everyone would recognize" from the standpoint of our familiar moral perspectives (DR, 64). In presenting readers with literary depictions of situations that resist contemplation within the framework of our habitual moral conceptions, and by asking us to dwell on them in the way they do, the stories and memoirs Diamond examines thereby leave us exposed to the often strange and stunning pain of others. Such works challenge us to look on this unaccountable pain and to recognize it in our own bafflement and in all its incomprehensibility. Works of art like these thereby have the creative power to lead us beyond the page toward a deeper and more expansive understanding of the human condition, an understanding that includes bafflement.

The initial raw, paralyzing experience that Woolf exemplifies in her childhood moments of blows or shocks is an experience Diamond describes, with regard to Hughes's "Six Young Men," as a difficulty of reality marked by a sudden inability of the mind to comprehend the situation it finds before it. The shock of a such a difficulty of reality leaves the subject to cope with an experience of near-madness, trying to bring

together in thought what cannot be thought: the impossibility of anyone's being more alive than the smiling men in the photo, and of nothing's being more dead (DR, 44).

It is plainly possible, Diamond tells us, to describe the photo in
Hughes's poem so that it does not seem mind-boggling at all: here we
have an ordinary snapshot of a group of men who died young in battle
not long after the photo was taken. If we look at the picture that way,
there is no problem about the adequacy of our concepts to describe it.
The person faced with a difficulty of reality, however, finds herself isolated in linguistic and personal bewilderment, utterly *shouldered out*, in
Hughes's words, from ordinary ways of comprehending the world and
what happens in it. No amount of explanation can put into perspective
this "shuddering awareness of living in the contradiction of death and
life together" (DR, 73). As Banfield writes, "'the return of the dead' in
the photograph for the viewer meets then with the results of Orpheus's
look: the annihilation of sight, of perception, of consciousness, *within* it
and their banishment to some no man's land outside it" (OI, 80).

A difficulty of reality has to do with the capacity of reality not just to
exceed our conceptual grasp but to present a tormenting inexplicability, a resistance to our ordinary modes of thinking and talking. It is a difficulty marked by a coming apart of thought and reality, a repudiation of
the ordinary that, in a terrible irony, is nonetheless an enduring feature
of that same flesh-and-blood everyday.

Woolf, Diamond, and the Realistic Spirit

I return briefly once again to Woolf. For in "Modern Fiction," she claims
that writers like Tolstoy and Dostoevsky see into this flesh-and-blood
everyday "further than we do and without our gross impediments of
vision" (MF, 163). In her own critical writing, she proposes new approaches to correcting the blind spots and myopia she sees as characteristic of the novels of the early twentieth century. She calls for an improved focus on aspects of everyday life that novelists have previously
ignored in their efforts to offer robust descriptions of reality. "Look
within and life, it seems, is very far from being 'like this,'" she writes.
What she wants (from both an aesthetic and an ethical point of view) is
"a different outline of form . . . difficult for us to grasp, incomprehensible to her ["materialist," Edwardian] predecessors" (MF, 160–62). If
modern novelists are to be realistic about "the spirit we live by, life itself," they must learn to move beyond established convention, to attend
to "the life of Monday or Tuesday" in such a way as to "tolerate the

spasmodic, the obscure, the fragmentary, the failure" (MF, 160).[91] To faithfully represent "the thing we seek," something she describes (admitting further indexical "vagueness") as "life or spirit, truth or reality, this, the essential thing," writers must look after the "little deviations which the human spirit seems to make from time to time." They must turn their attention to the moments when "life escapes," when it veers off course, refusing to be contained by traditional narrative and linguistic conventions (MF, 159–60). For Woolf, realistically representing the complexity and mystery of human character and "what life is really like" means focusing on the oddities and anomalies of everyday human existence and quest for meaning. "Is it not the task of the novelist," she asks, "to convey this varying, this unknown and uncircumscribed spirit, whatever aberration or complexity it may display?" (MF, 160–61).

The complex anomalous moments Woolf would have us bear in mind in our efforts to speak to "what life is really like" are precisely what is at stake, with a vengeance, in Diamond's exploration of the difficulty of reality. In casting her eye on the role of these moments of incomprehensibility in everyday life, and the way they resist fitting into established conceptual narratives, Diamond, too, attends to the "little deviations which the human spirit seems to make" when "life escapes," as it were. In her treatment of the difficulty of reality, we find a philosophical response to Woolf's rhetorical question about the task of the novelist. For in Diamond's view, it is most certainly the task of the philosopher to convey life's varying, unknown, and uncircumscribed spirit, whatever aberration or complexity it may display. For striving to do just this is the only way to remain true to the realistic spirit she ascribes to Wittgenstein.[92]

In a discussion of her work on literature, riddles, and the range of linguistic phenomena associated with expressions of ethical experience and religious belief, Mulhall examines how Diamond's writing bears the mark of her inheritance from Wittgenstein in its commitment to representing the realistic spirit of life as accurately as possible—even when it resists established Wittgensteinian conventions of perspicuous representation. Diamond's own way of flouting inherited conventions of realism (in both its philosophical and its literary traditions) is consistent with the modernist novel's commitment to "questioning the generic conventions it inherits in the name of a more faithful representation of the real."[93] In an effort to remain true to Wittgenstein's realistic spirit, Diamond shows herself willing to sacrifice the signature concepts with which his work is so often identified—"language games," "grammar," "forms of life," and so on. Wittgenstein forged these representational devices in the service of redirecting our attention to the ways in which we actually use words in our lives, to return us to our actual life with language. Forged by Wittgenstein as tools to be used in the work of clarification, such concepts should possess the inherent flexibility needed to accommodate any pattern of word use that a person might employ. But if we allow these concepts to become hardened, they may in the end only narrow our sense of what the ordinary might be, and thereby risk betraying Wittgenstein's most fundamental legacy. Of Diamond's treatment of the difficulty of reality, Mulhall writes:

> Diamond can properly acknowledge such difficulties only by . . . sacrificing one of the supposedly defining features of a distinctively Wittgensteinian approach to philosophy. For its business of returning words from their metaphysical to their everyday use (PI, §116) is usually glossed as a matter of rehousing words in the Heimat of ordinary language games. But properly to register the essential nature of a difficulty of reality asks us to acknowledge the capacity of reality to shoulder us out from our familiar language-games, to resist the distinctively human capacity to word the world, and thereby to leave us as bewildered and disorientated as a bird that suddenly finds itself incapable of constructing a nest, or a beaver of building a dam.[94]

What Diamond would have us see is that riddle phrases and nonsense phrases (forms of speaking that either lack meaning, exceed it, or defy our ordinary assignments of sense), as well as the failure of words in the face of momentous experience in which reality surpasses our sense-making capacities, all nonetheless play a key role in the rich life with language that Wittgenstein seeks to display to us with clarity, even if they cannot be accounted for through his signature concepts. Such expressions are techniques of our language as any other. They are empty of linguistic sense, to be sure, but not of human use and significance.

In her examination of these phenomena, Diamond draws on the insights she delivers in "Ethics and Imagination and the Method of Wittgenstein's *Tractatus*," *The Realistic Spirit*, and elsewhere about Wittgenstein's view of nonsense, and our need—as good readers and moral agents—to enter imaginatively into taking nonsense for sense in order to diagnose the confusion or understand the ethical impulse that lies at the source of that nonsense in the heart of its speaker. In the *Tractatus*, as we have seen, Wittgenstein seeks to disabuse us of our tendency to succumb to metaphysical nonsense. In the "Lecture on Ethics," however, he gives us new insights into the role of nonsense in his thinking: Nonsensicality, he says there, is the "very essence" of sentences with which we give voice to our ethical experience (LE, 44). As we saw in chapter 2, expressions of ethical experience or religious belief represent cases in which our linguistic intentions are such that what we want to say is essentially incompatible with making sense. As Diamond writes, "sometimes the purposes with which we speak would not be served by sentences that makes sense" ("Ethics and Imagination," 164). Any attempt to render an ethical sentence meaningful, Wittgenstein declares, he would reject, *ab initio*, "on the ground of its significance" (LE, 44). Nonsense that "springs from a desire to say something about the ultimate meaning of life," he continues, is a "document of a tendency of the human mind" that he "cannot help respecting deeply" (LE, 46). Diamond pays her own respects to the complex function of nonsense in our ethical lives through her attention to the riddles and difficulty so significant to the spirit of everyday reality.

Beauty Is Strong. Non-being Sprawls.

In her essay on the difficulty of reality, Diamond draws on Cavell's reflections in "Notes and Afterthoughts on the Opening of Wittgenstein's *Investigations*" on the philosophical difficulty of seeing the obvious, and how this difficulty bears on the hardness of philosophy.[95] "What is the everyday, that it is so hard to achieve?" she asks. "It is within the everyday that there lie the forms and varieties of repudiation of our language-games and distance from them, the possibility of being tormented by the hiddenness, the separateness, the otherness of others" (DR, 77). An integral part of what makes the experience of such difficulty so traumatizing or astounding is this: what the shouldered-out person sees as incomprehensible (whether it is awesome or astonishing in its beauty or grace or agonizing in its horror) is seen by others as utterly banal. What haunts the person in the throes of a difficulty she takes to be not fittable-in with the world as she understands it, that is, may leave others entirely unfazed. A person who suffers such a difficulty is thus cut off from other people, suffering also in (and from) solitude. As Mulhall puts it, "difficulties of reality thereby serve to isolate individuals, disclosing others as opaque to them and themselves as opaque to others; reality's resistance to our understanding reveals us as essentially resistant to one another's understanding."[96]

In *To the Lighthouse*, Woolf grapples with a reality marked by such difficulty. She first creates a community of characters who are all, to different degrees, isolated from one another and ambivalent in their desire for contact, each laboring continuously to guard his or her own individual privacy in the "inadequacy" and "extreme obscurity" of human relationships, "all of them bending themselves to listen," Woolf writes, thinking, "pray heaven that the inside of my mind may not be exposed" (TL, 96). The central figures of Woolf's novel nonetheless reach out to make vital contact with each other, striving in vain to gain access to what Lily Briscoe describes as the "dome-shaped hive" of their sealed inner lives. They yearn to enter the chambers of other minds, to read the "tablets bearing their sacred inscriptions," which if deciphered could "teach one everything," but which remain private (KA, 67; TL, 175, 43, 54). Woolf's free indirect technique of entering into the minds of her characters also reveals the difficulties they have communicating significant ethical experience. Lily's desire to wake up Mr. Carmichael to share with him a sense of nostalgia communicated through an expression of wonder at what Wittgenstein calls the "existence of language itself" is thwarted by her realization that

> one only woke people if one knew what one wanted to say to them. And she wanted to say not one thing, but everything. Little words that broke up the thought and dismembered it said nothing. "About life, about death; about Mrs. Ramsay"—no, she thought, one could say nothing to nobody. The urgency of the moment always missed its mark. Words fluttered sideways and struck the object inches too low. (TL, 178)

In her essay, as I have said, Diamond explores a range of phenomena to describe the difficulty of reality she has in mind. And although her first examples deal with the traumas of life and death and the horror of what we do to animals, she also includes in her account "instances of goodness or beauty [that] can throw us" (DR, 60). One of the things Woolf offers at the center of her elegiac novel is a sense of general astonishment and awe at the existence of beauty and a yearning not only somehow to grasp its mystery and grace, but to come to terms with the depth of its loss. The beauty at the center of the novel is represented most fully in the figure of Mrs. Ramsay (whom Prue pronounces "the thing in itself," Mr. Bankes "the happier Helen of our days," and Mr. Ramsay "the beauty of the world" [TL, 118, 51, 40]). The sight of her "reading a fairy tale to her boy" has on Mr. Bankes "precisely the same effect as the solution to a scientific problem" (TL, 51). Her presence gives rise in Mr. Bankes to the kind of existential questions it brings out in Lily Briscoe, but which would otherwise not occupy him: "Is human life like this? Is human life like that?" (91). Bankes declares her beauty, her face, "incongruous," yet "there she was" (TL, 13).

By offering us the reflections of the characters for whom the range of phenomena associated with the difficulty of reality is a pressing issue, Woolf also shows us that the reality of the Ramsay's thriving world in "The Window" is one whose integrity war and death and the passage of time are always poised radically to alter if not obliterate. In a precursor to the enigmatic narrative of "Time Passes," the Ramsays' middle daughter, Nancy (who shares her mother's photographic consciousness and sense of the contingency of life as well as a Wittgensteinian affinity for the sense of fantastic, cosmic magic, and sometimes monstrous God-like power explored in the Grimm tale Mrs. Ramsay reads to James), stands alone over a tidal pool, intermittently casting "vast clouds over [the] tiny world by holding her hand against the sun" and bringing "darkness and desolation, like God himself, to millions of ignorant and innocent creatures," before taking her hand away to let the sun stream down again. The interlude continues, from Nancy's perspective:

> Out on the pale criss-crossed sand, high-stepping, fringed, gauntleted, stalked some fantastic leviathan (she was still enlarging the pool), and slipped into the vast fissures of the mountain side. And then . . . she became with all that power sweeping savagely in and inevitably withdrawing, hypnotized, and the two senses of that vastness and this tininess . . . flowering within it made her feel that she was bound hand and foot and unable to move by the intensity of feelings which reduced her own body, her own life, and the lives of all the people in the world, for ever, to nothingness. (TL, 78)

The narration of Nancy's interlude with being, nothingness, fate, and will on the beach is given to the reader as a lengthy parenthetical account that begins with the peevish narrative from the girl's perspective of how she was diverted from her attempt to retreat to the privacy of her attic, "to escape the horrors of family life." Instead of retreating into solitude, she is conscripted into the role of a third-wheel chaperone to Paul Rayley and Minta Doyle, destined for marriage at Mrs. Ramsay's Angel-in-the-House urging. Chapter 14, set off from the rest of the narrative by parentheses, both takes place at a physical remove from the family's house and represents a kind of narrative aside, occurring as it does in the interstices between Mrs. Ramsay's question "Did Nancy go with them?" at the end of chapter 13, and chapter 15, which contains only Prue's more considered affirmation that she thinks she did. Shut out of the lovers' intimacy, Nancy seeks her own privacy, letting "that couple look after themselves" (TL, 78). Seeking the solitude pursued by all the adult characters in the novel, she wades out to "her own rocks" and searches for "her own pools" (TL, 78). Before the tide can rush in to cut the party off from the shore and "cover the place where they had sat in a minute," Nancy distracts herself by creating, out of a pool of anemones and minnows, a fabulist's microcosm that bears all the weight of the world (TL, 79). "We might all sit down and cry, she felt. But she did not know what for" (TL, 80). In this parenthetical chapter, Woolf adds a measure of poignant affect to Mrs. Ramsay's quiet dread at the island's eventual "engulfment in the sea" and Mr. Ramsay's consideration of his fate as "a desolate sea bird, alone," "on a spit of land which the sea is slowly eating away" (TL, 20, 47).

If Diamond's "difficulty of reality" finds a central locus in *To the Lighthouse*, its punctum is surely to be found in moments like the one we get in this parenthetical episode. But it is more deeply rooted still in the abrupt, bracketed reports of the deaths of Mrs. Ramsay, Andrew, and Prue in "Time Passes." That these death notices stand in apparent contrast with the content of that section's final bracketed statement— which delivers news of Mr. Carmichael's successful volume of poems ("the war, it seems, had revived people's interest in poetry") is a question I will return to in relation to Woolf's own successful postwar volume in this chapter's conclusion (TL, 138).

A Source of Our Gratitude to Poetry

The sudden incursion of these asides into the quizzical narrative, "eyeless and so terrible," of a world falling into and being "fetched up" from oblivion, underscores Nancy's apprehension of the insignificance, when seen against the vastness of the universe, of individual human beings— even of those who have been, but moments ago, absolutely alive and absolutely significant to the fictive community for which they were central, as they have been for the reader, engaged imaginatively in that community (TL, 143). The shocking impact of these understated reports of bracketed death thus also gives readers a sense of the "contradictory permanent horrors" of a difficulty of reality and works to shoulder them out from their experience of the world of the novel (thus far).

As we have seen, when describing the difficulty of reality, Diamond turns to literary examples that depict the bewildering phenomenon as a profound anomalous disturbance of the soul, a shocking experience of horror, grace, or beauty, that is anchored in a concrete, particular event or object (a photograph, a dead infant, the industrial slaughter of animals farmed for human consumption, a seemingly miraculous act of sacrifice, the architecture of a tree). In *To the Lighthouse*, however, the difficulty of reality is more or less untethered from any acute particular event in the story and haunts the novel in a pervasive, general way. By offering us a novel whose most significant affective experience is the uncanny feeling of living in a present "now" run through with the melancholy foresight of an uncertain future in which that "now" is preserved photographically as a past moment of loss—suspended, incomplete, and imperfect—Woolf speaks to the predicament of human existence more broadly.

The difficulty of reality is present in the onslaught of darkness and undoing of "Time Passes," and the searching, enigmatic existential questions that pervade it. Indeed, the difficulty of reality makes itself known from the novel's very beginning. The "horrible permanent contradictions" within it take root in the tension between the "yes . . . but" of the book's opening lines. The sense of possibility that Mrs. Ramsay puts forth in her comforting response to her youngest child's implicit question (can we go to the lighthouse?): "Yes, of course, if it's fine tomorrow," is quickly staunched by her husband's denial of the antecedent of his wife's *modus ponens*, her "way that affirms by affirming": "but it won't be fine" (TL, 8). Mr. Ramsay damns his wife for hiding from their children that "life is difficult," by saying things that "flew in the face of facts, made his children hope what was utterly out of the question, in effect, told lies" (TL, 35). Mrs. Ramsay, as we have seen, is herself deeply aware of "that lie"—that we are all in the hands of the Lord, as well as the lie implicit in her generously hopeful phrases and repeated promise to James. For the sense of possibility that she presents to her son and represents for her whole entourage is one she proffers in order to shield them from the darker and more threatening sense of possibility she herself intuits: that it won't be at all fine tomorrow, that the uncertain future is perhaps but an abyss.

Mrs. Ramsay's sense of possibility is always infused with an uncanny prescience of the passage of time as leading to potential annihilation, a ringing down of unimaginable death or oblivion on a world of people so visibly present and alive. Her difficulty of reality has to do with the strange sense that all that is alive and flourishing before her "has now come to an end," is over and done with, that "the lights of the town and of the harbour and of the boats seemed like a phantom net floating there to mark something which had sunk" (TL, 85, 71). Already.

The difficulty of reality is likewise present in Mr. Ramsay's recognition of "all sorts of horrors," in his melodramatic "phrase-making" about the "poor little world," and in the refrains from Tennyson and Cowper he is overheard to recite in his moments of broken privacy (and which Woolf echoes pointedly in "Time Passes" [TL, 72–73]).[97]

In the first section of the novel, Mr. Ramsay is seen intermittently lumbering across the lawn, thundering phrases from Tennyson's "Charge of the Light Brigade." He bears down repeatedly on his family and invited guests while "boom[ing] tragically" his pronouncements about "shot and shell" and riding "through the valley of death" before turning abruptly to slam "his private door on them" (TL, 154, 29). Mr. Ramsay's shouts about blunders, search parties, and shipwrecks in the novel attest to more than just a need for an elevated script through which to dramatize his plight and ventriloquize his distinguishing tyrannical need for sympathy. For his deep acquaintance with Cowper's "The Castaway," with its "obscurest night" in which all "transient respite past" and "toil subdued," "we perish'd, each alone," provides him with the words to express the pain of his loss and his sense of human separateness and isolation "in a world of woe" (TL, 156). What Cavell says at the end of "Knowing and Acknowledging" about the relationship between the privacy of the self and a human need (indeed a thankfulness) for poetry speaks deftly to Mr. Ramsay's connection to the fragmented lines he delivers throughout the novel, as well as to the dignity and humanity that Woolf accords the novel's otherwise often irritating patriarch (based, of course, on her father). "A natural fact underlying the philosophical problem of privacy," Cavell writes,

> is that the individual will take *certain* among his experiences to represent his *own* mind—certain particular sins or shames or surprises of joy—and then take his mind (his self) to be unknown so far as *those* experiences are unknown. . . . There is a natural problem of *making* such experiences known, not merely because behavior as a whole may seem irrelevant (or too dumb, or gross) at such times, but because one hasn't forms of words at one's command to release those feelings, and hasn't anyone else whose interest in helping to find the words one trusts. (Someone would have to *have* these feelings to know what I feel.) Here is a source of our gratitude to poetry. (KA, 265–66)

Mr. Bankes describes Mr. Ramsay early in the novel as a man "hung round with the solitude which seemed his natural air" (TL, 24). His effusions of bits of poetry provide him with a public, canonical conduit for his otherwise private feeling about war, love, and loss. By quoting poetic phrases written by others, phrases that sum up an experience he recognizes to be somehow like his own, he finds a solution to the problem of making his inner experience known to others. His eruptions of representative phrases from poetry grant brief glimpses into an interior life that he releases to his intimates only on these performative occasions.

Mr. Ramsay's sudden recitation of Charles Isaac Elton's "A Garden Song" contributes to the cohesion of a happier communal moment at the end of the dinner scene in "The Window." Mr. Ramsay's oration of the little-known poem engages the whole party, even the otherwise silent and sphinx-like Augustus Carmichael (who is moved to emerge from his characteristic silence and immobility to utter the poem's final lines, bowing to Mrs. Ramsay as she departs the scene). For Mrs. Ramsay, the words her husband recites first seem meaningless, "cut off from them all, as if no one had said them, but they had come into existence of themselves." "She didn't know what they meant," Woolf's narrative continues, but she eventually finds herself communing with them nonetheless. For "like music, the words seemed to be spoken by her own voice, outside her self, saying quite easily and naturally what had been in her mind the whole evening while she said different things" (TL, 112–13).

Mr. Ramsay's inscrutable channeling of poetic phrases by Tennyson, Cowper, and Elton becomes his mode of seeking what Cavell calls acknowledgment from his closest others. These same others, his youngest children in particular, suffer the pain of Mr. Ramsay's tendency to withhold his acknowledgment from them. What James and Cam look for in their father is something all the characters in Woolf's novel search for in each other: a form of acknowledgment that entails a recognition (rather than an evasion) of others, and a responsiveness to (and a sense of responsibility for) their experience of independent personhood. This experience includes the feelings they are inclined to suppress, or that they find hard to put into words (their pain and suffering, for example, their love, longing, and sense of finitude).

Malheur

Mrs. Ramsay's sense of these things is something we see in her attunement to the "darkness, spreading and unfathomably deep," of a general difficulty of reality that few others around her see or understand. It is marked by an awareness of what Simone Weil calls "affliction" ("unhappiness," "woe"—*malheur*) (TL, 65). Diamond calls our attention in her essay to Weil's notion that human thought is unable to acknowledge the reality of affliction [*malheur*]. To acknowledge the reality of affliction means saying to oneself: "I may lose at any moment, through the play of circumstances over which I have no control, anything whatsoever that I possess, including those things which are so intimately mine that I consider them as being myself. There is nothing that I might not lose. It could happen at any moment that what I am might be abolished and replaced by anything whatsoever of the filthiest and most contemptible sort." To be aware of this in the depth of one's soul is to experience non-being.[98]

In Simone Weil, Diamond finds an example of a philosopher who saw the difficulty of her philosophical work as the difficulty of *keeping to* the awareness of affliction and of the difficulty of reality, of not being "deflected" from it, in Cavell's sense, by turning to established related philosophical or moral debates and arguments apparently in the vicinity as a way of resolving the problem at hand.[99] One of Diamond's primary aims in her "Difficulty" essay is to examine the ways in which certain works of literature can remain similarly engaged in a mode of understanding difficulties of reality that may be present "only in a diminished and distorted way in philosophical argumentation" that gives in to a tendency to turn what Cavell calls a "metaphysical finitude"—a limit or difficulty of the human condition so painful that it unseats reason, into an "intellectual lack" or a factual problem (KA, 68; DR, 69). Professional philosophy, Diamond points out, certainly knows how to deal with hard problems. But the hardness of a difficulty of reality is of a different order of difficulty from the hardness of a philosophical argument (DR, 58).

It is the non-being Weil speaks of that Mrs. Ramsay experiences as she vacillates between a sense of coherence, plenitude, and freedom ("It is enough! It is enough!") on the one hand and doom as a wedge-shaped core of darkness on the other in her solitary reverie, and which Nancy experiences as a sense of nothingness before the tidal pool (TL, 68). It is this non-being that encroaches on Woolf's narrative in the bracketed reports of "Time Passes." That Mr. Carmichael's creation of a volume of poetry, with its power to fill a need for the postwar audience, should also be reported in these same brackets, however, provokes important questions about Woolf's own sense of the power of literature in a postwar context—her literature in its context—to offer a creative, productive salve to combat the difficulty and affliction she takes up in her novel (and this includes the skeptical problem of her surviving characters' opacity to each other). I want to probe, by way of conclusion, this question, which seems especially pressing when considered alongside Diamond's own questions about how certain works of literature can be more adept in their treatment of the philosophical complexities of our ethical experience of the world than certain applied philosophical approaches and theories can be.

Conclusion: We Remain

A few weeks after *Mrs. Dalloway* appeared in 1925, Woolf wrote down her now-famous speculation about a new name for her future work, a generic designation to supplant "novel": "A new _____ by Virginia Woolf. But what? Elegy?"[100] Christine Froula has argued that in *Mrs. Dalloway* and *To the Lighthouse*, Woolf adapts the tradition of pastoral elegy to a more modern public elegy, transposing to prose fiction the elegiac form of postwar mourning and moving on to (Milton's) fresh woods and pastures new.[101] I want to end here by reflecting on the ways in which *To the Lighthouse* is a work in which a search for lost time *does* become a therapeutic means of reanimating the novel's present (and Woolf's own). But attending to Woolf's elegiac project as one that entails struggles with difficulties of reality, in Diamond's sense, helps us to see that if the novel resolves with a productive sense of creative possibility, it is not quite because it aims to *console*. Rather, Woolf plumbs the depths of life's most painful and confounding difficulty and contingency and only then offers "some incorrigible hope" "twined about her dirge" (TL, 135). There are no fresh woods and pastures new for the Ramsays or even for Lily Briscoe. Only the same "poor little place," now "much changed" (TL, 72, 152). What Woolf offers us in the place of a neat, fully consoling resolution to her surviving characters' attempts to emerge from their mutual isolation and affliction—through continued questions and quests for vision and unity—combines a transposed Russian commitment to inconclusiveness with a sort of frayed fairy-tale ending to a novel in which the power of fairy-tale magic has served as a consistent leitmotif: Woolf sets the scene of separateness by endowing it with a magical simultaneity and parallel perspective (James, Cam, and Mr. Ramsay in the boat, making their long-postponed ritual trip to the lighthouse, and Lily with her long-postponed painting on the lawn). It is not an enchanted flounder in Woolf's story, as it is in the Grimms', but a mutilated mackerel that is thrown back into the sea. Nor is the integrity of this world threatened by a fantastic leviathan, as Nancy's tidal pool microcosmos is; Woolf's novel tells the story of ordinary people struggling only with the "formidable ancient enemy" of "truth" and "reality" (TL, 162). By and by the standstill at the center of the book's final section, in which all parties are stuck (the boat in the Mariner's windless harbor and Lily puzzling before the "hideously difficult white space" of an empty canvas), is magically broken, as if to make way for a transformative forward movement toward the final culmination of their respective projects, and with it the evolution of the characters themselves toward an improved mutual understanding they reach only through their shared individual experience of the difficulty of reality (TL, 186–90, 163).

But does Woolf solve the problem of other minds so central to her novel by establishing a long-sought unity among her characters? Not quite. Mr. Ramsay, for one, remains mysterious and unknown, still guarding his privacy and "conducting some secret symphony" as he makes his leap onto the lighthouse rock as if proclaiming: "there is no God." "What he thought they none of them knew" (TL, 193). From his youngest children's point of view, "he might be thinking, We perished, each alone, or he might be thinking I have reached it, I have found it; but he said nothing" (TL, 191, 210). Does Woolf "get at the truth of things" through Lily's culminating vision? Not exactly. Lily's revelation endures for but a fleeting epiphanic moment. It represents an "attempt at something that must be perpetually revisited and remade." It has, after all, taken four separate moments of revelation and composition over a period of more than a decade for Lily to "smooth out something she had been given . . . years ago, folded up; something she had seen" and represent it "with a sudden intensity, as if she saw it clear for a second" in the line at the center of her completed painting (TL, 211). Her vision, in spite of its position in the novel, signaling finality and apparent plenitude, is still a revision. Her search, the narrative suggests, will continue even in its wake.

What Woolf *does* do by the end of the novel is to make us think about how the experience of the difficulty of reality, although it may isolate us from others, in certain cases, or to certain degrees, can also work to bring people together in shared acknowledgment. Through this acknowledgment we find kinship with others, and a sympathy that lies not only with the mind—"for it is easy with the mind," Woolf reminds us, quoting Militsina—"but with the heart. With love towards them" (RPV, 183). Woolf's masterful representation in her novel of multiple overlapping consciousnesses allows us to enter imaginatively into the lives of others in the way that Diamond describes as central to the ethical teaching of the *Tractatus*, and which Simone de Beauvoir cites as the miracle of literature—its power to give us the "taste of another life," and

insights into the perspective of the other that help to bridge the separation between human beings.[102]

What Woolf leaves us with at the close of *To the Lighthouse* is the
"incorrigible hope" of a continued (and shared) engagement with ambivalence and ambiguity, with others who remain remote to us, questions that remain unanswered, quests that are always incomplete, and
visions that are always revisions. All these questions go sounding on,
long after the novel has ended. And it is with these questions and quests,
Woolf seems to say, that separately and yet somehow, alongside one another, "we remain" (TL, 133).[103]

4

Wittgenstein, Joyce, and the Vanishing Problem of Life

At first I thought the questions pointless and irrelevant. I felt . . . I would find all the answers. But the questions repeated themselves over and again, demanding answers with more and more urgency. They fell like full stops, always on the same spot, uniting in one large black spot.
—Leo Tolstoy[1]

He reflected on the pleasures derived from literature of instruction rather than amusement as he himself had applied to the works of William Shakespeare more than once for the solution of difficult problems in imaginary or real life.

Had he found their solution?

In spite of careful and repeated reading of certain classical passages, aided by a glossary, he had derived imperfect conviction from the text, the answers not bearing on all points.
—James Joyce[2]

We feel that even if *all possible* scientific questions are answered, the problems of life have still not been touched at all. Of course there is then no question left, and this is just the answer. The solution of the problem of life is seen in the vanishing of this problem. (Is not this the reason why men to whom after long doubting the sense of life became clear, could not say wherein this sense consisted?)
—Ludwig Wittgenstein[3]

The Formulation of the Question

I ended the previous chapter with attention to Woolf's treatment of what it is "to remain," to survive in the present and into the future by living among others with whom we are bound, even in our alterity, isolation and ambivalence, in mutual acknowledgment and a shared investment in questions and quests. In this chapter, I turn to an examination of the "Ithaca" chapter of Joyce's *Ulysses* read alongside Wittgenstein's *Tractatus* in an effort to explore Wittgenstein's thinking about the need to overcome these same questions.

The pairing of the *Tractatus* and "Ithaca" would seem to be one of rather strange bedfellows. In the first text, we have a solemn aphoristic philosophical meditation on language and world, which famously culminates in an ostensibly epiphanic, stylized authoritative pronouncement ("what one cannot speak about one must be silent about"). The other presents us with a tongue-in-cheek impersonal catechism that unfolds in a single episode of a novel with epic ambitions, in a chapter whose long series of questions and answers ends abruptly. It is narrative progression and dramatic climax lost amid the garbled refrain of a final somniloquy curtailed by an outsized punctuation mark: a full stop. In some ways, "Ithaca" constitutes an ending for Joyce's novel. Joyce wrote of it as "in reality the end, as 'Penelope' [Molly Bloom's soliloquy in the book's final chapter] has no beginning, middle or end," as Molly weaves and unweaves the tapestry of her life.[4] Indeed, "Ithaca" was the last chapter of the book that Joyce composed. "In its role as conclusion to *Ulysses*," Andrew Gibson writes, "the chapter even ostentatiously parades the fact that all its questions have answers. Yet it remains none the less anticlimactic and inconclusive for that."[5] As Frank Kermode writes in *The Sense of an Ending*, realist Joyce (admired by T. S. Eliot for modernizing myth, and attacked by Wyndham Lewis for celebrating mess) "chooses a Day; it is a crisis ironically treated. The day is full of randomness. There are coincidences, meetings that have a point, and coincidences which do not. We might ask whether one of the merits of the book is not its *lack* of mythologizing." For Joyce's commitment to the novel's unfinishedness is still evident in the novel as Molly weaves and unweaves the tapestry with which she makes sense of her life.[6]

I bring these two disparate texts together here in a continued effort in this book to account for how studies in Wittgenstein can shed light on the literature of the modernist context from which his own thinking emerged, and how high-modernist literature, in turn, can offer us a better understanding of Wittgenstein's aesthetic commitments as a thinker and writer, as well as of the ethical stakes and aims of his philosophical method. Looking at Wittgenstein and Joyce together casts certain features of Joyce's project in a new philosophical light that also grants us insights into literary modernism more broadly. But just what is it about the Joyce of *Ulysses* that makes him a worthy interlocutor for the Wittgenstein of the *Tractatus*? And why turn to the "Ithaca" episode in particular in an effort to make the two texts communicate in fruitful ways?

Beginning with a characteristically Ithacan inventory of the concerns common to the *Tractatus* and the penultimate chapter of *Ulysses* can help us understand what looking at them together has to tell us about each of these texts and their modernist context. So, we might ask, in an Ithacan vein, what parallel courses do Wittgenstein and Joyce follow? What points of contact exist between them? (U, 666, 689).

Both are dedicated to exploring the questions and quests associated with what Joyce's protagonist, Leopold Bloom, calls a "different order of difficulty" through the mundanely difficult "propositions of natural science" (TLP, 6.53). Both rely (Joyce's chapter to a more "jocoserious" degree) on (pseudo-)scientific precision in their treatment of matters of the soul—precision intimately related to both the search for the meaning of life and a striving to make the decisive shift in ethical attitude that will lead to living it in the best way (TLP, 6.521; U, 677). In spite of their apparent exclusivity, both challenging texts reflect their authors' shared aspirations for their qualified universality. Both rely on a performance or parody of dogma, didacticism, and appeal to the language and tone of scripture alongside that of science and logic.

Wittgenstein and Joyce both treat with suspicion the notion that systematic solutions can ever adequately put to rest the questions that they deal with in the predominantly cold prose of their texts. They offer methods aimed at transforming their readers' understanding of the questions we ask when we want to express our astonishment at the world or our curiosity about it. The transformation they prompt us to make also involves getting us to imagine what it might look like to *overcome* our attachment to these same questions. Both distinguish the responses we seek to these "Big" life concerns from the kind of senseful propositions that offer explanations of how things stand, for example, or that appeal to the laws of physics, or to useful definitions, the rules of translation, and so on. Both texts induce us to imagine that we can get from a book a comprehensive description of the world, or the answers to "all scientific questions," thereby getting us to see that no such book can provide us with the answers we seek when we pose existential questions. Both Wittgenstein and Joyce implicitly challenge readers to figure out their respective authorial (and deauthorizing) strategies as well as the puzzling relationship of their differently constructed faux doctrines to the literary, ethical, and philosophical aims of their works. Both are structured in the form of a catalogue of ordered assertions, questions, and answers that give the appearance of progressing toward a final conclusion that is ultimately withheld by the author.

Reading "Ithaca" with Wittgenstein in mind allows us to consider, within a wider modernist context, Joyce's decision to give the chapter the catechetical structure that he does. In "Ithaca," he conveys the affective aspects of Bloom's homecoming at the end of the male narrative of his modern quest epic through the medium of the coolly rational exchange (one that also acts as a send-up of a coolly rational exchange) afforded by the extended question-and-answer technique he described as a "mathematical," "impersonal catechism."[7] While the drama (or anti-drama) of the final lines of "Ithaca" pales in comparison to the bombshell of Wittgenstein's declaration of the nonsense of his text's constitutive sentences, the homecoming episode of *Ulysses* nonetheless culminates in a surprise ending that similarly flouts the reader's longing for closure. The chapter's long series of questions and answers—which considers an array of domestic, scientific, and spiritual problems; "difficulties of interpretation"; "hypothetical solutions"; and possible futures—comes to an exaggerated and abrupt full stop at the end of the chapter as Bloom falls into the sleep and dreams that give him temporary relief from the questions and quests that have occupied him throughout the course of the novel (U, 676, 686).

I have argued throughout this book that the *Tractatus* is a peculiarly modernist puzzle text, one that challenges its readers to engage in a philosophical activity of clarification that can help them to handle the most difficult questions of life, the search for their solutions, and the longing for transformative insights. Seeing the *Tractatus* as a modernist puzzle allows us to recognize Wittgenstein's investment in a set of interrelated issues that I take to be some of the fundamental concerns of the deliberately crafted group of monuments of modernist thought and literature of which Wittgenstein's *Tractatus* and Joyce's *Ulysses* (in their different ways—and according to different critical and historical criteria) have become recognized exemplars.

The central concerns of works of this high-modernist genre come into sharper relief in the passages from Tolstoy, Wittgenstein, and Joyce that serve as opening epigraphs to this chapter. I will return to a discussion of these excerpted passages below. For now, I want to call attention to the ways in which they each bring up some of the central concerns I explore in this book: textual and existential difficulty; ethical instruction and the work of self-improvement; a striving for personal transformation or transfiguration; a longing for revelations about, a deeper understanding of (or even liberation from), the weighty problems of life, the search for its meaning and for solutions that often prove intangible or inadequate. As the passages that serve as epigraphs above attest, Tolstoy's, *Confession*, Joyce's *Ulysses*, and Wittgenstein's *Tractatus* each explore a longing for answers, solutions, or transformative insights. In the end, though, the only answer they arrive at in the excerpts presented in the epigraphs is that no answer bears entirely on the questions they pose. The answers they seek are not the answers they find.

Tolstoy's autobiographical treatment of his own personal crisis of being, purpose, and faith, and subsequent search for understanding and meaning, adheres to the genre of the confessional narrative that tends toward an ultimate fulfilling revelation. In "Ithaca," Joyce hesitates before such revelation, ending the chapter with inarticulate muffled words and an exaggerated full stop. Wittgenstein leaves it to readers to continue to pursue the task toward which he aims to lead them in the *Tractatus*: to climb the ladder of the book's propositions and to figure out, once we've reached the top, what kind of clarifying insight comes with throwing that ladder away.

Each of the three writers uses a pedagogical method elaborated on the human project of asking and seeking with the aim of leading their readers toward a new kind of clarity about language and life by transforming our relation to the questions we ask and the answers that will satisfy us. Some elaboration of momentary epiphanic experience plays a role in each of these authors' works. Or, to put it more aptly, the instructive methods of each involve urging their readers to keep alive the insights that such passing revelatory moments can offer, in such a way that they can have a more lasting transformative effect on readers' general perspective and the kind of attention we pay to life and the world.

Epiphany and Counter-epiphany

As we saw in chapter 3, Virginia Woolf details the epiphanic experience that informs her own thinking in descriptions of what she calls "moments of being." But it is of course Joyce who is most closely associated with this sort of "sudden spiritual manifestation," since it was he who first gave a literary application to the word "epiphany," the sublime moment of presence pursued in so many works of modernist fiction (most notably by such writers as Conrad, Joyce, Woolf, Mansfield, Proust, Faulkner, Rilke, Mann, and others). Derived from the Greek, in which it signifies a manifestation of the divine, in Christian theology it represents a hidden message offered for the salvation of others and refers to the celebration of the revelation of Jesus's divinity to the Magi. Joyce gave the name "epiphany" to a set of short sketches he wrote from 1898 to 1904. Although he left off writing these sketches after January 1904, the epiphany was to become a central mode of the early stories he published in *Dubliners*. In *Stephen Hero*, an early version of *A Portrait of the Artist as a Young Man*, Joyce's character, Stephen Dedalus, believes epiphanies to be "most delicate and evanescent of moments," something for a man of letters to handle with care.[8] He sums up the epiphany to his friend Cranly as a sudden, momentary showing forth of a person's authentic self, "whether in the vulgarity of speech or of gesture or in a memorable phase of the mind itself" (SH, 211). As Stephen explains it, building on Aquinas, the sublimity of the epiphany can be rooted in an object, which "epiphanises" when its *quidditas*, its "whatness," shows forth:

> First we recognise that the object is one integral thing, then we recognise that it is an organised composite structure, a thing in fact: finally, when the relation of the parts is exquisite, when the parts are adjusted to the special point, we recognise that it is that thing which it is. Its soul, its whatness, leaps to us from the vestment of its appearance. The soul of the commonest object, the structure of which is so adjusted, seems to us radiant. The object achieves its epiphany. (SH, 212)[9]

Wittgenstein's interest in epiphanic experience is evident in his own writing, and especially apparent in his sporadic remarks about seeing the everyday world *sub specie aeternitatis*. But as we shall see below, this way of seeing the world is not, for Wittgenstein, a strictly epiphanic one. For what Wittgenstein is after in his thinking about the value of seeing the world against the background of eternity and all logical form is not a mere momentary experience of capturing the essence of the world as if from a position of relative remove. What he is trying to get readers to do is achieve a long-term transformation in our way of *seeing* the ordinary world around us. This way of seeing, he suggests, is made available to us by works of art, and the modes of aesthetic contemplation they solicit from us.

Like Woolf's exploration of a modern sublime experience she describes in terms of raptures, ecstasies, and "moments of being," Wittgenstein's consideration of the ephemeral experience of the sublimity of the world viewed *sub specie aeternitatis* is conducted with the grander ambition of transforming our outlook on the model of such moments of aesthetic contemplation, and making these moments compel us to see the world differently on a more ongoing basis. The sublime moments Woolf experiences as a child and discusses in *A Sketch of the Past* ultimately act as catalysts to her writing life. The "shocks" and "blows" that marked her past existence are experiences she works to transfigure (and thereby redeem) in her literary art, art in which she seeks in turn to offer a picture of the world that can transform our understanding of life. And Wittgenstein thought that a philosophical work—his *Tractatus*, for example—could be as powerful as a work of art when it comes to transforming the way we look on the world.

What I have been building up to here is that it is important to see that although modes of epiphany do function in both Joyce's and Wittgenstein's writing, whatever revelation their texts seek ultimately to leave us with, it is not an epiphanic one. One of my main claims in this chapter is that Wittgenstein's and Joyce's different modernist treatments of searches for answers turn on their use of *counter-epiphanic* aesthetic strategies that run against much received wisdom about modernism (including its attraction to epiphany) and both authors' relationships to it. The works of both authors are ultimately directed not at grasping after fleeting epiphanic insights but at getting readers to make a more lasting change, one that depends on imaginatively considering what it would be like to step back from our questions and let go of our quests for answers.

Joyce's move away from the attention he paid to the figure of the epiphany in his earlier writing and toward an exploration in *Ulysses* of searches for the lasting understanding and sense of being at home in one's language and world runs parallel to the transition that occurs between Wittgenstein's early and later work in the philosophical method with which he approaches the search for clarity. I trace the shared aspects of Wittgenstein's and Joyce's respective counter-epiphanic, transfigurative aesthetic practices here with an eye to attending, toward this chapter's conclusion, to the important differences between their respective projects.

I will return to a discussion here of Wittgenstein's statements about the worldview he calls "happy" in the *Tractatus*, and in the philosophical notebooks he kept between 1914 and 1917. Entries in both texts attest to the influence of Tolstoy's *Gospel in Brief* and *A Confession* on Wittgenstein's thinking as he composed the *Tractatus* during the First World War. As we saw in the context of Diamond's and Woolf's different treatments of the Grimm Brothers' tale "The Fisherman and His Wife" in the previous chapter, the opposing attitudes Wittgenstein calls "happy" and "unhappy" (expressive of an outlook of satisfaction and dissatisfaction, respectively) involve a creative kind of willing that radically changes a person's perspective in a way that thus also "changes the world" (TLP, 6.43). What Wittgenstein says about the "happy" is deeply connected to his notion of "seeing the world in the right way" and to his enigmatic statement that the solution to the problem of life is to be seen in only its vanishing.

In my discussion of Woolf, I examined the Grimm story's eponymous fisherman's wife, a character Diamond points to as exemplary of a person whose "deep dissatisfaction with the world's not meeting the conditions she lays down," one who expresses a deep and defining sort of discontent with the independence of the world from all that she herself would like to bring about and who therefore demonstrates an "unhappy" outlook on the world.[10] I then suggested that in spite of Mrs. Ramsay's deep sense of the connection of her fate with a potentially "terrible" force beyond her control, in *To the Lighthouse*, Woolf gives us a character who strives overtly to uphold a faith in possibility (in spite of her lack of belief in religious salvation) by facing an uncertain world with an attitude of acceptance and plenitude. Toward the end of this chapter, I go on to explore important ways in which Bloom, Joyce's own long-doubting, questioning, and questing modern "Everyman or Noman," becomes an unexpected literary exemplar of a person who looks on the world and its problems with this "happy" attitude (U, 727). Bloom's outlook is infused with a satisfaction born of an imaginative affirmation of his own life and quiet endorsement of it as a whole—its setbacks as well as its triumphs.

In his story of Bloom's own circuitous wanderings around Dublin and return home to 7 Eccles Street, I will argue below, Joyce gives us a literary representation of the kind of performance of the ordinary that Wittgenstein describes in a 1930 notebook entry. Wittgenstein's remark includes a thought experiment featuring "someone who thinks himself unobserved engaged in some quite simple everyday activity." "Let's imagine a theatre," he says. "The curtain goes up & we see someone alone in his room walking up and down . . . seating himself etc. so that suddenly we are observing a human being from outside in a way that we ordinarily can never observe ourselves. . . . We should be seeing life itself" (CV, 4). For Wittgenstein, a work of art (like Joyce's *Ulysses*, I will argue, though it is not a book Wittgenstein ever concerned himself with) can give us perspective from which to view the world *sub specie aeternitatis*.

The work of art compels us to look on things in the world not as "a piece of nature like any other," but as something worth contemplating aesthetically from the "right perspective," from the "outside," as Wittgenstein puts it (CV, 4).

Wittgenstein's aim in the *Tractatus* is to get readers to adopt such a stance toward our ordinary lives. One of the ways he seeks to do this in the book is by turning our attention toward the general form of a proposition, which gives us the rule by which all senseful propositions can be constructed (TLP, 6). Because the general form of proposition also expresses the possibility of every possible situation (everything that can happen and be the case), it thus gives us both language and world. The will of the ethical subject attaches to the language and world revealed by the general form of a proposition in one of two ways. We can yearn to find genuine value that we imagine lies out of our reach (beyond the limits of language and beyond the world of accident and happening and being the case Wittgenstein describes at proposition 6.41), and so face the world with sense of dissatisfaction or resignation. Or we can, as Diamond suggests, learn to "re-see" things, to occupy a figurative perspective from which the limits of language are but figurative constraints, and thereby gain a transformed perspective of the world seen figuratively from "outside" ("Limits of Sense," 261).

In Leopold Bloom, Joyce creates a fictive character who manages figuratively to "view the world as a limited whole," in Wittgenstein's sense. In the novel, Bloom regards the world (in which, as Wittgenstein says at proposition 6.41, everything is accidental, everything is as it is and happens as it happens) as an object worthy of aesthetic contemplation and ethical engagement. Joyce's Bloom is also a questing figure who finally manages to reach a point in the novel where he can "stand back," as it were, from what Diamond calls "the asking and answering of questions" that provides "Ithaca" with its proper catechetical form. And he does so with the recognition that "no satisfaction is to be had from any answer" ("Limits of Sense," 259–63).

Joyce's Odyssean Bloom is, as Emily Wilson's recent translation of the *Odyssey* puts it, a "complicated man" who "wandered and was lost." He is also Richmond Lattimore's "man of many ways." He is also Friedrich Nietzsche's creator and guesser of riddles and redeemer of accidents.[11] The state of relative peace in which we find Bloom at the end of *Ulysses*, I argue, speaks to the correspondences between Nietzsche's concept of redemption (as creative transfiguration) and Wittgenstein's (as ethical clarity). Both of these involve a kind of "re-seeing," one that itself depends on making a willed shift in attitude toward the world and one's questions. I argue further that the differences in Joyce's and Wittgenstein's divergent treatments of what Wittgenstein describes in the *Tractatus* as "seeing the world in the right way" not only shed light on the continuity of Wittgenstein's "early" and "late" philosophy; they also give us new purchase on the evolution of Wittgenstein's philosophical method from the *Tractatus* to the *Philosophical Investigations*.

Precision and Soul in the "Modernist Masterpiece"

In 1922, the year in which the *Tractatus* and *Ulysses* first appeared in book form, Wittgenstein's and Joyce's Austrian contemporary Robert Musil lamented what he called "an abiding miscommunication between the intellect [*Verstand*] and the soul [*Seele*]" that typifies the modern age. "We don't have too much intellect and too little soul," he continues, "but too little intellect in matters of the soul."[12]

Allan Janik, Stephen Toulmin, and Michael André Bernstein, among others, have likened Musil's philosophical commitments to Wittgenstein's in a variety of ways.[13] Like Wittgenstein, Bernstein emphasizes, Musil began his career in the sciences and consistently sought to distinguish his own brand of modernist writing by making a conscious effort "to combine a commitment to the most stringent principles of mathematical logic with a mystical yearning for a new, less alienated way of living," one that would integrate spiritual feeling and idea.[14] Musil drew on his technical, scientific, and mathematical training as well as his literary imagination to construct an ethical framework within which to grapple with the difficult questions associated with the search for an elusive understanding that would bring about what he speaks of in his complex unfinished novel, *Der Mann ohne Eigenschaften*, as "Das rechte Leben," the right life, the right way of living.[15]

Wittgenstein, for his part, sought to lead readers of his own logical-philosophical treatise to overcome philosophical confusion through an activity of clarification aimed at getting them to see "die Welt richtig," "the world in the right way" (TLP, 6.54). We can see Joyce as offering another response to Musil's call to combine precision and soul in modern letters in "Ithaca," the chapter that Joyce called a "mathematico-astronomico-physico-mechanico-geometrico-chemico sublimation of Bloom and Stephen (devil take 'em both)."[16] By speaking of sublimation here, Joyce thereby speaks to an effect of sublimity that is part of his purpose in the episode. In "Ithaca," he merges sublimation in the scientific sense (the chemical action of converting a solid into a vapor); sublimation in the sense of a transmutation into a purer substance, related to a kind of sublation close to a Hegelian *Aufhebung*; and sublimation as elation or ecstasy.

In "Ithaca," Bloom's and Stephen's thoughts, actions, and interactions are all rendered, as Joyce puts it, in their "cosmic physical, psychical . . . equivalents . . . so that . . . the reader [will] know everything and know it in the baldest, coldest way." Bloom and Stephen "thereby become heavenly bodies, wanderers like the stars at which they gaze."[17] In the arid interrogative mode of the Q&A he uses in "Ithaca," Joyce finds a meditative narrative technique that offers a poignant (and at times hilarious) depiction of Bloom's wanderings through an everyday fraught with questions big and small in his stargazing search for conclusive solutions that will put his all-too-human problems (of life and love, past and future) to rest.

Musil's call for a balanced relationship between the broad opposing nodes of "intellect" and "soul," along with the attention he pays in his writing not only to the inspiration of epiphany (that mainstay of critical modernism) but also to the more arduous and lasting quests for the *right way of living* and looking on the world that must go beyond such ephemeral epiphanic moments, testify together to what I see as an axial concern of the European high-modernist canon in which Wittgenstein's *Tractatus* and Joyce's *Ulysses* have come to figure so prominently. That is, an investment in transforming our ways of seeing the world and living in it, and a commitment to striving to rise to demands like the one articulated in the (deceptively straightforward) command Rilke issues in his "Archaïscher Torso Apollos": "Du mußt dein Leben ändern." You must change your life.[18] Because this persistent concern with transformation is especially pressing in a work like the *Tractatus*, which seeks to engage readers in the personal and philosophical work that will ultimately allow us to see "the world in the right way" (to put Wittgenstein's own grand gesture, his obscure directive, in a similar deceptively straightforward way), it is important to attend to it in our efforts to account for Wittgenstein's kinship with modernist literature.

Far from expressing just one man's idiosyncratic concern, then, Musil's postwar maxim points to a central preoccupation of a whole class of texts—Joyce's *Ulysses* and Wittgenstein's *Tractatus* chief among them—that Michael André Bernstein has identified as a distinct literary subgenre and historically circumscribed form unto itself: the self-consciously crafted "modernist masterpiece."[19]

In his attempt to articulate the stakes of the so-called modernist masterpiece as genre and goal, Bernstein isolates three imperatives to which representative works are answerable. The ambition (indeed, the *claim*) to satisfy these imperatives, taken together with the inexorable failure ultimately to do so, are definitive of the sort of works that fall under this category. Paying homage to the form of Wallace Stevens's "Notes toward a Supreme Fiction," Bernstein adds to the unofficial injunction that works of high modernist experimentation, in T. S. Eliot's words, "must be difficult," the further requirements that the modernist masterpiece "Must Seem Universal" and, finally, also "Must Be Redemptive."[20]

In spite of their apparent exclusivity, both Wittgenstein's and Joyce's challenging texts are crafted to reflect their authors' shared aspirations for achieving a qualified universality. Qualified, I say, because the availability of both texts is decidedly not immediate. Their accessibility turns on the rather arduous demands they place on readers, who must grapple with the different levels of difficulty active within them if they are ever to grasp successfully the insights their authors aim to convey and get readers to put into play in their lives. It is of course a main point of this book that the role of this attraction to the weighty questions of existence that becomes so pressing in early twentieth-century thought and literature comes into better view if we examine it in the context of its relationship to modernism's well-known obsession with difficulty. For the puzzles, riddles, and unanswered questions and quests for their solutions on which the signature texts of high modernism are so fixated function not only to hone the reader's intellect but also to call for intelligent work on what Musil calls the soul.

It is by beginning with attention to the first of these "musts"—difficulty, in all its complexity—that the interdependent relationship among these three requirements (and in turn their relationship to a Musilian call for sufficiently intellectual precision in matters of the soul) becomes clearest. For we see high modernism's trademark "requisite" difficulty—and Wittgenstein's unique deployment of it in the *Tractatus*—at its most acute and challenging when we examine the way it functions within narratives of universal human yearning (and attendant search) for meaning, enlightenment, and redemption.

I argue here that the searches for revelation and redemption that animate the works Bernstein designates as decidedly *modernist* masterpieces are carried out with the prior recognition that the revelation and redemption sought are hardly imminent. Clarity about, resolution of, or even deliverance from the age-old problems of life that such works offer often bear little resemblance to the goal conceived at the outset of the quest. The sense of a foregone inconclusiveness (deriving more from a pragmatic worldliness than from any straightforward pessimism or optimism) that haunts these texts is a definitive aspect of their modernism. To understand the project of modernist masterpiece-making as one that conforms to the last of Bernstein's "musts," then, we need to see that whatever redemptive power a representative modernist work can be said to possess is itself predicated on the ancillary demand that it must demonstrate a desire for redemption or improved understanding that may, in the end, never be satisfied. Bernstein's "must be redemptive" might be more aptly recast, then, as "must express a *longing* for redemption." For it is this sense of longing, I claim, rather than any final grasp of its elusive object or aim, that catalyzes the searches that proliferate in the "big" works of high modernism, especially Joyce's and Wittgenstein's. This longing for the peace and repletion that is redemption's promise is one that persists even in the face of redemption's possibly infinite deferral.

The notion of redemption for which texts like Wittgenstein's and Joyce's express a longing diverges from the Christian concept from which it nonetheless also draws. The concept of redemption at issue in each of their works is something I will examine in closer detail below with reference to the Nietzschean notions of redemption and transfiguration that R. Lanier Anderson clarifies in a deft discussion of these questions.[21]

Perennial Questions and Great Riddles

The "difficult problems in imaginary or real life" so central to Joyce's and Wittgenstein's texts give rise to the kind of unanswered questions that Maria DiBattista identifies as the "perennial questions" of "errant, questing beings," who venture out into the unknown world where the human drama of becoming unfolds.[22] These are the questions that haunt the modernist novel and leave intact the enigmas on which it turns. They are urgent, repetitive questions that "recur without respite, . . . preoccupy and often confound us because we can neither answer nor refrain from asking them."[23] Although such questions signal some of the foundational problems of philosophy and emerge in modernity to become the core questions of the human sciences, they become especially acute in the modernist novel, with its affinity for uncertainty, unknowing, and inconclusiveness.

DiBattista offers two examples of perennial questions to indicate the different kinds of perplexity (equally but differently generative of narrative movement and mystery) that such questions address. The first is the question of more a civic and spiritual order that Bloom asks in the Hades chapter, echoing Jesus in the Gospels: "Who is my neighbour?" (Luke 10:25–29; U, 77). That question is one that is always in need of new answers, none of which may ever be final. Because the answer it solicits must be "performed as well as thought," the ideal form for its answer to take, DiBattista points out, is the parable, whose meaning is never fixed. The form of response Christ adopts in answer to this question is the parable of the Good Samaritan. The second type of unanswerable perennial question DiBattista points to has to do with "love's bitter mystery" and the sadness and enigma of life and death. The example she provides is the disconsolate question Stephen comes out with as he recalls the scene of his mother's crying on her deathbed: "Where now?" Whether or not such a forlorn question can have an answer, DiBattista notes that it does have a future in "Ithaca," since it prefigures the last question the novel asks its peripatetic hero, Bloom, at the end of the chapter: "Where?" (U, 607).[24]

Cora Diamond has called such questions the "great riddles."[25] She compares the role of nonsensical propositions in the elucidatory procedure of the *Tractatus* with impossibility proofs in mathematics and with "riddle reasoning" and riddle solving. Riddles demand our rational and reflective capacities as arguments do, but they also differ radically from other more straightforward forms of argumentative reasoning in which the successive steps of an argument are fixed before we reach its conclusion.[26] Following Wittgenstein's lead, she draws a comparison between the difficult riddles in life and literature and problems given to the mathematician in the absence of any clear method of solution. Such questions are "spurs to mathematical activity, stimuli for the mathematical imagination."[27] "Trying to solve them," she continues, "is like trying to move one's ears when one has never done so, like trying to unravel a knot which one does not even know is actually a knot—and setting someone such a problem is like asking him how white can win in twenty moves in a game whose rules have still to be invented."[28] Such problems are utterly unlike the kind of problems one gives a child, to which an answer can be given according to rules already established. Wittgenstein himself compared riddles to problems given to the mathematician without a method of solution. He writes that the latter are

> like the problem set by the king in the fairy tale who told the princess to come neither naked nor dressed, and she came wearing fishnet. That might have been called not naked and not yet dressed either. He didn't really know what he wanted her to do, but when she came thus he was forced to accept it. It was of the form "do something which I shall be inclined to call 'neither naked nor dressed'." It's the same with the mathematical problem "Do something which I shall be inclined to accept as a solution, though I don't know now what it will be like."[29]

Diamond recalls to us a remark of Pascal's: that we understand the prophecies only when we see their fulfillment. With a riddle, she tells us, "it is only when one has the solution that one knows how to take the question, what it is for it to have an answer. This is clear in the case of the Sphinx's riddle, or that of the king and the princess."[30] Confronted with a riddle to which we do not know what the solution might be, we must guess at or invent solutions that will satisfy the conditions given by the question, which the solution must meet. Of course, we need not know the solution to a riddle in advance to be able to reject candidates that do not satisfy the conditions given in the question.

And yet, Diamond asks, "what sort of game is it . . . in which what seems to be a clear non-solution turns out to be the solution after all, if only you are ingenious enough in determining what is to count as fulfilling the conditions?" She offers this example of a "riddle" that itself comments on this feature of riddles:

> A: What's green, hangs on the wall, and flies?
> B: I don't know. What?
> A: A herring.
> B: But a herring's not green.
> A: You can paint it green.
> B: It doesn't hang on the wall.
> A: You can hang it on the wall.
> B: It doesn't fly.
> A (shrugs): So it doesn't fly![31]

I want to suggest here that we look at Wittgenstein's and Joyce's shared attraction to such questions (and the sense of possibility and failure attendant to them) in the larger context of modernism's investment in what Diamond describes as "a kind of groping search" for answers. Such a search involves

> seeking for something not specifiable in advance, and which perhaps is not for anything that can be intelligibly described at all. . . . [It] includes searching for an answer to "the riddle of life in space and time," "the riddle '*par excellence*'" as Wittgenstein called it, and which he said was not a question. It includes seeking God, as Anselm described it—what we look for we do not know, and what we find is not what we looked for. The discussion of riddles is thus meant to bear on the great riddles, and on the notions of ignorance and mistake with which they are correlative. And so also on the related idea in such contexts of the *hidden*: the hiddenness of God is akin to the hiddenness of the solution to a riddle.[32]

Diamond's discussion of the relationship among mathematical questions, literary riddles, and the "great" riddles of mythological and religious traditions (all of which, because they prove resistant to established methods of solution, demand innovative responses on our part—along with a willingness to err and to revise) offers us a thought-provoking means of examining Wittgenstein's and Joyce's shared concern with presenting in their work a desire for (unforeseen) solutions to the riddles that appear within them. Both "Ithaca" and the *Tractatus* suggest that if answers to life's enduring questions did not exist, we would have to invent them. Diamond's point that mathematical problems and literary riddles alike bear on the great riddles she points to provides us with an approach to understanding the different ways the *Tractatus* and "Ithaca" endeavor to explore the relationship between mathematical, scientific, or even simple everyday problems and the great, timeless riddles of life that she invokes.

Theolologicophilolological Commitments

Joyce's and Wittgenstein's engagement with the pressing problems of life in their respective texts is further complicated by the combination of irony and sincerity that arises from their shared ability to see such age-old problems from the perspective Wittgenstein described as a "religious point of view" in spite of the fact that neither was, as he says, "a religious man."[33] As Cranly observes of Stephen Dedalus in *A Portrait of the Artist as a Young Man*, Joyce's mind was "supersaturated with the religion in which [he claimed to] disbelieve."[34] Indeed, in spite of their shared commitment to a human investment in the spiritual aspects of life, both Joyce and Wittgenstein are, in Ithacan terms, "indurated by . . . an inherited tenacity of heterodox resistance"; "profess[ing] . . . disbelief in many orthodox religious . . . ethical doctrines" (U, 554).[35]

Joyce's portmanteau "theolologicophilolological" offers an apt description of the secular-spiritual investments Joyce and Wittgenstein share (U, 205). "Ithaca" and the *Tractatus* seek in their different ways not only to combine the theological with the philosophical and the logical (to speak not at all of the philological) but also—and perhaps more importantly—to infuse their secular explorations of the concrete everyday with attention to wonder and a yearning for truth, existence, meaning, and transcendence. In doing so, both aim to open readers to everyday experience—as it is revealed through ordinary language—by leading us beyond the dichotomies of the earthbound and the spiritual, and toward a recognition of the possibility of seeing our ordinary dealing with the world as endowed with significance.

"Ithaca" and the *Tractatus* are both enlivened by a secular engagement with traces of narrative traditions of spiritual instruction and quests for enlightenment to which their authors adhere in spite of their eschewal of institutional religious commitment or belief in God. In the *Tractatus*, Wittgenstein adopts the prophetic tone of a spiritual guide or teacher who would lead his pupils to overcome illusion. His pedagogy relies on his use of the theological image of a ladder; he engages in a mode of oblique instruction verging on the parabolic; he speaks of God, "the higher," "the mystical," "the unsayable" and of solving the riddle of the meaning of life. Themes of pedagogical training also permeate *Ulysses*'s penultimate chapter. Through the catechetical interrogations that make up the "Ithaca" episode, structured around the *figurae* of St. Paul, Dante, and the Bible (as well as *Hamlet* and the *Odyssey*), Bloom becomes both an "advertising Elijah, restorer of the church in Zion" and the "traditional figure of hypostasis" delivering prophetic "light to the gentiles" (U, 676, 689, 476).[36] Bloom's attraction (both scientific and spiritual) to all that is higher, along with his concomitant sense of the contrasting absurdity of the human condition, is evident throughout the "Ithaca" chapter in his consistent interest in constellations and stargazing.[37]

In "Ithaca," even acts as banal as shaving are interrupted by thoughts of being and nothingness. The "thought of aught" Bloom seeks is "fraught with naught" (U, 674). His meditations beneath the spectacle of the "heaventree of stars hung with humid nightblue fruit" touch intermittently on existential questions about life and death; "ipsorelative" and "aliorelative" existence; "the irreparability of the past" and "the imprevidibility of the future" as well as the absurdity of the human condition in the "cold of interstellar space" (U, 708, 667, 696, 704, 734). Charles Peake writes of the deep connection between the chapter's reflection of a "materialist vision" that "makes man's scientific control of nature possible," and its evocation of a "bleak and terrifying universe in which man seems minute, insignificant and at the mercy of powers beyond his imagination."[38] Bloom contemplates the mundane against the backdrop of a firmament "evermoving from immeasurably remote eons to infinitely remote futures in comparison with which the years, threescore and ten, of allotted human life formed a parenthesis of infinitesimal brevity" (U, 698). The narrative arrangement of the catechism of "Ithaca" conflates Bloom's thoughts about a human fascination with space and time and attempts to account for our place in it via developments in physics and cosmology, mathematical progress, and so on, with the questions of moral redemption that represent for him difficulty of "a different order":

> Did he find the problem of the inhabitability of the planets and
> their satellites by a race, given in species, and of the possible so-
> cial and moral redemption of said race by a redeemer, easier of
> solution?
>
> Of a different order of difficulty. Conscious that the human
> organism, normally capable of sustaining an atmospheric pres-
> sure of 19 tons, when elevated to a considerable altitude in the
> terrestrial atmosphere suffered with arithmetical progression of
> intensity, according as the line of demarcation between tropo-
> sphere and stratosphere was approximated, from nasal hemor-
> rhage, impeded respiration and vertigo, when proposing this
> problem for solution he had conjectured as a working hypoth-
> esis which could not be proved impossible that a more adaptable
> and differently anatomically constructed race of beings might
> subsist otherwise under Martian, Mercurial, Venereal, Jovian,
> Saturnian, Neptunian or Uranian sufficient and equivalent con-
> ditions, though an apogean humanity of beings created in vary-
> ing forms with finite differences resulting similar to the whole
> and to one another would probably there as here remain inalter-
> ably and inalienably attached to vanities, to vanities of vanities
> and all that is vanity.
>
> And the problem of possible redemption?
>
> The minor was proved by the major. (U, 699–700)

In other words, the catechism of "Ithaca" declares the possibility of social and moral redemption to be a rather grim prospect. The major premise of Bloom's response is that humanoid existence on other planets is
not impossible, considering the adaptability of the species. But in spite of
its variability, humanity cannot overcome its fixed attachment to vanity.
So even though extraterrestrial humanoid existence is theoretically possible, given that humanoid existence will be vain wherever it flourishes,
redemption is doubtful.

Bloom's earthbound experience of the everyday is fraught with a
yearning to take flight, to seek a better understanding of a "higher reality" that he already knows he will never quite grasp, at least not in
any way he might envision in advance. One of the things that "Ithaca"
conveys to us is that a longing for answers to life's eternal questions is
a deep aspect of our experience of the everyday. A corollary to that lesson is that when it comes to arriving at satisfying answers to the questions about meaning toward which the catechism gestures, in Diamond's

words, "what we look for we do not know, and what we find is not what we looked for."

We can regard Wittgenstein's own claim that although he was not a religious man he could not help seeing every problem from a religious point of view not only in terms of what it can tell us about his own way of thinking and approaching problems (of both a philosophical and an everyday variety), but also as providing an apt description of many avowedly atheistic modern writers (Woolf, Kafka, and Rilke are notable examples) whose works are underwritten by the seemingly incongruous outlook of spiritual yearning that shows forth within them.

The Difficulty to Think at the End of the Day

The philosophical commitments Wittgenstein shares with literary modernists show themselves in the passages that serve as epigraphs at the heading of this chapter. In the three quoted passages, we will recall, Tolstoy confesses his plight facing the proliferation of questions each urgently demanding an answer; Joyce invokes the "pleasures derived from literature of instruction" in a narrative of questions and answers arranged in search of solutions to "difficult problems in imaginary or real life" yet "not bearing on all points"; and Wittgenstein suggests that we feel that answers to scientific questions do not touch the problems of life, before declaring that solutions to such problems are found in their disappearance. These three excerpts thus take up several issues that I claim in this book lie at the heart of the monuments of modernist thought and literature that establish Bernstein's subgenre of the "modernist masterpiece": difficulty, indirect ethical instruction, questions and quests for elusive answers, and a yearning for transformation. Wittgenstein addresses each of these concerns obliquely in the *Tractatus*. He also touches upon them in his meditations on the role of the work of art in seeing the world *sub specie aeternitatis*, which I also want to examine here in terms of Nietzschean transfiguration.

The urgent questions that arise from the crisis of existence, faith, and reason Tolstoy describes in the excerpt from his *Confession* that serves as the first of the epigraphs ("what am I? . . . why do I live? . . . what must I do?")—the very kind of existential question we have seen Lily Briscoe to pose repeatedly in *To the Lighthouse*—are first met only with what Tolstoy describes as an accumulation of periods forming one large black spot.[39] And again, it is with this same graphic image of the outsized full stop (one he demanded that the printer enlarge still further) that Joyce ends his own questioning chapter, thereby "sabotaging the climax" of his novel by punctuating it with a huge black dot that represents an aperture into unknown future possibility as much as it gestures at the accumulated dark events of the past or provides improvised closure to the story of Bloom's question, quest, and homecoming.[40]

The attitude of clarity that Wittgenstein describes enigmatically as related to seeing the solution of the problem of life in its vanishing is also nascent in the counter-epiphanic realizations conveyed in "Ithaca" through such questions as the following: "What selfevident enigma pondered with desultory constancy during 30 years did Bloom now having effected natural obscurity by the extinction of artificial light, silently suddenly comprehend?" The catechetical rejoinder: "Where was Moses when the candle went out?" (U, 729). The answer called for by the second question (itself positioned as a catechetical response to the first) is the punch line that is never explicitly given in the text: that like Moses, that biblical "seeker of pure truth," Bloom must quest in darkness both literal and figurative.

The variety and superabundance of the information that enriches the thoughts and conversations of "Ithaca" does not succeed in providing Bloom with the clear answers that will show him the way out of "the incertitude of the void." Nor does it lay a path for him from the "known to the unknown" or the "unknown to the known" (U, 697, 676, 689, 701, 697). The "literature of instruction or amusement" alluded to throughout "Ithaca" fails to provide answers that would belie the words of Solomon in Ecclesiastes that occur to Bloom in the chapter as they do to Tolstoy at the height of the existential crisis he describes in *A Confession*: that "all is vanity" (U, 700). There is nothing new under the sun.[41]

The epigraph passages thus offer an indication of the unique ways in which Wittgenstein's and Joyce's different texts both turn on an exploitation of modernism's trademark difficulty. They also reveal the shared commitment to exploring the yearning for answers that plays such a crucial role in their attempts to speak to the modern human condition.

As I argued in the introduction, observations about modernism's fascination with difficulty have become a sort of a critical commonplace. I contend in this book, however, that modernism's investment in and use of difficulty merits still closer scrutiny if we are better to understand the quality of the difficulty at stake in Wittgenstein's gnomic *Tractatus* and the book's place among the literary and cultural productions that have come to define the principal aesthetic movement of the twentieth century. The passages that serve as epigraphs point to two main levels of difficulty at work in notoriously demanding texts like Wittgenstein's and Joyce's.

At issue first of all is the more straightforward kind of contingent difficulty related to the pursuit of knowledge through attentive study of literary and philosophical texts and commentaries, "scientific questions," and the "literature of instruction rather than amusement." But the excerpts with which this chapter opens also remind us that modernism's trademark difficulty (whether it is thematized within a given text or activated through the overall demands it makes of its readers) is at its most difficult when it is rooted in searches for answers to the "difficult questions in imaginary or real life" pondered in them. The passages gesture at the most universal and least resolvable questions of existence we have examined throughout this book, and which are also at issue in the works from which they are excerpted: the age-old questions of the meaning of life, problems of identity and alterity, the possibility of redemptive change, the contrast between how things are in the world, and their significance from the point of view of the "higher." As we have seen, they are thus also expressive of struggles with the kind of problems that Joyce's narrative arranger has Bloom, his central character (contemplating the search for truth, the enigmas of life, and the possibilities of "social and moral redemption" in the early hours of June 17, 1904), refer to as problems "of a different order of difficulty" (U, 687, 729, 700, 699).

Problems of this order, as Wittgenstein suggests in a notebook entry about Tolstoy, engage our attention at the level of the *will* rather than just the intellect.[42] The hard work toward a kind of redemptive shift in attitude that both Wittgenstein and Joyce call for or attend to in their work has to do with a subtly strenuous kind of willing. The gauntlet they throw down amounts to more than the multiple calls for erudition that works like Joyce's and Wittgenstein's also famously entail. If such works testify to the accuracy of Joyce's own glib declaration that all the "enigmas and puzzles" he had put in it would "keep the professors busy for centuries," and to James Conant's and Michael Kremer's apt portrayals of the plight faced by first-time readers of the *Tractatus*, it is because the puzzles they present to us both include and exceed the kind of reader-be-damned conundrums we can turn to commentaries and concordances to solve.[43]

Wittgenstein's and Joyce's different treatments of problems of a different order of difficulty in their respective texts turn on their adherence to Wittgenstein's credo "anything your reader can do for himself, leave to him" and his view that the true difficulty of philosophy lies not in the difficulty posed by doctrines or theories that provide us with systematic answers, but in the ethical difficulty of working to bring about a change of (spiritual and philosophical) attitude characterized by a certain clarity of outlook that gives us peace from our questions and allows us to approach life with courage and wonder and without resignation (CV, 77). The different order of difficulty that animates "Ithaca" and the *Tractatus* has to do with the ethical significance of a yearning for—and self-perfecting work toward—an unspecified personal and philosophical clarity that would, ideally, culminate in our "seeing the world in the right way," or living "happily" in Wittgenstein's sense.

But from a practical standpoint, just what the world would look like when seen from the enlightened position Wittgenstein seeks to lead us to in the *Tractatus* remains rather mysterious. And Wittgenstein, who consistently eschewed explanation, gives us none. Joyce and Wittgenstein attend in their separate works to the human striving for resolution of the ongoing questions that Tolstoy thematizes in his *Confession*. Yet their more modernist formal and pedagogical commitments render the conclusions they offer in "Ithaca" and the *Tractatus* (the abrupt closure of the first in a larger-than-life full stop; the illuminating self-destruction of the second, and its announcement that the propositions we have struggled to make sense of come to nothing more than nonsense we are to overcome) far more immediately baffling. Wittgenstein and Joyce both leave to engaged readers the ongoing interpretive work of trying to figure out the stakes of the endings of their respective texts well beyond their final pages. Thus, neither Wittgenstein's overall project, nor Joyce's, is, strictly speaking, conclusive. Their shared commitment to leaving readers with such endings is something we can view in the wider context of modernist authors working under the influence of what Virginia Woolf has called the "inconclusiveness of the Russian mind."[44]

If Joyce's and Wittgenstein's projects leave us with questions that resound in the wake of their books' culminating points, it is because they depend, each in their different ways, on defying (and thereby revising) their readers' expectations about the sort of answer (or nonanswer) able to grant us relief from the search for satisfying resolutions to the significant problems of life. Although the epigraphic passages from Joyce and Wittgenstein express a failure to find, or inability to put into meaningful words, any clear-cut answers to the questions they pose about life's meaning, they speak as strongly to a sense of satisfaction in the yearning they convey as they do to any despair at its lack of fulfillment. Internal to Wittgenstein's remarks and those from the "Ithaca" chapter's catechetical Q&A is the suggestion that it is possible to arrive at a certain kind of peace—either *with* or *from*—the kind of difficult questions at issue in these two texts, and to come to take an attitude of acceptance in the face of these recurring questions and the kind of answers one *does* find (even when such answers consist only in the disappearance of the question or appear at the moment the quest is relinquished and are somehow seemingly ineffable).

Books of Facts and Ethics

As we saw in chapter 2, in his "Lecture on Ethics," Wittgenstein asks us to imagine two "fantastic or impossible books." The *Tractatus*, Eli Friedlander observes, strives to incorporate aspects of both. The first, a book of ethics, deals with pure transcendence. The second "presents us with the world as the sum total of facts, letting us survey or contemplate all that is the case extensively or exhaustively."[45] Wittgenstein describes that imaginary book as follows:

> Suppose one of you were an omniscient person and . . . knew all the movements of all the bodies in the world dead or alive and that he also knew all the states of mind of all human beings that ever lived, and suppose this man wrote all he knew in a big book, then this book would contain the whole description of the world; and what I want to say is, that this book would contain nothing that we would call an ethical judgment or anything that would logically imply such a judgment. There will simply be facts, facts, and facts but no Ethics. . . . It seems to me obvious that nothing we could ever think or say should be the thing. . . . Our words used as we use them in science, are vessels capable of containing and conveying meaning and sense, natural meaning and sense. Ethics, if it is anything, is supernatural and our words will only express facts; as a teacup will only hold a teacup full of water even if I were to pour out a gallon over it.[46]

Joyce's encyclopedic modernist "big book," *Ulysses*, aspires in its way to the comprehensiveness and omniscience exemplified in Wittgenstein's imagined book of facts. The "Ithaca" episode is the storehouse of facts in *Ulysses* and repository of bits of knowledge missing from earlier parts of the novel, the place the reader must go for solutions to the remaining puzzles.[47] It also withholds crucial information about the thoughts and feelings of its characters and leaves gaps in our understanding. As Wolfgang Iser has pointed out, each time "Ithaca" fills a lacuna of the book with its proliferation of answers, a host of new questions become possible. In this way, "Ithaca" demonstrates the impossibility of resolving questions by getting the "right" answers.[48]

The episode provides us with a "description of the world" (in "the character of a proposition of natural science" [TLP, 6.111]). Like the *Tractatus*, "Ithaca" positions itself between the extremes of the exhaustive book of facts and the apocalyptic book of transcendence by exploring the middle ground of our yearning to grasp life's significance within everyday experience.[49] This is a gap adjacent to the one between the parabolic words of the wise and our mundane daily struggles we saw Kafka problematize in his "On Parables." Joyce's authorial tactics in "Ithaca" are similar to Wittgenstein's in the *Tractatus* not only because he tells his story in the guise of a pseudodoctrine, uttering a litany of "facts, facts, and facts . . . capable of containing and conveying meaning and sense" and leaving it to the reader to figure out for herself the relationship between the episode's peculiar form and the way it engages ethical questions. Joyce also puts his citational use of logical-scientific language to work in support of the view he shares with his philosophical contemporary: that the "ethical spirit" that pervades everyday life is something that defies systematic scientistic explanation. Rather than being a subject that can be summed up in a doctrine or taught directly, this spirit shows forth in everyday language and is best conveyed by aesthetic means.

In a discussion of the kind of instruction we can hope to find "in" a book of nonsense, whose most important "part" is not to be found among its pages, Diamond turns to yet another of the imaginary books that figure into Wittgenstein's philosophical lessons. Wittgenstein's thought-experiment text, *The World as I Found It*, provides her with a point of departure for her exploration of the way the *Tractatus* works to change our conception of what (and how) a book of philosophy can teach us (TLP, 5.631).

Diamond's reading of Wittgenstein, and the relation of his thought to literature, is informed by Iris Murdoch's understanding of moral philosophy as reflecting the idea that the world is not fundamentally comprehensible but ultimately mysterious.[50] For Diamond, what links the *Tractatus* with the works of literature Wittgenstein admired is that those works explore our ethical sense of life's mysteriousness not by treating it as something to be explicitly narrated and explained, but, as Wittgenstein wrote to Engelmann of Uhland's poem, "unutterably *contain[ed]* in what is uttered" in the work.[51] Works of literature that deal with the ethical in this way, Diamond points out, place on readers demands similar to those Wittgenstein makes of readers of the *Tractatus*. They must "respond to what is not there by making of the book something that can be significant in the spirit in which they meet what happens, what needs to be done, and what has to be suffered."[52]

In spite of all it has to say about the world of 1904 Dublin, there is nothing in *Ulysses* that can provide Bloom, or the reader, with definitive answers to the problems of life. Joyce's book, like Wittgenstein's, prompts us to transform our desires for certain kinds of answers and to reassess our conception of the ways in which scientific explanation, or works of literature or philosophy, can provide them. As we have seen, Joyce constructs "Ithaca" in such a way that "what happens, what needs to be done and what has to be suffered" by Bloom and Stephen (and Molly, upstairs in the bedroom at 7 Eccles Street) is rendered in the chapter's impersonal catechism in its "cosmic physical, psychical . . . equivalent . . . so that . . . the reader [will] know everything and know it in the baldest, coldest way."[53] Despite Joyce's claims about the chapter's stark transmission to the reader of "everything" in its most crystalline form, "Ithaca" nonetheless demands that we pay attention to ways in which he, like Woolf, "writes absences," created by the excess of diverse bits of information delivered in the questions and answers of his chapter.[54]

Whereas Woolf writes into absence by drawing on the affective force of her characters' private fragmented and intertwined thoughts, words, and continuing sense of loss, Joyce steers clear of surface appeals to emotion, addressing Bloom's and Stephen's shared human predicamen through a stark geometrical form. Joyce's readers get a first hint of the absences he writes into the volley of facts in "Ithaca" in their initial contact with the episode's structure. The impersonal catechetical form of "Ithaca" keeps readers at a critical and affective distance from which to observe all that transpires in the quizzical episode and interpretively assess its meaning and retrospective illumination of the larger novel. As Frank Budgen maintains, "Ithaca" "is the coldest episode in an unemotional book. . . . The skeleton of each fact is stripped of its emotional covering. One fact stands by the other like the skeletons of man and woman, ape and tiger in an anatomical museum at twilight, all their differences of contour made secondary by their sameness of material, function and mechanism."[55] In the place of human feelings, Karen Lawrence writes, in the episode, "we are given a record of scientific phenomena" that obscures the emotional drama of the characters.[56]

In "Ithaca," Bloom explores a wide range of issues of popular science and culture, history, linguistics, and mathematics. The scientific and historical data that enriches "Ithaca" animates Bloom and Stephen's interaction by providing them with access to creative and informed explanations for a such things as "the generic conditions imposed by natural, as distinct from human law," the progression of Darwinian evolution, the development of the "guttural sounds, diacritic aspirations, epenthetic and servile letters" of different languages, the properties of a molecule of water, and the "various features of the constellations" (U, 697, 671, 700). In his canvassing of ways to "elucidate the mystery" of the world, Bloom broaches questions about such topics as the multisecular and mystical properties of water, the quadrature of the circle, the ineffability of the tetragrammaton, and the possibility of redemption (U, 702, 671, 699, 724, 700).

Throughout his musings on these diverse bits of practical, theological, and theoretical knowledge, he also reflects on more poignant topics of "interindividual relations" (U, 668). Before him lies a present haunted by an "accumulation of the past" that includes the premature death of his son and the suicide of his father. Also lying before him is the "predestination of the future" shaped by the anticipation of his impending old age, his daughter's immanent adulthood and departure, and the question of how to proceed in the wake of his wife, Molly's, adultery (U, 689). For this is the looming domestic problem that "as much as, if not more than, any other most frequently engage[s] his mind: What to do with our wives?" (U, 685)

But despite the fact that "Ithaca" touches on such socially and politically charged issues as religion, racism, and anti-Semitism, and such personally charged issues as marital infidelity, jealousy, and mourning, because of its style, "Ithaca" is more successful at disrupting the reader's emotional connection with the characters and their story than any other chapter in *Ulysses*. Bloom and Stephen's long-awaited interaction at 7 Eccles Street is often represented in "Ithaca" with the same rigorous impersonality that characterizes their parting handshake. Here Joyce withholds the external trappings of an affecting farewell, describing their departure from one another with stark geometrical precision: "How did they take leave, one of the other, in separation?" The response provided is the following: "Standing perpendicular at the same door and on different sides of its base, the lines of their valedictory arms, meeting at any point and forming any angle less than the sum of two right angles" (U, 73–74).

Like Bloom and Stephen, readers of "Ithaca" are "competent keyless citizen[s]." The geometrical principles of Joyce's chapter deny us the more intimate access to the minds and emotional lives of the novel's characters that Woolf offers in her own more affective brand of formal "interindividual" narrative and free indirect style. If Joyce's chosen form seeks to block our ability to enter imaginatively into the thoughts of his characters in the way Woolf's free-indirect style solicits, it challenges us instead to find a way of entering imaginatively into the form of the catechism itself, and to engage in the unaccustomed kind of interpretive work of grappling with an onslaught of questions if we are to attend to all that is said in the chapter in relation to all that goes unsaid there (U, 697).

Joyce echoes Wittgenstein's caveat to von Ficker about the *Tractatus* when he warns in a letter that his chapter is "strange," a "great piece of nonsense."[57] Although, unlike Wittgenstein, Joyce never goes so far as to advise readers to toss aside his book once they have finished it, the candor of his description of the authorial technique in "Ithaca" (i.e., as one enabling the transparent delivery of total knowledge) will nonetheless appear questionable to readers who have put in the work of following the challenging text only to be frustrated by its ultimate denial of the dramatic resolution we have been craving. Rather than tell us what will become of his characters at the end of the episode, Joyce leaves us staring at a big punctuation mark and wealth of possible outcomes and unresolved questions. And as with Woolf's *To the Lighthouse*, it is with these questions that "we remain." Seeking a final answer to the final question of the catechism in "Ithaca," "Where?" (which might seem to be pointing us toward somewhere in Stephen's, Bloom's, and Molly's future) the response we find in the place of a narrative ending is an outsized period that puts a full stop to the chapter's questions and answers. The episode's final sentence points to a where of which it does not speak, but is instead silent about:

> Womb? Weary?
> He rests. He has travelled.
> With?
> Sinbad the Sailor and Tinbad the Tailor and Jinbad the Jailer and Whinbad the Whaler and Ninbad the Nailer and Finbad the Failer and Binbad the Bailer and Pinbad the Pailer and Minbad the Mailer and Hinbad the Hailer and Rinbad the Railer and Dinbad the Kailer and Vinbad the Quailer and Linbad the Yailer and Xinbad the Phthailer.
> When?
> Going to a dark bed there was a square round Sinbad the Sailor roc's auk's egg in the night of the bed of all the auks of the rocs of Darkinbad the Brightdayler.
> Where? (U, 737)

As DiBattista points out, the catechism is "the anti-narrative form par excellence." It is therefore uniquely suited to the counter-epiphanic aesthetic strategy I argue both Joyce and Wittgenstein use in their respective works. It is suited to Joyce's version, first of all, because the traditional catechetical form is crafted to work against inventions of the mind or flights of insight. Its task is to make interlocutors stick to a preestablished set of questions and answers that serve the express purpose of elaborating and teaching doxa. The catechism functions to reinforce the already converted person's commitment to a creed or code (or the outward pretense of such commitment). It is an instructive form that preaches to the choir, as it were, rather than aspire to lead its interlocutor toward any real change in spirit. By adopting the form of the catechism in "Ithaca," Joyce engages parodically in a pedagogical method widely employed in religious and secular education from the late eighteenth century on. Involving rote memorization and recitation, the catechism is a discursive practice based on the form of a dialogue but expressive of the monologic voice of the institutionalized dogma it is meant to teach. It is a mode of questioning that serves a fixed pedagogical purpose. It not only provides pupils with systematic instruction; it offers proof of their mastery of a given doctrine through their ability to respond to each of its questions with the definite answer the form requires. As such, the catechism intrinsically "foreclose[s] all possibilities of error and improvisation."[58] It is a mode of questioning that, in effect, brooks no interrogation.

Joyce works throughout *Ulysses* to subvert totalizing ideologies through his changing styles and multivocalism. One of his aims in adopting the style of an impersonal catechism in "Ithaca" is to call into question our reliance on closed epistemological systems. By appropriating the catechism's pseudodialogical form, Joyce adopts an antitheoretical stance akin to Wittgenstein's. The form enables Joyce to issue, in imitation of a voice of totalizing authority (or at least of a mischievous altar boy making fun of such a voice), a humorous critique of the institutional claims to complete knowledge that the rote exchange represents. His loose imitation of methods of drilling dogma into young minds seeks to undermine our faith in systematic questions and the answers they provide. Even the pretense of complete and thorough encyclopedic knowledge still leaves us longing for elusive solutions.

More importantly, by casting Bloom and Stephen's conversations, thoughts, and hopes in an impersonal catechism that attests to a craving for (and urge to come up with) answers to every imaginable question, Joyce also brings us closer to our own longing for answers. This longing is expressive of a desire not for knowledge, but for redemptive responses to the recurring, irresolvable questions of existence DiBattista calls the "perennial questions" and Diamond calls the "great riddles." Such questions present us with a mode in which to address (ethically and aesthetically) a world that is, in Diamond's and Murdoch's sense, fundamentally incomprehensible yet all too familiar.

The "perennial questions" at issue in "Ithaca" and the *Tractatus*, DiBattista points out, "never admit to definitive answers but encourage us to devise solutions that answer to our own specific needs and ends."[59] The catechism in "Ithaca" provides Bloom with a mode of devising unforeseen solutions to the "difficult problems in imaginary or real life" in the episode.

We will recall that in "Ithaca," Bloom finds the answers to his search "not bearing on all points." Wittgenstein speaks in the *Tractatus* of problems resolving only in their vanishing. He declares that the value of his book consists first in its treatment of the ultimate solution of the problems it deals with and second in its demonstration of how little is accomplished by this solution (TLP, 6.521; pp. 29–30).

Both Joyce's and Wittgenstein's texts defy conclusive readings and exceed the reader's attempts to grasp and sum them up in any neat fashion. In his depiction of Bloom's and Stephen's interrogations of the world in "Ithaca," Joyce, like Wittgenstein, is far more interested in displaying the ways people struggle to order their lives than he is in giving us decisive answers to the questions they pose. Through the ordered series of questions and answers in "Ithaca," Joyce conveys the chaotic and unfinished nature of life. He pays homage, if not to truth itself, then to our yearning to search for it. Instead of giving us a straightforward account of the final "truth" about what will happen to Bloom and Molly and Stephen, Joyce offers us a representation of the many ways the subject of truth and ethics and the meaning of life can be discussed, deferred, avoided, or (both literally and figuratively) put to rest. Joyce's narrative (which, he claimed, is meant to render the myth of Odysseus *sub specie temporis nostri*), like Musil's unfinished novel, then, is to some degree an essay in *Möglichkeitssinn*, a sense of possibility for a life lived, if not *sub specie aeternitatis*, in Wittgenstein's epiphanic sense, then *sub specie possibilitatis*.[60] For Joyce is more concerned with refining readers' interpretive skills by confronting them with a wealth of possibilities than he is with giving definitive answers.

The World of the Happy Is Different from That of the Unhappy

Tolstoy's narration of his own crisis of meaning and chronicle of his attendant quest for answers in *A Confession* ultimately resolves in his reaching a point of peace and acceptance through his reverence for (and eventual attunement to) the outlook of faith and simplicity that marks the life of the Russian peasant community he aspires to inhabit. However inconclusive their endings, Wittgenstein's and Joyce's texts, underwritten as they are by narratives of quest and transfiguration, also strive toward such a sense of understanding, clarity, and at-homeness in everyday life. This sense of understanding, both writers suggest, is intimately related to a striving for the *Nostos* Joyce revives in the final chapters of *Ulysses*. It is imbued with a sense of longing to be at home (again) in the language and world we already know.

The attitude of harmony Tolstoy achieves at the end of his confession becomes a source of the outlook Wittgenstein calls "happy." In his view, just as the ethical spirit of the world can be contained and conveyed in literature or poetry (like Tolstoy's or Uhland's, for example) that makes no explicit mention of ethics, or in music or visual art that involves no spoken language, it can also be seen in the attitude we take toward the world, and in the ways in which we take up the tasks life presents to us. As we saw briefly in chapter 3, in the *Tractatus* (and at much greater length in the notebooks he kept as he was finishing it), Wittgenstein talks of two different attitudes toward the world: that of the "happy" and that of the "unhappy." His talk of these opposing ethico-spiritual existential attitudes is characteristically condensed. At *Tractatus* 6.43, Wittgenstein writes simply: "Good or bad willing changes . . . the limits of the world, not the facts, not the things that can be expressed in language. . . . The world of the happy is a different one from that of the unhappy." In order to gain a clearer idea of what he means with this remark, it is helpful to supplement the abridged description Wittgenstein offers in the *Tractatus* with some of his earlier remarks about a happy attitude in the notebooks from which many of the propositions of the *Tractatus* were culled.

In those notebooks, Wittgenstein writes that just as there can be no single objective mark of ethics that, taken by itself, can describe what ethics is, neither is there a single distinguishing characteristic of a happy, or what he calls a "harmonious" life.[61] In the "Lecture on Ethics," we will recall, Wittgenstein prefers a series of examples of the kind of verbal expression we take to be ethical to any single definition of ethics seen as a topic or area of philosophy. And in much the same way, he refrains from offering any rigid definition of the ethical spirit revealed in the attitude he calls "happy" in the *Tractatus* and in the preliminary notebooks he kept for it. He offers instead a series of brief descriptions of the distinguishing character traits of a person who looks on the world with such an attitude.

A person who lives happily, Wittgenstein writes, is someone who lives in agreement and harmony with the world, and who knows whether or not she is living in this way by paying attention to what her conscience tells her (N, 75). Living happily means "fulfilling the purpose of existence" (N, 73). A person can live in this way when she is content with life, and "no longer needs to have any purpose except to live" (N, 73). Wittgenstein also indicates that in order to live with the happy attitude he speaks of, a certain kind of personal work is required. For, as he says, "man cannot make himself happy without more ado" (N, 76). The person who lives with this attitude is one who lives not in time but in an eternal present, without hope or fear, even in the face of inevitable death (N, 74–76). But living in the eternal present also means living without hope. (N, 74–75, 76). Such a person, Wittgenstein writes, lives with the understanding that "wanting does not stand in any logical connection with its own fulfillment." A person who lives with this attitude can want and yet not be unhappy if fate does not grant her desires (N, 77). Living "happily" means recognizing that the world is independent of the human will and that "even if everything that we want were to happen, this would still only be, so to speak, a grace of fate." Living in agreement with the world, then, means living with the knowledge that one is powerless to bend the happenings of the world to meet one's desires (N, 73). And it is with this understanding that one can live happily even in the face of the world's misery (N, 81).

Furthermore, seeing the world with a happy eye means viewing it not only with an attitude of acceptance, but also with courage and creativity (N, 77; TLP, 6.421). Elaborating on his compressed statement in the *Tractatus* that "ethics and aesthetics are one," Wittgenstein writes in the *Notebooks* that "the work of art is the object seen *sub specie aeternitatis*; and the good life is the world seen *sub specie aeternitatis*. This is the connection between art and ethics" (N, 83). He suggests that adopting the kind of attitude that accompanies the living of a "good life" means looking at the world aesthetically, in much the same way one might regard certain works of art. But what does this mean?

In the remarks that immediately follow, Wittgenstein writes that in the course of our everyday affairs, prior to any transformation that can be produced by art, we most often tend to view the objects of the world as it were from "the midst of them" (N, 83). In our daily encounters with the world, we tend to view the things around us rather matter-of-factly, instrumentally, or even disinterestedly. We can fail to engage in really *looking* at the world. Instead of allowing ourselves to attend closely to or to be moved by the things or happenings in the world, we take them for granted. We don't really *see* them. They are as if obscured for us by a veil of what Woolf, as we saw in the last chapter, calls the cotton wool of "non-being."

Wittgenstein tells us in both the notebooks and the *Tractatus* that each thing in the world stands on a par with all others, and that thus no one thing can be less insignificant than any other. And yet, he points out, each thing in the world is also equally *significant* (N, 83; TLP, 6.4). For Wittgenstein, as for Woolf, there are moments in our lives in which, for whatever reason, a given thing suddenly discloses itself to us, and we experience an acute awareness of its meaningfulness. During such moments, a thing in the world can seem so strikingly present to us that with it the entire world in all its significance appears to rise up to meet our gaze. At these times, we see the world not prosaically but somehow *poetically*, or as we would a work of art. We see the world not in terms of *how* it is, but with wonder *that* it is. In Wittgenstein's words, we see the world against the background of the whole of logical space. We see its very presence from the point of view of eternity, as it were. This is the way of seeing things that Wittgenstein is talking about in proposition 6.45 of the *Tractatus*, where he says: "To view the world *sub specie aeterni* is to view it as a whole—a limited whole. Feeling the world as a limited whole—it is this that is mystical."

In his war notebooks, Wittgenstein offers an example of what it is to see the world in this way in a remark he makes about the kind of concentrated contemplation of an everyday thing in the world (in this case, a stove) that gives rise to the view *sub specie aeternitatis*. He draws a distinction here between looking at an object as but one more commonplace thing in the world and looking at it as having a significant place in the world, as representative of the world itself. He writes:

> If I have been contemplating the stove, and then am told: but now all you know is the stove, my result does seem trivial. For this represents the matter as if I had studied the stove as one among the many things in the world. But if I was contemplating the stove *it* was my world, and everything else colourless by contrast with it. (N, 83)

Wittgenstein first describes the stove as a thing among things, and then as "a world." As Diamond puts it, in the passage, the stove is seen as having a "*dignity* of being what it is" that is not in view in the course of one's ordinary dealings with it ("Limits of Sense," 267, my emphasis). In a later notebook entry, written in April 1930, Wittgenstein offers us an even more detailed depiction of just what such a way of looking at the world amounts to. In this remark, he stresses the importance of striving to remain receptive to the world around us, lest we lapse into an attitude of dull detachment from our lives. He cautions us not to look at things coldly or dispassionately and emphasizes the need to regard the world and the mundane things in it with a removed kind of attachment. For Wittgenstein, the significance of the whole world can resonate in things as simple and familiar as an ordinary gesture, a photo, a tree, a way of talking, the shape of a life. Seeing the world *sub specie aeternitatis* means looking on such things with a sort of receptiveness that allows us to see them as objects of wonder.

In the 1930 notebook entry, Wittgenstein discusses this perspective on the world in a passage that contains what Michael Fried calls Wittgenstein's most original and sustained contribution to aesthetic thought.[62] I quote it at length:

> Engelmann [Wittgenstein's close friend with whom he discussed literature and philosophy during the war years and beyond] told me that when he rummages round at home in a drawer full of his own manuscripts, they strike him as so glorious that he thinks they would be worth presenting to other people. (He said it's the same when he is reading through letters from his dead relations.) But when he imagines a selection of them published he said the whole business loses its charm & value & becomes impossible. I said this case was like the following one: Nothing could be more remarkable than seeing someone who thinks himself unobserved engaged in some quite simple everyday activity. Let's imagine a theatre, the curtain goes up & we see someone alone in his room walking up and down, lighting a cigarette, seating himself etc. so that suddenly we are observing a human being from outside in a way that ordinarily we can never observe ourselves; as if we were watching a chapter from a biography with our own eyes,— surely this would be at once uncanny and wonderful. More wonderful than anything that a playwright could cause to be acted or spoken on the stage. We should be seeing life itself.—But then we do see this every day & it makes not the slightest impression on us! True enough, but we do not see it from that point of view.—Similarly when E. looks at his writings and finds them splendid (even though he would not care to publish any of the pieces individually), he is seeing his life as God's work of art, & as such it is certainly worth contemplating, as is every life &

everything whatever. But only the artist can represent the individual thing [*das Einzelne*] so that it appears to us as a work of
art; those manuscripts rightly lose their value if we contemplate
them singly & in any case without prejudice, i.e. without being
enthusiastic about them in advance. The work of art compels
us—as one might say—to see it in the right perspective, but without art the object [*der Gegenstand*] is a piece of nature like any
other & the fact that we may exalt it through our enthusiasm
does not give anyone the right to display it to us. (I am always
reminded of one of those insipid photographs of a piece of scen-
ery which is interesting to the person who took it because he was
there himself, experienced something, but which a third parry
looks at with justifiable coldness; insofar as it is ever justifiable
to look at something with coldness.) But now it seems to me
too that besides the work of the artist there is another through
which the world may be captured sub specie aeterni. It is—as
I believe—the way of thought which as it were flies above the
world and leaves it the way it is, contemplating it from above in
its flight. (CV, 4–5)

I first want to compare Wittgenstein's contemplation of the stove in
the first of the two notebook entries above with Woolf's reminiscences in
A Sketch of the Past about the Wordsworthian "spots of time" that made
a lifelong impression on her in her earliest childhood, and in particular
her experience of a sudden (Blakean) sense of wholeness while contemplating an otherwise insignificant ordinary thing: the flower at St. Ives.
In her memoir, Woolf treats the flower with a respect akin to the dignity
with which Wittgenstein endows the stove in the notebook entry above.
As we will recall from chapter 3, Woolf distinguishes "non-being" from
the "feeling of ecstasy . . . of rapture" that characterizes the exceptional
moments of being that emerge from behind the cotton wool of everyday
existence, calling on her to focus on and involve herself in them.[63] She
describes the "shocks" and "blows" to which she is especially attuned.
Whether they manifest themselves in feelings of plenitude or of horror,
sadness, or despair, they act as catalysts for her creative work. The powerlessness and sense of hopeless sadness that overtakes her during her
fight with her brother, like her experience of "the whole" while looking
at the flower, leaves her with a newly heightened consciousness of her
power to translate that sensation into her writing.

In her memoir, Woolf narrates in the first person the "discovery"
she makes in childhood about the power of her own art to represent the

world through her experience contemplating the flower. But she does so while adopting a third-person perspective from which she sees herself, in Wittgenstein's words, "from outside," as it were, "in a way that ordinarily we can never observe ourselves; as if we were watching a chapter from a biography with our own eyes." In the longer 1930 notebook entry I quoted above, Wittgenstein describes his friend Engelmann looking on his own manuscripts from a similarly detached, externalized standpoint. From *that* point of view, Engelmann regards his writings as unique and "wonderful." From this estranged position, he can contemplate his life as a performance in what Friedlander calls the "theatre of the ordinary."[64] He looks on the everyday features of his existence as if contemplating a divine work of art. Similarly, in the thought experiment Wittgenstein considers, which asks us to imagine observing (by Fried's lights absorptively, antitheatrically) a performance on the stage of "life itself," watching a man who thinks himself unobserved going about his regular daily activities.

In his thought experiment, Wittgenstein describes a way of seeing the everyday world not from "in the midst" of things, not, that is, from within what Woolf calls the "cotton wool" of daily life, but as something that emerges as worthy of contemplation. For Wittgenstein, a work of art can transform the perspective of the viewer, listener, or reader in a way analogous to how he thought a philosophical work like the *Tractatus* could. Wittgenstein's claim in that book that "ethics and aesthetics are one" becomes clearer once we consider that in his view, just as the general form of a proposition he offers at *Tractatus* 6 gives us a rule for all senseful language, making available the evaluative purchase afforded by an ethical sense of wonder at what he calls in the "Lecture on Ethics" the "existence of language itself" (i.e., not *how* it is but *that* it is), so a work of art can transform our way of seeing by enabling us to contemplate the "thereness" of the world as a whole (LE, 44). Diamond links this evaluative sort of purchase on the world and senseful language to an ability to "stand back" from our questions and searches for answers that is relevant to our understanding of the mysterious claims Wittgenstein makes in propositions 6.45–6.521. There, we will recall, he says that if a question can be asked, it can also be answered, that a question can exist only where there is an answer, and that even if all possible scientific questions were answered, the problems of life will not have been touched at all. "Of course there is then no question left," he continues, "and this is just the answer. The solution of the problem of life is seen in the vanishing of this problem."

Diamond's claims about "standing back" from our questions and quests also presents us with ways of interpreting the stance (or, more accurately, recumbent position) Bloom takes toward questions and answers by the end of "Ithaca":

> Having our attention drawn to senseful language may lead us to stand back from the asking and answering of questions, as we recognize that no satisfaction is to be had from any *answer*. We are, that is, enabled to contemplate things, but no longer "from their midst," rather from a point of view that sees what is the case as whatever indeed is the case; *how* things are is not the centre of concern, and *that* they are is, in a sense, open to view. . . . Ethics and aesthetics are one in their relation to the world, the essence of which is given by the general form of a proposition. The idea, in Wittgenstein's conception of ethics and aesthetics, is of transformation in our relation to all that is accidental, all that happens and ordinarily absorbs us, all that we usually take ourselves to know, to be aware of. Insofar as "In the world everything is as it is, and everything happens as it happens" can be for us *satisfaction* or *dissatisfaction*, there is *will*, and thus ethics. ("Limits of Sense," 261–63)

Wittgenstein's notion of "happy" and "unhappy" attitudes plays a fundamental role in the outlook of philosophical clarity that he promises will be available to readers who set themselves to the task he presents them with in the *Tractatus* once they have mounted the elucidating rungs of his figurative ladder. The "happy" worldview Wittgenstein tersely describes there, I claim, is the attitude that Bloom has adopted by the end of "Ithaca." It is one that enables him to "stand back," in Diamond's sense, from the questions and quests at issue in the episode. The penultimate chapter of *Ulysses* (which Joyce declared was "really the end" of the encyclopedic "monster" novel) makes an overdetermined gesture at providing readers with the "facts, facts and facts," of the "world-book" Wittgenstein imagines in the "Lecture on Ethics," and at the array of answers to what Wittgenstein talks of at *Tractatus* 6.52 as "*all possible* scientific questions." Nonetheless, Diamond's words on the matter apply to Bloom. For "none of the gazillion speakable answers to questions will reach to [his] concern with the problems of life, that none of the speakable answers can be an answer to the questions [he takes himself] to be putting" ("Limits of Sense," 243). Bloom gives himself over to sleep as the end of the chapter resounds with a final unanswered general question (one that stands in for all the unanswerable existential questions Wittgenstein describes as ethical). That final question appears in the episode as a mysterious answer to all the questions that came before it: "Where?"

If Joyce's chapter gives us the figure of Bloom standing back from the multitude of questions it poses, it also represents the work of art that, as Wittgenstein has it, puts readers in a position to stand back in our regard of the world, and thereby work to gain new ethical perspective in much the same way. In his encyclopedic *Ulysses*, Joyce presents us with a localized slice of all that is the case. In "Ithaca" he presents readers with the stark geometrical figure of a world, and what Lawrence describes as a "curious sense of displacement about the writing, as if one story were being written, while another, more important story were taking place."[65] Joyce presents readers with a strange novelistic form and asks readers to read behind or within it a "responsiveness to life."[66]

Wittgenstein's notion of the "happy" also informs our understanding of the fallible kind of grace that characterizes Bloom's attitude of acquiescent self-possession at the end of "Ithaca." In the previous chapter, I discussed Diamond's characterization of the eponymous fisherman's wife of the Grimms' story, with her desire to exert her will on the world in a godlike fashion, to a person with an "unhappy attitude" toward the world. I went on to say that although Mrs. Ramsay's choice to read that particular fairy tale to her children speaks indirectly to her attraction to the magical power of Ilsibil's will to control, and to the story's ultimate cautionary tale about the limits of human willing. Mrs. Ramsay is a character whose outlook of satisfaction and "happy" plenitude is fraught with an uncanny attunement to a difficulty of reality, in Diamond's sense.

In Joyce's Bloom, however, we find a more straightforward, if unexpected, literary exemplar of a person living with a Wittgensteinian "happy" outlook. He faces his cuckolded situation with "more abnegation than jealousy, less envy than equanimity" (U, 733). In spite of his inability to reach a full understanding of human existence, and despite his dejection at its imperfections, Bloom takes an attitude of humor, curiosity, and ultimately of peace and humility. He faces the world with the knowledge that he is powerless to bend its happenings to meet his will.

But we misunderstand and oversimplify Bloom's plight as well as Wittgenstein's notion of the "happy" if we assume that to face the world with the kind of "happy" attitude of acceptance we see in Bloom is to be a mere passive victim of circumstance. For as we shall see below,

Bloom's understanding that he is powerless to bend the ways of the world to meet his will does not preclude his willing his own redemption by accomplishing a Nietzschean kind of transfiguration within the larger creative endeavor that is *Ulysses*, one that allows him to "see the world in the right way" as Wittgenstein would have it.

Bloom's clarity and sense of satisfaction in "Ithaca" is paradoxically reflected in the sense of purpose he achieves by navigating the "void incertitude" with a sense of wonder expressed in the continual questions he poses about everyday life as it passes inexorably "slowly, quickly, evenly, round and round and round the rim of a round precipitous globe" (U, 681). He finds satisfaction in the world despite the "apathy of the stars":

> His mood?
> He had not risked, he did not expect, he had not been disappointed, he was satisfied.
> What satisfied him?
> To have sustained no positive loss. To have brought a positive gain to others. Light to the gentiles. (U, 676, 734)

In the wake of Bloom's thoughts about the "many social conditions, the product of inequality and avarice and international animosity" he desires to amend, the catechism continues:

> He believed then that human life was infinitely perfectible, eliminating these conditions?
> There remained the generic conditions imposed by natural, as distinct from human law, as integral parts of the human whole: the necessity of destruction to procure alimentary sustenance: the painful character of the ultimate functions of separate existence, the agonies of birth and death: the monotonous menstruation of simian and (particularly) human females extending from age of puberty to the menopause: inevitable accidents at sea, in mines and factories: certain very painful maladies and their resultant surgical operations, innate lunacy and congenital criminality, decimating epidemics: catastrophic cataclysms which make terror the basis of human mentality: seismic upheavals the epicentres of which are located in densely populated regions: the fact of vital growth, through convulsions of metamorphosis from infancy through maturity to decay.
> Why did he desist from speculation?

> Because it was a task for a superior intelligence to substitute other more acceptable phenomena in place of less acceptable phenomena to be removed. (U, 697)

Bloom finds comfort in his misapprehension of Stephen's affirmation of his own syllogistic movement from the known to the unknown, realizing that "as a competent keyless citizen he had proceeded energetically from the unknown to the known through the incertitude of the void" (U, 697).

Joyce's early interest in epiphanies gives way in "Ithaca" to ruminations that grant Bloom a certain peace (achieved in satisfaction rather than resignation) and a new depth of understanding that allows him to go on, although his problems remain unresolved. It is worth noting here that if *Ulysses* is marked by the absence of epiphany, it is also marked by the absence of any outright depiction on the page of a dramatic shift or transformation in outlook on Bloom's part. It is as if Bloom is predisposed toward a "happy" outlook from the very beginning of the episode, if not the book itself. In that sense, Bloom's looks to be a transformation that is not one. In the progress of his "meditations of involution," he finds only that "nought nowhere was never reached," a pronouncement whose triple negative also suggests an opposite meaning (U, 699). The closest thing to a visible transformative turning point for Bloom comes when he finds implicit resolution (notably in yet another question positioned as a catechetical answer) to the "selfevident" last of his three enigmas. There his exploration of his problems finally coalesces in the strangely sudden, silent counter- or even *anti*-epiphanic realization that, like Moses when his candle went out, he too is fumbling in the dark.

Bloom's moment of enlightenment in the unlit night of his daylong odyssey is thus not the sudden unaccountably transformative illumination experienced by the allegorical blind man who gains sight in Tolstoy's reworking of the Gospels (thus inspiring Wittgenstein's parenthetical question at the end of *Tractatus* 6.521) and is able to metaphorically, spiritually, to "see the world in the right way." Bloom's experience of enlightenment through obscurity, instead, is perhaps better described as a more drawn-out process of coming to clarity on the part of the blind man's world-wearier (yet still reservedly optimistic) opposite, reached in the course of his wanderings through the everyday comedy of human life and realizing philosophically that the cosmic joke is somehow on him. What Joyce's Bloom sees in "Ithaca" is also something akin to what Cavell takes Socrates (with all the "faded irony" or "stuffy humility" of his own wisdom) to have seen in engaging in philosophy as an "effort to find answers and permit questions, which nobody knows the way to nor the answer to any better than yourself." What Socrates recognizes, Cavell writes in an almost Ithacan vein, is that "about the questions which were causing him wonder and hope and confusion and pain, he knew that he did not know what no man can know, and that any man could learn what he wanted to learn."[67]

At the end of the "Ithaca" episode's catechetical engagement with the "difficult problems in imaginary or real life," the phenomenon of the sudden revelation of epiphanic insight gives way to a depiction of a more muted, measured, and protracted understanding that goes beyond the epiphanic. As I indicated above, what is attained at the novel's close is a kind of a secular modernist state of grace (bestowed not from without by an external divine, but from within, through a receptiveness to it that Bloom achieves through the work of questing and questioning, and of revising his various searches until he arrives at an imperfect but satisfactory peace, clarity, and acceptance of life lived in the present but against the background of all eternity). The end of Bloom's Odyssey gives him rest from—or simply puts a seemingly arbitrary Ithacan full stop to—his unresolved questions, even if that profane state of grace provides only temporary respite. Though a "conscious reactor against the void incertitude," by the end of the chapter, Bloom is nonetheless able to find peace from his problems ("He rests. He has traveled"), if only for a night (U, 737).

As Derek Attridge reminds us in a discussion of the theological concept in relation to J. M. Coetzee's treatment of it in his fiction (to which I will turn in chapter 5), "grace is by definition not something given, not something earned. . . . Grace is a blessing you do not deserve, and though you may seek for grace, it comes, if it comes at all, unsought." Although the matter sounds like a recipe for moral lassitude—"for doing nothing, or doing whatever you like," he continues—"the paradox of the theological concept of grace . . . is that it is not a disincentive to good works, but a spur."[68]

To properly consider the peace and grace Bloom achieves by the end of the novel, it is important to note that his attitude of acceptance, like the attitude Wittgenstein calls "happy," does not amount to mere quietism. Bloom's is a lively contemplation of his world that represents neither a resistance to change nor a passive resignation to the way things stand. Nor does Bloom's attitude of acceptance entail a mystical abandonment of the will, or a still more ascetic Schopenhauerian self-annihilating denial of it. Rather, the Joycean catechism that provides the form of "Ithaca" thrusts Bloom into an active kind of interpretive work

toward a willed redemption in a transfigurative Nietzschean sense. Looking at R. Lanier Anderson's reading of Nietzsche's desacralized concept of
redemption through transfiguration offers us valuable insights into Wittgenstein's own gestures at the possibility of redemption in his philosophical writing, especially viewed in relation to Joyce's Leopold Bloom.[69]

Nietzschean Redemption and Transfiguration

Wittgenstein's and Joyce's "theolologicophilolological" commitments,
and their tendency to see problems from a religious point of view in spite
of their lack of straightforward adherence to any particular religious
belief, are rooted in their cultural inheritance from Friedrich Nietzsche.
Creator of the madman who declares the death of God in *The Gay Science*, Nietzsche announces the age of spiritual disorientation initiated by
modernity. In the world of disenchantment Nietzsche's madman proclaims, the human predicament becomes one of devastating disorientation and uncertainty. Having killed God, and thus figuratively "un-
chained this earth from its sun," humankind strays "as though in an
infinite nothing," seeking to fill the void left in God's absence by inventing alternative sacred games and modes of spirituality through which to
seek comfort, cleansing, and atonement in our practical lives.[70]
    Nietzsche is of course famous for his inflammatory denouncement of
the central tenets and dogmas of Christianity and his indictment of Christian moral values as both spurious and deleterious to the lives of believ-
ers. But, as Anderson emphasizes, in spite of the disenchantment of the
world he engenders, Nietzsche remains dependent on characteristically
religious, and even quasi-Christian concepts. His philosophy, including
the critique of Christianity he mounts within it, is organized around the
positive redeployment of desacralized versions of such religious notions
as atonement, salvation, transfiguration, and redemption (NRT, 226).
    For Nietzsche, there is a decisive difference between the compensa-
tory Christian notion of redemption he takes to be false, and the genuine path to redemption he offers by doing away with the structure of
compensation around which the Christian concept is built. According
to that understanding of redemption, Christ's sacrifice affords us cosmic
and spiritual compensation that fulfills a double duty: it satisfies divine
justice by repaying the debt we owe God for our sins while also delivering us from the evils and suffering of the world with the future-directed
promise of heavenly reward.
    If Wittgenstein's "happy" outlook is an ethical attitude connected
with a way of seeing the world "in the right way," Anderson too speaks

of Nietzsche's redemptive strategy as entailing a call for a willed shift in attitude, one that will restore spiritual wholeness and harmony to the human condition Nietzsche's Zarathustra now finds "in ruins," made up of "fragments and limbs and dreadful accidents—but no human beings" (Z, 250). Anderson points out that, like Christ, Nietzsche's Zarathustra promises a better future. But Nietzsche's prophet departs from the Christian view of redemption by insisting that it is we ourselves who must work creatively to shore up these fragments against our ruin. Zarathustra calls on each of us to be "a seer, a willer, a creator, a future himself as well as a bridge to the future." It is we ourselves who must "create and carry together into one what is fragment and riddle and dreadful accident" (Z, 251). Nietzsche's idea of redemption calls on us to tend to our own restoration in a future that we envision for ourselves. His main criterion is that we work to redeem our future lives by recreating all "It was" into a "Thus I willed it!" (Z, 251). What Nietzsche calls redemption, then, comes not via Christian deliverance from suffering and to an entirely different future in which we find compensation for past hardship, but instead from an effort to move forward with a radically new and affirming attitude toward that same past and all that is regrettable about it.

To clarify the difference between the stakes of the Christian notion of redemption and Nietzsche's, Anderson turns to Nietzsche's well-known doctrine of "eternal recurrence," seeing it not as a cosmological theory about the circular movement of time, but as a practical thought experiment that offers a way to assess the value of a life. At Nietzsche's provocation, the reader is asked to imagine how she would respond to the idea that she would have to live every moment of her life, exactly as it is, "every pain and every pleasure and every thought and sigh," over and over again in the same sequence, indefinitely. Here is the challenge issued by the demon when Nietzsche first introduces the practical thought experiment of eternal recurrence in *The Gay Science*:

> This life as you now live it and have lived it, you will have to live once more and innumerable times more; and there will be nothing new in it, but every pain and every pleasure and every thought and sigh and everything unutterably small or great in your life will have to return to you, all in the same succession and sequence. . . . If this thought gained dominion over you it would change you as you are, or perhaps crush you. The question in each and every thing, "Do you desire this once more and innumerable times more?" would lie upon your actions as the greatest

weight. Or how well disposed would you have to become to yourself and to life to wish for nothing more than for this eternal confirmation and seal? (GS, 341)

For the reader to imagine with joy the prospect of the eternal recurrence of every moment of her life as it has unfolded to date would indicate a fully authentic and unified existence, in which her life and values are merged. But for the reader to receive it with horror would indicate the need to engage in an active reevaluation and work toward redemption, as Nietzsche understands it.

Nietzsche's thought experiment induces us imaginatively to project our entire lived existence into the future. It thus forces us to consider the shape of our life as a whole, reanimated in a future in which we do not overcome its setbacks and sorrows by being redeemed *from* them, or by relegating these moments to a past from which we have been blessedly delivered as we would in the Christian tradition, but by adopting a new attitude toward them, one that requires us to look on all our past trials as constituting a vital part of the life that we seek to redeem.

If Nietzsche's notion of redemption turns on our ability to change our stance toward life, it therefore also depends on our desire and inclination to *do* something, namely, to creatively respond to the demon's call to "change as you are" by transforming the "It was" into a "Thus I willed it." For Nietzsche, redemption entails a new understanding of the importance of negative events in life; the fragmentary, accidental, or regrettable aspects or circumstances that we find too difficult or painful to wish to live through again. But if we can come to see these events as contributing in a powerful, positive way to the shape of a life that we can endorse as a whole, if we can actively, creatively change our life into one in which sorrows and apparent setbacks turn out to have been indispensable to our ongoing existence, we will have "saved" ourselves by redeeming our lives, and these moments along with it. "For Nietzsche," Anderson writes, "it is the particular troubling events that really need redeeming, and so a story can *count* as redemptive only insofar as it incorporates each of the very same events in the life and gives it a significance that can be affirmed, rather than living it mired in regret" (NRT, 253).

To illustrate this idea, Anderson offers the example of Jimmy Carter's response following his crushing loss of his presidency during the 1980 election. To avoid capping off his career with a stunning failure, Carter had to *do something* to redeem this defeat, to positively change the meaning of his life as a whole. He had to face his dramatic loss affirmatively, and creatively "turn it from a debilitating setback into something that could be accepted—even willed." Carter's response to this challenge was to turn his presidential library into the Carter Center, under the auspices of which he went on to fight for peace and against poverty and disease. In the process, he would gain a moral credibility as an ex-president that he is unlikely to have achieved had he beat Ronald Reagan in that election. Carter's later successes redeem his earlier failure, in Nietzsche's sense. "To wish for such an ex-presidency," says Anderson, "is also to wish for the defeat, and precisely that fact allows the later successes to redeem the earlier failure. To wish away the defeat would also be to wish away Carter's genuine achievement—namely, the invention of a whole new kind of public life" (NRT, 240). The period of his life following his defeat thus becomes not just another chapter to add onto a sequence of others leading up to it; it utterly transfigures his life as we know it.

Anderson's discussion of Nietzsche's claims about redemption in *The Gay Science*, *Zarathustra*, and elsewhere, much like Diamond's claims about Wittgenstein's related concerns in the *Notebooks* and *Tractatus*, centers around these philosophers' shared conceptions of the importance of a shift in attitude. And yet the proposed change in outlook that Nietzsche's thought experiment is supposed to provoke in us leaves us with some of the same questions we face when trying to understand what "seeing the world in the right way," as Wittgenstein conceives it, would require of us. The need for a change in attitude that Nietzsche hopes to impress on us with his thought experiment presents us with what Anderson calls "a real puzzle," one that also applies to the change that the *Tractatus* demands. The difficulty in question, Anderson says, has to do with "whether (and how) a *mere* change in attitude can make the dramatic difference Nietzsche suggests." He asks: "Is changing your *attitude* really sufficient to change your *life*. . . ?" (NRT, 241).

Anderson makes it clear that the creative shift in attitude necessary to "change as you are," as Nietzschean redemption demands it, must amount to more than what he, following Bernard Reginster, calls mere *counteradaptation*.[71] Counteradaptation involves a capitulative kind of "settling" for the status quo that we achieve by redirecting our desires in such a way that we come to want what we actually have (NRT, 241). The kind of redemption that Nietzsche is urging, Anderson argues, rests on another sacred concept he draws on and redeploys to his own ends—transfiguration. In the Christian context, the transfiguration signifies a crucial moment in the life of Jesus, when he is revealed in radiant glory to his disciples in his special status as the son of God (Matthew 17:2; Mark 9:2–3; Luke 9:28–36). For Nietzsche, who draws on the Hellenistic tradition of the concept as well as the Christian, redemption operates through transfiguration, the identity-preserving process of a thing's metamorphosis into another form while its matter and identity remain constant. My affirmation of the trials of the past, taken as a part of my endorsement of my life as a whole, is meant to transform my life while leaving me the same person. "In Nietzsche as in the Christian case," Anderson writes, "transfiguration is always a spiritualizing change, even though it loses all mystical or otherworldly connotations. Transfiguration takes something mundane and ordinary, and bestows upon it some wider significance, deeper meaning, or new beauty" that gives it new artistic form (NRT, 243). Genuine redemption, for Nietzsche, requires an act of creation, or more aptly, according to Zarathustra's teaching, a re-creation of the past.

Anderson answers his own question about how a mere attitudinal shift can change a life by explaining that only a change in outlook that has real, deep effects can bring about redemption in a person's life. "My redemption depends on the invention of a new life story which becomes sufficiently central to my self-conception to produce ongoing effects on my actions and in my world, changing the meaning of what I do, plan, and become" (NRT, 256). In Nietzsche's view, the creative activity of self-transformation that redemption requires is not something an external force, divine or human, can perform in a person, but something a person must achieve for herself.

Creator and Guesser of Riddles and Redeemer of Accidents

It is Nietzsche's concepts of redemption and transfiguration, rather than the Christian version he rejects, that help us to understand both the kind of grace I am claiming Bloom attains in "Ithaca" and its relevance to Wittgenstein's notion of the "happy" as an ethical way of looking upon the world. I said earlier that Joyce's treatment of Bloom's questions and his quest in *Ulysses* features no overt description of a particular revelatory moment or acute dramatic transformative shift in outlook on Bloom's part. I also indicated that Bloom is characterized as in possession of a "happy" attitude, in a Wittgensteinian sense, from the very start. So, if Bloom is given to us more or less consistently just as he is, what kind of transfigurative shift in attitude can I be talking about?

The change in outlook that Bloom experiences over the course of "Ithaca" is one that occurs in keeping to the challenge that Nietzsche issues with his practical thought experiment of eternal recurrence. If Bloom changes within the course of "Ithaca," it is by rising to the challenge to "change you as you are." The peace he finds by the end of the chapter lies in the transfiguration he achieves by "becoming himself" and wishing for nothing more than the eternal affirmation of his life as it is. If he represents a Wittgensteinian "happy" man, it is in part because he is shown not to be "crushed" by the call to assess the value of his life in the present in accordance with the challenge of Nietzsche's demon's future-directed thought experiment. Bloom, a character of Joyce's own creation, is transfigured within the creative artistic will of the text itself.

It is the peripatetic interrogative form of "Ithaca," and what Joyce reveals through it about Bloom's views about his life, that allows his attitude of acceptance to show forth in the chapter as the aesthetically and ethically complex outlook Wittgenstein describes with the deceptively unassuming word "happy." Joyce's chosen form in the episode thereby distinguishes the moral gravitas of that attitude from a stance of merely passive forbearance or counteradaptive settling. The haphazard Q&A of the chapter drives Bloom's conscious self-assessment by formally calling on him to survey the discrete events of his life in a way that gives him (and the reader) a retrospective overview of his existence. The chapter's call to a general appraisal of a life is one that requires Bloom (and the reader) actively and intelligently to face the various "fragments," "riddles and accidents," and personal trials of his existence and bring them into meaning as a whole. The form of the episode thus effects a literary metamorphosis that is such a vital part of Nietzsche's idea of redemption. It puts into motion a creative transfiguration of the particular features of Bloom's life, giving them new form, holistic significance, and evaluative salience. The hardships and sorrows of Bloom's life, his loneliness, impotence, and bumbling social failures are presented along with all the miscellaneous information and points of speculation Joyce offers in the chapter. None of Bloom's problems are solved by the novel's inconclusive end. But whatever redemption Bloom achieves in the novel is achieved through an attitude of creative and re-creative willing and affirmation of the past that redeems his life in the present in which he is changed while remaining the same person.

The Place I Have to Get to Is a Place I Must Already Be at Now

The shift Joyce makes in his aesthetic philosophy from attention to epiphany in his earlier works (from an investment in achieving a flash of clarity about the soul or whatness of something) to *Ulysses*'s treatment of a more attenuated quest for understanding that would confer a sense of being at home in one's language and world runs parallel to the transition that occurs between Wittgenstein's early and later work in the philosophical method with which he approaches the search for clarity.

Although in his later work, Wittgenstein continues to pursue the therapeutic goal of achieving a change in his readers' self-understanding through an improved relationship with language, he comes to see his mode of philosophical engagement in the *Tractatus* as flawed because of its overly dogmatic assertions. Conant contrasts Wittgenstein's early and later philosophical methods by calling attention to his endeavors in the later work to use frequent exchanges with his interlocutor in order to maintain closer contact with his reader and his ongoing, evolving problems. In the *Investigations*, Wittgenstein relinquishes the Kierkegaardian strategy of "deceiving the reader into the truth" that he uses in the *Tractatus*. In that early book, Wittgenstein's method entails "leading his interlocutor through an elaborate structure of apparent claims in order finally to round on him," disabusing him all at once of the mistaken impression that what he was following all along was a progressive chain of arguments. The method he adopts in the *Investigations*, on the other hand, "is to round on his interlocutor at every point, to press at every juncture" in order to attend to our language and lives as they actually are.[72]

As we will recall from the introduction, Diamond has described Wittgenstein's attempts to resist his own attractions to dogmatism and false necessity by reshaping his life in the ongoing development of his therapeutic method over time in a conscious striving to "*own* [his] past philosophy in a new way."[73] Caleb Thompson also offers insights into the evolution of Wittgenstein's philosophical method from his early to his later writings that shed light on the fate of the Joycean epiphany in *Ulysses*. The difference between Wittgenstein's earlier and later methods, in his view, comes to a difference between a conception of philosophical activity as one that seeks to bring about a linear ascent to perfect clarity on the one hand, and one that sees it as an ongoing struggle against a persistent temptation to give into illusion on the other. The difference is visible in the difference between two remarks, one from the *Tractatus*, and another from a 1930s manuscript.

At *Tractatus* 6.54, Wittgenstein writes that his reader must throw away the ladder of his elucidatory nonsensical sentences once he has overcome his need for it. Returning to philosophy some years later, Wittgenstein again speaks of ladders, this time treating the image quite differently:

> I might say: if the place I want to get to could only be reached by way of a ladder, I would give up trying to get there. For the

place I really have to get to is a place I must already be at now. Anything I might reach by climbing a ladder does not interest me. (CV, 7)

In the *Tractatus*, Wittgenstein expresses the impulse to transcend his fallible human condition. He thus seeks a redemption that still adheres to the Christian compensatory model that Nietzsche criticizes, since it seeks to dispense with and be redeemed *from* the sins of the past, rather than be transfigured along *with* them. In the later passage, Wittgenstein is accepting of his human imperfection, as Bloom is of his in *Ulysses*. In the *Tractatus*, Wittgenstein talks of climbing to the heights atop a ladder, from which to survey the world "in the right way." In the passage quoted above, however, his focus falls closer to home, to "the place [he] must already be at now." He is committed to exploring the lay of the land as it is. Kremer supplements Wittgenstein's Tractarian ladder metaphor with his later call for more grounded, localized investigations: The "ladder" of the *Tractatus* leads us not to a point higher and higher above the world, but out of the pit into the world, in which we are now free to live.[74]

Wittgenstein seeks to engage us in a philosophical activity of clarification. He aims to lead us to a point where we can live comfortably in our own world—in part by dispelling the illusion of having transcended that world. His aim in the *Tractatus* is to lead us to achieve clarity by equipping us with tools that help us to use our ordinary capacity to distinguish what makes sense from what does not. His efforts to help us overcome our philosophical problems by transforming them involves detaching them from theses and from what Diamond refers to as the "Big Question" (whether that question takes the form of an interrogation of the nature of language, the how and why of existence, or something else), and its attendant the search for the Big Answer.[75] When he wrote the *Tractatus*, Wittgenstein believed himself to have solved the fundamental problems of philosophy, the confusions he would have us overcome. Yet, as we saw in the introduction, the fact that his method of clarification nonetheless remained held in the distorting grip of his own self-bewitchment by essentializing ideas that bring his practice into "unbearable conflict" with his conception of the proper practice of philosophy shows that he had not quite succeeded in carrying out his aim of overcoming them in his early work.

As Diamond and Conant see it, there are two kinds of metaphysical language at issue in the *Tractatus*. First, there is the metaphysical nonsense Wittgenstein employs self-consciously, ironically, as a transitional tactic to get readers to recognize their unconscious adherence to metaphysical theses. But there are moments in the *Tractatus* at which, in spite of his best intentions, Wittgenstein's own unwitting engagement with metaphysics shows forth in a number of his still rather dogmatic assumptions. Although the early Wittgenstein did not recognize his continued adherence to dogma, beginning around 1929, he would both acknowledge and criticize this problem.[76] The criticism of the method of the *Tractatus* Wittgenstein gives us in the *Investigations* centers on the fact that the method of his first book still labors in the shadow of a picture of language related to the Big Question it has not completely got past. "The search for the essence of language is, in theory, *überwunden*, overcome. But it is really still with us, in an ultimately unsatisfactory, unsatisfying, conception of what it is to clarify what we say."[77]

Wittgenstein thus clings, in spite of himself, to the notion that there is something higher, more essential, than the "ordinary language [that] is part of the human organism and is not less complicated than it" (TLP, 4.002). He thereby betrays the goals he set with that book, of attending to ordinary language as a means of "transforming our problems and our sense of where we are with them."[78] The metaphysical viewpoint of which the *Tractatus* aims to cure us still haunts the book and its method. Kevin Cahill, who sees the *Tractatus* as meant to render a cultural critique of the "entire modern worldview," points to the unwitting irony of Wittgenstein's effort to engage readers in a search of something like a *final* vision or ideal of a single method of clarification, thereby succumbing to one of modernity's greatest traps.[79]

Beginning in the late 1930s, Wittgenstein would come to see that the notion that all philosophical problems are resolvable through the application of a single clarificatory method presupposed the possibility of specifying in advance the structure of philosophical problems, and the meaningful use of language. He thus came to view his privileging of a single method of clarification as something that stood in the way of his efforts to look closely at the range and variety of ordinary language use. Using such a method also keeps us from attending to the specificity and variety of the problems we encounter in the course of living and philosophizing.

In the *Investigations*, Wittgenstein no longer organizes his propositions hierarchically to form a linear argument. His later philosophy faces particular problems, rather than seeking to solve *the* problem. As Diamond puts it, the *Investigations* conceives of problems as crosswise, rather than infinitely long lengthwise strips. Wittgenstein no longer imagines the possibility of completely overcoming philosophical problems. Instead, he searches for clarity in particular cases, using particular methods suited to those cases. He no longer holds out for a grand sort of revelatory discovery, but takes a new approach to getting readers to see their familiar ordinary language and life more clearly.[80]

In a remark from the 1940s, Wittgenstein speaks about self-expression in terms of ladders, this time in an attempt to disabuse his readers of the illusion of ascent. "You write about yourself from your own height," he writes. "You don't stand on stilts or a ladder, but on your bare feet" (CV, 33). By the time Wittgenstein writes the *Investigations*, his earlier talk of the solution of the problem lying in the vanishing of the problem is given a new formulation, in the context of a different conception of philosophical method. In *Investigations*, §133, Wittgenstein writes,

> The real discovery is the one that makes me capable of stopping doing philosophy when I want to—The one that gives philosophy peace, so that it is no longer tormented by questions that bring *itself* in question.—Instead, we now demonstrate a method, by examples; and the series of examples can be broken off.—Problems are solved (difficulties eliminated), not a *single* problem. There is not *a* philosophical method, though there are indeed methods, like different therapies.

Here, Wittgenstein no longer entertains a fantasy of ascent, a mystical overcoming of the Big Question. He has relinquished what Terry Eagleton has called the distinctively high-modernist gesture of irony with which the *Tractatus* cancels itself in favor of "the open-ended, pluralistic, generously demotic investigations of his later period."[81] In the *Investigations*, he no longer approaches problems as attempts to solve *the* problem, or answer the Big Question. Instead, he takes up the work of clarification meant to transform our relationships to such questions. His "criss-cross" approach uses multiple methods and ways of dealing with the unending problems with which we are presented every day. Particular problems are resolved, and so disappear, and so one can stop doing philosophy for a time, until the next problem presents itself and calls for a different therapy.

This, I want to say, is kind of peace that Bloom finds by the end of the "Ithaca" chapter's long exchange of questions and answers. If Bloom's outlook enables him to see the world clearly, it is not because it is part of a narrative of ascent of a kind we might attribute to the *Tractatus*. Bloom doesn't look on the world as if from atop a ladder. As Franco Moretti indicates, Joyce has him gazing poetically at the spectacle of the "heaventree of stars" above him with his feet planted firmly on the ground (U, 698).[82] In the striking lyricism of the passage, he concludes logically that the constellation the narrative describes as a "heaventree of stars hung with humid nightblue fruit" is but a utopia, there being "no known method from the known to the unknown" (U, 698–701). It's not that Bloom strives to transcend the ordinary to attain a higher perfection. He achieves clarity by "owning" his past and accepting his life in all its imperfections, trials, and tribulations. The problems and questions that the catechism tackles randomly on a serialized or piecemeal basis are not overcome all at once at the end of the chapter. Nor will they be. What Conant says about the later Wittgenstein also applies to Joyce's treatment of Bloom's predicament at the end of his Odyssean quest: the business of moral or religious life is never finished for him.[83]

Bloom conducts an investigation of "the place he is already at now." His "long and involved journeyings" compel him "to travel over a wide field of thought criss-cross in every direction" and finally lead him home, where he is capable of "stopping doing philosophy" at least until morning (PI, xxix). That Bloom's condition represents an alternative to a vertical climb is apparent even at the basic level of the horizontal posture he adopts at the episode's close. The last page of "Ithaca" finds Bloom and Molly lying down, head to foot, in bed together, "at rest relatively to themselves and to each other . . . each and both carried westward, forward and rereward respectively, by the proper perpetual motion of the earth through everchanging tracks of neverchanging space" (U, 737). At the end of "Ithaca," Bloom succumbs to Wallace Stevens's "difficulty to think at the end of day." He becomes "a self that fills the four corners of night," that "peacefullest time" in which "nothing need be explained."[84]

The kind of peace from quest and question that Bloom finds at the end of the long catechism of "Ithaca" can be understood in relation to a remark Wittgenstein made in a 1930 notebook entry, in which, as Sabina Lovibond observes, the influence of Tolstoy on his thinking is apparent, since he "seems to be rehearsing a very *Confession*-like point":

> If anyone should think he has solved the problem of life and feels like telling himself that everything is quite easy now, he can see that he is wrong just by recalling that there was a time when this "solution" had not been discovered; but it must have been possible to live then too and the solution which has now been discovered seems fortuitous in relation to how things were then. And it is the same in the study of logic. If there were a "solution" to the problems of logic (philosophy) we should only need to caution

ourselves that there was a time when they had not been solved (and even at that time people must have known how to live and think). (CV, 4)[85]

There is a sense in which the attitude Bloom adopts is reminiscent of a view Wittgenstein took from Tolstoy: in our efforts to come to terms with the complicated questions of language, thought, and being, we would be wise to take a cue from "those for whom there is no such thing as the 'problem' of life; for whom pseudo-questions, disengaged from the machinery of actual thought, do not arise; or who exemplify the un-selfconscious 'integration of language and activity.' "[86] For Bloom, as for Wittgenstein, the solution to the problem of life is indeed seen in the vanishing of the problem, if only because he allows (or the catechism's abrupt conclusion simply *obliges*) his problems to dissolve (and as water in the episode, to "hold in solution all soluble substances") at the close of day into the dreams of "sound repose" just before the chapter ends, facing a multitude of unresolved questions with an oversized *Punkt*. In silence.

5

A New Life Is a New Life: Teaching, Transformation, and Tautology in Coetzee's *Childhood of Jesus*

What I mean to say is that in our truest reading, as students, we searched the page for guidance, guidance in perplexity. We found it in Lawrence, or we found it in Eliot, the early Eliot: a different kind of guidance, perhaps, but guidance nevertheless in how to live our lives. . . . If the humanities want to survive, surely it is those energies and that craving for guidance that they must respond to: a craving, that is, in the end, a quest for salvation.
—**J. M. Coetzee**[1]

Ask yourself where we would be if there were no such thing as ladders.
—**J. M. Coetzee**[2]

It may be said that the historical narrative of the life and actions of Jesus is merely a vehicle for a message—a message which concerns the spirit in which we should live. While people may use the narrative in conveying the message (in teaching and preaching), and in helping to make the message alive to themselves, the story (of a man who supposedly did thus-and-so) merely *illustrates* the message.
—**Cora Diamond**[3]

I mean to say that it is human, it is the human drive to transcend itself, to make itself inhuman, which should not end until, as in Nietzsche, the human is over.
—**Stanley Cavell**[4]

Afterword: After Modernism after Wittgenstein

The overarching aim of *A Different Order of Difficulty* so far has been to recast understandings of the significance of Wittgenstein's philosophy for studies in literary modernism (and vice versa). This final chapter extends that project by considering how "literature after Wittgenstein" (this book's subtitle) can also lead us to a better understanding of the way the concerns I have identified as modernism's guiding preoccupations continue to shape works of contemporary literature like Coetzee's. In previous chapters, I have concentrated my efforts of reading early twentieth-century literature in a Wittgensteinian vein on the task of exploring these guiding concerns as they arise in a set of emblematic high-modernist texts by Kafka, Woolf, and Joyce. In this chapter, I turn to a discussion of Coetzee's 2013 novel *The Childhood of Jesus*.

My move from modernist to contemporary literature here might seem to suggest an abrupt shift in the primary focal point of this book. But a consideration of three important aspects of Coetzee's uncommon, overlapping connections to literary modernism and Wittgenstein alike (and this includes Wittgensteinian thinking after Wittgenstein) shows the relationship of continuity, interaction, adaptation, and renewal that links the unfinished project of modernism to its afterlife in the formal, ethical, and political advancements of contemporary literature that represent what Stephen Ross has called an "index of modernism's persistence."[5] Like the works of those modernist figures before him, Coetzee's complex, often inscrutable *Childhood of Jesus* deals internally with the textual and existential difficulties that loom in the challenges it poses for its readers. Coetzee also reconfigures the quests for solutions to the crises of meaning, language, identity, and faith that became such a pressing issue in modernist literature and thought. The interrelated philosophical, formal, pedagogical, and thematic commitments I have identified throughout this book as the defining preoccupations of the different modernist works I have explored here are the very issues Coetzee is concerned to recuperate and rework in his own "modernist-after-modernism" fashion.

It bears emphasizing that the contemporary novel in question here is one composed by an author long dedicated in his writing career to bringing modernism's dominant concerns and formal techniques to bear on his own literary efforts to represent the real in a philosophically and ethically attentive way. Derek Attridge and David James, among others, have made convincing cases for viewing Coetzee's ethical and aesthetic strategies in relation to the formal techniques of modernism (construed both in more traditional terms and according to the more capacious global and historical conceptions of the literary field made available in recent work in what Douglas Mao and Rebecca Walkowitz first called the "New Modernist Studies") rather than to those of a variously designated postmodernism.[6] "Coetzee has always maintained a more effective alliance with modernism than with the age of postmodern writing on whose cusp Coetzee published his debut novel, yet with which he would subsequently never remain in tune," James writes.[7] Attridge first proposes that it might be more accurate to characterize Coetzee's fiction as an instance of "late modernism" or "neo-modernism," only to express hesitation about whether the resonances of these designations made them entirely suitable. He finally speaks of Coetzee's mode of recuperating and expanding on modernist themes and devices in his fiction as entailing a "modernism after modernism," one that "necessarily involves a reworking of modernism's methods, since nothing could be less modernist than a repetition of previous modes, however disruptive they were in their time."[8]

Coetzee's novel speaks starkly to his predecessors' fixation on unanswerable existential questions exemplified in the many "questions as to what and why and wherefore" that resound in Woolf's oeuvre as well as in the pedagogical mode Joyce riffs on in the catechism of "Ithaca." This same genre of questions is an overriding concern of *The Childhood of Jesus*.[9] To indicate the extent to which such questions proliferate in Coetzee's novel, I offer here a representative list of the queries scattered throughout the text, posed mostly by David, the child at the center of the story, to his surrogate father (and teacher) figure, Simón: "What is human nature?" (CJ, 48); "Who am I?" (CJ, 193); "What is brotherhood?" (CJ, 195); "What is value?" (CJ, 167); "What is x?"; "What is a fable?" (CJ, 171); "Who is God?" (CJ, 218); "What is the moral weight of work?" (CJ, 109); "What is it all for?" (CJ, 110); "Why are we here?" (CJ, 17); "How is one to live?" (CJ, 54); "Is this the best of all possible worlds?" (CJ, 41). At one point, Simón finally hits bedrock in his attempt to provide patient answers to the boy's many nagging questions. Exhausted by his own series of explanations and justifications, the only response he manages to come out with is the timeless, exasperated parental version of Wittgenstein's "this is simply what I do": "*Because that is the way the world is.*" "No more questions," he adds. "Be quiet and watch the football" (CJ, 169).

The Childhood of Jesus also speaks to the attraction Coetzee shares with his modernist precursors to varieties of spiritual and transcendent experience, and to the human yearning for transformation, transfiguration, or conversion that figure variously in their different works. Writing under the influence of these earlier writers, Coetzee makes active, purposive use of the kind of unconventional methods of ethical instruction and enticements to the work of moral perfectionism that propelled their earlier modernist experiments. *The Childhood of Jesus* not only tells a story that features the pedagogical work of inculcating others in new ways of thinking; it is also a novel crafted to reflect its author's devotion to the possibility of effecting change in its reader's cognitive, ethical, and affective outlook. Coetzee's philosophically and ethically attentive literary approach has long been fed by source texts from each of these domains. In *The Childhood of Jesus*, Coetzee adds Wittgenstein to his intertextual repertoire, alluding to such signature aspects of Wittgenstein's later philosophy as the "private language argument" and investigations of rule following.

But as I claim here, at the level of the novel's pedagogical aims and chosen form of expression, Coetzee also makes subtler references to distinguishing features of Wittgenstein's early work. He registers his attraction to the oblique, ironic mode of instruction and solemn transformative ambition that he shares with Wittgenstein in the extended parabolic narrative form of his fiction, and in the aspirations for ethical instruction that not only figure prominently and thematically in the novel, but reach to touch the life of the reader beyond the book's pages.

As I have indicated in this section's heading, this chapter embodies more than just a study of Coetzee's *Childhood of Jesus* read in light of the author's investment in both literary modernism and Wittgensteinian philosophy. While it is certainly that, it is also an afterword. It carries that added designation in the most obvious sense that it serves the generic purpose of offering a conclusion to this book, one in which to gather together and turn a discerning retrospective gaze on the intertwining threads of the arguments I have offered in earlier chapters. But this last one also represents an afterword in the sense that it extends the book's primary subject matter beyond the scope of its initial focus on modernism. In doing so, this chapter offers a broader perspective from which to reflect back on preceding chapters from a standpoint after modernism (in both a historical and a critical sense). Or, to be precise, after a modernism read in turn in this book after Wittgenstein in a similar sense.

Because of Coetzee's unparalleled engagement with so many of the concerns that Wittgenstein shares with his literary modernist contemporaries, the after-modernist-after-Wittgensteinian perspective that allows for a fruitful retrospective gathering together of the themes and arguments at issue in *A Different Order of Difficulty* is one made available in Coetzee's novel as it is almost nowhere else. Coetzee's own living involvement with so many of the questions that preoccupied his predecessors gives us exceptional purchase on their work that both sharpens and enriches our understanding of it.

It bears mentioning here that Coetzee's *Elizabeth Costello*, and Cavell's *Claim of Reason*, like other texts I have examined in this book, start with the question of beginning—as if just to begin to say something, the writer needs to already cover infinite distance. *The Childhood of Jesus* ends in much the same way that it begins. Its to-be-continued sense of an ending finds a future only in its sequel volume. And with my opening gesture at conclusions, the present chapter also hails new beginnings for our continuing studies of Wittgenstein. These new beginnings promise richer conceptions of literary modernism and its afterlife by showing how the mutually enlightening relationship between Wittgenstein and modernist fiction opens fresh possibilities for ongoing critical work in philosophy and literature. They also anticipate renewed considerations of literature's role in our thinking about moral life more generally.[10]

In the course of my reading of *The Childhood of Jesus* in this chapter, I look back at the core guiding concerns of *A Different Order of Difficulty*, tracing the ways in which they arise in Coetzee's novel at the intersections of the parabolic and allegorical, the secular and the spiritual, inspired by what Coetzee calls his "attach[ment] to the notion of fantasy."[11] Coetzee's novel grants us unique understandings of the ancient quarrel between philosophy and literature and sheds light on the gap Kafka posits in "On Parables" between mundane, ordinary life and a fabulous realm of the "higher." In it, Coetzee returns to a meditation on the central question Kafka poses in his "On Parables": how, if at all, can the figurative language of literature, poetry, and the "words of the wise" bring about tangible change in our daily lives?[12]

But like Kafka's parable and Wittgenstein's *Tractatus*, the combination of tactical and "different-order" difficulty at stake in Coetzee's novel of migration and linguistic and ontological homelessness can leave readers perplexed, feeling lost and disoriented themselves. Early reviewers of *The Childhood of Jesus* framed their praise for the novel with expressions of dismay at its difficulty, using the same words readers have long applied to the *Tractatus*: "strange," "gnomic," "enigmatic," a "puzzle" they had trouble making sense of.[13]

In her essay on the novel, Elizabeth Anker expresses the sense of frustration readers experience in the face of this "difficult, confounding" text, with its author's notorious evasiveness, and refusal to explain his work during public readings.[14] For Anker, Coetzee's *Childhood of Jesus* blurs the boundaries between literature and theory, offering an illustration of how critique—viewed as a style of fiction writing as well as of interpretation—devolves into a kind of hermeneutic game. In her essay, however, Anker all but ironically turns what amounts to a sort of suspicious hermeneutic gaze on Coetzee's allusive fiction, claiming that by plunging readers into an experience of lostness it "enacts critique" by calling on readers to follow an impulse to decode, and thereby to engage with his writing according to a critique-based hermeneutic (Anker 199).[15] But such a reading is, in the end, less than productive.

In her *Revolution of the Ordinary*, Toril Moi offers an alternative way of working through the perplexity we experience as readers and critics that proves extremely helpful in our efforts to find our bearings in Coetzee's inscrutable novel. Moi emphasizes that for the later Wittgenstein, "philosophy begins in the acknowledgement of this lostness."[16] "A philosophical problem has the form: 'I don't know my way about,'" he tells us at §123 of the *Philosophical Investigations*.[17] If we think of the work of reading literature as something akin to Wittgenstein's notion of the work of philosophy as a therapeutic activity that begins with a recognition of our own sense of confusion, Moi suggests, then we come to see the practice of reading not as a method of explaining, or of unveiling hidden agendas, but as an attempt to respond to the questions that arise for us when we find ourselves surprised or confused and there is something we want to get clear about.

Moi's paradigm question in this regard is one Cavell sees as essential to criticism: "Why this?"[18] "Why this?" questions arise for readers every time we find ourselves puzzled by difficult or unexpected situations a text presents. For Moi as for Cavell, "Why this?" questions are the starting point for our critical investigations (RO, 193). To ask "Why this?" is to acknowledge the "blur or block" Cavell cites as the point of departure for textual inquiry. Such questions prompt us to take the risks necessary to read and write about challenging texts with a kind of daring, trusting our own interpretive convictions, intuitions, and responses.[19] We show our responsiveness to such questions not by attempting to unearth a text's hidden meanings or (in the worst-case scenario) adopting "a permanent pose of knowing cynicism," but by conducting ongoing investigations of what is *there* and what *happens* in the text (and how it discloses the world). Such investigations lead us toward what the later Wittgenstein speaks of as an *übersichtliche Darstellung* (PI § 122), a clear overview, a "perspicuous representation" (as Anscombe's translation renders it) that gives us a surveyable look at things (RO, 184).

Coetzee's difficult *Childhood of Jesus* gives rise with stunning frequency to the "Why this?" questions that are the source of our most productive thinking about a text. Taking stock of just a small sample of the host of questions Coetzee's novel elicits from readers shows just how robust and pervasive Coetzee's tactical use of difficulty is in the book, and points to the deeper order of difficulty at stake in it. For starters, we might ask: just what does the title of the book have to do with the childhood of Jesus (accounts of which are all but absent in the canonical Gospels themselves)?[20] What insights do we stand to gain from the interwoven references in the novel to the other literary and philosophical figures Coetzee invokes most centrally? What is the bearing of the circular nature of the novel's overall quest on its main character's guiding obsession with achieving self-transformation? In short: "Why all this?"

One way of improving our interpretation of Coetzee's complex novel in the context of this study—in the aim of reading it with the kind of understanding Wittgenstein sought from his own readers—is to respond to the book by attending to it in relation to a broader set of questions that arise in our experience of reading the *Tractatus*. Thus, in this chapter I strive to account for the dialectical relationship that Coetzee sets up between his text and its readers, and for how we can see *The Childhood of Jesus* as a novel dedicated to training us to be not just better readers of literature, but more complex and attentive ethical thinkers as well. I examine the kind of lessons Coetzee's parabolic book aspires to convey to us and consider what his indirect method of teaching asks us to *do* in response. I explore the question of whether Coetzee's depiction in his novel of an unrelenting desire for new ways of seeing and living is also meant to provide a model, in the manner of Wittgenstein's *Tractatus* and the works of Coetzee's literary modernist forebears, for the decisive moral shift that the author hopes to inspire in his readers. In this chapter, I look at how Coetzee's book operates therapeutically by prompting us to see life and the world more clearly through its intertextuality and references to a broad array of formal literary genres (novel, poetry, fairy tale, scripture, philosophical dialogue), as well as through the obscurity of the extended parabolic narrative it represents.

These are the questions that steer my discussion of *The Childhood of Jesus* in this chapter. Having spoken just above about the "lessons" the book aspires to "convey" to us, however, I feel moved to qualify. After all, my talk of "lessons" might give the impression that there is a particular "takeaway" to be extracted from the interpretive guidance Coetzee offers in his complex novel. "Convey" would seem to suggest a rather smoother communicative transaction between text and reader than Coetzee's challenging fiction generally allows. "Aspire," in turn, would seem to indicate a more solicitous authorial spirit than Coetzee characteristically manifests in his writing, one motivated by a will to adhere more readily to an ethos of disclosure than to one of withholding. Like his modernist predecessors, Coetzee prompts us to engage in a process in which we must grapple with the unanswerable existential, ontological questions of a "different order of difficulty" at stake in his novel. Convinced, like Wittgenstein, that such questions defy explanation, Coetzee offers none.

Fiction and the Recognizable World

"If the world of my fictions is a recognizable world," Coetzee writes, "that is because (I say to myself) it is easier to use the world at hand than to make up a new one."[21] As I argue below, Coetzee's *Childhood of Jesus* is a novel that is more autonomous than committed. It hews more closely to the form and spirit of the parable than it does to allegories of the most straightforwardly applicable political kind.

On one level, *The Childhood of Jesus* does potentially offer a timely allegory of the worldwide plight of migrants and refugees in what Coetzee (as if in echo of Wittgenstein) so frequently refers to as "these dark times."[22] After all, *The Childhood of Jesus* first emerged into a global refugee crisis that had swelled to overwhelming proportions by the time the novel's sequel appeared in 2016. As such, it is a text that would not be out of place were it examined, for example, alongside the allegorical reelaboration of the scene of the nativity erected on the lawn of Christ Church Cathedral in Indianapolis in July 2018. There, church activists encaged existing crèche statues of the Holy Family on cathedral grounds within chain-link fencing to mount a scathing protest of the Trump administration's "zero-tolerance" policy and the separation of families, and detention of refugees (including the youngest of children) at the US southern border. Their protest was mounted simultaneously to censure self-avowed Christian supporters of that policy for their hypocrisy.

Coetzee's main characters, Simón and David, arrive in the fictive port of entry much like the millions of real refugees currently displaced worldwide by war, genocide, poverty, oppression, and violence. They come seeking the promise of a safe haven, one largely retracted in the era of the ever-constricting (and increasingly restrictive and xenophobic) welfare state. The "holy family" Coetzee improvises in his novel—child, father figure, and adoptive virgin mother—first comes together in a town called Novilla, which they later flee to keep David out of state-mandated detention at a remotely located "special school." In the novel's sequel, *The Schooldays of Jesus*, we find the threesome still on the run from census takers.

In Coetzee's adopted home of Australia, more specifically, refugees arriving by sea, as Simón and David do, are met with forced incarceration in tent cities in the desert, or on Pacific islands kept outside of the nation's migration zone. As Jennifer Rutherford observes,

> David and Simón are met with a contradictory logic that resonates with the Australian state's "benevolent" governance of refugees and, more generally with the rich West's response to the global refugee crisis (charity and push-backs; humanitarian rhetoric and deterrence strategies). A reception centre awaits them, but they end up sleeping rough in the welfare worker's backyard. They are provided with money to purchase immediate provisions, but no food is to be found. Work is available for Simón, but it involves labouring like a beast of burden, unloading impossibly heavy sacks of grain at the docks in perilously dangerous conditions. . . . Life in Novilla is similarly ordered, rule-bound and devoid of the chaos of lives governed by appetites and drives. And yet, as new subjects entering into this ordered society, David and Simón are treated "like dirt" and they become *like* the world's millions of stateless and displaced people.[23]

The initial setting of *The Childhood of Jesus* is a strangely benign abstract realist version of smoothly ordered relocation-camp bureaucracy, one that stands in marked contrast to the violent militarized camps and outposts Coetzee describes in *Michael K* and *Waiting for the Barbarians*, and certainly more benign than the very real detention centers and migrant encampments respectively popping up and being destroyed all across the globe. But as much as Simón and David's arrival at the gate of the new migrant reception center in Novilla speaks as a kind of political allegory for the current ongoing refugee crisis, it is also reminiscent of the highly literary scene set at another gateway: to the caricatured Kafkaesque setting Coetzee gives us in the last chapter of *Elizabeth Costello*. There, the title character's purgatorial existence is one of "becoming parable" in the sense Kafka proposes in "von den Gleichnissen." Coetzee's depiction of the fantastical scenario in which his fictive novelist, Elizabeth Costello, must await her Kafkaesque fate "before the law" is marked by the self-reflexive irony that arises from her writerly insight and sense of historical perspective. Both of these aspects of Coetzee's portrayal of his main character equip her to identify her new transitory place of residence not only in terms of its likeness to a Nazi concentration camp or Soviet gulag but as a "literary theme park" of clichés "straight out of Kafka" (EC, 209).[24]

The characters in *The Childhood of Jesus*, however, perform no such reflexivity. Simón, who can draw on only the barest traces of his past identity, and any education he might retain from his now-unknown past life, not only fails to register the citational nature of the lines from the Gospel that infiltrate much of the advice he gives to David, he also fails to detect the absurdity of the intertextual echoes that shape his literary context as much as they permeate Costello's unnamed town.

Given the prominence of *Don Quixote* in the novel, the stripped-down setting Coetzee creates in Novilla calls to mind "hot, dusty, tedious La Mancha," he describes it in his Jerusalem Prize acceptance speech.[25] From the start of his career as a novelist, Coetzee has shown a fondness for grounding his characters' searches for survival and transcendence in indeterminate yet Defoe-inspired, Robinsonesque *terra incognitae* of economy, isolation, and confinement. Set in an unspecified time, a remote, vague, and colorless present, utterly shorn of history, *The Childhood of Jesus* is no exception. As Julika Griem describes it, the diegetic world Coetzee develops in the novel is one that "yields only a sense of 'here and now,' but not of '*beyond.*'" It is a world characterized by what she calls a "grammar of reduction."[26] The sense of a timeless present-ness and indeterminacy of place that Coetzee creates is something he enhances further with his chosen narrative mode. The bare simplicity of the novel's style serves to isolate Simón's singular voice and perspective, for it is his thoughts and point of view that steer the narrative. Coetzee keeps his story to the present tense and, in his telling, sticks primarily to the back-and-forth of his characters' direct speech, thereby thwarting the reader's sense of any normatively or spatio-temporally orienting narrative authority.

Robert Pippin makes a philosophical connection between the sparseness of Coetzee's prose and the conceptual and tonal minimalism of Wittgenstein's *Tractatus*, thereby positing a bond forged consciously by Coetzee between his own contemporary writing and the aesthetic and philosophical modernism he draws on so scrupulously in his fiction and essays.[27] As James has convincingly argued, Coetzee's characteristic lean and frugal style was first engendered by his early interest in Ford Madox Ford, and various other models of high and late modernist writers (Beckett and Kafka chief among them). Coetzee himself once declared his commitment to "spare prose and a spare, thrifty world," and to creating in his own fiction even "more sparseness than Ford practiced."[28] Indeed, in *The Childhood of Jesus*, Coetzee takes us to altogether new heights of stylistic austerity, using the novel's extreme phenomenological frugality to act as a catalyst to a complex exegetic abundance.[29]

At the opening of the novel, we are introduced to Simón (whose name is assigned administratively along with his age—forty-five—upon his arrival a resettlement camp in the fictive town of Belstar). We also meet David (likewise assigned a name and an age, five), a boy who has been separated from his mother as well as from the letter, explaining his origin, that he wore in a pouch around his neck).[30] The two arrive together as seekers of asylum and a "new life" at the gateway to the novel world of Novilla, the Spanish-speaking limbo town that is the first permanent point of contact for boat people like themselves, who have voyaged across Lethean waters to be "washed clean" of their mother tongue and all but the barest traces of memory of their previous lives.

Shortly after their arrival, the pair sets out to find their new life in Novilla. Simón announces that there are "no signposts" to guide them on their path, and no key to grant them entry to a dormitory room where they can "lay their heads" for the night, much less to unlock metaphorically any other mysteries they face. This last phrase refers to Matthew 8:20, "the foxes have holes, the birds of the air have nests. But the son of man has nowhere to lay his head." As Pippin points out, in that New Testament fragment, as in Coetzee's novel more generally, the human condition is cast as one of ontological and linguistic homelessness.[31] David and Simón are restless wanderers on an unending, cyclical quest for a "new life" of philosophical and spiritual transformation that will satisfy their deep yearning for more or other than they find.

In Novilla, these two figures of pastlessness and rebirth take their place in a new community—among the docile, somewhat bovine townspeople of the somewhat Nietzschean herd that populates Novilla. The town's name most obviously suggests a no-town, a novel-town—both in the sense that it is the stuff of that genre of fiction and a place of newness and novelty. Yet it is also relevant that in Spanish, the language of the town, "novilla" also designates a heifer, a young cow that has not yet borne a calf. With this in mind, Pippin suggests that Coetzee is also making a veiled reference in the novel to Nietzsche's *Thus Spoke Zarathustra* and its city of the "many-colored cow," as well as to Nietzsche's general description of the herd mentality of modern society, and his characterization of modern human beings as the "last men, who have invented happiness, and blink."[32] Novilla exists in the abiding now of a *nunc stans*. The place is a city of "last men," marked by the death of curiosity that worried Nietzsche, where all longbows available to shoot "the arrow of longing" have lost their tension, and all ambitious desire for the higher realms of humanity that lie beyond mere necessity (love, philosophy, art, music) are dead.[33]

Upon arrival, Simón, the seeker (suggestive of a New Testament Peter), at once denies the child and claims him as kin with the repeated refrain equally indicative of an ambiguous paternity (suggestive of Joseph), "I am not his father, not his grandfather, but responsible for him nonetheless," he declares, in various formulations (CJ, 1, 2, 20). Simón has vowed, since the moment of the "shipwreck" they experienced on their way to Belstar, to find David's lost mother. And if an overriding yearning for transformation in a new life breeds the cycle of quest narratives that makes the world of this novel spin, it is this quest for David's mother that is its most glaring one. The search promises to be fruitless from the outset, since the mother, like all denizens of Novilla, will have been stripped upon arrival not only of the memory that would allow her to recognize the son lost in transit, but also of any known name or identity with which to track her down.

The novel's first phase is itself marked by a number of transformative movements. The first, an arrival at a "new life" in Novilla, is attained at the story's outset, though whether that movement represents a postapocalyptic or politically motivated migration or the passage from life to death to afterlife or reincarnation is never entirely clear. Simón and David's quest for basic mastery of their new surroundings is also soon drained of its urgency. The two refugee figures, who already coexist with an easy intimacy and sense of familial solidarity as the novel opens, strive quietly at this formative point only to adapt and settle into their everyday Novillan life. They attend to the task at hand: to get the lay of the land. They quickly forge a community of trusted colleagues (Simón soon finds work at the docks as a stevedore) and even build a sort of nascent domestic life with their neighbors, the more established newcomers Elena and her son, Fidel. But, having tried to "lay his head" in this new place, Simón soon becomes restless, and a yearning for greater fulfillment (both sexual and existential) becomes his distinguishing imperative.

The second phase of Coetzee's novel unfolds from a radical move on Simón's part to explode any semblance of stability he may have achieved in his life in Novilla's bland socialist idyll. Passing through yet another significant gate—"a rusty gate, overgrown with ivy"—while on a walk with David, he spies three people in tennis whites in front of an upscale residence like figures from a Stefan Zweig hotel (CJ, 68). Among them is a woman, the virginal Inés, whom Simón approaches shortly thereafter, bearing the proposal that she take up the role of David's "real" "true" mother. As Attridge observes about the title character from Coetzee's *Life and Times of Michael K*, however, we are never made privy to Simón's decision making in *The Childhood of Jesus*; "it is almost as if he acts without going through the process of what to do next."[34]

Simón's move to pass the child in his care off to a total stranger initially strikes the first-time reader as the character's strangely misguided attempt to trade in his anodyne Novillan existence for a potentially quite dangerous alternative. It would be an understatement to say that the act he performs spices up the easy daily existence he has grown accustomed to and already bored by. Simón's move at this juncture strikes the reader as outrageous, unaccountably reckless, at least when read as a realist depiction of events (as do Elena and Simón's friend and fellow worker, Álvaro, from their position within the novel). Simón is often figured in the text in his role as a reluctant Sancho, didactic straight man to David's questing Quixote, correcting and attempting to put his patient avuncular instruction to the task of leading the child out of his flights of fancy. In his role as author of this strange narrative thread, however, it is Simón who tilts at the windmills of his own creation. In his new story line, it is now Simón who is impervious to irony. At this pivotal point in the novel, he gives himself over inexorably (but unlike Elizabeth Costello, unquestioningly, without skepticism) to an unerring faith in the unfolding of his own newly established authorized narrative. The plot twist Simón puts into play is related, in deep ways he seems unaware of, to a preestablished set of intersecting narratives: the story of Christ, the mythology of the mother, and not least of all Cervantes's nonreligious Bible of the modern novel. Simón, the father figure, also becomes in the novel a figure of Abraham. He is the "father of many nations," ready to sacrifice his beloved son, and a Kierkegaardian knight of faith, refusing to give up hope for something higher.

Following an eerie moment of a suggestively predatory, sexualized version of a ritual of adoption one might find in Frazer's *Golden Bough* (or as fodder for Wittgenstein's *Remarks on Frazer's "Golden Bough"*), David is reborn into Inés's care.[35] In this second transformative phase of the story, David, now living alone with Inés, at first regresses into a petulant thumb-sucking enfant terrible. Under the threat that the child, whom Inés and Simón see as "exceptional," will be moved to a reform school in a distant town because of his intractably wayward approach to math and reading, the family flees to a town to the north. Soon it is David who invites others to follow him (a hitchhiker John-the-Baptist figure called Juan, the proprietors of their campsite, the doctor who tends to him after an accident with "magic" powder—magnesium given to him that leaves him temporarily blind yet in this state able to "see the whole world"). The book ends with the company looking to start another new life, in another new place—in a new book, as it turns out. For *The Childhood of Jesus* is followed by a sequel, *The Schooldays of Jesus*, in which Coetzee extends the narrative life of his three main figures, renewing the sense of possibility that seemed all but cut off at the knees with the abrupt, inscrutable, even failed ending of the original volume.

In the place of a denouement leading to some kind of final revelation at the end of *The Childhood of Jesus*, then, Coetzee offers us a resumed pilgrimage that is itself a cyclical repetition of the quest with which the novel began. The reader's desire for some kind of resolution in revelation at the end of *The Childhood of Jesus* (a desire that coincides in important ways with Simón's yearning for revelatory change throughout the book) is thwarted by the ambiguity and static circularity of its final pages. The novel thus "both rekindles and relativizes the idea of new beginnings and also of other worlds."[36] *The Childhood of Jesus* delivers neither the revelation nor the "new life" that Simón craves. Instead, Coetzee resumes the course of Simón's quest in a sequel. For nothing creates and gives shape to a new life or a new world, he seems to suggest, like a new work of literature—or indeed, the existence of literature itself.

Coetzee's Formative Fictions

The Childhood of Jesus is a text, as I said above, that functions as a puzzling kind of philosophical fable or parable. Yet even while the novel deals overtly with such themes as the struggle of the immigrant, the reading of "sacred" texts both religious and secular, collective goodwill, parental love, patient ethical teaching, and self-transformative quests, it defies our attempts to come up with easy encapsulations of any lessons in moral thinking it has on offer. The novel flouts our desire to sum up its overall message in several ways. One of these is how it presents readers with a text structured around a multiplicity of intertextual citations and denies us a single, stable theoretical foothold.

The primary intertexts of Coetzee's novel are what Joshua Landy calls "formative" fictions—texts whose difficulty works to train us as a readers in a way that helps us to refine our thinking and strengthen our ethical character.[37] Given its title, *The Childhood of Jesus* points us most obviously to the bearing on his work of Jesus's parables in the synoptic Gospels of the New Testament and the method of ethical and religious instruction they epitomize. Plato's *Republic* provides another key philosophical intertext, particularly in casting Novilla as an idealized "just" city where reason and philosophy hold sway. Also haunting the background of this novel, as it does so many of Coetzee's others, is Kafka's own brand of parabolic and aphoristic teaching about the bearing of literature and "the words of the wise" on everyday life.

Just as central to Coetzee's novel as Plato's dialogues and the Christian Bible is the book Coetzee has declared the secular bible of modern literature: Cervantes's *Don Quixote*. By invoking *Don Quixote* alongside the Gospels as a competing major intertext, Stephen Mulhall argues, Coetzee declares literature religion's successor.[38] Coetzee's use of Cervantes's text in *The Childhood of Jesus* brings to the fore the themes of quest, translation, and the distinctions between realism and idealism, and appearance and reality that Coetzee explores in his novel. Cervantes's archetypal novel is one Coetzee sees as a testament to the power of the imagination, and of literature itself, to participate in and respond to a human yearning to transcend the everyday real it simultaneously describes. In his Jerusalem Prize speech, Coetzee speaks of Cervantes's literary project in the following question and answer: "how do we get from the world of violent phantasms to a true living world? This is a puzzle that Cervantes' *Don Quixote* solves quite easily for himself. He leaves behind hot, dusty, tedious La Mancha and enters the realm of faery by what amounts to a willed act of the imagination."[39]

And at times just above the surface of the novel, and others just below, alongside references to Wittgenstein's remarks, early and late, Coetzee gestures at Tolstoy's confessional writing and synthesis of the Gospels in his *Gospel in Brief*. Tolstoy's *Gospel* had a powerful effect on Wittgenstein's own philosophical commitments and "religious point of view." In that work, Tolstoy fuses the Gospels, stripping them of their supernatural events—no miracles, no resurrection—only Christ's teachings about how we should live. Indeed, there are moments, especially in the first phase of *The Childhood of Jesus*, in which Tolstoy's synthesized *Gospel*—and its relationship to Wittgenstein's ethical aim in the *Tractatus*—seems a more compelling intertext for Coetzee than the canonical Gospels themselves.

To say that Coetzee's general body of work is allusive of many figures of the realist and modernist literary canon comes as no surprise (we have long known how much Kafka, Beckett, Dostoevsky, Defoe, and others have informed his writing), but as far as his connection with Wittgenstein is concerned, Coetzee presents us with a rather special case. *The Childhood of Jesus* reverberates with what Pippin has called "a kind of low, Wittgensteinian rumble."[40] And yet, time was, any abiding connection between Coetzee and the philosopher (beyond, say, one arising from Coetzee's broad linguistic and philosophical interests and academic training) was achieved not so much as a result of his reaching actively toward Wittgenstein as from the attraction his own novels of thinking have exerted on philosophers of a "resolute" ilk, and on other thinkers broadly sympathetic to that interpretive program (EC, 188).

In *The Childhood of Jesus*, however, Coetzee engages with Wittgenstein rather in earnest—pointedly enough, in fact, to have prompted one reader to comment in the "community reviews" section of a popular online platform that a more appropriate title for the book might have been *The Childhood of Wittgenstein*.[41] One might even go so far as to suggest—as I mean to do here—that if Coetzee chose to bring aspects of Wittgenstein's thinking to bear on his recent novel, it is not unlikely that he was prompted to do so under the influence of the Wittgensteinian philosophers who have long drawn on his writing in the elaboration of their own moral thinking. To attend closely to Coetzee's 2013 novel, then, is to hear an even lower, second-order Wittgensteinian roar reverberating beneath the principal rumble. For Coetzee's focus on Wittgenstein in his later writing arguably speaks to an effort on his part to respond in turn to the philosophers who have made a responsiveness to his literature a part of their own meditations on Wittgenstein, philosophy, ethics, and literature.

This is of course not to say that *The Childhood of Jesus* embodies any kind of direct reply to the work of these philosophers. But it *is* to say that their thinking about literature and moral thought in explicit relation to Coetzee's own literary engagement with these matters is something we should consider while canvassing the texts he draws on more or less overtly in *The Childhood of Jesus*. Griem and Yoshiki Tajiri, in separate essays, point to how Coetzee's novel represents not only a "literary themepark" of his most influential literary precursors, but also a "museum" of carefully orchestrated references to the themes he explores in his own existing body of work.[42] I would extend the intertextual archive they account for to include the growing body of significant work on philosophy and moral thought written in connection with Coetzee's writing before *The Childhood of Jesus* (especially by Raimond Gaita, Cora Diamond, Stanley Cavell, Stephen Mulhall, Alice Crary, Robert Pippin, and Jonathan Lear). Although these thinkers' work is not something Coetzee takes up explicitly in his later fiction, it would seem unlikely that it does not obliquely inform it.[43]

As for the "low Wittgensteinian rumble" of the first order, it can be heard in Coetzee's engagement with the "philosophical difficulties" of rule following and private language that are a hallmark of the *Philosophical Investigations* (CJ, 229).[44] First of all, the father-son pair at the center of the novel embodies a variation of a dual figure that runs throughout the *Investigations*—that of the child learner and the adult responsible for his education and induction into the human social and linguistic community. David, the child in Coetzee's story, becomes an extreme literary embodiment of Wittgenstein's "deviant pupil," who has difficulties grasping how to generate a sequence of correctly related numbers. Simón becomes in his paternal relation the teacher left to figure out effective ways of responding to the child's divergent practices and of leading him to the right next step in applying rules that will enable him to *go on* in his mathematical or linguistic endeavors. In this scenario, the teacher-parent must also question his own authority and the claims that he takes for granted can justify what that (culturally, linguistically appropriate) step will be, and whether he has found the most effective and ethical way of communicating it to the pupil for whom he is responsible. Coetzee's Wittgensteinian deviant pupil moves predictably from divergent rule following to the use of a private language made up of nonsense syllables like *la la fa fa yam ying tu tu*. David claims that these sounds mean something to him. But Simón responds by explaining to the child that what he is saying does not amount to language but only gibberish. His retort gives expression to the Wittgensteinian commonplace that a private language is a nonsensical idea, since in order for a language to be authentic, it has to be communal: "Language has to mean something to me as well as to you," he tells the child, "otherwise it doesn't count as language" (CJ, 186; "Health and Deviance," 23).

Coetzee's allusions to Wittgenstein in *The Childhood of Jesus* are never more overt than they are when he invokes the *Investigations* in these scenes. Beyond these explicit references to rule following and the private language argument, however, Coetzee's insinuations of Wittgenstein's thought are less immediately recognizable. They have their origins in Wittgenstein's earliest philosophical writing, and are less easily summed up in relation to Wittgenstein's historical context, biography, or best-known signature concepts of his later philosophy (e.g., language games, forms of life, rule following, family resemblance, "meaning is use," etc.) that are so often the focus of literary works that explicitly take up Wittgenstein's thought.

Still more crucial to my purposes here, Coetzee's general investment in Wittgenstein in *The Childhood of Jesus* shows itself in its main character's abiding obsession with transfiguration and the search for a new life. Wittgenstein's impact also reverberates in the novel's secular engagement with the language and tone of scripture, and with obscure, prophetic teaching related to Jesus's parabolic instruction in the Gospels, at which Coetzee gestures throughout. *The Childhood of Jesus* presents readers with a puzzle text that demands of us the kind of interpretive work that Wittgenstein saw as ethical. The book is at its most Wittgensteinian in the way it deploys difficulty and obscurity in relation to the yearning at its center for a grounded transfigurative movement toward living in the world in the right spirit.

Difficulty and Intertextuality

In *The Childhood of Jesus*, Coetzee works on many levels—structural, stylistic, narrative, and intertextual—to immerse readers in a tenuous subjunctive. This grammatical mood is the native form of expression of the realm of possibility, wish, and imagination that Coetzee champions as the site of the fantastic in which fiction thrives. But it is also the lingua franca of the domain of uncertainty and ambiguity in which he embeds his literary characters. The modes of possibility and negative capability that thrive in Coetzee's text lend gravity and authenticity to his literary efforts to respond to our craving for guidance in how to live our lives. But the guidance in perplexity he offers, fraught as it is with the perhapses and as-it-weres of the world, also serves itself to perplex. Readers of *The Childhood of Jesus* must cope with bewilderment in the face of the hefty interpretive challenge it levels at us. Our experience as readers and critics is a bit like Simón and David's upon their somewhat dazed arrival in Novilla. Like them, we search in vain for signposts to orient us and to point to ways of speaking about the novel in a more straightforward indicative mood. And like them, we follow the winding paths on the map of Novilla searching for the marked "beauty spot" we thought we would reach at the next turn, only to find ourselves at an altogether unexpected destination, standing before a gate that gives way to entirely different narrative directions (CJ, 67).

Coetzee's novel works to create an overriding sense of puzzlement in its readers, a feeling that the story is a cipher whose key has been lost (as Adorno famously wrote of Kafka's tales). Early reviews feature lists of the questions that go unanswered in the book.[45] To begin with, Coetzee conspicuously fails to explain the bearing of the title, with its religious overtones, on the story he tells, and on the interpretive task he allocates to the reader.

In prefatory remarks he made to a reading of his then still-unpublished manuscript at the University of Capetown in early 2013, Coetzee explained that he "had hoped that the book would appear with a blank cover and blank title page, so that only after the last page had been read would the reader meet the title, namely, *The Childhood of Jesus*." Had he done so, the story would have come into the world as unadorned and unannounced as the refugees arriving at their new destination.[46] "But," Coetzee continues, "in the publishing industry as it is at present, that is not allowed."[47]

So, as it stands, Coetzee's title, *The Childhood of Jesus*, quite precedes the story he has to tell. As readers, we do indeed meet the title (or are met *with* it) but not according to his stated fantasy ideal—not as a title disclosed only belatedly, in a final surprise revelatory twist, offering retrospective illumination of our initial naive reading. Instead, our interpretive engagement with the book is largely conditioned from the outset by the fact that we are never innocent of its provocative title. The figure of religious faith and tradition it invokes establishes Christian scripture as a primary intertext among others—none of which, as I have said, presents the reader with a single isolated key able to unlock the text's meaning.

As we first work our way through *The Childhood of Jesus*, we may find ourselves confused about just how it is that this canonical parallel text is meant to guide us in our reading of the novel before us. The connections between the two are not always obvious. For starters, no character bears the name "Jesus" in Coetzee's story. Nor is anyone called Jesús, the common, secularized Spanish rendering of the name that one might expect to find among the characters in the narrative, given its translational device. And as Mulhall points out, Christianity (and indeed the topic and practice of religion in general) is quite absent from life in Novilla. In contrast, however, Coetzee's more overt allusions in the novel to the other primary intertexts by Cervantes, Plato, and Wittgenstein are related to the active role both philosophy and literature play in Novillan life. Philosophy is woven explicitly into the social construction, educative pursuits, and daily existence in the town. Literary works manage to arrive and survive there too, if only in a vestigial state ("Health and Deviance," 32).

The Childhood of Jesus shows its surface attachment to its prominent religious intertext through references to the Gospels (some more pointed than others), and loose riffs on recognizable New Testament motifs. The composed holy family that takes shape in the book includes Simón, at once an uncertain father figure, teacher, and disciple of the child, and provider of the family's daily bread. It is most often Simón who scatters fragments of scripture and Christian theology throughout the narrative. He does so not because he is knowingly quoting scripture, however, but because within the novel's strange logic, he is either giving voice to traces of a past life and cultural literacy not "washed clean" with the rest of his memories when he arrives in Novilla, or he is somehow compelled by the uncanny force of narrative itself to ventriloquize lines from a powerful, immediately recognizable urtext about which he appears blissfully unaware. Simón declares that "one cannot live on bread alone" (CJ, 36). He confesses to David on one occasion that he failed to look out for him because he "slept when [he] should have watched" (CJ, 242). He talks of consubstantiation—you eat pig, you are pig (CJ, 171). He tells the child that his primary task is to grow up to be a good man, like "the seed that goes deep into the earth and puts forth strong roots, and then when its time comes bursts forth in light and bears manifold" (CJ, 246). Simón exhorts him not to hide his talents, to honor his mother, to save the oppressed, to protect the poor (CJ, 43, 246). Bearing traits of Peter and Joseph, as he does, Simón also acts as the archangel Gabriel, announcing the incarnation to the child's virginal adoptive mother, Inés (Agnes, pure and holy patron saint of virgins). And he does so, furthermore, in a room wallpapered with a motif of lilies (CJ, 72).

David, the "exceptional" godson in whom Simón is "well pleased," is Christ-like in his confident flouting of authority; disregard for rules; love of magic and fable; potentially revelatory insights into an unknown, possibly higher realm of understanding; longing to be an escape artist; and desire to "save" his friends and bring renewed life to the dead—in his case, a stevedore named Mariano and a horse reminiscent of *Don Quixote*'s Rocinante that he calls El Rey, and a duckling tortured by a schoolmate (CJ, 49, 199, 157, 244). David renounces his immediate family repeatedly in favor his worldly brothers and sisters, some of whom see him as a mascot, a kind of lamb, whom they prove surprisingly ready to follow (CJ, 275, 255). He experiences strange visions at the hand of an attractive devilish trickster figure named Daga. And finally, when a philistine teacher directs him as punishment for apparent dishonesty to write out on the blackboard, I must tell the truth, he writes instead "yo soy la verdad," I am the truth (CJ, 225).

In spite of these biblical connections, however, in relation to Coetzee's narrative, the book's title, with all the associations it implies, may nonetheless seem somehow ill fitting, hung somewhat askew or too easily unstuck from the text readers feel driven to strive interpretively to contain within the frame it announces. In many ways, the title of the novel stands as a tantalizing provocation of sorts, an invitation to interpretation, always implicitly demanding that we try to account for it, to make sense of its banner presence and explain its relevance to the contemporary work of fiction at hand. If the title confers spiritual gravitas on Coetzee's tale, it does not do so by laying down an Eliot-style mythical order to undergird the novel's significance to the zeitgeist, or to tame its excesses of meaning. By taking as its titular subject matter a period of Jesus's life about which the Christian Bible is notoriously all but silent, and offering a divergent supplement to that story, Coetzee gestures at a gap between title and tale in this novel that is every bit as significant as any connection he asks us to make between them.[48] Indeed, gaps of different kinds (in memory or understanding, between translation and original, appearance and reality, irony and sincerity, zero and one, nowhere and somewhere, "old life" and "new life") are an abiding concern in this novel (and others by Coetzee).

In an essay on *The Childhood of Jesus*, Mulhall draws on his previous analysis of *Elizabeth Costello*, a novel that points self-consciously at narrative gaps throughout its opening interrogation of realism, and still more significantly in the title character's claim that realism in modernist literature is exemplified by the way that Kafka "stays awake during the gaps when we are sleeping" (EC, 32). Kafka does this in his "Report to an Academy," Costello tells her son John, by fantastically embedding one reality (that of a captured ape) into another (early twentieth-century European culture) and then attending carefully to how the logical unfolding of this strange, impossible conjunction of one reality and another can grant us important insights into both. Mulhall focuses on Coetzee's attention to gaps and skips, and to concern with the notions of embedding and embodying he voices in his earlier novel (where they are the preferred, mutually inflecting terms of title character and narrator, respectively), bringing it to bear on his reading of *The Childhood of Jesus*. He uses these notions to examine how Coetzee uses the intertexts in this later novel to explore new possibilities for exploring realism and the relationship between ideas and reality in a fictive medium. Coetzee embeds shreds from each of his literary, religious, and philosophical source texts in his novel, allowing his characters to embody and give voice to the ideas at issue in them in the new context into which he has brought them. By using this intertextual strategy, Coetzee is able to direct, from his astute and sometimes ironic authorial position within the gaps Elizabeth Costello posits, the elucidations his novel as a whole has to offer as a composite work of fiction composed of the various conjunctions of idea and reality he has created. We can understand more clearly what is at stake in *The Childhood of Jesus*, and the clarity about reality (in all its bewildering complexity) to which Coetzee would awaken us with his general intertextual strategy, by remaining actively attentive to the combinations he orchestrates among the particular texts he chooses to embed in the novel, and the particular ideas his characters embody there.

Jean-Michel Rabaté argues that *The Childhood of Jesus* is less an *Imitatio Christi* than a *Projectio Christi*, since it never falls into traditional Christian eschatology but promotes a messianism without a messiah.[49] I argue that by invoking the New Testament as he does in the book, Coetzee calls to mind the Gospels' investment not only in spreading the "good news" by telling the story of Christ's life, but also in laying a path for us to follow in our work toward salvation in the "new life," the quest for which is so central to Coetzee's novel. Giving his book the title that he does also allows Coetzee to gesture at another key feature of the Gospels: Jesus's preferred mode of instruction and spiritual guidance, the parable. I will explore in greater depth in this chapter's conclusion how Coetzee's use of this pedagogical literary device in his own more extensive parabolic narratives ties his novel not only to religious scripture, but also to modernism, and the provocative modernist modes of transformative teaching. Coetzee's intertextual use of the Gospels to make obscure parabolic instruction a part of his novelistic form thus ties him to modernism via Kafka especially, and also the early Wittgenstein.[50]

Master Keys and Critique

As I have said, Coetzee's novel refuses answers to the questions it poses and resists the theorizing it simultaneously tempts readers to engage in. Anker points out that because of its intertextuality, Coetzee's novel "contains a wealth of what at first appear freighted, instructive signs and allusions." Thus, although it holds out "the promise of a master theory," she claims, "the narrative consistently refutes the expectation that any given theory or theorist could possibly resolve or explain anything" (Anker, 188). Anker is certainly correct that Coetzee's *Childhood of Jesus* is rife with apparently loaded references, the proliferation and unusual combination of which may sometimes overwhelm readers. She is also correct that Coetzee actively works in the novel to frustrate our attempts to account for its meaning on the basis of a single *explanatory* theoretical model. Anker is no doubt also correct that certain readers will chose to approach *The Childhood of Jesus* in search of a master theory with which to unite the text's extraneous allusions, and to resolve its open riddles by appeal to ideology. But her claim that Coetzee is concerned to extend the promise of a master theory in the novel is harder to swallow.

To begin their new life in Novilla, Simón and David must also embrace a new language. Though the book is written in English, readers are to understand that its characters are actually speaking a developing but still rudimentary Spanish, the language of all that transpires within its diegetic world. Coetzee flags the problems with language and interpretation that the two refugees have upon arrival with a momentary flash of grave humor that calls to mind, once again, the kind of joke that would certainly count among those Wittgenstein would call "grammatically deep" (PI, §111).[51] Finding himself standing before a locked door to the dormitory room he and the child have been allotted at the resettlement center that is their first point of arrival in the town, Simón asks whether there might not be a skeleton key to grant them access. He asks an attendant, in his faulty new Spanish, not for a master key, a *llave maestra*, but for a *llave universal*, a universal key. In the context of the existential stakes of Coetzee's puzzling parabolic work, and the depiction within it of a fictional place otherwise as devoid of incisive wit and irony as it is of sexual desire or spicy food, the comeback Simón gets in response stands out from the somber austerity of the novel like a dark punch line out of Kafka or Beckett: "If we had a *llave universal*," he is told, "all our troubles would be over" (CJ, 4).

Anker cites this exchange, with its use of the metaphor of a *llave maestra*, as a dialogue that "actively court[s] theorization," and "begs for a metaphorical or allegorical reading," claiming that moments of dialogue like this one "rouse the reader to quest for a key or code capable of cracking the text's many conundrums" (Anker, 187). She argues more broadly that Coetzee's fiction in general solicits readers invested in critique-based hermeneutics to apply a range of theories to his work in order to respond to his call to "look to theory as something of a *llave maestra*: a cipher capable of decrypting the many allegories, allusions, and hermeneutic puzzles staged within his novels" (Anker, 187).

I would not disagree that certain critics have been and will be tempted to respond to Coetzee's puzzling text with a theoretical plug-and-play approach. And yet, I find it difficult to see the line about the *llave universal* as entailing anything but the very *opposite* of a call to search for a key that will unlock the code of Coetzee's text. It seems to me (and surely to Coetzee) that to take seriously the notion that readers can approach a text of any substance with the governing idea that it can be unlocked with a key is to operate with a very questionable notion of how literature—at least Coetzee's literature—works, and the kind of engagement it seeks to elicit from us as readers and critics.

The way I read Coetzee's passage, the remark in question operates as a witticism that gives comfort to the world-weary seeker, the critic who already knows that our troubles (not only as living beings but also as readers of Coetzee's challenging fiction) are hardly over, and that there is no such thing as a "universal key" that can put our troubles to rest. Rather than court our impulse to theorize, the final line from that passage calls on us to recognize a joke made at our expense, a joke any human who has ever longed for universal resolution of his problems can be expected to be in on (Coetzee included). The line also invokes a familiar cliché, one often pronounced in relation to Kafka's writing in the wake of Adorno's well-known comments about it. For it seems to announce that, like Kafka's stories, *The Childhood of Jesus* unfolds in "a parabolic system the key to which has been stolen; yet any effort to make this fact itself the key is bound to go astray by confounding the abstract thesis of [the] work, the obscurity of the existent, with its substance. Each sentence says, 'interpret me,' and none will permit it."[52]

In my view, Coetzee is not soliciting his readers' knowing formalism or affinity for reductive theory. Instead, he urges us to engross ourselves in a reading practice driven by productive questioning of the kind Moi urges us to engage in. He calls on us to pay close attention to the network of confounding details that make up the novel in a way that obliges us to think long and hard about what his fiction is trying to get us to see and understand about the world. If in fact he does, as Anker says, "summon the application of theory," or pander to his readers' intellectual predispositions, I would argue that it is not because he is merely toying with his readers in a glib postmodern "game" that entails his creation of "a parade of gimmicks and ploys" in the way she suggests (Anker, 186, 189). Nor, as she also suggests, does Coetzee compose the complex novels he does only to invite his readers to impose on it a variety of mutually embattled modes of critique characteristic of a bygone era of literary theory, one now eclipsed by what she tends to represent in her essay as something akin to a new theoretical program of the "postcritical."

While Anker emphasizes the ways in which Coetzee moves to "appease" critics by creating for them the opportunity to employ critique, I am more interested in the ways he productively *unsettles* critique in a manner more consonant with the interpretive outlook associated generally with postcritique. Such an outlook is one Rita Felski describes as an "attitude," "mood," or "mindset"—words that dovetail with those Diamond and Conant use to speak about the ethical stance or worldview

Wittgenstein adumbrates in his talk of the world of the "happy," and "right way" of seeing things.[53]

As I see it, if Coetzee is to be understood as an author concerned to create challenging and highly allusive texts with the aim of soliciting his readers' theoretical engagement with his novel, it is not because he is convinced of the power of institutionally recognized methods of scholarly critique (which is not to say that he is not savvy enough to recognize in advance that literary critics will certainly rise to the temptation to ply our trade with the customary application of theory to his fiction). Nor is it because the position he seeks to occupy vis-à-vis his readers is an aloof, manipulative one, from which to seduce us to theorize about his writing in predictable ways, all with the aim of entrapping us in his cleverly overwrought literary-theoretical snare.

If Coetzee does use his novel to solicit his interpreters' application of any number of critical theories, he does so by taking a Wittgensteinian, Kierkegaardian *anti*theoretical mirroring strategy. As Anker herself puts it, he writes a novel that functions as "a hall of mirrors that at first verify whatever theories we expect to see although only to reflect them back to us warped and perverted." He is thereby able to "dramatize the stranglehold any given metric can exert on the limitless possibilities of interpretation (Anker 206, 205).[54] Anker is right to point to Coetzee's academic high-theory wherewithal, and to the way his proliferation of allusions to literary and philosophical ideas and systems functions to lure readers in to the temptation to meet them with the relevant theoretical approach (be it Marxist, postcolonial, postsecular, poststructural, etc.). And her performance in the essay—from the title onward—of the reader's vacillating experience of excitement at the myriad discoveries that await us in Coetzee's layered texts, on the one hand, and of worry that he might just be pulling the wool over our eyes, or baiting us with a bunch of red herrings and false leads, on the other, certainly resonates with anyone struggling to make sense of a novel as suggestive—and yet mysterious—as *The Childhood of Jesus.*

And yet in spite of all this, I maintain that Coetzee's novel is decidedly *not* the "prime occasion for critique" Anker makes it out to be (Anker, 187). If Coetzee seems at first to "goad the critic to pursue a methodological (and, arguably, metaphysical) heuristic that can explain the novel's otherworldly, disconcerting elements," then he works even harder to show readers that no shrewd critical move to explain, decode, decipher, or expose with the help of a single heuristic system is ever going to do the trick of summing up what is at stake in this novel as a whole. As Maria DiBattista says of the questioning works of high modernism, *The Childhood of Jesus* functions in a way that guards its central enigmas intact.[55] In so doing, the novel calls its readers to an attentive interpretive work that neither gives way to straightforwardly explanatory models nor responds to the hermeneutics of suspicion.

In her *Revolution of the Ordinary*, Moi offers a persuasive account of how the tradition of ordinary language philosophy elaborated after Wittgenstein, Cavell, and Austin offers us a powerful way of renewing critique by providing us with an alternative to the hermeneutics of suspicion and the driving notion that we must "read against the grain" in order to detect and expose the ideology that lies hidden within the texts we read. Ordinary language philosophy, for Moi, thus also offers us an important new perspective from which to regard recent debates about surface and depth reading. She argues that suspicious or paranoid methods of interpretation are "not required to produce subtle, complex, critical, and far-reaching readings" of texts. Such methods need not be seen as the sine qua non for the production of compelling critiques of injustice and oppression aimed at contributing to social justice and political change (RO, 5).[56]

What *is* needed as we face literature as what Moi figures a "loosely configured network of texts and practices" is the knowledge that we bring to it, the circumstances in which it touches us, and a practice of Cavellian acknowledgment that requires the kind of attention that Diamond calls for, drawing on the thinking of Simone Weil and Iris Murdoch (RO, 50). Understood as a practice of acknowledgment, reading is a "a conversation between the work and the reader" that demands our receptiveness to the claims even the most inscrutable hermetic texts makes on us, and the way they work on us existentially and ethically as well as cognitively to lead us toward new ways of thinking that are potentially transformative of our understanding of ourselves and the world (RO, 219).

Ethical Guidance Unsettled and Unsettling

One thing that seems clear about Coetzee's fiction is that it is not motivated by argument. As we saw in chapter 3, in her discussion of *The Lives of Animals*, Diamond undermines the status of argument as a primary mode of critical intervention. Attridge suggests that the frustrating, failed arguments presented in the various lessons of that text should more strictly be called *arguings*, events staged within the work that "invite the reader's participation not just in the intellectual exercise of positions expounded and defended but in the human experience, and the human cost, of exposing convictions, beliefs, doubts, and fears in a public arena."[57] Speaking of the kind of conversion experience he sees as the source of Coetzee's ethical outlook, Attridge turns to Diamond's account in "Anything but Argument?" of the way literature works on us ethically by calling not for argument but "a loving and respectful attention" that is the "root of morality in human nature."[58]

As Attridge points out, "one consistent aspect of Coetzee's technique as a novelist is to deny the reader any ethical guidance from an authoritative voice or valorizing metalanguage. We are left to make the difficult judgments ourselves."[59] For Lear, Coetzee's authority lies in his ability to divest himself of authority.[60] What drives him to adopt a style that lets him do so is not a desire to be coy or calculating or to demonstrate that he can do "postmodern hip." His aim, instead, is a morally serious one: to defeat ersatz ethical posturing and banish the transmission of "ethical arguments" representative of what Wittgenstein decried as mere "gassing," chit-chat that deflects our attention from our actual lives. Coetzee attends to the morally serious aim Lear attributes to him by using a narrative style crafted to promote authentic ethical thought in his reader.[61]

As we have seen, Wittgenstein announces at *Tractatus* 6.521 that the solution of the problem of life lies in its disappearance. Years later, he declares that he has no new truths to teach, only new methods, and announces his credo that anything the reader could do for himself should be left to him to do (CV, 88).[62] Woolf models her own commitment to inconclusiveness and the philosophical grounds of her refusal to offer pat solutions to the complex questions she takes up in her writing on the Russian writers whose style and treatment of life so captivated her.

Like Wittgenstein, and each of the high-modernist literary figures I have examined in this book, Coetzee is not in the business of delivering in his fiction—nor eliciting from his readers—easy answers to the timeless, transcendent questions that haunt it. Nor is he in the business of proposing straightforward solutions to the pressing moral and political dilemmas we face in the current era. As Jan Wilm puts it, in a Heideggerian vein, Coetzee's fiction "urges us to rethink worlds."[63] "What Coetzee's novels do not do is tell us how to live," adds Martin Woessner.[64] In the fashion of the modernist literary figures whose legacy he has long solicitously executed, however, the work of facing bewilderment and frustration in an attempt to rise to his challenge of transforming our own vision as we grapple with the perennial questions of the human predicament is work he leaves up to us. Coetzee's move to leave his readers to their own devices is, as Lear asserts, no mere literary device; it is an ethical *strategy*. It proactively generates thought in the reader by first "defeating an easy desire to defer to an author or a surrogate for the author in the text."[65]

In her "Difficulty of Reality" essay, Diamond draws our attention to what Elizabeth Costello says alternately about Ted Hughes and Wolfgang Köhler in *The Lives of Animals*: writers teach us more than they are aware of; the book we read is not the book the author thought he was writing. Diamond uses the gist of Costello's point to cast light on Coetzee's own literary-philosophical treatment of the moral complexity of our difficult reality in those lectures. In the stories about Elizabeth Costello he offers in the Tanner Lectures, according to Diamond, "Coetzee gives us a view of a profound disturbance of soul, and puts that view into a complex context." "What is done by doing so he cannot tell us, he does not know. What response we may have to the difficulties of the lectures, the difficulties of reality, is not something the lectures themselves are meant to settle. This itself expresses a mode of understanding of the kind of animal we are, and indeed of the moral life of this kind of animal."[66]

Coetzee does not eschew answers and explanations on principle, in good Wittgensteinian fashion, as a merely cosmetic gesture of latter-day high-modernist authorship. If he deliberately abstains from offering solutions to the hard problems he explores, and adopts the perplexing formal strategies he does, it is because as an ordinary human animal himself, who must struggle with the incomprehensible wounding difficulties of reality along with the rest of us, he doesn't actually hold them in his grasp any more securely than we do. The textual and existential difficulties he probes in his writing are not settled for him, and not meant for him to settle. What Coetzee offers readers in the place of ready answers or pathways to theory that can settle difficulties for us are complicated stories and philosophical investigations that are crafted to *unsettle* us, and thereby challenge us to expand our minds, imaginations, and moral sympathies in a way that makes us more receptive to understanding the mysterious aspects of life and the kind of animal we are.

In our attempts to grapple with these questions about Coetzee's authority before the unsettled complexities of real life and the human condition his difficult fiction asks us to confront in these "dark times" (as Wittgenstein did in his), it is helpful to regard Coetzee's pedagogical stance in relation to the philosophical and literary methods of ethical instruction employed by the modernist forebears he draws on so consistently in his writing. It is worth considering in the context of the present discussion a passage from Walter Benjamin's perceptive commentary on Kafka. Benjamin's astute reading of his early twentieth-century contemporary offers us guidance that can help us find our way about in the obscure fiction of our own contemporary, a writer as committed as his precursor to casting light on reality by embracing its deepest mysteries

and riddles, and to rejecting all ersatz explanations available to him.
Benjamin writes:

> Kafka wished to be numbered among ordinary men. He was
> pushed to the limits of understanding at every turn, and he liked
> to push others to them as well. At times he seems to come close
> to saying with Dostoyevsky's Grand Inquisitor: "So we have
> before us a mystery which we cannot comprehend. And pre-
> cisely because it is a mystery we have had the right to preach
> it, to teach the people that what matters is neither freedom nor
> love, but the riddle, the secret, the mystery to which they have to
> bow—without reflection and even against their conscience." . . .
> Kafka had a rare capacity for creating parables for himself. Yet
> his parables are never exhausted by what is explainable; on the
> contrary, he took all conceivable precautions against the inter-
> pretation of his writings.

To read Kafka's parables with understanding, Benjamin advises, "one
has to find one's way in them circumspectly, cautiously, and warily."[67]

As readers of Kafka's obscure texts, we do often feel lost, pushed to
the limits of our understanding in the way Benjamin describes. As I have
indicated, we experience a similar sense of lostness as readers of Coetzee's *Childhood of Jesus*. But by exhorting readers to try to find our
way about in Kafka's parables (which of course provide Coetzee with
one important model for his own mode of engagement with the reader
in novels like *The Childhood of Jesus*) with the advice that we should
proceed "circumspectly, cautiously, and warily," Benjamin is pointedly
not advising us to try to find our bearings by seeking out explanatory
approaches that promise to tame or unseat the "riddle, the secret, the
mystery" on which they turn. Instead, he suggests, we should regard the
mystery at issue in them with a certain attitude of reverence.

We do our best reading of Kafka's stories when we attend to the
points where his texts confound us the most. For it is often in these moments that we find the source of our best interpretive, philosophical
thinking. And by calling on us to be "circumspect" and "wary" as we
wander, flummoxed and adrift, through Kafka's texts, Benjamin is certainly not calling on us to read them with a hermeneutic of suspicion.
To read Kafka in that way, it seems to me as to Benjamin, would be to
read him in the wrong spirit. To follow Benjamin's advice, on the other
hand, is to strive self-consciously to inhabit the predicament of lostness
in which Kafka's writing submerses us. Our confusion can thus play a

decisive role in a generative reading practice that plays out in an ongoing quest toward perspicuity if we strive actively to respond to our perplexity by paying meticulous attention to the textual details in which it is rooted.

If we face our confusions in this way, we are more apt, in our work of "figuring out," to remain responsive to whatever it is that the mystery Benjamin says Kafka claims the right to "preach" stands to "teach" us about "what life is really like" in the community of ordinary people in which, Benjamin declares, Kafka counted himself a member. The work of reading that Benjamin urges us to take up in the passage above entails actively drawing on our own deep sense of bafflement in the face of the mysteries Kafka places before us. It involves letting the questions that arise from our confusion guide our investigations of the text and what it shows us. I see this as the kind of work Coetzee demands of readers of his texts, rather than the engagement in hermeneutical methods that Anker worries he is all too keen to solicit.

Kafka, and Coetzee after him, both strive to endow their readers with a clearer vision of the modern world by bringing the most obscure and pressing aspects of human life into relief in their writing. Part of the point of literary works that function parabolically in the way Kafka's and Coetzee's do is that they don't easily, if ever, give way to transparency, even at the adept hands of the most inventive master readers. Nor should they. The same ordinary life they seek to shed light on is itself run through with extraordinary mystery that mounts a resistance against summarizing gestures at explanation and theorization. The struggles with understanding that Kafka and Coetzee enact in their texts, like the work of interpretation they demand, reflect the plight of the fallible human condition just as they engage readers in the quest for an outlook of clarity that galvanizes Wittgenstein's philosophical investigations from the *Tractatus* onward. Gaining an understanding of these authors, and the kind of clarity about life and the world toward which they would guide us (like Wittgenstein, by setting us to the task of contending with the obscurity of their texts), depends in part on our ability to recognize that clarity—the kind Wittgenstein imagines will give us peace from our problems, however temporary—will also endow us with a vision of life and literature as always bound up with mystery that refuses easy neutralization.

Our creative modes of finding satisfying resolutions to our problems don't, in the end, lead us to definitive solutions. Nor, as even common sense tells us, do problems just dissolve magically on their own. And for Wittgenstein, we can't just resolve them counteradaptively either. As we've seen, what Wittgenstein is getting at when he says at *Tractatus* 6.521 that the solution of the problem of life is seen in the vanishing of this problem is that the philosophical activity of clarification neither solves nor dissolves our problems. We gain peace from them only when they cease to appear to be problems.

To achieve an outlook of clarity about life or literature is to see that both are fraught with a lingering obscurity that we can't always just resolve away. Nor do we always *want* to resolve it away (any more than Wittgenstein would have us attempt the impossible by trying to make sense of the nonsense with which we give voice to the ethical experience he discusses in his "Lecture on Ethics," for example, or than Diamond would ask us to diffuse the range of stunningly unintelligible experiences of the difficulty of reality she explores by trying to do the impossible and make sense of them). To work with that notion of what resolution amounts to would be to fail to register the strange and haunting aspects of reality that literature so creatively makes us struggle to understand. There are also experiences of life that do not seem mysterious but can be expressed only by a kind of mystery, might only look mysterious under the wrong kind of analysis. If we look at the task we face as readers of challenging literature as one in which we can achieve clarity only through our relation to obscurity, we come to appreciate that the work of "finding our way about," "finding clarity," "finding peace from our problems," relief from our questions, and so forth, does not rest on banishing all forms of mystery, uncertainty, or ambiguity. If it did, then the enduring, unanswerable questions of life's meaning that preoccupy so much of twentieth-century literature and philosophy would be divested of the urgency, the potency, and the poignancy they continue to have for us.

When facing difficult texts that seek the kind of attentive engagement that Wittgenstein's, Kafka's, and Coetzee's require, we manage to find ways of resolving our confusions by adopting an attitude of curiosity, even daring, born of a trust in our own readerly intuitions (rather than our suspicions) and an openness to the experience of obscurity and mystery that is not only alive in them but nurtured there. Adopting such an attitude can transform the way we read, the questions we ask, the answers we seek, and the way we look on and talk about literature and what it can reveal to us about ordinary life in all its strangeness.

Though Toril Moi is not concerned in her book with exploring the religious or spiritual valence of Wittgenstein's philosophical revolution, she nevertheless reminds us that the radical change in outlook he seeks for his readers—a shift from a complacent adherence to illusory conceptions of philosophy to a clear overview of things—is something we can experience not just as a far-reaching adjustment of our thinking, but also as a deep-seated transfiguration that also has a spiritual resonance and a parallel in religious writing: "I was blind, but now I see" (RO, 188).[68]

Attention to the conversional investments of Wittgenstein's therapeutic philosophy brings us back to questions about how his way of seeing every problem "from a religious point of view" (though he affirmed he was not a religious man) coincides with his investment in the literature and practice of confession, view of philosophy as a clarificatory activity, and use of authorial guile in the *Tractatus* with the aim of leading his readers indirectly to take up the work on the self this transformative practice demands. It also returns us to a consideration of how each of these aspects of Wittgenstein's philosophical thinking, moral outlook, and instructive method can offer us guidance in our reading of Coetzee's *Childhood of Jesus*, a novel whose obsession with personal transformation unfurls under the heading of an inscrutable allusion to religious scripture and in formal relation to a literary pedagogy that compels readers toward transfigurative change, all while denying us authoritative lessons and leaving the work of understanding up to us.

Religious Underpinnings and Transformative Reading

As I began to indicate above, the kind of indirect guidance in perplexity that Coetzee offers readers not only serves an ethical purpose; it has religious underpinnings as well—throughout his body of work. Rabaté describes the reader's sense of "theological mystery and apocalyptic promise in each page of the novel."[69] Attridge argues that "in his reaching for a register that escapes the terminology of the [Marcusean] administered society, Coetzee has often turned to religious discourse, and there is a continuity among several of his characters who find that, although they apparently have no orthodox religious beliefs, they cannot talk about the lives they lead without such language" ("Age of Bronze," 180). Indeed, all the protagonists of Coetzee's novels, from *In the Heart of the Country* and *Waiting for the Barbarians* onward, express a concern with the state of their soul and a desire for salvation or redemption. The "lessons" of *Elizabeth Costello* offer a series of meditations on the different ways in which religious or supernatural ideas and commitments enliven the human imagination and even our most reasoned secular dealings with the world. Coetzee's interest in the theological notion of grace, for example, begins to manifest itself centrally in his novel

Disgrace, a work that, like *The Childhood of Jesus*, is suffused with religious ideas.[70]

In chapter 4, I argued that in *Ulysses*, James Joyce draws on this
same religious notion of a condition of receptiveness to the divine by be-
stowing a profane, fallible sort of grace on his character Leopold Bloom,
the Odyssean father figure to Stephen's Telemachus and Hamlet, whom,
it seems worth repeating in the current discussion of *The Childhood of
Jesus*, Joyce also characterizes as a light-giving figure of hypostasis.[71]
The profoundly human state of grace that Bloom inhabits at the end of
"Ithaca," as I have described it, is one that informs his attitude of acquiescent self-possession and agreement with the world. The stance Bloom
takes toward life in Joyce's novel is related to the outlook Wittgenstein
describes as "happy" in his early writing, where he characterizes it as a
mode of living marked by a steadfast recognition that the world is independent of the human will and that "even if everything that we want
were to happen, this would still only be, so to speak, a grace of fate."[72]

To clarify a point I will discuss in greater detail below, I want to
draw attention here to the decisive contrast between the attitude of peace
and agreement that Bloom adopts in Joyce's book (favorable, in Wittgenstein's and Nietzsche's views), and the kind of passive compliance
and weak satisfaction that characterizes the figures who inhabit Coetzee's Novilla (unfavorable, by Wittgenstein's and Nietzsche's lights). Although at first blush they may seem collectively to have achieved the spirit
of peace and harmony of the Wittgensteinian "happy" man that I argue
Leopold Bloom resembles in Joyce's novel, this turns out not quite to be
the case. The Novillans' acceptance of the way things are in their world
represents an extreme abstraction of the kind of counteradaptive capit-
ulation to the status quo that, as we saw in the previous chapter, stands
in important contrast to the creative act of imaginative willing (to affirm
the past in a spiritualizing change that gives it new form and significance)
that Nietzsche saw as capable of bringing about the kind of authentic
redemption I associate with Bloom's achievement within the narrative
of *Ulysses*.

In *Ulysses*, Joyce translates the theological concept of grace to a transnational literary context, employing it as a part of his own secular method
of representing a modern worldview shaped by an active kind of interpretive work toward a willed redemption in the form of transfigurative
change. Coetzee's move in *The Childhood of Jesus* to combine faith and
imagination by making religious concepts like grace and transfiguration a
central part of his novel gives him a way of pushing against the boundaries of traditional realism.

The focus on the imagination's transformative possibilities and treatment of self- and world-transcendence that drives Coetzee's novel calls our attention to the religious dimensions of his fiction, especially in *The Childhood of Jesus* and its sequel, *The Schooldays of Jesus*, in which an overriding reference to the story of Christ and a preoccupation with theological notions of transcendence, redemption, salvation, and grace take center stage.[73] Yearning for self-transcendence lies at the heart of Coetzee's attempt to shed light on the human condition in the novel. Crary observes that since the idea of self-transcendence is sometimes associated with religious experience, "it would not be unreasonable to speak in this connection of a *religious* dimension of thought."[74] There is an apparent tentativeness conveyed in the qualifying remark that brackets her claim here ("it would not be unreasonable"). But that qualifying remark itself ends up lending support to one strand of her argument: that in Coetzee's secular literary project, "reasonable" thinking (in contrast to rational thinking, which he is more reluctant to embrace) is entangled with religious ideas.

I turn first, however, to another strand of her argument, one that underlies her claim that Coetzee uses the religious aspects of the novel's structure first of all as a means of giving us a powerful picture of what it is like to be compelled to think or act *without* reason. Literature that features such experience is something he explores in relation to Tolstoy's writing. In an essay on *The Death of Ivan Ilyich*, Coetzee emphasizes the lengths to which Tolstoy goes to undermine the notions of causal reason that lie at the core of his realism. In his later stories, he points out, Tolstoy presents us with characters and situations in which causal reason and plausibility give way to the inscrutable, the out of character, the inexplicable, the act of God. In "bringing God as an actor into his story," Coetzee claims of "Master and Man," "Tolstoy issues a challenge to the rational, secular basis of fictional realism."[75]

We may or may not decide that what Coetzee is doing in the novel he so provocatively titles *The Childhood of Jesus* represents for him some way of "bringing God as an actor into his story." His title certainly introduces the possibility that the child David offers a new literary instantiation of the "traditional figure of hypostasis" appropriate for "these times." But if we choose to look for ways in which Coetzee might be said to follow Tolstoy's lead by bringing some form of godliness to the center of his own story, there are other less obvious, less embodied figures of divine or semidivine intervention in the novel we might point to: the saving grace of parental love, for example; or the quest for self-transformation in relation to such love; or perhaps the intervention of

God's successor—the enduring power of literature itself. Whatever our reading of what "bringing God as an actor" might entail for Coetzee's story, I think that we should underestimate neither the awe Coetzee expresses in his account of Tolstoy's dramatic move as an author, nor his commitment to challenging the rational, secular basis of fictional realism in some related way.

Coetzee also demonstrates what it is like to be compelled to think or act without reason in his treatment of Simón's ethical stance with regard to David in the novel. When we are moved to cut ourselves off from reason in our thoughts and actions, it is most often out of a faith in (and acknowledgment of) other people, even when what they think, do, or say makes little sense to us. To illustrate this experience, Coetzee uses the novel's structural religious aspects in combination with the details of its unfolding plot. On a narrative level, he tells the story of the mundane tasks (and occasionally life-altering decisions) associated with Simón's responsibility of rearing, educating, loving, and believing in the sometimes unfathomable child in his care—a mathematically aberrant, nonsense-spouting boy who, what's more, may or may not have access to higher insights.[76] "In urging us to imaginatively follow Simón in believing in David," Crary writes, "the novel asks us to leap without any clear sense of where we are going and, in doing so, to experience what it depicts as the religious moment of thought in its starkest and most terrifying aspect. *The Childhood of Jesus's* simultaneously formal and descriptive treatment of this dimension of thought is in this respect singular."[77]

We can also regard Coetzee's attempt to get his reader to take such a leap of faith in relation to another religious notion related to such a move. In Coetzee's view, reading that awakens our ethical instincts can bring about "something like a conversion experience." He places this experience of an unexpected, unchosen shift in outlook at the very origin of ethical thinking. He describes it as the experience of a world-renewing assent to life, one that happens without warning.[78]

As Attridge argues, Coetzee sees the act of reading literary (as opposed to nonliterary) texts as uniquely suited to opening us up to the possibility of ethical conversion. This is because what it gives us is not just information, moral exempla, or philosophical truths, but *experiences* that acquaint us with new ideas and a variety of possible meanings. The experience of going through a time of strife or joy is not the same as the experience of reading a compelling literary description of such an experience. Being in "the midst of things," in a Wittgensteinian sense, can mean standing too close to gain purchase on it. But reading about such experience in good literature may give us the distance required to adopt new perspectives on it. The nuanced, varied moral experience that literature exposes us to can have a transformative effect on our lives, however lasting or significant such change might ultimately be.[79] Questions about *how*, or to what degree, a text can change us ethically, or about just what the change in question will look like, however, are not questions that lend themselves to definitive answers. These are questions that remain unsettled, in the sense in which Diamond talks of settling questions about Coetzee's authorship and the kind of solutions he can be said to offer. They are questions we must settle for ourselves, in ways that will be relevant to the particulars of our own varied ways of responding to the ethical experience to which a given text gives rise in us.

The account Attridge offers of Coetzee's views about the potential for personal change achieved through the experience of reading a literary text is a relatively moderate and pragmatic one. He concedes, after all, what we all know to be true: that any such shift in outlook will most likely be fleeting, and in that sense perhaps ultimately inconsequential in the grand scheme of things. But in what Coetzee says about his own stance on literature's power to effect readerly transfiguration, and how he imagines such a thing would play out, he articulates a rather stronger position on the matter. Coetzee is adamant that if we face it with a sincere receptiveness to its dramatic transfigurative power, literature (including, I take him to imply, his own) can bring about in us a change that can be swift, dramatic, and deeply life altering.

Writing about the sudden manifestation of grace in the conversional moments that occur at the end of Tolstoy's "Master and Man" and *The Death of Ivan Ilyich*, Coetzee draws a distinction between a conception of literature as something to be consumed for entertainment, and one that rests on a recognition that the goal of good literature is not the reader's diversion, but her authenticity:

> Whatever it is that "suddenly" happens to Brekhunov or to Ivan Ilyich is unforeseeable and at the same time inescapable. The grace of God manifests itself, and suddenly, all at once, the world is new. In both of these stories, Tolstoy pits his powerful rhetoric of salvation against the commonsense scepticism of the consumer of fiction, who like Ivan Ilyich in his heyday looks to works of literature for civilized entertainment and no more.[80]

The more radical stance Coetzee adopts here with regard to the question of literature's capacity to bring about transfigurative change (which in the context of the Tolstoy tales he examines here does, in the end, satisfy what Elizabeth Costello calls a "quest for salvation"), and the high stakes that Coetzee, like Wittgenstein, attributes to the potentially transformative relationship between text and reader, call to mind the bold assessment Adorno makes about the kind of receptivity to understanding that Kafka demands of his own readers. As Adorno sees it, working to figure out what Kafka aims to get us to see and do in response to his writing requires an attentive engagement that exceeds aesthetic contemplation, and which must go deeper than the proving ground of intellectual acuity. As Adorno describes it, the challenge issued by Kafka's texts is an existential and moral matter of life-or-death proportions.[81]

The Childhood of Jesus is a puzzling novel whose challenge to our intellectual powers of interpretation also necessarily involves a demand for an attentiveness to the story's religious references and quest structure. In writing such a novel, Coetzee engages readers dialectically in a literary tradition of parables and conversion narratives with the aim of contributing to a secular transfiguration of our own very real thinking, feeling lives. Coetzee's transformative strategy is one he develops on (and beyond) the foundation of a more general conception of the transaction between text and reader. That more basic conception is one I would describe as follows: Coetzee crafts the form of his novel as he does with the aim (ethical, in Wittgenstein's sense) of honing the interpretive powers of his readers in such a way that they will gain, as he says using phrases that echo Kafka's "On Parables," "access to another world beyond this one," something he says is achieved neither by doing good works nor by a properly Christian grace but by "giving the self up to fiction."[82] Coetzee thinks that certain works of literature can sharpen and expand our vision of things and thus effect a kind of change in us that spurs us on to take up (now more perspicuously) genuine ethical thinking of our own. Understood in this general way, the dialectical ethical strategy operating in Coetzee's spare, complex work of fiction bears a resemblance to the overall method that Wittgenstein uses in the *Tractatus*.

To be sure, in its generality, this basic sketch of the transformative strategy attributable to both Coetzee and Wittgenstein suppresses certain salient formal peculiarities of Wittgenstein's early dialectical method (just as it fails to attend to related aspects of Coetzee's own). Crary suggests that Coetzee's novel invites us to remake ourselves in a religious register.[83] In connection with that claim, and with attention to the role the novel's stylistic features and intertextual structure play in the way it formulates that invitation, I want to point here to a relevant feature of the *Tractatus* that my adumbrated version of the basic form of Coetzee's and Wittgenstein's complex transformative strategies overlooks: the tone of quasireligious fervor that lends Wittgenstein's framing enunciations in the *Tractatus* their distinguishing prophetical intensity and stylized high-modernist élan.

This tonal feature of the book resonates in the koanic quality of its numbered aphoristic propositions, as well as in the transformative call it issues to readers. The unusual tone of Wittgenstein's obliquely instructive book attests to the deeper aesthetic and spiritual sensibilities that animate the transformative ethical strategy elaborated in it. Wittgenstein refined the aesthetic and spiritual sensibilities that inform the *Tractatus* through his engagement with literature, religious texts, and works of cultural criticism. Attention to these sensibilities points us in turn to the twin sources from which they arise, intertwined, in his early writing. Construed most broadly, these sensibilities derive, on the one hand, from an interest in Socratic-Kierkegaardian irony (used to "deceive the reader into truth") that I have spoken of in previous chapters. They arise on the other hand from an affinity for irony and polemic that is exemplified in Wittgenstein's long and vocal devotion to Karl Kraus.[84]

In Kraus's combination of biting aphoristic wit and essayistic expressions of social despondency, we hear the voice of the apocalyptic prophet sounding off beneath the words (and the silence) of his more climactic Tractarian double. The voice with which that climactic prophet expresses the propositions of the text that he ultimately declares to be nonsense stands in ironic relation to the sincere commitment to ethical transformation that he is silent about.

Wittgenstein's combined use of voice and silence in the book attests to the second source of the spiritual and aesthetic sensibilities active in it. For Wittgenstein's beckoning gesture to readers who "understand him" to follow his lead in mounting the figurative ladder he offers them as a path toward surmounting the illusion and self-deception that impedes their vision in order finally to see the world in the right way calls to mind his lifelong commitment to courage, confession, and atonement, and the equally enduring related fascination with narrative and scriptural accounts of religious conversion that led Wittgenstein to bring Tolstoy's confession to bear on the *Tractatus* and Augustine's on the *Investigations*.

Coetzee's novel is a work animated by a "religious point of view" of the nonreligious kind Wittgenstein espoused. It is equally committed to the hard-going interpretive work the philosopher demands of his readers—the work of change and moral perfectionism that he saw as ethical in its capacity to bring us clarity about the world and our relationship to it. For Coetzee as well as for Wittgenstein, then (to talk of these matters in the combined language of Woolf, Diamond, and Murdoch), our attunement to calls for transcendence and transfiguration is very much a part of the mysterious spirit we live by. It is a part of our form of life as the kind of animal we are. With this in mind, any genuinely realistic picture of the world and the way life is must attend to its enigmatic aspects in much the same way that it must account for other instances of what Woolf describes as the "deviations which the human spirit seems to make from time to time"—the "difficulties of reality" that Diamond draws our attention to, for example; and the human tendency to give strange secondary or poetic sense to the language we use to express our ethical, aesthetic, and religious experience of the world, a tendency Wittgenstein swore he would not, for the life of him, ridicule. [85]

Ladder Lessons

As we saw at the end of chapter 4, between 1921 and 1930, Wittgenstein's thinking about (and use of) ladder metaphors undergoes an evolution that signals the beginnings of a concomitant development in his philosophical method. At *Tractatus* 6.54 he declares the constitutive sentences of his book to be sheer nonsense. But they serve a clarifying purpose, he indicates, for the reader who understands him. Once readers have worked through Wittgenstein's sentences (or as he puts it in that proposition, "climbed through them, on them, over them"), they will finally recognize them for the nonsense that they are.

The recognition Wittgenstein speaks of is gained in the course of what Coetzee's Elizabeth Costello describes in an epigraph for this chapter as the "truest reading." This committed kind of reading is one I contrast with that of any particular "ideal" reader or member of a chosen elect. I also contrast it with the "hermeneutics of suspicion" and "symptomatic readings" carried out in what Felski calls a "spirit of disenchantment," and dedicated to exposing hidden or repressed ideologies in the text through strategies of excavation, interrogation, and decoding that Anker (following Latour, Sedgwick, Best and Marcus, Felski, Moi, and other proponents of postcriticism) is concerned to criticize, and which she claims Coetzee elicits in his fiction.[86]

The "truest reading," as I see it, is marked by an investment in a search for clarity and a craving for "guidance in perplexity" that goes hand-in-hand with the reader's understanding *that* (if not necessarily yet of exactly *how*) Wittgenstein's nonsense sentences stand to offer her (and indeed are composed with the express *aim* of offering her) such guidance. The perplexity in which a reader of the *Tractatus* finds herself arises not just as a result of the complex reading experience Wittgenstein creates with the composition of his extraordinary text. It originates in the philosophical and existential confusions that he thinks act to distort the reader's practice of philosophy, use of language, and view of life. Wittgenstein's method of offering the reader therapeutic guidance in overcoming these confusions involves first submersing her in a pressing and immediate experience of perplexity at a textual level. He does this with the aim of getting the reader to recognize her experience of this more trivial perplexity as a scaled-down version of the more pervasive experience of personal and philosophical bewilderment she must work to overcome. Once the reader has gotten over [*überwinden*] the need for reliance on the sentences of the *Tractatus*, as Wittgenstein says she has to do to attain the clarity and "right" view of life toward which the book seeks to lead her, she must, so to speak, "throw away the ladder" they represent.[87]

I have spoken of the religious valence of Wittgenstein's famous culminating metaphor in the *Tractatus*. His use of the figure of a ladder in his bravura announcement of the resolution of perplexity (and indeed the fundamental problems of philosophy) in that book speaks to the high stakes he attributes to his instructive method, and to his conception of how the "different kind" of philosophical guidance in "how to live our lives" that he offers in his book represents an apt response to a human craving for guidance that, as Coetzee describes it in *Elizabeth Costello*, is merged with a deeply spiritual "quest for salvation."

But, as I indicated at the end of my discussion of Bloom's predicament at the end of "Ithaca" in chapter 4, by the time Wittgenstein had returned to professional philosophy in the late 1920s, he had changed his tune about the utility of the ladder to provide an apt metaphor for his philosophical method. By 1930, we will recall, he favors demotic figures of groundedness over those of transcendence, declaring that anything reachable by climbing ladders no longer interests him. He would "give up" trying to reach any place accessible only by ladder, he says, since the only place he really has to get to is the one he must already be at now.[88] A decade later, he uses the same figure to address his changes in style and ambition, calling for philosophical writing that emanates not from the heights attained with the help of stilts or ladders, but from those reached by standing on one's own bare feet (CV, 33).

Ladders also figure, both literally and metaphorically, in Coetzee's Wittgenstein-infused *Childhood of Jesus*, a novel that unfolds in an earthbound cycle of quests for transcendence and transfiguration. From a realist perspective, within the novel's fictive envelope, ladders serve quite literally as tools of the trade for Simón, and his fellow dockworkers in their adopted town of Novilla. In this place where the industrial progress whose absence he questions is presumed an exercise in futility, ladder climbing is, after all, a necessary part of the arduous physical labor they do every day to move from ship to storage the grain that provides sustenance to the local population.

Midway through the story, however, Coetzee makes a pointed figurative reference to ladders in his narration of a philosophical exchange that takes place—in the most mundane of settings, a bus stop—between Simón and Eugenio, a fellow stevedore (and night-school philosophy student at the free local Institute). Simón brings the discussion to a close with an open-ended bit of advice he delivers to his colleague in the form of a rhetorical question that turns on the metaphorical figure of a ladder. The two discuss the question of sexual desire, something that is all but entirely lacking in the people of Novilla. In this utopic society, in certain aspects a flat, cardboard pop-up version of Plato's ideal city, the notion that desire must be mastered by reason is taken to the extreme. Simón, a recent immigrant to the town (who stands out in the community by being decidedly *not* deficient in sexual longing), wants to know what the members of the local population do to satisfy their "physical urges" (CJ, 141).

The owlish Eugenio, whose sexual experience seems all but limited to seminar room discussions, does his best to respond to Simón's question by appeal to a recent class lesson on the abstract essences of the crude Platonism that structures life in Novilla. Sexual desire has no specific object, Eugenio intones, since it impels the subject not toward the particular, but toward the ideal. To attempt to satisfy erotic desire via "union with an inferior copy," a mere manifestation of the ideal, is only to "traduce the urge" in a way that "can only leave the searcher disappointed and saddened" (CJ, 141). But, Simón asks provocatively in response, "if it is of the nature of desire to reach for what lies beyond its grasp, should we be surprised if it is not satisfied?" He suggests to Eugenio the alternate lesson that "traducing the urge" by embracing inferior copies might just be a necessary intermediary step in the ascent toward the good, the true, and the beautiful. "Think about it," Simón says, before catching his bus. "Ask yourself where we would be if there were no such things as ladders" (CJ, 142).

One way of summing up what Simón is getting at here is this: In the course of any quest for an ideal that lies beyond one's grasp (and this includes attempts to satisfy a yearning for transcendence, a longing for "access to another world" or a "new life" beyond this one"; a craving for salvation; efforts to climb beyond appearance to a higher truth or reality; and searches for a better, more authentic way of living), one might well have to content oneself by kissing a lot of frogs before finding satisfaction in the proverbial prince. For any seeker of perfection stands to find disappointment and dissatisfaction in the failures, imperfections, and facsimiles that she will inevitably encounter (and learn from, he would seem to imply) in the successive steps she takes along the way. Before we can overcome the appearances and illusions that impede our ability to see things in the right way, as the Wittgenstein of the *Tractatus* would have it, we must put in the hard, reflective work of climbing through, on, and over them. This is one way of interpreting what Simón aims to convey to Eugenio with his talk of ladders.

But an alternate way of answering the rhetorical question Simón leaves suspended in the wake of his departure would be to respond with the deceptive simplicity of the middle and later Wittgenstein, who had lost interest in such figures of ascent (having recognized the goal of a final vision they imply as every bit as antithetical to his ongoing antimetaphysical philosophical project—or at least every bit as misleading to the reader the project seeks to engage—as the figurative talk of the limits of language in the *Tractatus*, which, as he points out by reconfiguring these same imagined boundaries in the "Lecture on Ethics," speak more aptly to the "perfectly, absolutely hopeless" tendency of anyone writing or talking about ethics or religion to run up against the walls of a cage).[89]

To answer Simón's question according to the post-*Tractatus* development of Wittgenstein's ideas would be to say that if there were no such things as ladders, we would all be standing on our bare feet, grappling with our problems, and seeking satisfaction at ground level, right where we are. This, I argued in chapter 4, is where Bloom stands by the time he has returned home from his daylong wandering across Dublin at the end of his neo-Odyssean quest. Rather than strive to transcend the ordinary to attain a higher perfection, Bloom conducts his "criss-cross" investigations of the past, present, and future of a varied, lively world with an attitude of satisfaction and curiosity, facing the imperfections of his life and the questions that remain unresolved for him with a redemptive outlook of curiosity, clarity, and acceptance characteristic of a Wittgensteinian "happy."

The culminating moment of Bloom's retreat to his rest, which puts a stop to the barrage of questions and answers that provide "Ithaca" with its catechetical form, exemplifies the kind of "discovery" Wittgenstein describes as attendant to such an outlook. This breakthrough is one Wittgenstein credits with making him capable of stopping doing philosophy when he wants to, of finding peace by putting all questions into abeyance—at least for a time, or until the next question arises to activate a new quest or resumed philosophical investigation (PI, §133).

Coetzee's *Childhood of Jesus* leaves both ways of interpreting Simón's question about ladders open to readers. The novel is centrally concerned with an everyday reality (albeit a decidedly dustier and duller everyday reality than the one offered by Joyce's "new Bloomusalem") that is also fraught with a persistent yearning for transcendence (U, 395). That everyday reality exists in Coetzee's novel in the realm of appearance and nearly static presence that is the town of Novilla. The persistent yearning for transcendence and a "new life" that is this novel's central obsession is Simón's defining characteristic. The yearning for transcendence at issue in Coetzee's novel represents a longing for a very different sort of redemptive transfiguration than the earthbound mode of satisfaction that Bloom imaginatively wills for himself within the narrative arrangement of Joyce's fiction. In *The Childhood of Jesus*, with its stark religious overtones, Coetzee seems to suggest, along with his character Elizabeth Costello, that the craving for transcendence at issue in the novel ultimately amounts to a quest for salvation.

In spite of Eugenio's commitment to educating (and so, presumably, bettering) himself, and in spite of his mechanical privileging of ideal forms in the canned speech he makes to Simón, he is nonetheless representative of the prevailing outlook of a place that is utterly lacking in general ambition or desire for advancement or moral perfectionism. For Eugenio, as for all the people of this town, governed as it is by reason and goodwill rather than by passion or desire, Simón's first question and stimulus for further discussion—"if it is of the nature of desire to reach for what lies beyond its grasp, should we be surprised if it is not satisfied?"—has little meaning. In the end it has only a stultifying effect on their exchange. Through his studies at the Institute, Eugenio has mastered the theoretical concept of the ideal, at least in some loose sense. But he has no active understanding of "the nature of desire," or of what it would be to really *want* and, risking failure, *reach* to achieve such elusive perfection at some uncertain point in the future.

Despite their general restraint and much-touted adherence to a benevolent ethos of "goodwill," the Novillans seem to lack developed faculties of wanting and willing. Thus, absent in Eugenio is a related understanding of the kind of satisfaction (or alternately, frustration) that Simón is talking about. Simón's point, what he is trying to get Eugenio to see, is most likely quite lost on the man. And the suggestion that Eugenio, or his fellow Novillans, might be "surprised" if the desire Simón speaks of were not satisfied seems not quite believable either. For bland contentment and predictable routine are both the condition and the aim of the Novillan form of life. Narratives of ascent to imagined higher realms offer no inspiration to the characters who see things from the compliant, literalist worldview associated with that form of life.

Simón's words lack persuasive force for Eugenio because they have no real resonance in a Novillan context. Like everyone in the world of Novilla, where all basic needs are met, Eugenio *is* satisfied in his current life. Or perhaps more accurately, he is neither satisfied nor unsatisfied. In any case, he is not *dis*satisfied. He is not frustrated in his aims like Ilsibil is, as we saw in chapter 3, in the Grimm story that Mrs. Ramsay reads to her youngest son in Woolf's *To the Lighthouse*, and which Diamond uses to clarify the ethical outlook of "unhappy" dissatisfaction that, for Wittgenstein, makes the world "quite another" from the one viewed from the perspective of its "happy" opposite (TLP, 6.43).

Eugenio is thus representative of a Novillan outlook that is decidedly not "unhappy," in Wittgenstein's sense. The people of Novilla are neither dissatisfied nor resigned, exactly. They do not, that is, regard life in Novilla as something unpleasant they must simply endure. Just the opposite, in fact, for they openly reaffirm the value of their way of life at every opportunity.

There is an attitude of spiritual resignation and lack of moral and political agency that pervades Novilla. Simón notes that the town's inhabitants "do not see any doubleness in this world, any difference between the ways things seem and the way things are" (CJ, 64). And their response to criticism of "the way things are" is prim and defensive. Because (like all denizens of Novilla) he lacks any conception of irony, Álvaro has trouble grasping the joke (and the critical assessment delivered within it) when Simón snidely complains about the unproductive logic of Novilla's industry and form of life with the Voltarian remark that "all is for the best in this best of all possible worlds" (CJ, 41). In response, Coetzee writes:

> Álvaro frowns. "This isn't a possible world," he says, "it is the only world. Whether that makes it the best is not for you or me to decide."
>
> [Simón] can think of several replies, but refrains from airing them. Perhaps, in this world that is the only world, it would be prudent to put irony behind him. (CJ, 42)

The people of Novilla can, in a sense, be said to follow in the spirit of Wittgenstein's 1930 remark in having, as it were, "given up" trying to reach any place accessible only by ladder, since they do, in their weak satisfaction (or weak non-dissatisfaction), hold to life in the place they are already at *now* (CV, 7). But the life they live in the present is not a life lived fully, in the Tolstoyan-Christian sense that informs Wittgenstein's aims in the *Tractatus*. As Coetzee depicts them, they do not, indeed cannot, live fully because they dwell only counteradaptively, rather than poetically, on the earth. By creating characters defined by a fundamental obtuseness in the face of irony and metaphor, Coetzee prompts readers to wonder whether the strange fictive residents of his invented town are truly capable of following in the spirit of Wittgenstein's or any other such figurative claim in the first place. It is not at all clear in the novel that the Novillans, such as they are, would be imaginatively or creatively able to grasp the Wittgensteinian ladder trope I just used above in order to convey (albeit with the qualifiers indicative of a grain of skepticism) the possibility that the Novillans' mode of *holding to* their world might derive from some actively willed ethical attitude or social commitment on their part to living life as fully as possible in the present.

The Novillans pay lip service to upholding a general ethos of collective goodwill in their community. But in the absence of the kind of passion that would foster real solidarity among them, it is hard to see just how the collective they represent could cohere around any living commitment on their part beyond that of a steadfast bond of inertia. Their bond is forged by a complacent kind of torpor born of their having together somehow really *given up* trying to reach anyplace else (or of having relinquished the will to reach after different ways of looking at the place in which they find themselves). Expressed in terms of their literalist relation to Wittgenstein's trope, then, the Novillans' social and ethical commitments seem more the result of abdication than satisfaction. They seem more indicative of a passive surrender to the way life *is* (or happens to be) in the place they are already at now than of any active devotion to dwelling poetically in that place. Dwelling poetically, the art of living both Wittgenstein and Coetzee would have their readers strive for, entails trying in good faith to be responsive to the "ethical" nonsense, secondary sense, jokes, irony, and figurative speech of others. But the Novillans' social and ethical commitments and aspirations seem to extend no further than their current situation. Here they already are now. In this only-world. Why strive to climb metaphorical ladders?

The Novillans' uninspired, nongenerative relationship to learning, shown in their rote civic-minded affirmations of the town's govern-

ing social tenets and catechetical recitations of the philosophical doctrines they encounter at the Institute, represents just the kind of sterile
scholasticism that Joyce lampoons with his chosen catechetical form in
"Ithaca." With their collective tin ear for poetic language and notions of
transformative change, the Novillans are also like the figures who speak
within Kafka's "On Parables"—players trapped within the hermeneutic
form of an endless, unfathomable joke they aren't in on. Like Kafka's
sparring interlocutors, the people of Novilla cannot bridge the gap between ordinary life and an unknown "higher" realm any more than they
can travel the distance between recognizing the generic form of a parable
and understanding what that parable aims to get us to see and to do going forward. For Eugenio and the rest of Novilla, then, Simón's talk of
ladders would seem to be without metaphorical significance.

Understood in this way, the strangely flat fictive community Coetzee
creates as the setting for the novel epitomizes the most literal interpretation of the space opened up by the thought experiment Simón proposes
to Eugenio in his parting provocation. By inventing a place whose inhabitants lack both transformative aspiration and an ear for figurative language, Coetzee makes available yet another response to Simón's question about where we would be if there were no such things as ladders:
Right where we are now, in Novilla itself.

Much to Simón's chagrin, it is in this place, so inhospitable to any
longing for change, depth, and significance, that he must make his home.
In his newly adopted town, he is marked by his own foreignness. But
what makes him seem strange in his Novillan context is not his recent-
immigrant status. For every member of this apparently young society has
come to the town, more or less recently, from somewhere else. Simón
stands out from the rest of Novilla's inhabitants in his stubborn refusal
(or perhaps fictive psychic inability) to conform or (counter)adapt entirely to the ethos of the place. He is alienated from local life by an un-
willingness to suppress his unwavering desire for transcendence and self-
transformation. What he wants is "a new life," brought about by some
shift in the narrative that will compel him beyond the fictive real he occupies in the novel and deliver him from his current predicament to a better, fuller existence.

Republic of the Happy

Not far into the novel, we find Simón trying to verify that the word "an-
odino" exists in Spanish, for he grasps at this word in an effort describe
the generally soothing, dull lifestyle and worldview that is the order of

the day in his new home. Novilla's uncannily anodyne sort of quasiso-cialist utopia is constructed on the basis of the authorizing theoreti-cal model that was its original source, but from which it now appears largely cut off, marked as it is by the general remoteness of any control-ling, overseeing governing body. The theoretical foundation of Novilla's prevailing ethos is one constructed in a composite of various philosophi-cal ideas, each similarly ripped from its ideological origin and reassem-bled, with some irony, in Coetzee's fiction.

Novilla is a place of untrammeled rationality, where measured good-will and a deep commitment to the value of labor, education, and sexual and gender equality preside. Imbued with what Simon calls "the spirit of the agora," where passion is held in check by reason, and citizens engage daily in philosophical debates (about universals and abstract essences—the chairness that unifies all chairs despite local differences; reality's par-ticipation in ideas, and the internal relation of ideas and ideals; the as-cent to the beautiful and the good), the place is clearly evocative of the ideally just city Socrates elaborates in Plato's *Republic* (CJ, 115).[90]

But in the comportment of the people of Novilla, Coetzee also gives us a version of the outlook of peace and acceptance that Tolstoy speaks of achieving at the end of his *Confession* and which, as we have seen, becomes a source of the idealized ethico-spiritual outlook Wittgenstein calls "the happy" in the *Tractatus*, an outlook closely related to his trans-formative notion of what it is to "see the world in the right way" once one has overcome one's philosophical confusions. Although the attitude Wittgenstein calls "happy" involves a kind of willing that "changes the world" (TLP, 6.43) as Simón would do, it also, of course, points us to living as the Novillans seem to do: with purpose, in agreement and har-mony with the world, not in time but in an eternal present, without hope or fear, even in the face of inevitable death (N, 74–76).

The combined Platonic-Tolstoyan-Tractarian-infused utopian vision of a new life and ethical perspective toward the world (a perspective given in these source texts as attainable only through confession, hard work on the self and the formation of collective well-being, and an ar-duous spiritual or philosophical climb—as if up a figurative ladder) is something Coetzee holds up for ironic scrutiny in his novel. If Coetzee concocts a Kafkaesque landscape overlaid with newsreel footage of early twentieth-century European life in wartime as the setting for the last chapter of *Elizabeth Costello*, the society he gives us in *The Childhood of Jesus* looks more like a send-up "Republic of the Happy." His depic-tion of the Novillans' earnest investment in this idealized way of living quickly gives way to a parody in which their principled commitment to simplicity, harmony, and a set of philosophical ideals begins to look more like the uninspired complacency of an almost robotic population of well-meaning but ethically vacuous simpletons. Social existence in Novilla is kind of benign life-in-death of collective lassitude in which there is no change, no yearning, no revolution, no politics, no desire, no excess, no error.

One of the things Coetzee's novel asks us to see is that if we think that the Novillans' outlook is expressive of any ideal it might resemble in appearance (whether that of the Platonic polis or a Tolstoyan-Wittgensteinian "happy" attitude) we would be mistaken. For surely the outlook of the Novillans is not what we want to think "seeing the world in the right way" would amount to. That the actual world (the one Álvaro declares the only world) might be found wanting in relation to certain ideas or ideals (of justice, freedom, progress) is something utterly opaque to the people of Novilla. And in this way, the Novillans' manifest lack of irony goes hand in hand with the unimaginative leadenness and ethical complacency that characterizes their approach to life. Their complacency leaves them skeptical about the possibility of the kind of change that Simón has constantly in his sights. As Stephen Mulhall points out, the Novillans are incapable of doing what Wittgenstein's stance on the plurality of "forms of life" enables: the conviction that making sense of the world means also being able to *see the world otherwise* (TLP, 5.634). What's more, their opacity also leaves them at odds with Plato's Socrates, "master of the irony which operates in the space between seeing and being, appearance and reality—the very gap that Plato's theory of ideas opens up and exploits to lead us out of the cave of illusion and up towards a genuine understanding of reality." For the inhabitants of Novilla, "the theory of reality as dependent upon its participation in ideas is used not to reveal a gap between imperfect actuality and ideal reality that we might close, but rather to identify the actual with the ideal, and so to disavow any real distinction between seeming and being" ("Health and Deviance," 21–22).

In *The Childhood of Jesus*, Coetzee uses the novel medium to convey to us just how easily we can misunderstand Wittgenstein's notion of the happy. With his parody, Coetzee exposes the problematic aspects of this composite ascetic idealization of simple, grounded acceptance that texts like Tolstoy's *Confession* and the *Tractatus* seem to fetishize through his depiction of Simón's frustrations about the place he finds himself in. Novilla presents him with an overdetermined fictive realization of something that feels like an established system based on a once longed-for and agreed-on ideal, now become an unquestioned, community-enforced status quo. Novilla is a place where affect is flat, the food bland, the sex without passion, and the conversation without ironic imagination. It is a utopian society cut off from any sense of struggle, or hunger, or human fallibility, or sense of possibility that would make it a compelling place for Simón. If Woolf's *To the Lighthouse* presents us with a deep anxiety about the future, and a longing to hold life at a still point in time, and "Ithaca" offers a frank assessment of a life, and a picture of what it looks like to imaginatively will satisfaction in the present, even when one's problems remain unresolved, then Coetzee's novel is about the stultifying experience of occupying a present that is maddening because it gives way to nothing new. As such, life in Novilla represents not the apex of Simón's yearning for the arrival at the goal of his quest for transformation, but a place he yearns to move beyond.

Whether or not Coetzee crafted Novilla and its inhabitants with the aim of offering a deliberate indictment of Tolstoyan or Tractarian "happy" point of view, by depicting the ethos of Novilla the way he does, Coetzee diagnoses a problem with overly simplistic understandings of Wittgenstein's thinking about the aim of the *Tractatus*. By doing so, Coetzee cannily if indirectly prompts us to see something wrong with an understanding of "the happy" that too easily takes the peace and repletion that is the earnest goal of long (spiritual or quasispiritual) struggles (across so many religious traditions) for transformative personal and philosophical change and turn it into a caricature. In *The Childhood of Jesus*, Novilla is presented as a kind of sappy, ersatz Western nirvana in which the goal of acceptance is turned into the absence of all yearning for change. Enlightenment, such as it is in Novilla, seems pat. It is something that is presumed to be already attained, but that seems severed from (or perhaps "washed clean" of) the trials one must undergo along the path toward its achievement.

Novilla, where all basic needs are met and where human interaction is handled in apparent goodwill, nonetheless offers a cautionary picture of what life looks like when we labor under the disillusion that we need to put an end to the curiosity, yearning, and restlessness that define us as human beings. "Everyone I meet is so decent, so kindly, so well-intentioned," says Simón. "No one swears or gets angry. No one gets drunk. No one even raises his voice. You live on a diet of bread and water and bean paste and you claim to be filled. How can that be, humanly speaking? Are you lying, even to yourselves?" (CJ, 30).

Frustrated with what she sees as a cliché of his midlife crisis, Simón's friend Elena voices her concern for her friend by taking the pragmatic position that what he really needs to overcome is not his current life, but "this endless dissatisfaction, this yearning for the something-more that is missing. . . . *Nothing is missing*," she tells him. The nothing that you think is missing is an illusion. You are living by an illusion" (CJ, 63). "A new life is a new life," she tells him later. But the kind of "strictly correct method" Elena tries to adopt in her attempt to talk sense to Simón fails to cure him of his investment in poetic, existential nonsense conveyed in expressions of his ethical experience of yearning (TLP, 6.53). Her attempt to disabuse him of illusion is indeed unsatisfying to him. It amounts to a mere tautology, logically without sense, without heft. What she says to Simón doesn't help him philosophically, because Simón already understands that whatever answer or solution to his problems he's seeking, he is not going to find it in Novilla's realm of sense. Nothing that makes sense in Novilla would give him the satisfaction he wants.

"But what is the good of a new life," he responds to Elena's challenge, "if we are not transformed by it, transfigured, as I certainly am not?" (CJ, 143). What Simón seeks as an alternative to the prevailing ethos and metaphysical constructs of Novilla is a philosophy that allows for the passion missing in his current world. In his words, what he wants is "a philosophy that shakes one. That changes one's life" (CJ, 238). Simón's desire for a transformative shift in personal and philosophical outlook runs parallel to the one Wittgenstein calls for in the readers of the *Tractatus*. But there is something deeply unsatisfying, Coetzee indicates, about the inauthentic complacent version of an attitude of "happy" acceptance that has come to flourish in Novilla, as the pay-off, writ large, for yearning and the work of transformation.

Elena's argument in defense of how things stand with the Novillans and their way of thinking and being emerges ostensibly not from any blind defense of the status quo per se, nor does it represent any forceful indictment of Simón's lack of adherence to it. Elena's straight talk to Simón is motivated in the text instead by a desire to communicate her concern for her friend and moral judgment of the strange recent decisions (e.g., choosing at random, and on misplaced faith, in her view, an unsuitable mother for David) that have taken his life in a new direction she finds insalubrious. Elena confronts Simón with appeal to common sense, aiming to enlighten him and shake him out of what she sees as a sort of entitled, self-indulgent delusion on his part (that there is something more and better out there than what he already has and finds dissatisfying; that there is a different kind of life he feels compelled to search for). Look around you and be grateful that your needs are fulfilled, that goodwill abounds, and you have a child who loves you, she tells him (CJ, 107). Be happy with what you have.

What Elena is advocating to Simón is a counteradaptation of the kind Anderson discusses in relation to Nietzsche's thinking about transfiguration and redemption, and which I examined in relation to Joyce's Bloom in the previous chapter.[91] As readers, from a practical, realistic point of view, we understand quite well where Elena is coming from in her worry about Simón's unaccountable choice of Inés as David's mother. Her desire to bring her friend peace from his questions also resonates with us. We can thus easily identify what it is she wants to convey to Simón by suggesting the resolution to his frustrations that she does. But the path to resolution she proposes will not lead to the resolution he wants. Elena's kind, commonsense call to counteradaptation is one we also come to see as deeply at odds with what Coetzee aims to get us to see in the larger context of his parabolic novel of quest. Coetzee's story would be wholly other, after all, were Simón to respond to Elena's call in the way she suggests. And in the end, he refuses to quell his yearning for change with the inauthentic satisfaction achieved by making the counteradaptive move Elena encourages him to make. He adheres instead to the family narrative he has initiated, following the migratory movement it affords him in his continued quest for a new life.

Allegory and Parable

As I pointed out earlier, Coetzee's treatment of migrant life in *The Childhood of Jesus* has real-world resonance, due to its timely relevance to pressing current political events. In our endeavors to account for a tangible relationship between Coetzee's fiction and everyday life, regarding his texts as politically applicable allegories can seem like the obvious place to start. If we feel the impulse to allegorize Coetzee's texts along these lines, it is because we find them so puzzling when taken at face value. We want to *make sense of* the elements of his texts by accounting for the way we take them to function symbolically or metaphorically for further-reaching sociopolitical, philosophical, or critical ideas or issues.

In works like *Waiting for the Barbarians*, *Michael K*, and *The Childhood of Jesus*, Coetzee's way of gesturing allegorically at real-life political events is to create enigmatic characters, place them in timeless, unspecified historical settings, and suppress any guiding authorial presence. The ethical force of those works derives from the fact that he pays more attention in them to lines of thought and questioning than to lines of plot. Combined with our own critical awareness of the shifting political contexts in which he wrote his individual works, each of these facets of Coetzee's writing contributes to our desire as readers to look beyond the limits of what Coetzee *says* in his texts, and to search elsewhere in the world for clarity about the human condition, somewhere beyond the text itself, in Attridge's words, "in a realm of significance which the novel may be said to imply without ever directly naming" (AA, 32).

Attridge's claim that attempts to allegorize complex literary works like Coetzee's (by mapping them on to pressing real-life social or political situations that lead readers to search for meaning in a sphere beyond the limits of what is said in the text itself) resonates with Wittgenstein's stance on the importance of working to attend to what is said *in* a text—and indeed to all that we can say in our everyday language (something he takes himself to have clarified for us with his presentation of the general form of a proposition at *Tractatus* 6). It also resonates with his views about the importance of our not falling to the temptation of thinking we need to look to the other side of the figurative limits he posits in his early writing to find satisfaction in meaning. Conversely, it also reminds us of the importance Diamond attributes to what an author *does not* say in a text and to the absences he writes into them.

Ben Ware's reading of the *Tractatus* as an example of Adorno's modernist conception of an autonomous artwork is also relevant to the present discussion of Coetzee.[92] According to Ware, the *Tractatus* is a text we can place alongside Adorno's own examples of autonomous works of literature—Kafka's stories, Beckett's plays. Unlike a committed work— one by Brecht or Sartre, say—which has a more overt ethical or political message, the autonomous modern artwork offers critique not through its content but through its *form*. "Kafka's prose and Beckett's plays," Adorno writes, "have an effect in comparison to which official works of committed art look like children's games. . . . In dismantling illusion they explode art from the inside, whereas proclaimed commitment only subjugates art from the outside, hence only illusorily. Their implacability compels the change in attitude that committed works only demand."[93]

The *Tractatus* does not communicate a straightforward philosophical "message," overt lesson, or clearly delineated assignment specifying the specific kind of ethical work we are supposed to take up. Instead, to paraphrase both Adorno and Wittgenstein, it dismantles illusion by exploding traditional philosophy (including ethics) from the *inside*. The book's ethical point is not, in this respect, contained *in* the book (as Diamond reminds us). It is not something one might discover in anything it *says*. It inheres instead in the perspectival shift it aspires to achieve in its readers by engaging them in the absence of overt ethics. In order to find the ethical "in" the *Tractatus* and to learn from what the book aims to teach us about how we might look on and live in the world, we must first give up the idea that the work provides any kind of ethical theory for us to grab onto and follow.

And as we saw in chapter 3, Wittgenstein expressed a deep appreciation for literary and poetic works that, as Diamond observes, strive to communicate in an ethical spirit by speaking to a sense of life's uncertainty and mystery, rather than resolving or closing down all negative capability by anchoring the text in a particular moral or political doctrine, or by attaching it to an ultimate, deliverable message for which the prose or poetry in question serves as a mere conduit.[94] Criticisms of the prevailing tendency to try to *explain* the meaning of Coetzee's complex works of fiction by appeal to applied allegorical readings of them in this way is also related to the aversion Diamond shares with Wittgenstein and Woolf to interpretive approaches that read creative literary works as if they were merely attempts to present philosophical arguments clothed in fictional form.[95] And it is for engaging in just this mode of philosophical practice that Diamond criticizes the philosophers and literary critics who contributed response essays to Coetzee's Tanner Lectures in *The Lives of Animals*. One of the central points of Diamond's criticism of these respondents in "The Difficulty of Reality and the Difficulty of Philosophy" is that by looking at Coetzee's lectures as little more than conveyors of arguments, the contributing philosophers and critics end up missing the raw ethical significance of what Coetzee actually accomplishes in those lectures by leaving us at rather loose ends. To read the lectures as they do—with their focus restricted by argumentative blinders, Diamond argues, is to miss the full richness and complexity of Coetzee's provocative thinking art. The respondents' efforts to deflect from the ethical difficulty of the problems Coetzee presents in those lectures onto a range of established and seemingly related philosophical or moral debates and arguments not only fails to resolve the problems at stake for Elizabeth Costello; it shows them up as readers who have failed utterly to recognize the depth and complexity of Coetzee's treatment of those problems in the first place.[96]

As Griem says of Coetzee's two most recent novels, "the strange cast populating the minimized series of *The Childhood of Jesus* and *The Schooldays of Jesus* cannot be domesticated as philosophical 'beasts of burden'; rather, they invite us to reconsider how philosophical questions can be tied to aesthetic and philological questions."[97] That Coetzee's individual works defy readerly efforts to boil them down to any singular sociopolitical or ethical message is also something he has long thematized in his fiction. To cite just one salient example, when an interviewer approaches *Elizabeth Costello*'s title character to pose the question

"What would you say your main message is?" Costello, a woman (so her son muses) not interested in the "big questions," responds: "My message? Am I obliged to carry a message?" (EC, 10). And in a discussion about storytelling and the novel, Coetzee makes a claim that speaks to his own counter-allegorical project:

> No matter what it may appear to be doing, the story may not really be playing the game you call Class Conflict or the game called Male Domination or any of the other games in the games handbook. While it may certainly be possible to read the book as playing one of those games, in reading it in that way you may have missed something. You may have missed not just something, you may have missed everything. Because (I parody the position somewhat) a story is not a message with a covering, a rhetorical or aesthetic covering.[98]

We will recall from chapter 3 that Wittgenstein once wrote to Norman Malcolm that he hoped his friend would get a lot out of Tolstoy's *Hadji Murad*, since there was "a lot *in* it."[99] But as we have seen, when Wittgenstein spoke of there being a lot "in" Tolstoy's novella, he was not talking about a specific moral takeaway he hoped Malcolm would be able to sum up after reading it. For as Coetzee advises with his parodic diagnosis of the impulse to discover a text's meaning or message, as long as one is concerned primarily with the task of figuring out what a story means in connection with a particular sociopolitical context, or theoretical or philosophical game, agenda, or message, one stands to miss entirely what is "in" in the story in the sense in which Wittgenstein describes it to Malcolm. For when Wittgenstein talks of what is "in" a work of literature or poetry, what he is getting at what is contained in the work *as a whole* (as he says of Uhland's *Graf Eberhards Weißdorn*), the development of a "picture of a life" that it gives us through its form, tone, and manner of description, and the ways it works affectively and cognitively to move or even to bemuse us. For the works he is talking about are works he thinks have the imaginative and philosophically instructive potential to expand our moral understanding by getting us to see the familiar things in our everyday world quite differently.

Attridge does not deny the critical insights allegorical modes of reading make available to us. If he is "against allegory," it is in the sense that Susan Sontag asks us to work "against interpretation," rather than in any strict reductive sense. He concedes Northrop Frye's and Fredric Jameson's shared view that all literary interpretive endeavors are essentially extended modes of allegory, since in seeking to pin down or sum up what a given work is "about," commentators must strive to attach ideas to the images, situations, and complications presented in the text.[100] Nonetheless, he is takes a stand against methods of reading that seek pointedly to locate hidden ethical political meanings beneath, beyond or outside the text, but toward which it gestures obliquely. Attridge shows his affinity with Moi's view of our work as readers (and how ordinary language philosophy offers us ways of reading in which we are not hung up on interrogating texts in order to make them cough up their hidden meaning) when he asks, "what happens if we *resist* the allegorical readings that the novels seem half to solicit, half to problematize, and take them, as it were, at their word?" (AA, 35). That is, would reading and discussing such texts *without* looking for messages or ultimate meanings in the end only empty them of their potential political or ethical significance? Or, on the contrary, does sticking to close readings of what the texts themselves say—and working to avoid reading them with an eye to affixing them to a particular idea, event, or message we take them to point to, but instead to follow our confusions and trust our own intuitions about what they are *doing* at their most inscrutable moments—offer us a richer engagement with his texts and what they aim to get us to see.

This question, and the interpretive approach to Coetzee's fiction Attridge advocates in response, are inspired by Donald Davidson's "What Metaphors Mean" as well as Sontag's "Against Interpretation."[101] Both essays are motivated by a shared impulse; they call for paying critical attention not to what an artwork or metaphor *means* (i.e., over and above what it presents most literally), but what it *does*. For both Sontag and Davidson, then (to put their overarching claims in the vocabulary of the later Wittgenstein), the meaning of a work of art or a metaphor lies in its *use*. It is to be found, that is (to put matters in a Wittgensteinian way), in the philosophical or interpretive activity of clarification in which it engages the reader, viewer, or hearer.

The alternative interpretive approach that Attridge advocates in opposition to allegorical reading, in the restricted sense in which he casts it, is one he calls "literal." A "literal" reading is an interpretation that is grounded in the *experience* of reading as an unfolding *event*, one in which the text in question is treated not as an object of interpretation whose meaning we must determine via reference to things and ideas that lie beneath or outside of it, but as "something that comes into being only in the process of understanding and responding that I, as an individual reader in a specific time and place, conditioned by a specific history, go through" (AA, 39).

The experience of reading "literally," in this sense, is a bidirectional one. On the one hand, it is an experience having to do with how the reader's situated position in the world, her intellectual and sociohistorical embeddedness in it, shapes her perspective on the text in question. But the event of reading also has to do, conversely, with how the text, in turn, goes on to *reshape* the reader's perspective toward the aspects of the world (including her embeddedness in it) that the text reveals to her. To experience reading as an event, readers must go through a process of coming to understand that changes our way of seeing what we read by enhancing our responsiveness to both text and world.

Sometimes this enhanced responsiveness is achieved relatively smoothly, as a result of the reader's preexisting engagement with a given text's presentation of ideas, situations, or relationships that are intellectually or affectively already familiar (whether owing to the knowledge she already possesses, or a critical acquaintance with a particular literary genre and the customary ingredients of its form, her personal history or cultural background, or familiarity with such "games" as would facilitate a reading of the story in terms of Class Conflict, or Male Domination). But in other reading experiences, there is more that happens. In these cases, we register a "a strangeness, a newness, a singularity, an inventiveness" and an otherness in what we read (AA, 40). In such cases, increased receptiveness is not brought about in the reader because a text speaks clearly or directly to the specific, individual historically conditioned situation we already inhabit and bring to bear on our reading. It happens instead because the literary work in question leads us into unfamiliar affective, cognitive, and ethical terrain, and thus threatens to destabilize our original viewpoint and shake us out of our comfort zone precisely by presenting us with forms and ideas that are utterly alien to it. As Crary describes it, in works like *Disgrace* and *The Childhood of Jesus*, Coetzee presents the cognitive and moral development in his characters in a way that that "impresses on us the possibility of having our sensibilities engaged in a manner that stretches us beyond ourselves, bringing into view things previously inaccessible."[102] Coetzee's thematic treatment of such development in his fiction is a part of a broader narrative strategy in which by positioning the reader imaginatively to experience difficulty, confusion, and self-transformation at issue in his story, he also invites us to make a living change of our own that allows us to occupy new evaluative perspectives that grant us new visions of the world.

Reading "literally" opens up possibilities and a space for the unknown. Rather than attempting to announce a text's connection with a preestablished meaning or moral code, "literal" reading opens us up to confusion, surprise, and humility and invites an inventive ethical response. Coetzee issues such an invitation to ethical responsiveness in the possibility he leaves open and the indeterminacy of his treatment of the moral complexities of human (and animal) life. His repeated defense of and privileging of the possible over the actual undermines efforts to take narrowly construed allegorical approaches to reading his fiction. As Attridge writes, "if Coetzee's novels and memoirs exemplify anything, it is the value (but also the risk) of openness to the moment and to the future, of the perhaps and the wherever" (AA, 64). When faced with texts that challenge us imaginatively to make something of their unaccustomed strangeness in the way that Coetzee's (like Kafka's and Wittgenstein's) do, we must rise to that challenge in a way that leaves us open to the sense of possibility and uncertainty that allows us to make the kind of change in outlook such texts strive to give rise to in us.

Although Attridge chooses to describe the kind of reading he is keen to advance with the somewhat confounding term, "literal," a better name for the approach he is describing becomes available in an explanatory footnote in which he quite buries the lede. He writes there that another term that might signal something closer to the kind of reading he advocates than the simple kind of allegory to which he opposes it is "parable." This is because, unlike the kind of allegory that seeks to resolve textual perplexity by appeal to an adjacent repository of signification, parables do not gesture at a fixed meaning or alternate content beyond the text itself. Instead, they work performatively on the reader's grasp on meaning, training the reader in the more active and open-ended critical work of thinking and imagining possibilities. Parables offer us a literary form that is compatible with the postcritical reading practices that Moi argues ordinary language philosophy makes available to us. Coetzee's fictions are parabolic not because they are obliquely suggestive of remote meanings, but because they bear a likeness to Kafka's brand of parabolic narrative.

Again, Benjamin's commentary on Kafka's unique form of parabolic writing is instructive. He reflects on the interminable quality of Kafka's parables and notes that the priest's peculiar interpretation of "Before the Law" in *The Trial* gives the sense that the whole novel is but the unfolding of that parable. But "the word 'unfolding,'" he says, "has a double meaning." In the first sense, a parable can unfold as a bud does into a blossom. The second sense he describes is one he likens to the unfolding of a "boat which one teaches children to make by folding paper unfolds into a flat sheet of paper." "This second kind of 'unfolding,' he says, "is really appropriate to the parable; it is the reader's pleasure to smooth it out so that he has the meaning on the palm of his hand."[103]

Benjamin's second sense of unfolding figures the parable as if it were a message written out on the verso side of a piece of paper, and then hidden within the folds of a complex origami shape it has been given. In this sense of unfolding, the secreted message can be easily retrieved (to the destruction of its previous aesthetic form) by simply spreading the paper flat and thereby rendering the message clearly legible and open to view. This second sense of unfolding, because it features a hidden message we can bring to light, bears a likeness to readings offered in search of tangible lessons. But Benjamin distinguishes this kind of unfolding from the way a Kafka parable does it. He continues:

> Kafka's parables, however, unfold in the first sense, the way a bud turns into a blossom. This is why their effect resembles poetry. This does not mean that his prose pieces belong entirely in the tradition of Western prose forms; they have, rather, a similar relationship to doctrine as the Haggadah does to the Halakah. They are not parables, and yet they do not want to be taken at face value. But do we have the doctrine which Kafka's parables interpret and which K.'s postures and the gestures of his animals clarify? It does not exist; all we can say is that here and there we have an allusion to it. Kafka might have said that these are relics transmitting the doctrine, although we could regard them just as well as precursors preparing the doctrine. In every case it is a question of how life and work are organized in human society.[104]

Kafka's poetic parables preserve within them a level of uncertainty and open-endedness. They are not rooted in religious doctrine and do not function to illustrate or explain it. Instead, they speak in what Crary calls a religious *register* to the incertitude of the human experience that is so important to Coetzee. Unlike interpretive approaches that call on us to apply preexisting norms and make fixed moral judgments, parables like Kafka's (and extended parabolic texts like Coetzee's after them) embrace difficulty, ambiguity, the contingent, and the provisional. They keep moral questions alive by keeping the enigmas they touch on alive in their works.

Conclusion: Parabolic Teaching

In its Greek origins, "parable" means, of course, "comparison," "illustration" (think of the *Gleichnis* of Kafka's "Von den Gleichnissen").

In Matthew, it is synonymous with "mystery." Parables are "dark sayings," stories that cannot be taken at face value, that "mean more and other than they seem to say."[105] They are marked by a gap between what they say and the meaning we must make of what they say, a gap between the figurative and the real. Necessarily incomplete because always awaiting (potentially endless) exegesis of an original sense that may be remote or untraceable, our interpretation of them is in some ways always doomed to failure—if a breed of failure that also sparks further interpretive work. Barring moments of creative inspiration that may emerge from that failure, though, like the man from the country in Kafka's *Vor dem Gesetz*, though we seek access to the hidden sense of the story, the radiance streaming from behind the door just beyond our reach, we remain outsiders to all but its "radiant intimation."[106]

But then the question is, how is it that parables, and extended modern parabolic works (like some of Coetzee's novels, Kafka's *Trial*, the *Tractatus*, for example), function to teach us, to change our perspective or understanding by revealing to us something about the world and the meaning of life, if interpretive exclusion, or an appeal to a set of elect readers, is inherent to the form of that narrative device? Parables seek to challenge and train us by requiring that we hone our interpretive insights through a difficult kind of philosophical work that we are, ideally, to translate into the way we think and live.

In his lectures on Jesus's method of "teaching many things in parables," and on the complexity of the ostensibly simple narrative form and the kind of training it offers, Kermode gets to the crux of the matter of whether parabolic narrative is meant to usher us into understanding or to keep us out with a deliberate obscurantism by pointing to the discrepancies between Jesus's telling of the Parable of the Sower as it is presented in the Gospels of Mark 4:1–20, and Matthew 13:1–23.

In Mark, when the apostles ask Jesus the meaning of the parable, he replies that they, his elect, know the mystery of the kingdom and don't need to be addressed in parables. It is those who stand outside that he addresses this way, "*so that* seeing they may see and not perceive, hearing they may hear but not understand (Mark 4:11–12). In other words: to you insiders I give the secret of the kingdom, but for those outside the fold, I tell everything in parables to keep them from getting the point. But the fact that Jesus's stated aim here of transmitting lessons in a such a way as to make them intentionally opaque would seem at odds with his aim of reaching people with his good news. And this, Kermode explains, has led some commentators to argue that Mark's *so that* or *in order that*, the Greek ἵνα (hina) is a mistranslation of a word that in the lost

Aramaic original meant *in that*, so that Mark's Greek distorts the true sense, which says something like "I have to speak to them in parables, *in that*, or *since* the people in the crowd are the kind of people who can take stories but not straight up doctrine." This attempt to make "hina" mean "since" in this way, rather than "so that" speaks to a desire to shift Jesus's expression of the aims of using parables from one of uncompromising exclusion that seems almost intolerable to one of generosity in teaching. When the same parable is related in Matthew, who must have found Mark's "hina" intolerable too, as Kermode points out, the word "hina" is replaced in Mark 13:13 by the word ὅτι (hoti), "because," with causal force that ends up making the phrase even milder: I speak to them in parables because they see without perceiving, hear without understanding." In Matthew, the implication is that the exclusion arises not from the speaker's intention but from the daftness and laziness of his hearers, to whom he must (or kindly deigns to) minister, not to exclude. If "hina" says "I keep my stories obscure on purpose in order to keep the dull and imperceptive outside," then "hoti" says "I tell outsiders stories because they're too dull and imperceptive to get their point. They are not necessarily impenetrable, but the outsiders, being who they are, will misunderstand them anyway."[107]

Kafka is an example of a writer who, like Mark, supports the "hina" obscurantist doctrine of narrative. The question for readers of Coetzee, a writer whose own attraction to (and peculiar brand of) parabolic ethical instruction is in many ways inspired by Kafka (and in recent work, Wittgenstein), is whether, or to what degree, he adopts either a "hina" or "hoti" stance in his own deployment of difficulty in *The Childhood of Jesus*. Like Kafka and Mark, he is a doorkeeper of sorts, but in that capacity, he too stands outside the gate. Neither Kafka nor Coetzee makes Matthew's move of trying to reduce or tame the bleak mystery and unavailability imposed by Mark's "hina." Neither, for that matter, does Wittgenstein—who eschewed explanation of his puzzling first work throughout his lifetime, never ministering to his readers' indolence.[108] But as we have seen, the author of a book as complicated as the *Tractatus* nevertheless also claimed to address his works to his readers' understanding, rather than to their ignorance.[109] Wittgenstein was committed to the notion that his philosophy could act on us therapeutically. Not in spite of the "hina" implicit in it, but because of it, because of the difficult work of interpretation and clarification it charges us with before we can even begin to attend to what it aims to teach us. *The Childhood of Jesus* embraces the "hina" doctrine in a similar way. Alive with allusions to other stories of yearning and quest for ideal ways of life, Coetzee's book, like the source texts he draws on, prompts us to ask what the relationship is between the sense of puzzlement with which we face the interpretive gaps and difficulties it presents us with and the deeper, spiritually galvanizing perplexity it also thematizes in its obsession with the new life.

Toward the end of *The Childhood of Jesus*, Simón laments that "something is missing." "I know it should not be so, but it is. The life I have is not enough for me. I wish someone, some savior, would descend from the skies and wave a magic wand and say, *Behold, read this book and all your questions will be answered*. Or, *Behold, here is an entirely new life for you*" (CJ, 239). Simón's longing for the answers to be found in a book (or to be gratefully relieved of his longing by getting answers from a book)—whether that book is the omniscient book of facts, or the exploding Big Book of ethics that Wittgenstein uses as thought experiments in his "Lecture on Ethics," *Don Quixote*; Joyce's encyclopedic *Ulysses*; the *Tractatus*; *The Gospel in Brief*; the Good Book; or *The Childhood of Jesus* itself—is a longing left unsatisfied, incomplete, figuratively and literally to be continued (in its sequel, *The Schooldays of Jesus*, and perhaps in an upcoming third volume that would form a textual Holy Trinity).

In the preface to the *Tractatus*, we will recall that Wittgenstein declares "the *truth* of the thoughts communicated in the book . . . unassailable and definitive." He believes he has found "the final solution of the problems." In other words, he says, as if echoing Simón in answer to his wish: *Behold, read this book and all your questions will be answered*. The boldness of Wittgenstein's statement is quickly undermined, however, by the addendum he makes shortly thereafter: "And if I am not mistaken in this belief, then the second thing in which the value of this work consists is it shows how little has been done when these problems are solved" (TLP, pp. 3–5).

As we have seen throughout the chapters of this book, the commitment to ethical instruction in twentieth-century literature and in Wittgenstein turns on an absence. There is nothing in the texts examined here that provides definitive answers to the problems of life. These books and parables respond to our yearning for answers to the questions of being and meaning that resound in them by teaching us to respond to them by willfully, creatively transforming our own desire for an answer to the meaning of life. In the absence of the explicitly ethical in them, we must make of them something from which ethics can be learned, something that gives us new ways of looking at the world and our lives in it.

Acknowledgments

A Different Order of Difficulty was written at Tulane University, but the project has evolved in my travels from place to place and across years since my thinking about it began. It is my pleasure to acknowledge here the various debts I owe the friends and colleagues who helped to nurture the ideas alive in this book, and who made my life and work so much richer as I wrote it.

Figuring out where to begin my litany of gratitude is the easiest part of this book about difficulty. First thanks go to Cora Diamond, whose thinking and writing about Wittgenstein, ethics, and literature, and whose deep, imaginative wisdom in the face of riddles and hard problems, have been a formative inspiration to me. The spirit of her oblique instruction and attentive guidance over the years has shaped my own practices of reading, teaching, and being in the world. I am thankful for her insightful humor, her kind support, and her friendship.

Lanier Anderson and J. P. Daughton have also been cherished advisers. Together and individually, they improved my work immeasurably with their distinct and equally uncanny abilities to lay bare the structure of any argument while remaining alert to the vague unsaid that lurks beneath, and to the possibilities for further exploration there. I am incredibly lucky to have been a member of the Fellowship of Scholars in the Humanities at Stanford

University under their codirection, and to be a continuing beneficiary of their complementary brilliance and jovial sense of doom.

Since any attempt to convey the depth of my gratitude to Nancy Ruttenburg would necessarily fall short, I will say only that she has been a role model in all respects from the moment I met her. A smarter, fiercer, funnier mentor and friend is more than anyone could reasonably hope for. Living the life of the mind as she so superbly does, she makes excellence look effortless. I am thankful for her unwavering support in all things.

I undertook this project with the encouragement of four exemplary teachers and scholars. Tony Cascardi expertly guided me toward new ways of thinking about philosophy and literature, and seeing the *Tractatus* in the context of literary modernism and aesthetics. Michael André Bernstein helped me to recognize the conversional tendency of the modernist novel, and its fascination with quests for the right way of living. John Bishop showed me the joy of Joycean jokes and puzzles and imparted his love of minutiae, startling coincidences, and multiple degrees of entendre. Ann Banfield modeled rigorous original thinking about the combined epistemologies of Bloomsbury and Cambridge philosophy. I am deeply thankful to each of them for their enduring enthusiasm for this project.

I will be forever grateful for the wonderful intellectual community that is the University of California, Berkeley, and especially for its Department of Comparative Literature. If the place ended up being everything it promised, it was the superb faculty and my extended cohort who made it so. The critical intelligence and eye-opening creativity of each of its members continue to inform and instruct me. For the many maieutic discussions that helped bring to life a book once distilled in a Mallard haiku, I am especially thankful for Robby Adler-Peckarar, Mary Akatiff, Michael Allan, Ayelet Ben-Yishai, Michael Cowan, Louise Hornby, Joshua Jordan, John Lurz, Joseph Nugent, Allison Schachter, Ben Tran, and Jenny L. White.

For dynamic workshops and discussions around our big table at the Stanford Humanities Center, I remain tremendously indebted to my fellow fellows Kate Elswit, Brendan Fay, Shana Goldin-Perschbacher, Andrew Goldstone, Danielle Heard, Alan Mikhail, and Edith Sheffer. In the Stanford English department, Claire Jarvis, Michelle Karnes, Saikat Majumdar, Vaughn Rasberry, Hannah Sullivan, Jennifer Summit, and Blakey Vermeule each have my gratitude for their friendship and for conversation that helped my work to change and grow.

In comparative literature at Harvard University, I thank David Damrosch, Sandra Naddaff, John Hamilton, Karen Thornber, and Judith Ryan for their generous guidance; Christina Svendsen, François Proulx,

Isaure Smith, and Wanda Di Bernardo for their friendship and solidarity. Each of these people, along with the members of my cohort of Faculty of Arts and Sciences faculty and fellows (and our weekly palavers) made my years in Cambridge as happy as they were productive.

It has been my great privilege to work in the English department at Tulane alongside an excellent group of colleagues. I am extremely grateful to Kate Adams, Michelle Kohler, Rebecca Mark, Scott Oldenburg, Molly Rothenberg, and Molly Travis, who were such supportive friends to this project and to me during my first years in New Orleans.

Audiences at the Johns Hopkins University Department of Comparative Thought and Literature and the Center for the Study of the Novel at Stanford offered valuable feedback that helped me to hone the arguments in this book. Financial support was provided by the Andrew W. Mellon Foundation, the Faculty of Arts and Science at Harvard, the Institute for European Studies, the Newcomb College Institute, and the Louisiana Board of Regents. I am also grateful for grants from the Lurcy and Lavin-Bernick Foundations, and the School of Liberal Arts at Tulane University. In addition, I wish to thank Alois Pichler at the Wittgenstein Archive at the University of Bergen, and the librarians at the Berg Collection at the New York Public Library, the British Library, and the National Library of Ireland. An early version of chapter 2 appeared in *Comparative Literature* 64, no. 4 (2012): 429–46, and is reprinted in revised form here with permission from Duke University Press. Material from chapter 3 first appeared in *Modern Language Notes* 130, no. 5 (2015): 1100–29, as "Our Toil Respite Only: Woolf, Diamond, and the Difficulty of Reality," and is reprinted here by permission of the Johns Hopkins University Press. A shorter version of chapter 4 was published as "The World as Bloom Found it," in *Wittgenstein and Modernism* (© 2017 by The University of Chicago. All rights reserved).

Alan Thomas and Randy Petilos at the University of Chicago Press have all my gratitude for taking on this project and for bringing this book into existence with great patience and care. I am also indebted to the anonymous readers whose comments helped me to make it a better one.

The life of this book has also been much enriched by the invaluable advice I received from participants in a community in philosophy and literature that transcends institution. Very special thanks are due Joshua Landy for his perceptive reading of the manuscript, and for our many thoughtful conversations since. Kevin Cahill I thank for countless debates about Wittgenstein over the course of a long friendship that began in tears and continues in shared confession and cultural criticism. Megan Quigley, Michael LeMahieu, Reshef Agam-Segal, Jami Bartlett,

Toril Moi, Yi-Ping Ong, Rebecca Schuman, and Marc Caplan offered wise suggestions at various stages of the book's development. I am exceptionally grateful to all these readers and interlocutors, each of whom, it goes without saying, is entirely innocent of any enduring errors here.

I owe an extraordinary debt to Jenny White for coming to the rescue with her keen editorial eye just in the nick of time. Kerry Chance's astounding certainty that this book was already a foregone conclusion helped me go above when nerve denied me. Louise Hornby, my accomplice in modernism, has for years been the cleverest reader of my indirection and my most incisive critic. And because I am always delighted by the visions emanating from her odd juxtapositions, I derived warmth and a sense of possibility from Katherine Ibbett's dream totem of my radiator tome.

Heartfelt thanks go to Cathy O'Sullivan, who created the peace in which to get this project started, Sandy Richmond for her incredible kindness in Dwinelle and beyond, and Susanna Corcoran for her wry regard of my process. This book also owes much to my extended Smyth-Fernwald family. Although the ground beneath our feet was sometimes shaky on that precarious scarp on the Hayward fault, the wild clan that came together there will always be intact, no matter how far apart the earth has flung us.

Sara Edelman, fearsome advocate, has long been the driving force and loving source of support for both this project and its author. Sarah Wheelock has made New Orleans a true home for me. My gratitude to each one of them is boundless.

Finally, for their gift of real joy in the art of living, and a lifetime of encouragement in all that I do, I thank my parents, Patricia Burns Zumhagen and Conrad F. Zumhagen, and my brother, Brian Zumhagen.

My deepest thanks go to my children, Finn Yekplé and Hazel Yekplé. Like it or not, they have more or less grown up with this book. It is infused with their presence even though I often had to absent myself to write it. I am glad for Finn's authentic sense of wonder and fairness, and for his sweetly ironic modulations of same. His unremitting curiosity about all things is a constant spur to my own reflections. Hazel transformed the world as she entered it, with her song of the *force douce*. The mindful strength of her character and the power of her creative autonomy amaze, sustain, and teach me at all hours. Above all, I am thankful for Léo Yekplé, who resolves all manner of difficulty by steadily, soulfully filling all our lives with love and significance.

This book is dedicated to the three of them. And to Stylo, my muse.

Notes

INTRODUCTION

1. James Joyce, *Ulysses* (New York: Random House, 1934), 699. Henceforth cited parenthetically as U.

2. J. M. Coetzee, *Elizabeth Costello* (New York: Penguin, 2003), 108.

3. These remarks, made in 1948 and 1940, respectively, appear in Ludwig Wittgenstein, *Culture and Value*, ed. G. H. von Wright, with Heikki. Nyman, trans. Peter Winch (Chicago: University of Chicago Press, 1980), 76, 36. Henceforth cited parenthetically as CV.

4. "Die Arbeit ist streng philosophisch und zugleich literarisch." Ludwig Wittgenstein, *Briefe an Ludwig von Ficker*, ed. G. H. von Wright (Salzburg: Otto Müller Verlag, 1969), 33; Ludwig Wittgenstein, "Letters to Ludwig von Ficker," ed. Allan Janik, trans. Bruce Gilette, in *Wittgenstein: Sources and Perspectives*, ed. C. G. Luckhardt (Ithaca, NY: Cornell University Press, 1979), 94–95.

5. The spate of books on Wittgenstein and literary studies published since 2015 alone includes Michael LeMahieu and Karen Zumhagen-Yekplé, eds., *Wittgenstein and Modernism* (Chicago: University of Chicago Press, 2017); and Anat Matar, ed., *Understanding Wittgenstein* (London: Bloomsbury, 2017); along with the following monographs: Cora Diamond, *Reading Wittgenstein with Anscombe, Going on to Ethics* (Cambridge, MA: Harvard University Press, 2019); Toril Moi, *Revolution of the Ordinary: Literary Studies after Wittgenstein, Austin, and Cavell* (Chicago: University of Chicago Press, 2017); Robert Chodat, *The Matter of High Words: Naturalism, Normativity,*

and the Postwar Sage (Oxford: Oxford University Press, 2017); Henry W. Pickford, *Thinking with Tolstoy and Wittgenstein: Expression, Emotion and Art* (Evanston, IL: Northwestern University Press, 2016); Marjorie Perloff, *Edge of Irony: Modernism in the Shadow of the Habsburg Empire* (Chicago: University of Chicago Press, 2016); Charles Altieri, *Reckoning with the Imagination: Wittgenstein and the Aesthetics of Literary Experience* (Ithaca, NY: Cornell University Press, 2015); Rebecca Schuman, *Wittgenstein and Kafka* (Evanston, IL: Northwestern University Press, 2015); Ben Ware, *The Dialectic of the Ladder: Wittgenstein, the "Tractatus" and Modernism* (London: Bloomsbury, 2015); André Furlani, *Beckett after Wittgenstein* (Evanston, IL: Northwestern University Press, 2015); and Megan Quigley, *Modernist Fiction and Vagueness* (Cambridge: Cambridge University Press, 2015), which includes a chapter triangulating Wittgenstein, Ogden, and Joyce.

6. The way of reading the *Tractatus* that has come to be known as "resolute" is best understood, as Conant, Diamond, and others have suggested, as a general program capacious enough to accommodate the development of a variety of emerging interpretations elaborated in conformity to the three interrelated basic features (all concerned with how the *Tractatus* ought *not* to be read) that suffice to make a reading "resolute." A reading is resolute if it is committed to recognizing (1) that the book rejects a substantial conception of nonsense; (2) that the nonsensical propositions of the *Tractatus* do not convey ethical insights; and (3) that just as the book does not advance a theory of meaning, neither does coming to understand it depend on any other theory. See James Conant and Cora Diamond, "On Reading the *Tractatus* Resolutely," in *Wittgenstein's Lasting Significance*, ed. Max Kolbel and Bernhard Weiss (London: Routledge, 2004), 46–99; James Conant, "Wittgenstein's Later Criticism of the *Tractatus*," in *Wittgenstein: The Philosopher and His Works*, ed. Alois Pichler and Simo Säätelä (Frankfurt am Main: Ontos Verlag, 2006); and Rupert Read and Robert Deans, "Nothing Is Shown: A 'Resolute' Response to Mounce, Emiliani, Koethe and Vilhauer," in *Philosophical Investigations* 26, no. 3 (2003): 239–68. For a comprehensive overview of the varieties of resolute readings, from "Girondin" to "Jacobin" and beyond, as well as of the specific disputes resolute readings have engendered among Wittgenstein commentators, see Silver Bronzo, "The Resolute Reading and Its Critics: An Introduction to the Literature," *Wittgenstein-Studien* 3 (2012): 45–80.

7. In his book-length presentation of Diamond's and Conant's arguments in *Dialectic of the Ladder*, Ben Ware offers a helpful account of the resolute program for literary scholars and a useful summary of current debates in Wittgenstein studies. Although Ware's examination of the *Tractatus* in the cultural context of modernism and modernity does in its final pages gesture "*towards* a literary use of Wittgenstein" (as the subtitle of his final chapter promises) by turning briefly to Kafka's "der Bau," Ware generally appeals to Wittgenstein's ideas in order "to inform our thinking about modernism" in a broader cultural sense (119).

8. James Conant and Cora Diamond, "Reading the *Tractatus* Resolutely: A Reply to Meredith Williams and Peter Sullivan," in *Wittgenstein's Lasting Significance*, ed. Max Kolbel and Bernhard Weiss (London: Routledge, 2004), 49.

9. Ray Monk, *The Duty of Genius* (New York: Penguin, 1990), 206.

10. Ludwig Wittgenstein, *Tractatus Logico-Philosophicus*, trans. C. K. Ogden (London: Routledge and Kegan Paul, 1922), 6.54.; Ludwig Wittgenstein, *Tractatus Logico-Philosophicus*, trans. D. F. Pears and B. F. McGuinness (London: Routledge and Kegan Paul, 1961), 6.54. Henceforth cited parenthetically as TLP, followed by proposition number (or page number from the Pears-McGuiness 1961 edition for passages from Russell's introduction or Wittgenstein's preface).

11. Wittgenstein, *Briefe an Ludwig von Ficker*, 35; Wittgenstein, "Letters to Ludwig von Ficker," 94–95.

12. James Conant describes the reading of the *Tractatus* that he urges along with Diamond as a "dialectical" one, in the spirit of Kierkegaard. See James Conant, "The Method of the *Tractatus*," in *From Frege to Wittgenstein: Perspectives on Early Analytic Philosophy*, ed. Erich H. Reck (Oxford: Oxford University Press, 2002), 374–462; and Cora Diamond, "Throwing Away the Ladder: How to Read the *Tractatus*," in her *The Realistic Spirit: Wittgenstein, Philosophy, and the Mind* (Cambridge, MA: MIT Press, 1991), 179–204.

13. Stanley Cavell, "Introductory Note to 'The *Investigations*' Everyday Aesthetics of Itself,'" in *The Literary Wittgenstein*, ed. John Gibson and Wolfgang Huemer (London: Routledge, 2004), 19; Ludwig Wittgenstein, *Philosophical Investigations*, 4th ed., ed. P. M. S. Hacker and Joachim Schulte, trans. G. E. M. Anscombe, P. M. S. Hacker, and Joachim Schulte (Oxford: Blackwell, 2009). Henceforth cited parenthetically as PI, followed by section number.

14. Charles Taylor, *Sources of the Self* (Cambridge: Cambridge University Press, 1989), 272.

15. See Martha Nussbaum, "'Finely Aware and Richly Responsible': Moral Attention and the Task of Literature," *Journal of Philosophy* 82, no. 10 (1985): 516–29.

16. I am grateful to an anonymous reader for the press for urging me to consider this issue.

17. See Beth Blum, "Modernism's Anti-advice," *Modernism/modernity* 24, no. 1 (2017): 117–39; and Beth Blum, "The Self-Help Hermeneutic: Its Global Histories and Literary Future," *PMLA* 133, no. 5:1099–117.

18. See Cora Diamond, "Ethics and Imagination and the Method of Wittgenstein's *Tractatus*," in *The New Wittgenstein*, ed. Alice Crary and Rupert Read (London: Routledge, 2000), 157. Henceforth cited parenthetically as "Ethics and Imagination."

19. Citing Cavell's brand of moral perfectionism, Ben Ware points to a problem with Wittgenstein's own, namely, that it is underpinned by a notion of "'magical voluntarism'—the view that one can transform one's outlook, and indeed one's life, through the sheer force of individual will." In answer to Foucault's analogous question why everyone's life cannot become a work of art, Ware writes, "the lives of most people are constrained in innumerable ways—by a lack of access to productive resources; by the demand that they sell their labour power in order to survive; and by the general hollowing-out of everyday social and political life. The problem is not, therefore, as Cavell suggests, that individuals *choose* to guard themselves against the kinds of intellectual and aesthetic awakenings which perfectionism entails, but rather that '(re)claiming one's

voice,' 'becoming intelligible to oneself,' and changing what Foucault calls one's 'style of life' would, for the majority, necessarily entail a wholesale change in *political and economic reality*: a transvaluation of the everyday neoliberal values which condemn so many to a life which does not live." Ben Ware, *Modernism, Ethics and the Political Imagination: Living Wrong Life Rightly* (London: Palgrave Macmillan, 2017), 75.

20. Stanley Cavell, *Conditions Handsome and Unhandsome: The Constitution of Emersonian Perfectionism* (Chicago: University of Chicago Press, 1990), xxxi, 1, 3, 21, 62; and Stanley Cavell, *Cities of Words: Pedagogical Letters on a Register of a Moral Life* (Cambridge, MA: Belknap Press of Harvard University Press, 2004), 13, 17, 42. Cavell's views on moral perfectionism coincide in important ways with those Foucault elaborates in his discussions of the care of the self in the third volume of *The History of Sexuality*, something Cavell acknowledges in *Cities of Words*, 11. See Michel Foucault, *The Hermeneutics of the Subject* (New York: Palgrave Macmillan, 2005). On the relation between Foucault's and Cavell's different formulations of ethical perfectionism, see Arnold I. Davidson, "Ethics as Ascetics," in *The Cambridge Companion to Foucault*, ed. G. Gutting (Cambridge: Cambridge University Press, 1994), 123–48; and Arnold I. Davidson and Frédéric Gros, eds., *Foucault, Wittgenstein: de possibles rencontres* (Paris: Éditions Kimé, 2011).

21. Cora Diamond, "Wittgenstein's 'Unbearable Conflict'" (paper presented at the American Philosophical Association Eastern Division Meeting, New York, January 10, 2019), 2.

22. Diamond begins her paper with a reflection on the puzzling verb tense with which Wittgenstein expresses his sense of an intolerable conflict at the center of his philosophy. At §107 of the *Investigations*, Wittgenstein writes: "The more closely we examine actual language, the greater becomes the conflict between it and our requirement. (For the crystalline purity of logic was, of course, not something I had *discovered*: it was a requirement.) The conflict becomes intolerable; the requirement is in danger of becoming vacuous.—We have got on to slippery ice where there is no friction, and so, in a certain sense, the conditions are ideal; but also, just because of that, we are unable to walk. We want to walk: so we need *friction*. Back to the rough ground!'"

23. Heinrich Hertz, *The Principles of Mechanics*, trans. D. E. Jones and J. T. Walley (New York: Dover, 1993), 7–8. For excellent discussions of Hertz's impact on Wittgenstein's conception of the activity of philosophy, see John Preston, "Wittgenstein, Hertz, and Boltzmann," in *A Companion to Wittgenstein* (Oxford: Blackwell, 2017), 110–24; and Michael Kremer, "Russell's Merit," in Wittgenstein's *Early Philosophy*, ed. José Luís Zalabardo (Oxford: Oxford University Press, 2011), 195–241. Both Preston and Kremer draw attention to the connections we can see in the following paragraph from Hertz and Wittgenstein's method:

> With the terms "velocity" and "gold" we connect a large number of relations to other terms; and between all these relations we find no contradictions which offend us. We are therefore satisfied and ask no further questions. But we have accumu-

lated around the terms "force" and "electricity" more relations than can be completely reconciled amongst themselves. We have an obscure feeling of this and want to have things cleared up. Our confused wish finds expression in the confused question as to the nature of force and electricity. But the answer which we want is not really an answer to this question. It is not by finding out more and fresh relations and connections that it can be answered; but by removing the contradictions existing between those already known, and thus perhaps by reducing their number. When these painful contradictions are removed, the question as to the nature of force will not have been answered; but our minds, no longer vexed, will cease to ask illegitimate questions.

Hertz, like Frege, emphasized how confusion and equivocation create philosophical puzzlement. What comes out in Hertz's paragraph is the significance of "clarification" as the central kind of response to philosophical problems, where clarification does not solve the problems but makes them cease to appear to be problems. Preston also draws attention to the connection between Hertz's passage and Wittgenstein's remark in the Big Typescript that "As I do philosophy, its entire task is to shape expression in such a way that certain worries disappear (Hertz)." (Ludwig Wittgenstein, *The Big Typescript: TS 213*, ed. and trans. C. Grant Luckhardt and Maximillian A. E. Aue [Oxford: Blackwell, 2013], 421)

24. Diamond, "Wittgenstein's 'Unbearable Conflict,'" 8.

25. Diamond, "Wittgenstein's 'Unbearable Conflict,'" 15–16.

26. Diamond, "Wittgenstein's 'Unbearable Conflict,'" 12.

27. See Jonathan Lear, "Wisdom Won from Illness," in *Wisdom Won from Illness: Essays in Philosophy and Psychoanalysis* (Cambridge, MA: Harvard University Press, 2017), 11–29.

28. Diamond, "Wittgenstein's 'Unbearable Conflict,'" 15.

29. Michael Kremer examines how Wittgenstein's criticism of his earlier thinking works on this formal level in the *Investigations* in his response to Diamond's paper (presented at the American Philosophical Association Eastern Division Meeting, New York, January 10, 2019), 14.

30. Secular modernism's seemingly inconsistent fascination with the religious or spiritual has been the focus of a number of recent scholarly treatments of the role of religion in modernist literature. For notable examples, see Steve Pinkerton, *Blasphemous Modernism: The 20th-Century Word Made Flesh* (New York: Oxford University Press, 2017); Matthew Mutter, *Restless Secularism: Modernism and the Religious Inheritance* (New Haven, CT: Yale University Press, 2017); Paul North, *The Yield: Kafka's Atheological Reformation* (Stanford, CA: Stanford University Press, 2015); John Bramble, *Modernism and the Occult* (New York: Palgrave Macmillan, 2015); Suzanne Hobson, *Angels of Modernism: Religion, Culture, Aesthetics 1910–1960* (New York: Palgrave Macmillan, 2011); Pericles Lewis, *Religious Experience and the Modernist Novel* (Cambridge: Cambridge University Press, 2010); Robert Alter, *Canon and Creativity*

(New Haven, CT: Yale University Press, 2000); Joshua Landy and Michael Saler, *The Re-enchantment of the World: Secular Magic in a Rational Age* (Stanford, CA: Stanford University Press, 2009); Gregory Erickson, *The Absence of God in Modernist Literature* (New York: Palgrave Macmillan, 2007); Robert Weldon Whalen, *Sacred Spring: God and the Birth of Modernism in Fin de Siècle Vienna* (Grand Rapids, MI: William B. Eerdmans, 2007). The topic of Wittgenstein and religion, first examined by Norman Malcolm and Peter Winch in Norman Malcolm, *Wittgenstein: A Religious Point of View?*, ed. Peter Winch (Ithaca, NY: Cornell University Press, 1994), has also been the subject of successful recent volumes. See especially Mikel Burley, ed., *Wittgenstein, Religion, and Ethics* (London: Bloomsbury, 2018); D. Z. Phillips and Mario von der Ruhr, eds., *Religion and Wittgenstein's Legacy* (Aldershot: Ashgate, 2005).

31. See Douglas Mao and Rebecca L. Walkowitz, "The New Modernist Studies," *PMLA* 123, no. 3 (2008): 737–48.

32. See David James, *Modernist Futures: Innovation and Inheritance in the Contemporary Novel* (Cambridge: Cambridge University Press, 2012); and *The Legacies of Modernism: Historicising Postwar and Contemporary Fiction* (Cambridge: Cambridge University Press, 2011).

33. See Rita Felski, *The Limits of Critique* (Chicago: University of Chicago Press, 2015); and Rita Felski, *Uses of Literature* (Oxford: Blackwell, 2008). See also "Feminist Investigations and Other Essays," special issue, *New Literary History* 46, no. 2 (Spring 2015); Elizabeth Anker and Rita Felski, eds., *Critique and Postcritique* (Durham, NC: Duke University Press, 2017); and earlier writing by Sontag, Ricoeur, Sedgwick, Latour, and others.

34. Wittgenstein's philosophy also provides a valuable model for broad work in "weak theory" in the sense that Lisi Schoenbach argues that Pragmatism does: "precisely because it makes such an exhaustive case for ethics . . . operating in the absence of a strong theory." Lisi Schoenbach, "Modernism Has Always Been Weak," "Responses to the Special Issue on Weak Theory," *Modernism/modernity Print Plus*, vol. 4, cycle 2 (2019). https://modernismmodernity.org/forums/posts/responses-special-issue-weak-theory-part-iv. See also Paul K. Saint-Amour's introduction to the special issue on weak theory, "Weak Theory, Weak Modernism," *Modernism/modernity* 25, no. 3 (2018): 437–59.

35. Two such postcritical readings are to be found in Stephen Best and Sharon Marcus, "Surface Reading: An Introduction," *Representations* 108, no. 1 (2009): 1–21; Toril Moi, *The Revolution of the Ordinary: Literary Studies after Wittgenstein, Austin, and Cavell* (Chicago: University of Chicago Press, 2017); and Toril Moi, "'Nothing Is Hidden': From Confusion to Clarity; or, Wittgenstein on Critique," in *Critique and Postcritique*, ed. Elizabeth S. Anker and Rita Felski (Durham, NC: Duke University Press, 2017), 31–49. In many ways, the practice of "surface reading" advocated by Best and Marcus offers an appealing alternative to symptomatic readings. But it rests too heavily on the false premise that all depth is suspicious and therefore a distraction from better uses of our critical attention. Depth is also a casualty of Toril Moi's articulation of a postcritical alternative to the idea that suspicion is the only attitude for serious literary critics. Moi challenges the understanding of a text as "a thing or object with

surface and depth," a picture she thinks holds captive surface readers and suspicious hermeneuts alike (Moi, *Revolution of the Ordinary*, 177). The solution she offers in the course of making a persuasive case for the importance of ordinary language philosophy to literary studies is to reject the surface/depth distinction entirely.

36. I am grateful to Joshua Landy for pressing me to take up these issues in the context of Wittgenstein's *Tractatus*. See his "In Praise of Depth; or, How I Stopped Worrying and Learned to Love the Hidden," *New Literary History*, forthcoming.

37. Moi invokes Wittgenstein's remark not to indicate that everything we read is self-evident, or to suggest that the search for clarity in which he seeks to engage us entails a rejection of difficulty or obscurity. What she wants to show is that the central claim of Wittgenstein's philosophy—that the meaning of a word lies in its *use* in the context in which it is uttered—opens up possibilities for reading practices that remain unavailable to us as long as we adhere to a post-Saussurean model of the split sign. The idea that a sign has two parts—a formal, material part on the visible surface (the signifier), and a hidden part that is its meaning (the signified)—provides a foundation for the hermeneutics of suspicion because it calls on readers to build "the idea of the hidden into their very idea of language." Any attempt to establish meaning according to this theory, Moi emphasizes, "will per definition become a hunt for the hidden" (*Revolution of the Ordinary*, 180). In contrast, Wittgenstein's view that "meaning is use" (see PI §43, "the meaning of a word is its use in the language") delivers us from an entrenchment in suspicious hermeneutics and the metaphysics of the hidden. It allows us to see utterances (and bodies of utterances in the form of novels, plays, poems, etc.) not as objects with surface and depth, but as complex actions and expressions that place claims on us as readers. It allows us to pursue meaning as something one *does* or *says* rather than as something hidden and accessible only through the excavation of critique.

38. See also Wittgenstein's remarks on the "deep and sinister" aspects of apparently trivial rituals of sacrifice in *Remarks on Frazer's "Golden Bough,"* in *Philosophical Occasions, 1912–1951*, ed. James Klagge and Alfred Nordmann (Indianapolis: Hackett, 1993), 146.

39. Landy addresses the problem of what readers stand to miss by striving to attend to the surface of a text in an effort to read it "on its own terms," in cases (like Wittgenstein's in the *Tractatus*) in which the very terms set by the text require coincident attention to depths hidden in it by the author's design, by turning to a parallel example offered by Lanier Anderson: Jane Austen's use of free indirect discourse in *Pride and Prejudice*. To understand the way her project is meant to work, readers must see how the sentences function differently on the surface than on a deeper level the text also asks us to intuit. As Landy writes, "there's a more illuminating way to read the Austen sentence, and there's a less illuminating way to read the Austen sentence. The less illuminating way is to take it at face value; the more illuminating way is to see behind its subtle trickery and realize that Austen is setting a trap for us. I see no reason not to call the less illuminating reading a *superficial* reading" (Landy, "In Praise of Depth," 1). The

deeper dimensions of Austen's texts aren't there because she made a mistake, or left traces of her own unconscious ideology for hermeneuts to detect and reveal. They are nonobvious effects of the surface narrative that Austen puts there on purpose, to help her do one of the things she wants to do in the text: shape her readers' capabilities and sharpen their ability to judge and suspend judgment.

40. Monk, *The Duty of Genius*, 498.

41. See George R. Clay, "Tolstoy in the Twentieth Century," in *The Cambridge Companion to Tolstoy*, ed. Donna Tussing Orwin (Cambridge: Cambridge University Press, 2002), 209.

42. Ann Banfield, *The Phantom Table: Woolf, Fry, Russell and the Epistemology of Modernism* (Cambridge: Cambridge University Press, 2000), 9; Jaakko Hintikka, "Virginia Woolf and Our Knowledge of the External World," *Journal of Aesthetics and Art Criticism* 38 (Fall 1979–80): 13.

43. J. M. Coetzee, *Elizabeth Costello* (New York: Penguin, 2003), 188.

44. Cora Diamond, "The Difficulty of Reality and the Difficulty of Philosophy," in Stanley Cavell et al., *Philosophy and Animal Life* (New York: Columbia University Press, 2008), 43–90.

45. For late twentieth-century fiction involving Wittgenstein, see especially Ingeborg Bachmann, *Malina* (Frankfurt: Suhrkamp, 1971); Ingeborg Bachmann, *Das dreißgste Jahr* (München: Piper, 1961); Thomas Bernhard, *Wittgensteins Neffe: Eine Freundschaft* (Frankfurt am Main: Suhrkamp, 1982); Ricardo Piglia, *Respiración artificial* (Barcelona: Editorial Anagrama, 1980); David Markson, *Wittgenstein's Mistress* (Chicago: Dalkey Archive Press, 1988); W. G. Sebald, *Austerlitz* (München: Carl Hanser Verlag, 2001); and David Foster Wallace, *The Broom of the System* (New York: Penguin, 1987). For theatrical, film, and radio pieces, see Terry Eagleton's screenplay for Derek Jarman's film, *Wittgenstein* (London: BFI, 1993); Tom Stoppard, *Dogg's Hamlet, Cahoot's Macbeth* (New York: Samuel French, 1979); and Ingeborg Bachmann, *Der Gute Gott von Manhattan* (München: Piper Verlag, 1976). See also the works Marjorie Perloff points to as examples of the growing body of Wittgensteiniana that includes Terry Eagleton, *Saints and Scholars* (London: Verso, 1987); Guy Davenport, "The Aeroplanes at Brescia," *Hudson Review* 22, no. 4 (1969): 567–85; and Peter Handke, *Kaspar* (Frankfurt am Main: Suhrkamp, 1968). Wittgenstein's impact on contemporary fiction is also explored in Martin Klebes, *Wittgenstein's Novels* (New York: Routledge, 2006); Stephen Mulhall, "Quartet: Wallace's Wittgenstein, Moran's Amis," in *The Self and Its Shadows: A Book of Essays on Individuality as Negation in Philosophy and the Arts* (Oxford: Oxford University Press, 2013), 283–321; and Marjorie Perloff, *Wittgenstein's Ladder: Poetic Language and the Strangeness of the Ordinary* (Chicago: University of Chicago Press, 1996).

46. The description of Coetzee's works as "novels of thinking" is Martin Puchner's. See his "J. M. Coetzee's Novels of Thinking," *Raritan* 30, no. 4 (Spring 2011): 1–12.

47. Laura Riding and Robert Graves, *A Survey of Modernist Poetry* (New York: Haskell, [1927] 1969); I. A. Richards, *The Principles of Literary Criticism* (London: Routledge and Kegan Paul, 1924); F. R. Leavis, *New Bearings in English Poetry: A Study of the Contemporary Situation* (Harmondsworth: Penguin

Books, 1932); Helen Gardner, *The Art of T. S. Eliot* (London: Faber and Faber, 1949). See Rachel Potter, *Modernist Literature* (Edinburgh: Edinburgh University Press, 2012), 2.

48. Leonard Diepeveen, *The Difficulties of Modernism* (New York: Routledge, 2003), x. Laura Frost discusses modernist difficulty in her study of pleasure in *The Problem with Pleasure: Modernism and Its Discontents* (New York: Columbia University Press, 2013).

49. Diepeveen, *Difficulties of Modernism*, ix.

50. Michael Levenson, *The Genealogy of Modernism: A Study of English Literary Doctrine 1908–1922* (Cambridge: Cambridge University Press, 1984), 218.

51. Theodor W. Adorno, "Lyric Poetry and Society," in *Notes to Literature*, vol. 1, trans. Shierry Weber Nicholson (New York: Columbia University Press, 1993), 39. Robert Scholes points out that modernism, with its emphasis on the connection between greatness and difficulty, has pushed the role of pleasure in modernist difficulty to the margins. See his *Paradoxy of Modernism* (New Haven, CT: Yale University Press), xiii.

52. T. S. Eliot, "The Metaphysical Poets," in *Selected Prose of T. S. Eliot* (New York: Harcourt, Brace Jovanovich and Farrar Straus and Giroux, 1975), 65. First published in *Times Literary Supplement*, October 20, 1921, 669–70. See also *The Use of Poetry and the Use of Criticism* (London: Faber and Faber, 1933), 151; and Diepeveen, *Difficulties of Modernism*, xiii.

53. Craig S. Abbott, "Modern American Poetry: Anthologies, Classrooms and Canons," *College Literature* 17 (1990): 209–21.

54. John Guillory, *Cultural Capital: The Problem of Literary Canon Formation* (Chicago: University of Chicago Press, 1993), 168.

55. See Walter Benjamin, "Franz Kafka: On the Tenth Anniversary of His Death," in *Illuminations: Essays and Reflections*, ed. Hannah Arendt, trans. Harry Zohn (New York: Schocken Books, 1968), 111–40; and Theodor Adorno, "Notes on Kafka," in *Prisms* (Cambridge, MA: MIT Press, 1983), 243–71.

56. George Steiner, "On Difficulty," in *On Difficulty and Other Essays* (Oxford: Oxford University Press, 1980), 19, 47. Henceforth cited parenthetically as OD. See also William Empson's *Seven Types of Ambiguity* (New York: New Directions, 1966). In her *Enigmas and Riddles in Literature* (Cambridge: Cambridge University Press, 2006), Eleanor Cook explores enigma as a basic literary category in which interest spiked sharply in the early twentieth century. Cook constructs a taxonomy of five sorts of enigmas (Pauline, Sphinxine, cyclic, random, and Sybilline) that serves as a companion piece to Steiner's.

57. See Frank Kermode, *The Genesis of Secrecy: On the Interpretation of Narrative* (Cambridge, MA: Harvard University Press, 1979). Joshua Landy also probes this issue in his *How to Do Things with Fictions* (New York: Oxford University Press, 2012).

58. Virginia Woolf, "Modern Novels," in *The Essays of Virginia Woolf*, vol. 3, *1919–1924*, ed. Andrew McNeillie (London: Harcourt Brace Jovanovich, 1988), 35.

59. Though the influence of Nietzsche, Kierkegaard, and Dostoevsky on the development of Heidegger's thinking is well known, the great debt he owes

Tolstoy for the latter's narrative depiction of authenticity and inauthenticity is something he acknowledges only in a single footnote in *Being and Time*, but which nonetheless helped to shape his thinking as it did Wittgenstein's. Tolstoy is thus a pivotal figure of influence in twentieth-century philosophy, since his writing helped give rise to existential thinking on the one hand, and ordinary language philosophy on the other. See Martin Heidegger, *Being and Time*, trans. John Macquarrie and Edward Robinson (San Francisco: Harper Collins, 1962), 298, 254. For a treatment of Tolstoy's influence on Heidegger, see William Irwin, "Death by Inauthenticity: Heidegger's Debt to Ivan Il'ich's Fall," *Tolstoy Studies Journal* 25 (2013): 15–21.

60. Ludwig Wittgenstein, "A Lecture on Ethics," in *Philosophical Occasions, 1912–1951*, ed. James Klagge and Alfred Nordmann (Indianapolis: Hackett, 1993), 38. Henceforth cited parenthetically as LE.

61. Diamond, "Difficulty of Reality and the Difficulty of Philosophy," 55.

CHAPTER ONE

1. Ludwig Wittgenstein, Ludwig Wittgenstein, *Culture and Value*, ed. G. H. von Wright, with Heikki Nyman, trans. Peter Winch (Chicago: University of Chicago Press, 1980), 77. Henceforth cited parenthetically as CV.

2. Ludwig Wittgenstein, *Wittgenstein's Lectures, Cambridge, 1932–1935: From the Notes of Alice Ambrose and Margaret MacDonald*, ed. Alice Ambrose (Chicago: University of Chicago Press, 1979), 97.

3. Marjorie Perloff, *Wittgenstein's Ladder: Poetic Language and the Strangeness of the Ordinary* (Chicago: University of Chicago Press, 1996), 25.

4. Ray Monk, *The Duty of Genius* (New York: Penguin, 1990), 137. Henceforth cited as DG.

5. Hermine Wittgenstein, "My Brother Ludwig," in *Ludwig Wittgenstein: Personal Recollections*, ed. Rush Rhees (Oxford: Basil Blackwell, 1981), 3.

6. Marjorie Perloff attends closely to the question of Wittgenstein's desire to become a different person in her coda, "Becoming a 'Different' Person: Wittgenstein's 'Gospels,'" in Marjorie Perloff, *Edge of Irony* (Chicago: University of Chicago Press, 2016), 153–70; and in her "'To Become a Different Person': Wittgenstein, Christianity, and the Modernist Ethos," in *Wittgenstein and Modernism*, ed. Michael LeMahieu and Karen Zumhagen-Yekplé (Chicago: University of Chicago Press, 2017), 41–56.

7. Ludwig Wittgenstein, *Ludwig Wittgenstein and the Vienna Circle: Conversations Recorded by Friedrich Waismann*, ed. B. F. McGuinness (Oxford: Blackwell, 1979), 117.

8. "I am not a religious man, but I cannot help seeing every problem from a religious point of view." M. O'C. Drury, "Some Notes on Conversations with Wittgenstein," in *Recollections of Wittgenstein*, ed. Rush Rhees (Oxford: Oxford University Press, 1984), 79.

9. A point of agreement among James Conant, Michael Kremer, and Kevin Cahill (who discuss the ethical aim of the *Tractatus* in terms of Kierkegaard, Augustine, and Heidegger, respectively) is that Wittgenstein strives indirectly to foster virtues vis-à-vis our use of language by bringing us to see that we are re-

sponsible for speaking either sense or nonsense, depending on whether we give meaning to all the signs in our propositions. The kind of authenticity associated with not fleeing this responsibility is connected to virtues like courage, character, humility, integrity, and honesty.

10. Ludwig Wittgenstein, *Tractatus Logico-Philosophicus*, trans. C. K. Ogden (London: Routledge and Kegan Paul, 1922); Ludwig Wittgenstein, *Tractatus Logico-Philosophicus*, trans. D. F. Pears and B. F. McGuinness (London: Routledge and Kegan Paul, 1961), 6.54. Henceforth cited parenthetically as TLP, followed by proposition number (or page number for passages from the Pears-McGuiness 1961 edition for Russell's introduction or Wittgenstein's preface).

11. See Ludwig Wittgenstein, *Philosophical Investigations*, 4th ed., ed. P. M. S. Hacker and Joachim Schulte, trans. G. E. M. Anscombe, P. M. S. Hacker, and Joachim Schulte (Oxford: Blackwell, 2009), §255, §109. Henceforth cited parenthetically as PI, followed by section number. See also *Remarks on the Foundations of Mathematics*, ed. G. H. von Wright, Rush Rhees, and G. E. M. Anscombe (Chicago: University of Chicago Press, 1980), 157.

12. Rainer Maria Rilke, "Archaïscher Torso Apollos," in *Neue Gedichte* (Leipzig: Iminsel Verlag, 1907), 1. Perloff also notes Wittgenstein's reformulation of Rilke's famous line in her *Edge of Irony*, 162.

13. Robert Musil, *Der Mann ohne Eigenschaften* (Frankfurt am Main: Rohwohlt Verlag, 1957).

14. Kevin Cahill, *The Fate of Wonder* (New York: Columbia University Press, 2011), 3.

15. M. O'C. Drury, "Some Notes on Conversations with Wittgenstein," 94.

16. For other notable discussions about Wittgenstein and modernism, see Stanley Cavell, "The *Investigations*' Everyday Aesthetics of Itself," in *The Literary Wittgenstein*, ed. John Gibson and Wolfgang Huemer (London: Routledge, 2004), 21–33; Stanley Cavell, "Declining Decline: Wittgenstein as a Philosopher of Culture," in *This New Yet Unapproachable America: Lectures after Emerson after Wittgenstein* (Albuquerque, NM: Living Batch, 1989), 59; Michael North, "Translation, Mistranslation and the *Tractatus*," in *Reading 1922: A Return to the Scene of the Modern* (New York: Oxford University Press, 1999), 31–64; Michael LeMahieu, "Nonsense Modernism: The Limits of Modernity and the Feelings of Philosophy in Wittgenstein's *Tractatus*," in *Bad Modernisms*, ed. Douglas Mao and Rebecca L. Walkowitz (Durham, NC: Duke University Press, 2006), 68–89; Michael Fischer, "Wittgenstein as a Modernist Philosopher," *Philosophy and Literature* 17 (1993): 279–85; John Gibson and Wolfgang Huemer, eds., *The Literary Wittgenstein* (London: Routledge, 2004); Ben Ware, *Modernism, Ethics and the Political Imagination: Living Wrong Life Rightly* (London: Palgrave Macmillan, 2017); R. M. Berry, "Wittgenstein and Modernism," *Symploke* 13, nos. 1–2 (2005): 303–7; Martin Puchner, "Doing Logic with a Hammer: Wittgenstein's *Tractatus* and the Polemics of Logical Positivism," *Journal of the History of Ideas* 66, no. 2 (2005): 285–300; Terry Eagleton, "My Wittgenstein," *Common Knowledge* 3, no. 1 (1994): 152–57.

17. North, *Reading 1922*, 6; Virginia Woolf, "Character in Fiction," in *The Essays of Virginia Woolf*, vol. 3, ed. Andrew McNeillie (New York: Harcourt, 1988), 421; Virginia Woolf, "Mr. Bennett and Mrs. Brown," in *The Essays of*

Virginia Woolf, vol. 3, *1919–1924*, ed. Andrew McNeillie (New York: Harcourt Brace, 1991), 384–89.

18. Allan Janik and Stephen Toulmin, *Wittgenstein's Vienna* (New York: Ivan R. Dee, [1973]1996). Henceforth cited parenthetically as WV.

19. Cahill, *Fate of Wonder*, 10; *Ludwig Wittgenstein: Personal Recollections*, ed. Rush Rhees; Drury, "Some Notes on Conversations with Wittgenstein"; Ludwig Wittgenstein, *Vermischte Bemerkungen*, ed. Georg Henrik von Wright (Frankfurt am Main, 1977). Michael LeMahieu and I discuss this in "Wittgenstein, Modernism, and the Contradictions of Writing Philosophy as Poetry," in *Wittgenstein and Modernism*, ed. LeMahieu and Zumhagen-Yekplé, 7.

20. See in particular Cavell, "The *Investigations*' Everyday Aesthetics of Itself"; Cavell, "Declining Decline."

21. See Oswald Spengler, *The Decline of the West*, ed. Helmut Werner, trans. Charles Francis Atkinson (Oxford: Oxford University Press, 1991); and Karl Kraus, "In These Great Times," in *In These Great Times: A Karl Kraus Reader* (Manchester: Carcanet, 1984). For extended discussions of the bearing of Spengler and Kraus on Wittgenstein's thinking, see Janik and Toulmin, *Wittgenstein's Vienna*; and Cahill, *Fate of Wonder*. Ben Ware also speaks briefly of both, and their relation to discourse in *Kulturkritik*, in his *Dialectic of the Ladder: Wittgenstein, the "Tractatus" and Modernism* (London: Bloomsbury, 2015), 75–78.

22. LeMahieu, "Wittgenstein, Modernism, and the Contradictions of Writing Philosophy as Poetry," 4.

23. See Marjorie Perloff, "'But Isn't *the Same* at Least the Same?': Wittgenstein and the Question of Poetic Translatability," in *Literary Wittgenstein*, ed. Gibson and Huemer, 39. Quoted in LeMahieu and Zumhagen-Yekplé, "Wittgenstein, Modernism, and the Contradictions of Writing Philosophy as Poetry," in 256n14.

24. Cora Diamond discusses Wittgenstein's characteristic resistance to explanation in "Introduction II: Wittgenstein and Metaphysics," in *The Realistic Spirit: Wittgenstein, Philosophy, and the Mind* (Cambridge, MA: MIT Press, 1991), 13. Wittgenstein's rather strong aversion to offering explanations of his own work can be seen in the occasionally impatient remarks he made in letters to Russell in response to the latter's questions about the *Tractatus* and about Wittgenstein's earlier work in logic. Near the end of 1913, for example, Wittgenstein wraps up his attempt to clarify certain issues of the *Tractatus* to Russell with the following outburst: "It distresses me that you did not understand the rule dealing with signs in my last letter because it bores me BEYOND WORDS to explain it. If you thought about it for a bit you could discover it for yourself! . . . I beg you to think about these matters for yourself: it is INTOLERABLE for me, to repeat an explanation which even the first time I gave only with the *utmost repugnance.*" See Ludwig Wittgenstein, *Letters to Russell, Keynes and Moore*, ed. G. H. von Wright and B. F. McGuinness (Oxford: Basil Blackwell, 1974), 42.

25. Another helpful account of Wittgenstein's ethical aims in the *Tractatus* can be found in Paul Engelmann's discussions of the exchanges he had with his friend Wittgenstein in the form of letters and conversations. See Engelmann, *Letters from Wittgenstein with a Memoir* (New York: Horizon, 1968), 60–148.

26. For a quotation of the entire letter in English translation, see G. H. von Wright, "Historical Introduction: The Origin of Wittgenstein's *Tractatus*," in

Prototractatus, ed. B. F. McGuinness, T. Nyberg, and G. H. von Wright, trans. D. F. Pears and B. F. McGuinness (London: Routledge and Kegan Paul, 1971), 15–16. Ludwig Wittgenstein, *Briefe an Ludwig von Ficker*, ed. G. H. von Wright (Salzburg: Otto Müller Verlag, 1969), 35:

> Von seiner Lektüre werden Sie nämlich—wie ich bestimmt glaube—nicht allzuviel haben. Denn Sie werden es nicht verstehen; der Stoff wird Ihnen ganz fremd erscheinen. In Wirklichkeit ist er Ihnen nicht fremd, denn der Sinn des Buches ist ein Ethischer. Ich wollte einmal in das Vorwort einen Satz geben, der nun tatsächlich nicht darin steht, den ich Ihnen aber jetzt schreibe, weil er Ihnen vielleicht ein Schlüssel sein wird: Ich wollte nämlich schreiben, mein Werk bestehe aus zwei Teilen: aus dem, der hier vorliegt, und aus alledem, was ich *nicht* geschrieben habe. Und gerade dieser zweite Teil ist der Wichtige. Es wird nämlich das Ethische durch mein Buch gleichsam von Innen her begrenzt; und ich bin überzeugt, daß es, *streng*, NUR so zu begrenzen ist. Kurz, ich glaube: Alles das, was *viele* heute *schwefeln*, habe ich in meinem Buch festgelegt, in dem ich darüber schweige. Und darum wird das Buch, wenn ich mich nicht sehr irre, vieles sagen, was Sie selbst sagen wollen, aber Sie arden vielleicht sicht sehen, daß es darin gesagt ist. Ich würde Ihnen nun empfehlen, das *Vorwort* und den *Schluß* zu lessen, da diese den Sinn am Unmittelbarsten zum Ausdruck bringen.

27. Diamond, "Ethics and Imagination," 149.

28. See, for example, Ian Proops, "The New Wittgenstein: A Critique," *European Journal of Philosophy* 9, no. 3 (2001): 375–404; and Peter Sullivan, "On Trying to Be Resolute: A Response to Kremer on the *Tractatus*," *European Journal of Philosophy* 10, no. 1 (2002): 43–78.

29. See James Conant, "The Method of the *Tractatus*," in *From Frege to Wittgenstein: Perspectives on Early Analytic Philosophy*, ed. Erich H. Reck (Oxford: Oxford University Press, 2002), 151n195; and James Conant, "Kierkegaard, Wittgenstein and Nonsense," in *Pursuits of Reason: Essays in Honor of Stanley Cavell*, ed. Ted Cohen, Paul Guyer, and Hilary Putnam (Lubbock: Texas Tech Press, 1993), 223n.

30. Michael Kremer, "The Purpose of Tractarian Nonsense," *NOÛS* 35, no. 1 (2001): 41–43.

31. Cora Diamond, "Introduction to 'Having a Rough Story about What Moral Philosophy Is,'" in *Literary Wittgenstein*, ed. Gibson and Huemer, 130–31.

32. In a letter he wrote to Russell just after the war, Wittgenstein reiterates his claim that the central concern of the *Tractatus*, "to which the whole business of logical prop[osition]s is only a corollary," is expressed in the claim that "what can be expressed [*gesagt*] by prop[osition]s—i.e. by language—(and which comes to the same, what can be *thought*) and what can not be expressed by prop[osition]s, but only shown [*gezeigt*]; which, I believe, is the cardinal problem

of philosophy." Letter dated August 19, 1919. Ludwig Wittgenstein, *Letters to Russell, Keynes and Moore*, 71.

33. David R. Cerbone, "How to Do Things with Wood: Wittgenstein, Frege and the Problem of Illogical Thought," in *New Wittgenstein*, ed. Crary and Read, 293.

34. Cora Diamond, "Throwing Away the Ladder: How to Read the *Tractatus*," in *Realistic Spirit*, 185.

35. See Diamond, "Ethics and Imagination," 155; James F. Conant, "What 'Ethics' in the *Tractatus* Is *Not*," in *Religion and Wittgenstein's Legacy*, ed. D. Z. Phillips and Mario von der Ruhr (Aldershot: Ashgate, 2005), 53.

36. In the *Tractatus*, Wittgenstein attempts to break the spell of the linguistic and philosophical confusions that arise from our failure to see language and life perspicuously. He is concerned with leading his readers out of a certain kind of temptation. Wittgenstein's use of the word *überwinden* in the penultimate remark of the *Tractatus* is thus worthy of note. He says at proposition 6.54 that the reader who aims to understand him "muß diese Sätze überwinden, dann sieht er die Welt richtig." Although the Pears-McGuinness translation renders *überwinden* in terms of transcendence, and Ogden in terms of surmounting, the primary meaning of the German word suggests the kind of overcoming one must do to get beyond temptation, or "getting over," as of an illness. The straightforward meaning of the German verb *überwinden*—to overcome, prevail, subdue, surmount (as an obstacle, one's inclinations, for example), or to outgrow (as a phase or a bad habit), then, is thus obscured by the translator's choice here of the English word "transcend," a word that historically has a quite different set of philosophical implications than those suggested by common usage of the word Wittgenstein employs in the original German. The German word usually used to express the English verb "to transcend" in the philosophical sense is not in fact "überwinden," but "transzendieren."

37. Ware, *Dialectic of the Ladder*, 59.

38. Walter Benjamin, "On Some Motifs in Baudelaire," in *Illuminations: Essays and Reflections*, ed. Hannah Arendt, trans. Harry Zohn (New York: Schocken Books, 1968), 155–200. Ware, *Dialectic of the Ladder*, 59–60; Walter Benjamin, *The Arcades Project*, trans. Howard Eiland and Kevin McLaughlin (Cambridge, MA: Belknap Press of Harvard University Press, 1991), K1, 1.

39. Ware, *Dialectic of the Ladder*, 59.

40. Michael Kremer, "Russell's Merit," in *Wittgenstein's Early Philosophy*, ed. José Luís Zalabardo (Oxford: Oxford University Press, 2011), 205; Heinrich Hertz, *The Principles of Mathematics*, trans. D. E. Jones and J. T. Walley (New York: Dover, 1993), 8.

41. G. E. M. Anscombe, *An Introduction to Wittgenstein's Tractatus* (London: Hutchinson, 1959), 171.

42. It seems clear, looking at the passage from *The Gospel in Brief*, that Wittgenstein is making a veiled reference to Tolstoy when he speaks of the problem of the meaning of life and its vanishing in propositions 6.52 and 6.521 of the *Tractatus*. Here is Tolstoy's rendering of the passage from John which contains the familiar line "I was blind, but now I see!"

The blind man whose sight has been restored remaining the
same man he was, can only say that he was blind but now
sees. And one who formerly did not understand the meaning
of life but now does understand it, can only say the same, and
nothing else.

Such a man can only say that formerly he did not know
the true good in life but now he knows it. A blind man whose
sight has been restored, if told that he has not been cured in a
proper manner and that he who restored his sight is an evil-
doer, and that he should be cured differently, can only reply: I
know nothing about the correctness of my cure or the sinful-
ness of him who cured me, or a better way of being cured; I
only know that whereas I was blind, now I see. . . . Formerly I
did not see the meaning of life, but now I see it and that is all
I know. (Leo Tolstoy, *The Gospel in Brief* [Oxford: Oxford
University Press, 1958], 281)

43. I offer a fuller treatment of Wittgenstein's notion that the resolution of
problems is to be found in their vanishing in chapter 4 in the context of a discussion of Tolstoy's influence on Wittgenstein's thought and the coincidence of
Joyce's creation of Leopold Bloom, a "happy" man in a Wittgensteinian sense,
whose problems, it turns out, are indeed effectively resolved only in their (temporary) disappearance.

44. See Anscombe, *Introduction to Wittgenstein's* Tractatus; and P. M. S.
Hacker, *Insight and Illusion*, rev. ed. (Oxford: Clarendon, 1986).

45. James Conant, "Throwing Away the Top of the Ladder," *Yale Review*
79, no. 3 (1991): 346; Conant, "Method of the *Tractatus*."

46. Anscombe, *Introduction to Wittgenstein's* Tractatus, 54

47. Perloff, Wittgenstein's Ladder, 15–16.

48. See Conant, "Method of the *Tractatus*"; James Conant, "Mild Mono-
Wittgensteinianism," in *Wittgenstein and the Moral Life: Essays in Honor of
Cora Diamond*, ed. Alice Crary (Cambridge, MA: MIT Press, 2007).

49. Anscombe, *Introduction to Wittgenstein's* Tractatus, 162. Hacker, *Insight and Illusion*, 26.

50. Diamond "Throwing Away the Ladder," 194.

51. Diamond, "Ethics and Imagination," 153; James Conant, "A Prolegome-
non to the Reading of Later Wittgenstein," in *The Legacy of Wittgenstein: Pragmatism or Deconstruction*, ed. Ludwig Nagl and Charles Mouffe (Frankfurt am
Main: Peter Lang, 2001), 93–130.

52. James Conant and Cora Diamond, "Reading the *Tractatus* Resolutely: A
Reply to Meredith Williams and Peter Sullivan," in *Wittgenstein's Lasting Significance*, ed. Max Kolbel and Bernhard Weiss (London: Routledge, 2004), 47.

53. See G. E. Moore, *Principia Ethica* (Cambridge: Cambridge University
Press, 1903).

54. See Moritz Schlick, "Ethics as a Factual Science," in *Problems of Ethics*,
trans. David Rynin (New York: Prentice Hall, 1939), §9.

55. Ludwig Wittgenstein, *Ludwig Wittgenstein and the Vienna Circle: Conversations Recorded by Friedrich Waismann*, ed. B. F. McGuinness (Oxford: Blackwell, 1979), 68.

56. Cavell, "'Introductory Note to 'The *Investigations*' Everyday Aesthetics of Itself,'" 19.

57. Thus, contrary to Russell's claim in his introduction to the *Tractatus*, Wittgenstein is not concerned with creating a "logically perfect language" (see Bertrand Russell, "Introduction," TLP, p. x). What Wittgenstein tells us at proposition 5.5563 is that "all of the propositions of our everyday language, just as they stand, are in perfectly logical order." For Wittgenstein, then, in order for language to be language, it must necessarily be logical (see TLP, 3.03). A desire to construct a logically perfect language is the expression of the view that there is something to be known that lies beyond the realm of our everyday language, and this is precisely the view that Wittgenstein is concerned to reject. In his view, the labor of philosophy is not one of construction of new truths, but one of elucidation of what we already know. For the early Wittgenstein, an ideal language can tell us no more about meaning than is already provided in the ordinary language we speak every day. Nonetheless, he does warn us that in our use of ordinary language, we often fail to pay proper attention to its logical form.

58. James Conant, "The Search for Logically Alien Thought: Descartes, Kant, Frege and the *Tractatus*," in *The Philosophy of Hilary Putnam: Philosophical Topics* 20, no. 1 (1991): 159–60; James Conant, "Elucidation and Nonsense in Frege and the Early Wittgenstein," in *New Wittgenstein*, ed. Crary and Read, 196–98.

59. At TLP, 4.112, Wittgenstein writes: "The object of philosophy is the logical clarification of thoughts. Philosophy is not a theory but an activity. A philosophical work consists essentially of elucidations. The result of philosophy is not a number of 'philosophical propositions', but to make propositions clear. Philosophy should make clear and delimit sharply the thoughts which otherwise are, as it were, opaque and blurred."

60. Alice Crary, "Introduction," *New Wittgenstein*, ed. Crary and Read, 13.

61. Conant, "Throwing Away the Top of the Ladder," 346; James Conant, "Putting Two and Two Together: Kierkegaard, Wittgenstein and the Point of View for Their Work as Authors," in *Philosophy and the Grammar of Religious Belief*, ed. Timothy Tessin and Mario von der Ruhr (New York: St. Martin's, 1995), 249.

62. Conant, "Putting Two and Two Together," 249. See also CV, 25.

63. Conant, "Method of the *Tractatus*," 374–462; Diamond, "Throwing Away the Ladder," 179–204.

64. Conant, "What 'Ethics' in the *Tractatus* Is Not," 53.

65. Ludwig Wittgenstein, "A Lecture on Ethics," in *Philosophical Occasions, 1912–1951*, ed. James Klagge and Alfred Nordmann, 36–44.

66. Regarding the philosophical ethical import that a joke can have, it is worth pointing to Wittgenstein's 1949 remark that "for a philosopher there is more grass growing down in the valleys of silliness than up on the barren heights of cleverness" (CV, 80). Also of note is his 1947 remark: "A typical American film, naïve and silly, can—for all its silliness and even *by means* of it—be instruc-

tive. A fatuous, self-conscious English film can teach one nothing. I have often learnt a lesson from a silly American film" (CV, 57). See also Wittgenstein, PI, § 111: "Let us ask ourselves: why do we feel a grammatical joke to be *deep*? (And that is what the depth of philosophy is.)" Finally, and perhaps still more relevant to my main concerns in this book, is Wittgenstein's 1948 remark about humor, and what it reveals about our attitude toward the world. He writes: "Humor is not a mood but a way of looking at the world. So if it is correct to say that humor was stamped out in Nazi Germany, that does not mean that people were not in good spirits, or anything of that sort, but something much deeper and more important" (CV, 78).

67. Regarding Wittgenstein's view of the relationship between his philosophical writing and poetic composition, it is also interesting to note a statement he made in a letter to Ludwig von Ficker in an attempt to persuade the latter to publish the *Tractatus* in his journal *Der Brenner*. In the letter, dated December 4, 1919, Wittgenstein makes it clear that in his view, the text of the *Tractatus* would not be out of place if it were to be published alongside the work of poets. Although von Ficker's journal generally dealt in literature and literary and social criticism, Wittgenstein clearly considered *Der Brenner* a publication to which his own work would be suited. He tells von Ficker, "I think I can say that if you print Dallago, Haecker, etc., *then* you can also print *my* book." Letter dated December 4, 1919, in Ludwig Wittgenstein, "Letters to Ludwig von Ficker," ed. Allan Janik, trans. Bruce Gilette, in *Wittgenstein: Sources and Perspectives*, ed. C. G. Luckhardt (Ithaca, NY: Cornell University Press, 1979), 96. Wittgenstein's statement to von Ficker speaks to the value of reading Wittgenstein's work in a literary-critical context and alongside literary works of his time. It also lends support to arguments for the merit of taking seriously the attention Wittgenstein paid to crafting the kind of literary devices that I maintain contribute to the astute reader's engagement with the *Tractatus*.

68. James Conant, "Must We Show What We Cannot Say?," in *The Senses of Stanley Cavell*, ed. R. Fleming and M. Payne (Lewisburg, PA: Bucknell University Press, 1989), 242–83.

69. Ludwig Wittgenstein, *Nachlass*, 120 145r 23 (April 1938), quoted in Cahill, *The Fate of Wonder*, 168.

70. Cavell, "*Investigations*' Everyday Aesthetics of Itself," 29.

71. Conant, "Kierkegaard, Wittgenstein and Nonsense," 185–224; Conant, "Putting Two and Two Together." See also M. Jaime Ferreira, "The Point Outside the World: Kierkegaard and Wittgenstein on Nonsense, Paradox, and Religion," *Religious Studies* 30, no. 1 (March 1994): 29–44.

72. Bertrand Russell claims that "in order to understand Mr. Wittgenstein's book, it is necessary to realize what is the problem with which he is concerned. In the part of his theory which deals with Symbolism he is concerned with the conditions which would have to be fulfilled by a logically perfect language." See Russell's "Introduction," in Ludwig Wittgenstein, *Tractatus Logico-Philosophicus*, trans. C. K. Ogden (London: Routledge, 2000), p. 7; trans. D. F. Pears and B. F. McGuinness (London: Routledge & Kegan Paul, 1961), ix–x. What Russell writes in that introduction confirmed for Wittgenstein, as for Frank Ramsey, Russell's misconception of Wittgenstein's concerns in the book. For a discussion

of Mallarmé in the wider context of European modernist aspirations for linguistic emancipation and ideal languages of perfect expressiveness—ranging from the avant-garde movements of the early twentieth century (especially André Breton and the French surrealists), to Filippo Tomasso Marinetti and the Italian futurists, to C. K. Ogden and I. A. Richards's "Basic English project," to Hofmannsthal's "Letter of Lord Chandos," and Eliot's *Four Quartets*—see Ware, *Dialectic of the Ladder*, 121–22. Megan Quigley discusses the efforts to investigate vagueness in attempts to reach ideal linguistic precision not only in the logic of Frege and Russell, but also in the work of Ogden and I. A. Richards, William James, Charles Sanders Peirce, T. E. Hulme, and others. See Megan Quigley, *Modernist Fiction and Vagueness* (Cambridge: Cambridge University Press, 2015), 6–7.

73. Quigley, *Modernist Fiction and Vagueness*, 18.

74. Russell, "Introduction," TLP, p. 8.

75. Quigley, *Modernist Fiction and Vagueness*, 103.

76. PI, §§ 81–86.

77. Ludwig Wittgenstein, letter to Bertrand Russell, March 13, 1919, in *Ludwig Wittgenstein: Cambridge Letters, Correspondence with Russell, Keynes, Moor, Ramsay and Sraffa*, ed. B. F. McGuinness and G. H. von Wright (Oxford: Blackwell, 1995), 111.

78. Ludwig Wittgenstein, *Letters to C. K. Ogden* (Oxford: Blackwell, 1983), 46.

79. Gottlob Frege, "Letters to Ludwig Wittgenstein," trans. Juliet Floyd and Burton Dreben, in *Interactive Wittgenstein: Essays in Memory of Georg Henrik von Wright*, ed. Enzo De Pellegrin (New York: Springer, 2011), 52.

80. Ludwig Wittgenstein, letter to Bertrand Russell (May 6, 1920), in *Letters to Russell, Keynes and Moore*, 88.

81. Wittgenstein, *Briefe an Ludwig von Ficker*, 33; Wittgenstein, "Letters to Ludwig von Ficker," 94–95.

82. Ludwig Wittgenstein, "Letters to Ludwig von Ficker," ed. Allan Janik, trans. Bruce Gilette, in *Wittgenstein: Sources and Perspectives*, ed. C. G. Luckhardt (Ithaca, NY: Cornell University Press, 1979), 94–95.

CHAPTER TWO

1. Franz Kafka, *Nachgelassene Schriften und Fragmente II*, ed. Malcolm Pasley (Frankfurt am Main: S. Fischer, 2002), (note 9) 63, 127–28. Commonly called "Zürau Aphorism No. 66."

2. Several recent philosophical and literary studies of Kafka and Wittgenstein attest to a growing critical interest in the connections between these two thinkers. For a comprehensive recent discussion of Kafka and Wittgenstein, see Rebecca Schuman, *Kafka and Wittgenstein: The Case for an Analytic Modernism* (Evanston, IL: Northwestern University Press, 2015). See also Yi-Ping Ong, "Lectures on Ethics: Wittgenstein and Kafka," in *Wittgenstein and Modernism*, ed. Michael LeMahieu and Karen Zumhagen-Yekplé (Chicago: University of Chicago Press, 2017), 206–30; Ben Ware, "Towards a Literary Use of Wittgenstein: The *Tractatus* and Kafka's 'Der Bau,'" in *Dialectic of the Ladder: Wittgen-*

stein, the "Tractatus," and Modernism (London: Bloomsbury, 2015), 125–41; James Conant, "In the Electoral Colony: Kafka in Florida," *Critical Inquiry* 27, no. 4 (Summer 2001): 662–702; Stephen Mulhall, *Wittgenstein's Private Language: Grammar, Nonsense, and Imagination in Philosophical Investigations,* §§243–315 (Oxford: Oxford University Press, 1990), 118–28; Henry Sussman, *Afterimages of Modernity: Structure and Indifference in Twentieth-Century Literature* (Baltimore: Johns Hopkins University Press, 1990), 50–59. For an earlier discussion of the *Tractatus* and Kafka's work, see Jorn K. Bramann, "Kafka and Wittgenstein on Religious Language," *Sophia* 14, no. 3 (1975): 1–9. Both Walter Sokel and Stanley Corngold offer thought-provoking readings of Kafka's late parable in their own treatments of Kafka's unique exploration of Gnostic spiritual yearning in the context of a modernist everyday: cf. Walter Sokel, *The Myth of Power and the Self: Essays on Franz Kafka* (Detroit: Wayne State University Press, 2002), and Stanley Corngold, *Lambent Traces* (Princeton, NJ: Princeton University Press, 2004).

3. Ray Monk, *Ludwig Wittgenstein: The Duty of Genius* (New York: Penguin Books, 1990), 498.

4. See, for example, David Stern and Béla Szabados, eds., *Wittgenstein Reads Weininger* (Cambridge: Cambridge University Press, 2004).

5. Ludwig Wittgenstein, *Tractatus Logico-Philosophicus*, trans. C. K. Ogden (London: Routledge and Kegan Paul, 1922), p. 23, propositions 6.54 and 7; Ludwig Wittgenstein, *Tractatus Logico-Philosophicus*, trans. D. F. Pears and B. F. McGuinness (London: Routledge and Kegan Paul, 1961), p. 3, propositions 6.54 and 7. Henceforth cited parenthetically as TLP, followed by proposition number (or page number from the Pears-McGuiness 1961 edition for passages from Russell's introduction or Wittgenstein's preface).

6. Cora Diamond, "Introduction to 'Having a Rough Story about What Moral Philosophy Is,'" in *The Literary Wittgenstein*, ed. John Gibson and Wolfgang Huemer (London: Routledge, 2004), 127–32.

7. Eli Friedlander, *Signs of Sense: Reading Wittgenstein's* Tractatus (Cambridge, MA: Harvard University Press, 2001), 152.

8. Franz Kafka, "Von den Gleichnissen," in *Kritische Ausgabe: Nachgelassene Schriften und Fragmente II*, ed. Jost Schillemeit (Frankfurt am Main: Fischer Verlag, 2002), 531–32.

9. Mark 4:34; Joshua Landy, *How to Do Things with Fictions* (New York: Oxford University Press, 2012), 50.

10. Landy, *How to Do Things with Fictions*, 58–60.

11. See Frank Kermode, *The Genesis of Secrecy: On the Interpretation of Narrative* (Cambridge, MA: Harvard University Press, 1979).

12. Diamond, "Introduction to 'Having a Rough Story,'" 128.

13. See James Conant, "Must We Show What We Cannot Say?," in *The Senses of Stanley Cavell*, ed. R. Fleming and M. Payne (Lewisburg, PA: Bucknell University Press, 1989), 242–83; and Michael Kremer, "The Purpose of Tractarian Nonsense" *NOÛS* 35, no. 1 (2001): 39–73.

14. Ludwig Wittgenstein, *Philosophical Investigations*, 4th ed., ed. P. M. S. Hacker and Joachim Schulte, trans. G. E. M. Anscombe, P. M. S. Hacker, and

Joachim Schulte (Oxford: Blackwell, 2009), § 111. Henceforth cited parenthetically as PI, followed by section number.

15. Ludwig Wittgenstein, "A Lecture on Ethics," in *Philosophical Occasions, 1912–1951*, ed. James Klagge and Alfred Nordmann (Indianapolis: Hackett, 1993), 44. Henceforth cited parenthetically as LE.

16. Ludwig Wittgenstein, *Ludwig Wittgenstein and the Vienna Circle: Conversations Recorded by Friedrich Waismann*, ed. B. F. McGuinness (Oxford: Blackwell, 1979), 69.

17. Ludwig Wittgenstein *Remarks on Frazer's "Golden Bough,"* in *Philosophical Occasions, 1912–1951*, ed. James Klagge and Alfred Nordmann (Indianapolis: Hackett, 1993), 133. See also Ludwig Wittgenstein, "Philosophy," in *Philosophical Occasions, 1912–1951*, 197.

18. Rush Rhees, "Introductory Note" to Ludwig Wittgenstein, *Remarks on Frazer's "Golden Bough," Human World* 3 (1971): 18n.

19. Paul Ernst, *"Nachwort,"* in *Kinder- und Hausmärchen Gesammelt durch die Brüder Grimm*, Band 3 (München: Georg Müller, 1910), 271. See also Josef G. F. Rothhaupt, *Ludwig Wittgenstein und Paul Ernst-*"Mißverstehen der Sprachlogik," *Wittgenstein-Studien* 2, no. 2 (1995); Josef G. F. Rothhaupt, *Paul Ernst-Nachwort zu den Kinder-und Hausmärchen der Brüder Grimm*, *Wittgenstein-Studien* 2, no. 2 (1995); and Wolfgang Künne, *Paul Ernst und Ludwig Wittgenstein*, *Wittgenstein-Studien* 3, no. 1 (1996).

20. Friedlander, *Signs of Sense*, 141.

21. Friedlander, *Signs of Sense*, 12–15.

22. Friedlander, *Signs of Sense*, 17.

23. Ludwig Wittgenstein, *Culture and Value*, ed. G. H. von Wright, with H. Nyman, trans. Peter Winch (Chicago: University of Chicago Press, 1980), 24. Henceforth cited parenthetically as CV.

24. Diamond, "Introduction to 'Having a Rough Story,'" 127–32; Cora Diamond, "Ethics, Imagination and the Method of Wittgenstein's *Tractatus*," in *The New Wittgenstein*, ed. Alice Crary and Rupert Read (London: Routledge, 2000), 157.

25. It should be said here that when he wrote the *Tractatus*, Wittgenstein did believe himself to have solved the fundamental problems of philosophy, and in that way to have found the "final answer" that would lead to their disappearance. As we will see in chapter 4, however, by the time he wrote the *Investigations*, Wittgenstein was to recognize (in a fundamental discontinuity in the unfolding of his later philosophy from his earlier) that his early method of clarification (which was to be free of all metaphysical commitments and laying down of philosophical requirements) in fact rested on the very metaphysics of language that he sought to put an end to with that earlier method. In the *Tractatus*, Wittgenstein recognized, he had inadvertently subscribed to a single conception of logical analysis, and so to a single correct method for overcoming philosophical confusion that is at odds with the goals of his philosophical project in that book.

26. Although Wittgenstein speaks at *Tractatus* 6.53 of the "correct method" of philosophy (which the reader would not find satisfying), he makes it evident at 6.54 that this is not the method he is following in the book. He never says

that the method he describes at 6.53 is not correct but simply implies that that method is not the one he is using in the book.

27. Ludwig Wittgenstein, *Wittgenstein's Lectures, Cambridge, 1932–1935: From the Notes of Alice Ambrose and Margaret MacDonald*, ed. Alice Ambrose (Chicago: University of Chicago Press, 1979), 97.

28. Michael Kremer, Response to "Wittgenstein's 'Unbearable Conflict'" (comments presented at the American Philosophical Association Eastern Division Meeting, New York, January 10, 2019), 12.

29. James Conant, "The Method of the *Tractatus*," in From *Frege to Wittgenstein: Perspectives on Early Analytic Philosophy*, ed. Erich H. Reck (Oxford: Oxford University Press, 2002), 422–23. Michael Kremer, "The Purpose of Tractarian Nonsense," *NOÛS* 35, no. 1 (2001): 60.

30. Cora Diamond, "The *Tractatus* and the Limits of Sense," in *The Oxford Handbook of Wittgenstein*, ed. Oskari Kuusela and Marie McGinn (Oxford: Oxford University Press, 2011), 261. Henceforth cited parenthetically as "Limits of Sense."

31. For a discussion of Wittgenstein and the "higher," see Piergiorgio Donatelli, "The Problem of 'the Higher' in Wittgenstein's *Tractatus*," in *Religion and Wittgenstein's Legacy*, ed. D. Z. Phillips and Mario von der Ruhr (Aldershot: Ashgate, 2005), 11–38.

32. Ludwig Wittgenstein, "Philosophy of Psychology—a Fragment," in *Philosophical Investigations*, 4th ed., ed. P. M. S. Hacker and Joachim Schulte, trans. G. E. M. Anscombe, P. M. S. Hacker, and Joachim Schulte (Oxford: Blackwell, 2009). Henceforth cited parenthetically as PPF. See also Cora Diamond, "Secondary Sense," in *The Realistic Spirit: Wittgenstein, Philosophy, and the Mind* (Cambridge, MA: MIT Press, 1991), 225–42.

33. Friedrich Waismann, "Notes on Talks with Wittgenstein," *Philosophical Review* 74, no. 1:12–13.

34. Rebecca Schuman addresses Kafka's way of offering up transformative possibility and dooming it in the same gesture. She begins her study of Kafka and Wittgenstein by attending to the double-twisting plots that run through Kafka's work, by looking at his "Kleine Fabel" as a perplexing microcosm of Kafka's fictional universe. In the case of the fable, the walls closing in on the mouse protagonist, and the trap that awaits her, not only show that she has "been going about the entire thing the wrong way"; it also points to the ways in which readers labor under their own illusions of the direction and progress in their search for the meaning of Kafka's stories. See Schuman, *Kafka and Wittgenstein*, 3–5.

35. See Ludwig Wittgenstein, *Lectures and Conversations on Aesthetics, Psychology and Religious Belief*, ed. Cyril Barrett (Oxford: Blackwell, 1966), 53. See also Cora Diamond, "Wittgenstein on Religious Belief: The Gulfs between Us," in *Religion and Wittgenstein's Legacy*, ed. D. Z. Phillips and Mario von der Ruhr (Aldershot: Ashgate, 2005), 99–139. See also Toril Moi's discussion, in terms of *Philosophical Investigations* §217, of gulfs that open up between two human beings when explanations fail to make others understand the world as we see it, when we are forced to face our finitude and the fact of our own separateness from others. At PI, §217, Wittgenstein writes: "Once I have exhausted

the justifications, I have reached bedrock, and my spade is turned. Then I am inclined to say: 'This is simply what I do.'" Toril Moi, *Revolution of the Ordinary: Literary Studies after Wittgenstein, Austin, and Cavell* (Chicago: University of Chicago Press, 2017), 171.

36. Landy, *How to Do Things with Fictions*, 60.

37. Diamond, "Ethics, Imagination and the Method of Wittgenstein's *Tractatus*," 157.

38. Landy, *How to Do Things with Fictions*, 61.

39. Landy, *How to Do Things with Fictions*, 55–57. The passages in question from the Gospel of Mark tell the following story:

> And from there he arose and went away to the region of Tyre and Sidon. And he entered a house and did not want anyone to know, yet he could not be hidden. But immediately a woman whose little daughter had an unclean spirit heard of him and came and fell down at his feet. Now the woman was a Gentile, a Syrophoenician by birth. And she begged him to cast the demon out of her daughter. And he said to her, "Let the children be fed first, for it is not right to take the children's bread and throw it to the dogs." But she answered him, "Yes, Lord; yet even the dogs under the table eat the children's crumbs." And he said to her, "For this statement you may go your way; the demon has left your daughter." And she went home and found the child lying in bed and the demon gone. (Mark 7:24–30)

40. Emily Dickinson, 466, "I dwell in possibility," in *Dickinson: Selected Poems and Commentaries*, ed. Helen Vendler (Cambridge, MA: Belknap Press of Harvard University Press, 2010), 222. I owe this example to Landy, *How to Do Things with Fictions*, 64.

41. Here one might think of the eponymous character in J. M. Coetzee's novel *Elizabeth Costello*. As I show in chapter 5, although she does, in a sense, become a Kafka parable in the Kafkaesque afterlife in the last chapter of that novel, the experience hardly delivers her from her daily cares.

42. The multiple genres Kafka simultaneously draws on and parodies in his piece (parable, scriptural exegesis, ethical teaching, stock platitudes, pastoral guidance, performative storytelling, and the well-timed joke) are each deployed to brilliant combined effect in Rabbi Nachner's story "The Goy's Teeth" in Joel and Ethan Coen's Kafka-inflected film *A Serious Man* (2009). The film as a whole explores many of the themes that Kafka takes up in his treatment of the parable, and in his wider body of work: oneiric realism; innovative critical engagement with established traditions in literary and religious instruction; the struggle to cope with mystery and uncertainty; the craving for answers and the quest for redemptive understanding; the question whether jokes, parables, and other obscure texts address a potentially wide audience, or a chosen group of elect insiders.

43. When considering Kafka's engagement with the Jewish joke tradition, it is also important to note that Hasidic stories were a rage among German-

speaking Jews, particularly Zionist-inclined ones such as Kafka and his friends, thanks to the influence of Martin Buber in the first three decades of the twentieth century. One source of information on this subject is Martina Urban's *Aesthetics of Renewal: Martin Buber's Early Representation of Hasidism as Kulturkritik* (Chicago: University of Chicago Press, 2008), which discusses Buber's early anthologies of Hasidic stories. Another is Gershom Scholem's collection of essays on Buber in his *On Jews and Judaism in Crisis*, ed. Werner J. Dannhauser (Philadelphia: Paul Dry Books, 2012); and *The Messianic Idea in Judaism and Other Essays on Jewish Spirituality* (New York: Schocken Books, 1971). At the same time as Buber's theological program is being laid out in his Hasidic anthologies—though not completely dependent on his influence—there was equally a vogue among German Jews for pseudo-Hasidic jokes; even Freud in his jokes book makes use of some of this material. The best philosophical use of the pseudo-Hasidic joke in Kafka's milieu is to be found in Ernst Bloch's *Spuren* (Frankfurt am Main: Suhrkamp, 1969), 97–99. I am grateful to Marc Caplan for pointing me to these texts.

44. Walter Sokel, *The Myth of Power and the Self: Essays on Franz Kafka* (Detroit: Wayne State University Press, 2002), 106.

45. James Conant, "Kierkegaard, Wittgenstein and Nonsense," in *Pursuits of Reason: Essays in Honor of Stanley Cavell*, ed. Ted Cohen, Paul Guyer, and Hilary Putnam (Lubbock: Texas Tech Press, 1993), 218.

46. Conant uses this Kierkegaardian mirror analogy in his discussions of changes, from the *Tractatus* to the *Investigations*, in Wittgenstein's notions about therapeutic solution. See his "Putting Two and Two Together: Kierkegaard, Wittgenstein, and the Point of View for Their Work as Authors," in *Philosophy and the Grammar of Religious Belief*, ed. Timothy Tessin and Mario von der Ruhr (New York: St. Martin's, 1995), 248–331; and most recently, James Conant, "What 'Ethics' in the *Tractatus* Is *Not*," in *Religion and Wittgenstein's Legacy*, ed. D. Z. Phillips and Mario von der Ruhr (Aldershot: Ashgate, 2005), 39–88.

47. Franz Kafka, *Briefe 1902–1924* (Frankfurt am Main: S. Fischer Verlag, 1958), 337.

CHAPTER THREE

1. Virginia Woolf, "Philosophy in Fiction" (1918), in *The Essays of Virginia Woolf*, vol. 2, *1912–1918*, ed. Andrew McNeillie (New York: Harcourt Brace Jovanovich, 1987), 208. Henceforth cited as E with corresponding volume and page number.

2. Cora Diamond, "Introduction to 'Having a Rough Story about What Moral Philosophy Is,'" in *The Literary Wittgenstein*, ed. John Gibson and Wolfgang Huemer (London: Routledge, 2004), 129.

3. Pamela L. Caughie, "Woolf and Wittgenstein," *Virginia Woolf Miscellany* 52 (1998): 2.

4. Leonard Woolf, *Letters of Leonard Woolf*, ed. Frederic Spotts (New York: Harcourt Brace Jovanovich, 1989), 539. Quoted in Ann Banfield, *The Phantom Table: Woolf, Fry, Russell and the Epistemology of Modernism* (Cambridge: Cambridge University Press, 2000), 394n41.

5. Ray Monk, *Ludwig Wittgenstein: The Duty of Genius* (New York: Penguin, 1990), 256. Henceforth cited parenthetically as DG.

6. Gaile Pohlhaus Jr. and Madelyn Detloff, "Making Sense of Wittgenstein's Bloomsbury and Bloomsbury's Wittgenstein," in *Queer Bloomsbury* (Edinburgh: Edinburgh University Press, 2016), 211.

7. Banfield, *Phantom Table*, 35.

8. Jaakko Hintikka, "Virginia Woolf and Our Knowledge of the External World," *Journal of Aesthetics and Art Criticism* 38 (Fall 1979–80): 13. Quoted in Banfield, *Phantom Table*, 36.

9. Banfield, *Phantom Table*, 35.

10. Banfield, *Phantom Table*, 35.

11. Rush Rhees, ed., *Recollections of Wittgenstein* (Oxford: Oxford University Press, 1984), 186.

12. Banfield, *Phantom Table*, 9. For works treating the relationship between Woolf and Wittgenstein in particular, see Pamela Caughie, *Virginia Woolf and Postmodernism: Literature in Quest and Question of Itself* (Urbana: University of Illinois Press, 1991); Pohlhaus and Detloff, "Making Sense of Wittgenstein's Bloomsbury and Bloomsbury's Wittgenstein"; Nir Evron, "Against Philosophy: Yaakov Shabtai's Past Continuous as Therapeutic Literature," *Partial Answers: Journal of Literature and the History of Ideas* 14, no. 1 (2016): 33–55; and Bernard Harrison, "Imagined Worlds and the Real One: Plato, Wittgenstein, and Mimesis," *Philosophy and Literature* 17, no. 1 (1993): 26–46. For other texts on Woolf and philosophy, see Megan Quigley, *Modernist Fiction and Vagueness: Philosophy, Form, and Language* (Cambridge: Cambridge University Press, 2015), especially chapter 2, "When in December 1910? Virginia Woolf, Bertrand Russell, and the Question of Vagueness"; Mark Hussey, *The Singing of the Real World: The Philosophy of Virginia Woolf's Fiction* (Columbus: Ohio State University Press, 1986); and Gillian Beer, *Virginia Woolf: The Common Ground* (Ann Arbor: University of Michigan Press, 1996). For other accounts of the relationship between Victorian Bloomsbury and modern Bloomsbury and Cambridge philosophy, see the work of S. P. Rosenbaum, especially *English Literature and British Philosophy* (Chicago: University of Chicago Press, 1971), including the chapter "The Philosophical Realism of Virginia Woolf," which explores connections between G. E. Moore's "Refutation of Idealism" and Woolf's depiction of matter. See also Christine Froula, *Virginia Woolf and the Bloomsbury Avant-Garde: War, Civilization, Modernity* (New York: Columbia University Press, 2005). For Wittgensteinian readings of Woolf from both an intellectual historical and a Cavellian perspective, respectively, see S. P. Rosenbaum, "Wittgenstein in Bloomsbury," in *Aspects of Bloomsbury: Studies in Modern English Literary and Intellectual History* (New York: St. Martin's, 1988), 161–90; and Martha Nussbaum, "The Window: Knowledge of Other Minds in Virginia Woolf's *To the Lighthouse*," *New Literary History* 26, no. 4 (1995): 731–53, henceforth cited parenthetically as Nussbaum. Michael Lackey sees Woolf's work as "anti-philosophical," concerned to challenge academic philosophy, and he argues that using philosophy to analyze and interpret her corpus thus places the critic at odds with Woolf's political and aesthetic agenda. See Michael Lackey, "Modernist Anti-philosophicalism and Virginia Woolf's

Critique of Philosophy," *Journal of Modern Literature* 29, no. 4 (2006): 76–98. See also a critique of Lackey in Timothy Mackin, "Private World, Public Minds: Woolf, Russell and Photographic Vision," *Journal of Modern Literature* 33, no. 3 (2010): 112–30.

13. Virginia Woolf, "The Leaning Tower," in *The Moment and Other Essays* (New York: Harcourt Brace Jovanovich, 1948), 130.

14. Ludwig Wittgenstein, *Philosophical Investigations* 4th ed., ed. P. M. S. Hacker and Joachim Schulte, trans. G. E. M. Anscombe, P. M. S. Hacker, and Joachim Schulte (Oxford: Blackwell, 2009). Henceforth cited parenthetically as PI, followed by section number.

15. Caughie, "Woolf and Wittgenstein," 3.

16. For further discussions of the larger lessons Diamond draws from Wittgenstein in her writing on ethics and literature, see especially Alice Crary, "Introduction," *Wittgenstein and the Moral Life: Essays in Honor of Cora Diamond* (Cambridge, MA: MIT Press, 2007), 1–26, and the essays compiled in that collection. See also Stephen Mulhall, "Realism, Modernism and the Realistic Spirit: Diamond's Inheritance of Wittgenstein, Early and Late," *Nordic Wittgenstein Review* 1 (2012): 7–34.

17. Cora Diamond, "The Difficulty of Reality and the Difficulty of Philosophy," in Stanley Cavell et al., *Philosophy and Animal Life* (New York: Columbia University Press, 2008), 43–90. Henceforth cited parenthetically as DR. Diamond's paper was first given at a conference in honor of Stanley Cavell at the New School for Social Research. It originally appeared in print in *Partial Answers: Journal of Literature and the History of Ideas* 1, no. 2 (June 2003): 1–26; and later in expanded proceedings of the New School Cavell symposium in Alice Crary and Sanford Shieh, eds., *Reading Cavell* (London: Routledge, 2006), 98–117. Reprinted a second time in *Philosophy and Animal Life*, Diamond's paper appears alongside essays by Stanley Cavell, Ian Hacking, John McDowell, and Cary Wolfe written as a set of alternative responses to the Tanner Lectures given by J. M. Coetzee at Princeton in 1997 and published, along with Amy Gutmann's introduction and reflections by Marjorie Garber, Peter Singer, Wendy Doniger, and Barbara Smuts as *The Lives of Animals* (Princeton, NJ: Princeton University Press, 1999).

18. For extended discussion of Diamond's ethical thinking and the ordinary sublime, see Espen Dahl, *Stanley Cavell, Religion, and Continental Philosophy* (Bloomington: Indiana University Press, 2014).

19. See Ludwig Wittgenstein, *Tractatus Logico-Philosophicus*, trans. C. K. Ogden (London: Routledge and Kegan Paul, 1922); Ludwig Wittgenstein, *Tractatus Logico-Philosophicus*, trans. D. F. Pears and B. F. McGuinness (London: Routledge and Kegan Paul, 1961). Henceforth cited parenthetically as TLP, followed by proposition number (or page number from the Pears-McGuinness edition for passages from Russell's introduction or Wittgenstein's preface).

20. Marjorie Perloff finds traces of the elegiac in the *Tractatus*. Pointing to Wittgenstein's dedication of the *Tractatus* to David Pinsent, his close friend from Cambridge who died in a plane accident during World War I, Perloff argues that "the 'logical' core of the *Tractatus* was subordinated to a larger scheme that is both poetic and at least subliminally elegiac." Marjorie Perloff, *Wittgenstein's*

Ladder: Poetic Language and the Strangeness of the Ordinary (Chicago: University of Chicago Press, 1996), 41.

21. For a discussion of Woolf's use of free indirect style to heighten the irony, intimacy, and perceptiveness of her novel *Mrs. Dalloway*, see R. Lanier Anderson, "Is Clarissa Dalloway Special?," *Philosophy and Literature* 41, no. 1A (July 2017): 233–71.

22. Stephen Mulhall, *The Wounded Animal: J. M. Coetzee and the Difficulty of Reality in Literature and Philosophy* (Princeton, NJ: Princeton University Press, 2009), 92–93. Hereafter cited parenthetically as WA.

23. John Gibson, *Fiction and the Weave of Life* (New York: Oxford University Press, 2007), 50.

24. Richard Eldridge, *Literature, Life, and Modernity* (New York: Columbia University Press, 2008), 106.

25. Virginia Woolf, *To the Lighthouse* (1927), ed. Mark Hussey (New York: Harcourt, 2005), 26. Henceforth cited parenthetically as TL.

26. For another perspective on modernism's engagement with question and quest, see Caughie, *Virginia Woolf and Postmodernism*; and Maria DiBattista, "*Ulysses*'s Unanswered Questions," *Modernism/modernity* 15, no. 2 (April 2008): 265–75. I examine DiBattista's arguments in that essay in chapter 4.

27. Virginia Woolf, "The Russian Point of View," *Essays of Virginia Woolf*, vol. 4, *1925 to 1928*, ed. Andrew McNeillie (London: Hogarth, 1984), 189. Henceforth cited parenthetically in the text as RPV.

28. Virginia Woolf, "Modern Fiction," in *Essays of Virginia Woolf*, 4:163. Henceforth cited parenthetically in the text as MF; Virginia Woolf, "Mr. Bennett and Mrs. Brown," in *The Essays of Virginia Woolf*, vol. 3, *1919–1924*, ed. Andrew McNeillie (New York: Harcourt Brace, 1991), 384–89; Virginia Woolf, "Character in Fiction," in *The Essays of Virginia Woolf*, vol. 3, ed. Andrew McNeillie (New York: Harcourt, 1988), 420–38, henceforth cited in the text as CF; RPV, 181–90. See also E, vol. 2, which contains "More Dostoevsky," "Mr. Sassoon's Poems," "On Re-reading Meredith," "A Minor Dostoevsky," "A Russian Schoolboy," "Tchekhov's Questions," and "The Russian View"; and E, vol. 3, which contains "The Russian Background," "Dostoyevsky in Cranford," "The Cherry Orchard," "Gorky on Tolstoy," "A Glance at Turgenev," and "Dostoevsky the Father." For an extensive treatment of Woolf's reading of these Russian writers, as well as edited transcriptions of her reading notes on Russian literature, see Roberta Rubenstein, *Virginia Woolf and the Russian Point of View* (New York: Palgrave Macmillan, 2009).

29. Virginia Woolf, "On Re-reading Meredith," E, 2:274.

30. Virginia Woolf, "Modern Novels," E, 3:35.

31. Virginia Woolf, "Tchekhov's Questions," E, 2:145.

32. Virginia Woolf, "Tolstoy's 'The Cossacks,'" E, 2:77.

33. Diamond, "Introduction to 'Having a Rough Story,'" 129.

34. Norman Malcolm, *Wittgenstein: A Religious Point of View?*, ed. Peter Winch (Ithaca, NY: Cornell University Press, 1994), 97.

35. See Cora Diamond, "Anything but Argument?," in *The Realistic Spirit: Wittgenstein, Philosophy, and the Mind* (Cambridge, MA: MIT Press, 1991), 291–309.

36. Paul Engelmann, *Letters from Wittgenstein with a Memoir* (New York: Horizon, 1968), 84.

37. Engelmann, *Letters*, 83. See also Wittgenstein's remark that "in art it is hard to say anything as good as: saying nothing." Ludwig Wittgenstein, *Culture and Value*, ed. G. H. von Wright, with H. Nyman, trans. Peter Winch, revised Alois Pichler (Oxford: Blackwell, 1998), 23. Wittgenstein and Engelmann's exchange about Uhland's poem and the effect of its language to "contain the unutterable" calls to mind Woolf's formal and poetic experiments in *Orlando*, yet another text whose title character ponders life from under a tree that becomes the inspiration for, and locus of, production, for her of "The Oak Tree," a poem that—in far more than twenty-eight lines, one imagines—also gives a picture of a life. Virginia Woolf, *Orlando: A Biography* (New York: Harcourt, 1928). Henceforth cited parenthetically as O.

38. "The Novels of George Meredith" (1928), reprinted in *Collected Essays*, ed. Leonard Woolf, 4 vols. (London Chatto and Windus, 1966–67), 1:230. See also "Philosophy in Fiction" (1918), E, 2:208–12.

39. Stephen Clark, *The Moral Status of Animals* (New York: Oxford University Press, 1977), 83.

40. Onora O'Neill, review of Stephen Clark, *The Moral Status of Animals*, *Journal of Philosophy* 77, no. 7 (July 1980): 445.

41. Iris Murdoch, "The Idea of Perfection," in *The Sovereignty of the Good* (London: Routledge and Kegan Paul, 1970), 34.

42. See Diamond, "Anything but Argument?" See also Stephen Mulhall's discussion of Diamond's debate with Onora O'Neill in chapter 1 of his *The Wounded Animal*.

43. J. M. Coetzee, *Elizabeth Costello* (New York: Penguin, 2003), 127.

44. Diamond, "Introduction to 'Having a Rough Story,'" 130–31.

45. M. O'C. Drury, "Some Notes on Conversations with Wittgenstein," in *Recollections of Wittgenstein*, ed. Rush Rhees (Oxford: Oxford University Press, 1984), 79. For a fuller discussion of Wittgenstein's remark to his friend and former student Maurice Drury, "I am not a religious man, but I cannot help seeing every problem from a religious point of view," see Peter Winch, "Discussion of Malcolm's Essay," in Norman Malcolm, *Wittgenstein: A Religious Point of View?*, ed. Peter Winch (Ithaca, NY: Cornell University Press, 1994), 95–137.

46. Virginia Woolf, *The Voyage Out*, ed. C. Ruth Miller and Lawrence Miller (Oxford: Shakespeare Head, 1995), 215.

47. Pericles Lewis, *Religious Experience and the Modernist Novel* (Cambridge: Cambridge University Press, 2010), 144–45.

48. Virginia Woolf, *A Sketch of the Past*, in *Moments of Being*, ed. Jeanne Schulkind (New York: Harcourt, 1985). Henceforth cited as SP.

49. Lewis, *Religious Experience and the Modernist Novel*, 149–50. For further discussion of Woolf and religious traditions, see also Mark Gaipa, "An Agnostic's Daughter's Apology: Materialism, Spiritualism, and Ancestry in Woolf's *To the Lighthouse*," *Journal of Modern Literature* 26, no. 2 (2002–3): 1–41; Jane Marcus, "The Niece of a Nun: Virginia Woolf, Caroline Stephen, and the Cloistered Imagination," in *Virginia Woolf: A Feminist Slant*, ed. Jane Marcus (Lincoln: University of Nebraska Press, 1983), 7–36.

50. Ludwig Wittgenstein, "Philosophy: Sections 86–93 of the So-Called 'Big Typescript' (Catalogue Number 213)," in *Philosophical Occasions, 1912–1951*, ed. James Klagge and Alfred Nordmann (Indianapolis: Hackett, 1993), 161–63, 171. See Richard Eldridge's treatment of this passage in a discussion of justice, culture, and the will in his *Literature, Life, and Modernity* (New York: Columbia University Press, 2008), 109.

51. Eldridge, *Literature, Life and Modernity*, 119. As I argued in chapter 1, we can gain a better understanding of the kind of transformative personal work Wittgenstein has in mind, as well as insights into his "religious point of view," by looking at his remarks collected in *Culture and Value* about character, courage, and confession, as well as at things Wittgenstein said in conversations with Rush Rhees and Maurice Drury and those described in personal recollections of Wittgenstein by Fania Pascal and Rowland Hutt. See Rush Rhees, *Wittgenstein: Personal Recollections* (Oxford: Basil Blackwell, 1981). See also James Conant, "Must We Show What We Cannot Say?," in *The Senses of Stanley Cavell*, ed. R. Fleming and M. Payne (Lewisburg: Bucknell University Press, 1989); James Conant, "Putting Two and Two Together: Kierkegaard, Wittgenstein, and the Point of View for Their Work as Authors," in *Philosophy and the Grammar of Religious Belief*, ed. Timothy Tessin and Mario von der Ruhr (New York: St. Martin's, 1995), 248–331; and James Conant, "Throwing Away the Top of the Ladder," *Yale Review* 79, no. 3 (1991): 328–64. See also Kevin Cahill, *The Fate of Wonder* (New York: Columbia University Press, 2011). For a different discussion of Wittgenstein and first-person expression, see Yi-Ping Ong, "Lectures on Ethics: Wittgenstein and Kafka," in *Wittgenstein and Modernism*, ed. Michael LeMahieu and Karen Zumhagen-Yekplé (Chicago: University of Chicago Press, 2017), 206–30.

52. Virginia Woolf, *The Diary of Virginia Woolf*, vol. 3, *1925–1930*, ed. Anne Olivier Bell and Andrew McNeillie (London: Harcourt Brace, Jovanovich, 1981), 62–63.

53. Friedrich Waismann, "Notes on Talks with Wittgenstein," *Philosophical Review* 74, no. 1:12–13.

54. Douglas Mao, *Solid Objects: Modernism and the Test of Production* (Princeton, NJ: Princeton University Press, 1998), 17. Henceforth cited parenthetically as *Solid Objects*.

55. See also Lucio Ruotolo, *Six Existential Heroes: The Politics of Faith* (Cambridge, MA: Harvard University Press, 1973), in which Clarissa Dalloway is one of the heroes explored, and Lucio Ruotolo, *The Interrupted Moment: A View of Virginia Woolf's Novels* (Stanford, CA: Stanford University Press, 1986). See also Pierre Nordon, "To the Lighthouse et l'experience existentielle," in *Genèse de la conscience modern: Etudes sur le développement de la conscience de soi dans les littératures du monde occidental*, ed. Yvon Brès (Paris: Presses Univérsitaires de France, 1983); and Radojka Verčko, "Existential Concerns and Narrative Techniques in the Novels of Ford Madox Ford, Virginia Woolf and Aldous Huxley," *Acta Neophilologica* 38, nos. 1–2 (2005): 49–59.

56. Ruotolo, *Interrupted Moment*, 7.

57. Ruotolo, *Six Existential Heroes*, 45.

58. Woolf, *Voyage Out*, 146.

59. Virginia Woolf, *Jacob's Room* (London: Harcourt, 1922), 64; *To the Lighthouse*, 18; *The Waves* (New York: Harcourt, 1931), 145.

60. Virginia Woolf, *The Years* (New York: Harcourt Brace and World, 1937), 133, 140, 160.

61. Perloff, *Wittgenstein's Ladder*, 19, 25, 45.

62. In her "Wittgenstein, Mathematics and Ethics: Resisting the Attractions of Realism," Diamond takes as a literary example Woolf's account of Andrew Ramsay's death (["A shell exploded. Twenty or thirty young men were blown up in France, among them Andrew Ramsay, whose death, mercifully, was instantaneous]" [TL, 137]) to bring out a point of resemblance between Wittgenstein's writing about philosophy and mathematics and her own interest in expressions of ethics that involve few (if any) specifically moral words. Diamond refers to Shuli Barzilai's claim that Woolf's sentence "serves to underscore (because, and not in spite of the inexact number) the importance of one particular life for one mother, one wife, or one friend." Shuli Barlizai, "The Politics of Quotation in *To the Lighthouse*: Mrs. Woolf Resites Mr. Tennyson and Mr. Cowper," *Literature and Psychology* 31 (1995), 22. Woolf's sentence, "A shell exploded. Twenty or thirty young men were blown up," Diamond suggests, "might be a record of what happened, might express moral thought—*which*, depends on its use." See Cora Diamond, "Wittgenstein, Mathematics and Ethics: Resisting the Attractions of Realism," in *The Cambridge Companion to Wittgenstein*, ed. Hans Sluga and David Stern (Cambridge: Cambridge University Press, 1996), 244. See also Cora Diamond, "Truth: Defenders, Debunkers, Despisers," in *Commitment in Reflection: Essays in Literature and Moral Philosophy*, ed. Leona Toker (New York: Garland, 1994), 195–221.

63. Ludwig Wittgenstein, "A Lecture on Ethics," in *Philosophical Occasions, 1912–1951*, 41–42. Henceforth cited parenthetically as LE.

64. Czesław Miłosz, "One More Day," in *The Collected Poems* (New York: Ecco, 1988), 108–9. Quoted in Diamond, DR, 60.

65. Louise Hornby, *Still Modernism* (New York: Oxford University Press, 2017), 179.

66. Hornby, *Still Modernism*, 179.

67. Ann Banfield, "*L'Imparfait de l'Objectif*: The Imperfect of the Object Glass," *Camera Obscura: A Journal of Feminism and Film Theory*, vol. 8 no. 3 (1990): 79. Henceforth cited parenthetically in the text as OI. Virginia Woolf, "The Cinema," in *The Essays of Virginia Woolf*, vol. 4, *1925 to 1928*, ed. Andrew McNeillie (London: Hogarth, 1994), 348–54. Timothy Mackin argues that Russell shares with Woolf a way of structuring the problem of the table for which the photographic provides a perfect vehicle. See Mackin, "Private World, Public Minds," 118. For an extensive treatment of photography and Woolf's novels, see Louise Hornby, "Still There: A Theory of Photography, chapter 4 of *Still Modernism*, 145–89.

68. Woolf, *The Waves* (New York: Harcourt, Brace, 1959), 285. For the term "camera consciousness," see Gilles Deleuze, *Cinema I: The Movement-Image*, trans. Hugh Tomlinson and Barbara Habberjam (Minneapolis: University of Minnesota Press, 1986), 74.

69. Roland Barthes, *Camera Lucida*, trans. Richard Howard (New York: Hill and Wang, 1981), 60. Henceforth cited parenthetically as CL.

70. Bertrand Russell, *My Philosophical Development* (London: Unwin Books, 1975), 79.

71. Roland Barthes, *Fragments of a Lover's Discourse* (New York: Hill and Wang, 1978), 216–17. Quoted in Banfield, OI, 75.

72. Hornby, *Still Modernism*, 180.

73. (What happiness back then! What liberty! What hope! What an abundance of illusions! None of them remained now!) Gustave Flaubert, *Madame Bovary, nouvelle version précédé ede scénarios inédits*, ed. J. Pommier and G. Leleu (Paris: Corti, 1949), 483. Quoted in Banfield, OI, 76.

74. Hornby, *Still Modernism*, 180.

75. See Stanley Cavell, "Knowing and Acknowledging," in *Must We Mean What We Say?* (Cambridge: Cambridge University Press, 1969), 242. Henceforth cited parenthetically in the text as KA. See also Stanley Cavell, *The Claim of Reason: Wittgenstein, Skepticism, Morality, and Tragedy* (Oxford: Oxford University Press, 1979), esp. part 4.

76. Cora Diamond, "Ethics and Imagination and the Method of Wittgenstein's *Tractatus*," in *The New Wittgenstein*, ed. Alice Crary and Rupert Read (New York: Routledge, 2000), 149–73. Henceforth cited parenthetically in the text as "Ethics and Imagination." In the essay, Diamond discusses of Wittgenstein's ethics in relation to the Grimms' "The Fisherman and His Wife" and "Rumpelstiltskin." For discussions of Wittgenstein's fondness for the Grimms' fairy tales, see especially Fania Pascal's memoir in Rush Rhees, *Wittgenstein: Personal Recollections*, 33–34. For a detailed and imaginative discussion of tone and ethical teachings of fairy tales that is especially relevant to many of the themes of Wittgenstein's ethical teaching that we have explored here, see G. K. Chesterton's "The Ethics of Elfland," and "The Flag of the World," in *Orthodoxy: The Romance of Faith* (New York: John Lane, 1908), 81–118, 119–47.

77. Ann Banfield makes a related point when she remarks that "in both *To the Lighthouse* and *Between the Acts*, the deictic tense statement 'It will be fine tomorrow' and its negation counterpose two mutually exclusive interpretations of the world." Woolf underscores their incompatibility in gendered terms, she explains, by making one outlook female and the other male. Mr. Ramsay and Charles Tansley, for example, negate the fact or possibility of light and sunshine that Mrs. Ramsay asserts. Ann Banfield, "Tragic Time: The Problem of the Future in Cambridge Philosophy and *To the Lighthouse*," *Modernism/modernity* 7, no. 1 (2000): 57.

78. Jacob W. Grimm and Wilhelm K. Grimm, *The Compete Fairy Tales of the Brothers Grimm*, trans. Jack Zipes (New York: Bantam, 1992), 72–80.

79. Ludwig Wittgenstein, *Remarks on Frazer's "Golden Bough,"* in *Philosophical Occasions, 1912–1951*, ed. Klagge and Nordmann, 146.

80. Wittgenstein, *Remarks on Frazer's "Golden Bough,"* 146.

81. In her effort in *The Realistic Spirit* to flesh out Wittgenstein's notion of an "ethical spirit," or "attitude to the world and life," that Wittgenstein calls "the happy," and to explain how it fits into the way he conceives ethics as more than just a field of philosophical discourse, Diamond points readers to G. K.

Chesterton's *Orthodoxy*. In the book, written some years before the *Tractatus*, Chesterton brings out the relation between what Diamond describes as an "ethical conception of the world as a marvel, of life as an adventure, and there being only logical necessity." While Wittgenstein contrasts two types of attitude to the world he speaks of as the happy and the unhappy, Chesterton characterizes these divergent attitudes as the spirit of attachment or loyalty and that of disloyalty. Here Diamond also points to Wordsworth, who "speaks of those who live in a world of life and of others in a universe of death," as well as to Hawthorne, whose central character in "The Birthmark," is shown to be unhappy through his willingness to destroy innocent beauty in his effort to make the world conform to his desires. Cora Diamond, "Introduction I: Philosophy and the Mind," in *The Realistic Spirit: Wittgenstein, Philosophy, and the Mind* (Cambridge, MA: MIT Press, 1991), 9–10.

82. On the "constitutively enigmatic," see Mulhall, *Wounded Animal*, 92. See also Fiona Jenkins, "A Sensate Critique: Vulnerability and the Image in Judith Butler's *Frames of War*," *Substance* 42, no. 3 (2013): 105.

83. Ruth Klüger, *Still Alive: A Holocaust Girlhood Remembered* (New York: Feminist, 2003), 103. Quoted in Diamond, DR, 61–62.

84. R. F. Holland, "The Miraculous," in *Against Empiricism* (Totowa, NJ: Barnes and Noble, 1980).

85. Ted Hughes, "Six Young Men," in *The Hawk in the Rain* (London: Faber and Faber, 1957), 54–55; quoted in Diamond, DR, 44.

86. Wilfred Owen, "Exposure," *Collected Poems of Wilfred Owen*, ed. and with an introduction by Cecil Day Lewis (New York: New Directions, 1965), 48–49.

87. Stanley Cavell, *The Claim of Reason: Wittgenstein, Skepticism, Morality and Tragedy* (Oxford: Clarendon, 1970), 433–54.

88. See Stanley Cavell, *The World Viewed: Reflections on the Ontology of Film* (Cambridge, MA: Harvard University Press, 1979), 18–19. Henceforth cited as WV. See also Stanley Cavell, "What Photography Calls Thinking," *Raritan* 4 (Spring 1985): 1–21; rpt. *Raritan Reading*, ed. Richard Poirier (New Brunswick, NJ: Rutgers University Press, 1990), 47–65; Diarmuid Costello, "Automat, Automatic, Automatism: Rosalind Krauss and Stanley Cavell on Photography and the Photographically Dependent Arts," *Critical Inquiry* 38 no. 4 (Summer 2012): 819–54. See also chapter 9 of Stephen Mulhall, *Stanley Cavell: Philosophy's Recounting of the Ordinary* (Oxford: Oxford University Press, 1994).

89. William Wordsworth, *The Prelude: Growth of a Poet's Mind* [1805], ed. Ernest de Selincourt (Oxford: Oxford University Press, 1970)] Book XII, lines 208–61, p. 213. "There are in our existence spots of time / Which with distinct pre-eminence retain / A vivifying Virtue, whence, depress'd / By false opinion and contentious thought, / Or aught of heavier or more deadly weight, / In trivial occupations, and the round / Of ordinary intercourse, our minds / Are nourish'd and invisibly repair'd, / A virtue, by which pleasure is enhanced / That penetrates, enables us to mount / When high, more high, and lifts us up when fallen."

90. William Blake, "Auguries of Innocence," *The Poems of William Blake*, ed. W. B. Yeats (New York: Charles Scribner's Sons, 1893), 90. The famous first

lines of Blake's poem are: "To see a World in a Grain of Sand / And Heaven in a Wild Flower / Hold Infinity in the palm of your hand / and Eternity in an hour."

91. Woolf, "Mr. Bennett and Mrs. Brown," 434.

92. Cora Diamond, "Realism and the Realistic Spirit," in *Realistic Spirit*, 39–72. See also Mulhall, WA, 145–50.

93. Mulhall, "Realism, Modernism and the Realistic Spirit," 8. In this essay, Mulhall discusses two papers by Diamond in addition to "The Difficulty of Reality and the Difficulty of Philosophy." They each focus on distinctly ethico-religious concerns. See "Riddles and Anselm's Riddle," in *The Realistic Spirit*, 267–90; "Wittgenstein on Religious Belief: The Gulfs between Us," in *Religion and Wittgenstein's Legacy*, ed. D. Z. Phillips and Mario von der Ruhr (Aldershot: Ashgate, 2005), 99–139.

94. Mulhall, "Realism, Modernism and the Realistic Spirit," 19; Mulhall, *Wounded Animal*, 82.

95. Stanley Cavell, "Notes and Afterthoughts on the Opening of Wittgenstein's *Investigations*," in *Cambridge Companion to Wittgenstein*, ed. Sluga and Stern, 261–95.

96. Mulhall, "Realism, Modernism and the Realistic Spirit," 29.

97. William Cowper, *Poems by William Cowper in Two Volumes*, vol. 2 (London: T. Bensley, 1800), 48. Alfred Lord Tennyson, *The Poetic and Dramatic Works of Alfred Lord Tennyson* (Boston: Houghton Mifflin, 1898), 226–67.

98. Simone Weil, "Human Personality," in *Simone Weil: An Anthology*, ed. Sian Miles (New York: Weidenfeld and Nicholson, 1986), 70. Quoted in Diamond, DR, 74–75.

99. See Cavell, "Knowing and Acknowledging," 238–66; and Stanley Cavell, "Declining Decline: Wittgenstein as a Philosopher of Culture," in *This New Yet Unapproachable America: Lectures after Emerson after Wittgenstein* (Albuquerque, NM: Living Batch, 1989), 29–76.

100. Woolf, *Diary of Virginia Woolf*, 3:33.

101. Christine Froula, "Mrs. Dalloway's Postwar Elegy: Women, War and the Art of Mourning," *Modernism/modernity* 9, no. 1 (2002): 92.

102. Simone de Beauvoir, "Que peut la littérature?," in *Que Peut la Littérature?*, ed. Yves Berger (Paris: Union Générale d'Editions, 1965), 83.

103. Virginia Woolf, "Tchekhov's Questions," E, 2:245–56. As Martin Woessner points out in the context of a reading of Coetzee's novels, works of literature that are concerned to foster in their readers an affective orientation or attunement toward the world do not seek to answer the transcendental questions they pose. Such works may not offer solutions to our most pressing moral questions, but they can help us to recognize, as Robert Pippin suggests in his study of Henry James, that "the key issue of morality may not be the rational justifiability with which I treat others, but the proper acknowledgement of, and enactment of, a dependence on others without which the process of any justification (any invocation of common normative criteria at all) could not begin." Martin Woessner, "Coetzee's Critique of Reason," in *J. M. Coetzee and Ethics: Philosophical Perspectives on Literature*, ed. Anton Leist and Peter Singer (New York: Columbia University Press, 2010), 241; Robert Pippin, *Henry James and Modern Moral Life* (Cambridge: Cambridge University Press, 2000), 10–11.

CHAPTER FOUR

1. Leo Tolstoy, *A Confession* (London: Penguin Books, 1998), 29.

2. James Joyce, *Ulysses* (New York: Random House, 1934), 677. Henceforth cited parenthetically as U.

3. Ludwig Wittgenstein, *Tractatus Logico-Philosophicus*, trans. C. K. Ogden (London: Routledge and Kegan Paul, 1922), 6.52–6.521; Ludwig Wittgenstein, *Tractatus Logico-Philosophicus*, trans. D. F. Pears and B. F. McGuinness (London: Routledge and Kegan Paul, 1961), 6.52–6.521. Henceforth cited parenthetically as TLP, followed by proposition number (or page number from Pears McGuinness's 1961 edition for passages from Russell's introduction and Wittgenstein's preface).

4. Letter to Harriet Shaw Weaver, October 7, 1921, in James Joyce, *The Letters of James Joyce*, vol. 1, ed. Stuart Gilbert and Richard Ellmann (New York: Viking, 1966), 172.

5. Andrew Gibson, *Joyce's "Ithaca,"* ed. Andrew Gibson (Atlanta: Rodopi, 1996), 4.

6. Frank Kermode, *The Sense of an Ending* (New York: Oxford University Press, 1967), 113.

7. Richard Ellmann, *James Joyce, New and Revised Edition* (New York: Oxford University Press, 1982), 501.

8. James Joyce, *Stephen Hero*, ed. John J. Slocum and Herbert Cahoon (New York: New Directions, 1944), 211. Henceforth cited as SH.

9. See James Joyce, *Epiphanies*, ed. Oscar Silverman (Buffalo, NY: Lockwood Memorial Library, University of Buffalo/Easy Hill, 1956); James Joyce: *Poems and Shorter Writings*, ed. Richard Ellmann and A. Walton Litz (London: Faber and Faber, 1991); Robert Scholes and Richard M. Kain, *The Workshop of Daedalus: James Joyce and the Raw Materials for* A Portrait of the Artist as a Young Man (Evanston, IL: Northwestern University Press, 1965).

10. Cora Diamond, "Ethics and Imagination and the Method of Wittgenstein's *Tractatus*," in *The New Wittgenstein*, ed. Alice Crary and Rupert Read (London: Routledge, 2000), 166. See also Cora Diamond, "The *Tractatus* and the Limits of Sense," in *The Oxford Handbook of Wittgenstein*, ed. Oskari Kuusela and Marie McGinn (Oxford: Oxford University Press, 2011), 262. Henceforth cited parenthetically as "Limits of Sense."

11. See Homer, *The Odyssey*, trans. Emily Wilson (New York: Norton, 2017), 105; and Homer, *The Odyssey*, trans. Robert Fagels (New York: Penguin, 1999), 77. Friedrich Nietzsche, "On Redemption," in *Thus Spoke Zarathustra*, trans. Walter Kaufmann (New York: Viking, [1888] 1954), 251. Henceforth cited as Z.

12. "Wir haben nicht zuviel Verstand und zuwenig Seele, sondern wir haben zuwenig Verstand in den Fragen der Seele." Robert Musil, "Das Hilflose Europa" [1922], in *Gesammelte Werke* vol. 8 (Hamburg: Rowohlt, 1981), 1092. Robert Musil, "Helpless Europe," in *Precision and Soul: Essays and Addresses*, ed. And trans. Burton Pike and David S. Luft (Chicago: University of Chicago Press, 1990), 131.

13. See Allan Janik and Stephen Toulmin, *Wittgenstein's Vienna* (New York: Ivan R. Dee, [1973] 1996). For analyses of the cultural relationship between

Wittgenstein and Musil, see also Allan Janik, *Wittgenstein's Vienna Revisited* (New Brunswick, NJ: Transaction, 2001); Aldo Giorgio Gargani, "Wittgenstein's 'Perspicuous Representation' and Musil's 'Illuminations,'" in *Robert Musil und die kulturellen Tendenzen seiner Zeit*, ed. Josef Strutz (Munich: Fink, 1983); Piergiorgio Donatelli, "Loos, Musil, Wittgenstein and the Recovery of Human Life," in *Wittgenstein and Modernism*, ed. Michael LeMahieu and Karen Zumhagen-Yekplé (Chicago: University of Chicago Press, 2017), 91–113; Pierre Fasula, "Wittgenstein, Musil and the Austrian Modernism," in *Understanding Wittgenstein, Understanding Modernism*, ed. Anat Matar (London: Bloomsbury, 2017), 113–25; Jacques Bouveresse, "'The Darkness of This Time': Wittgenstein and the Modern World," in *Wittgenstein: Centenary Essays*, ed. Phillips A. Griffiths (Cambridge: Cambridge University Press, 1991), 11–39.

14. Michael André Bernstein, *Five Portraits: Modernity and the Imagination in Twentieth-Century German Writing* (Evanston, IL: Northwestern University Press, 2000), 36–37.

15. Robert Musil, *Der Mann ohne Eigenschaften* (Frankfurt am Main: Rohwohlt Verlag, 1957).

16. James Joyce, in a 1921 letter to Claud W. Sykes, quoted in Ellmann, *James Joyce*, 516.

17. Ellmann, *James Joyce*, 501.

18. Rainer Maria Rilke, "Archaïscher Torso Apollos," in *Neue Gedichte* (Leipzig: Iminsel Verlag, 1907), 1.

19. Bernstein, *Five Portraits*, 1–10. Bernstein's catalogue of authors who strive in their works to attain the ambitious status he outlines includes the five writers (Rilke, Musil, Heidegger, Benjamin, and Celan) with whom his book is explicitly concerned. He also gestures at such usual suspects of modernist masterpiece making as Mallarmé, Yeats, Proust, Freud, Faulkner, and Stein as well as Joyce and Wittgenstein.

20. Wallace Stephens, "Notes toward a Supreme Fiction," in *Collected Poetry and Prose*, ed. Frank Kermode and Joan Richardson (New York: Library of America, 1997), 329–51. Eliot's oft-quoted claim states: "it appears likely that poets of our civilization, as it exists at present, must be difficult. Our civilization comprehends great variety and complexity, and this variety and complexity, playing upon a refined sensibility, must produce various and complex results." T. S. Eliot, "The Metaphysical Poets," in *Selected Prose of T. S. Eliot* (New York: Harcourt, Brace Jovanovich, Farrar Straus and Giroux, 1975), 65. First published in *Times Literary Supplement*, October 20, 1921, 669–70.

21. R. Lanier Anderson, "Nietzsche on Redemption and Transfiguration," in *The Re-enchantment of the World*, ed. Joshua Landy and Michael Saler (Stanford, CA: Stanford University Press, 2009), 225–58. Henceforth cited parenthetically as NRT.

22. Maria DiBattista, "*Ulysses*'s Unanswered Questions," *Modernism/modernity* 15, no. 2 (April 2008): 271.

23. DiBattista, "*Ulysses*'s Unanswered Questions," 171.

24. DiBattista, "*Ulysses*'s Unanswered Questions," 172–73.

25. Cora Diamond, "Riddles and Anselm's Riddle," in *The Realistic Spirit: Wittgenstein, Philosophy, and the Mind* (Cambridge, MA: MIT Press, 1991), 268.

26. Cora Diamond, "Introduction II: Wittgenstein and Metaphysics," in *Realistic Spirit*, 13–38.

27. Ludwig Wittgenstein, *Zettel*, ed. G. E. M. Anscombe and G. H. von Wright, trans. G. E. M. Anscombe (Oxford: Oxford University Press, 1967), §§ 696–97.

28. Diamond, "Riddles and Anselm's Riddle," 267.

29. The passage is taken from unpublished notes on Wittgenstein's lectures taken by Margaret MacDonald on May 22, 1935, quoted in Diamond, "Riddles and Anselm's Riddle," 267.

30. Diamond, "Riddles and Anselm's Riddle," 271.

31. Diamond, "Riddles and Anselm's Riddle," 272.

32. Diamond, "Riddles and Anselm's Riddle," 267–68. See also Wittgenstein's remarks in *Zettel*, §§ 696–97 that a mathematical question is a challenge that makes sense if it stimulates the imagination and spurs us on to mathematical activity.

33. M. O'C. Drury, "Some Notes on Conversations with Wittgenstein," in *Recollections of Wittgenstein*, ed. Rush Rhees (Oxford: Oxford University Press, 1984), 79.

34. James Joyce, *A Portrait of the Artist as a Young Man* (New York: Viking, 1964), 227.

35. Caleb Thompson and Peter Winch have both suggested that we can best understand Wittgenstein's statement about his "religious point of view" in relation to a claim we have seen him make elsewhere about his conception of philosophy as an activity of clarification—namely, that "work on philosophy is . . . actually more of a kind of work on oneself. On one's conception. On the way one sees things (And what one demands of them)" (CV, 16). Caleb Thompson, "Wittgenstein, Augustine and the Fantasy of Assent," *Philosophical Investigations* 25, no. 2 (2002): 153; Peter Winch, "Discussion of Malcolm's Essay," in Norman Malcolm, *Wittgenstein: A Religious Point of View?*, ed. Peter Winch (Ithaca, NY: Cornell University Press, 1994), 131. For Wittgenstein, religion is concerned not with the manipulation of the world or adherence to doctrine but with the state of a person's soul and ongoing progress toward self-perfection. He was deeply invested in the possibility of personal transformation and the power of religious experience—and the *literature* of religious experience—to bring it about. He himself turned (like Bloom, more than once) to the literature of instruction in search of solutions to the difficult problems of life. Wittgenstein read James's *Varieties of Religious Experience* with great interest, telling Russell, "This book does me a lot of good." Ludwig Wittgenstein, *Letters to Russell, Keynes and Moore*, ed. G. H. von Wright and B. F. McGuinness (Oxford: Basil Blackwell, 1974), 10. He turned for solace during the war to Tolstoy's *Confession* and *Gospel in Brief* and was an avid reader of Dostoyevsky's *Brothers Karamazov* and was later to read Augustine's *Confessions*, calling it "the most serious book ever written." See Drury, "Some Notes on Conversations with Wittgenstein," 79. As Pericles Lewis points out, Joyce was as shaped by his religious training as he was hostile toward organized religion. Though he fell away from the Catholicism of his upbringing, he nonetheless had a sacramental conception of his art, regarding it as a kind of alternative priesthood. In *Portrait*,

Stephen Dedalus sets himself up as a "priest of eternal imagination, transmuting the daily bread of experience into the radiant body of everliving life" (221). "What most inspires Joyce," Lewis observes, "is the power of the priest to transform the everyday into the eternal by performing the sacraments, rather than the power of God that lies behind those sacraments." Pericles Lewis, *Religious Experience and the Modernist Novel* (New York: Cambridge University Press, 2010), 179.

36. For further discussions of the patterns of figural visions of Dante and St. Paul in Ulysses, and in "Ithaca" particularly, see Stephen Sicari, *Joyce's Modernist Allegory*: Ulysses *and the History of the Novel* (Columbia: University of South Carolina Press, 2001); and Pericles Lewis, "The Burial of the Dead," in *Religious Experience and the Modernist Novel*, 170–92.

37. For a discussion of astrological symbolism in "Ithaca," see David Chinitz, "All the Dishevelled Wandering Stars: Astrological Symbolism in 'Ithaca,'" *Twentieth Century Literature* 37 (1991): 432–41.

38. Charles Peake, *James Joyce: The Citizen and the Artist* (London: Edward Arnold, 1977), 287.

39. Tolstoy, *Confession*, 36.

40. On Joyce's sabotaging the climax of the chapter, see Karen Lawrence, "'Ithaca': The Order of Things," in *Who's Afraid of James Joyce?* (Gainesville: University Press of Florida, 2010), 54. It was important to Joyce that the dot be a large one. The Rosenbach manuscript clearly shows Joyce's marginal note that "*La réponse à la dernière question est un point*" and his directions indicating that "*le point doit être plus visible.*" See Austin Briggs, "The Full Stop at the End of 'Ithaca': Thirteen Ways—and Then Some—of Looking at a Black Dot," *Joyce Studies Annual* 7 (Summer 1996): 125–44. The coincidence between Tolstoy's comment and Joyce's full stop is entirely accidental, though as I noted in the introduction, Joyce did share Wittgenstein's admiration for Tolstoy's "How Much Land Does a Man Need?" as "the "greatest story that the literature of the world knows." See George R. Clay, "Tolstoy in the Twentieth Century," in *Cambridge Companion to Tolstoy*, ed. Donna Tussing Orwin (Cambridge: Cambridge University Press, 2002), 209.

41. Tolstoy, *Confession*, 41.

42. Wittgenstein writes in a 1931 notebook, "Tolstoy: a thing's significance (importance) lies in its being something everyone can understand.—That is both true and false. What makes a subject hard to understand—if it's something significant and important—is not that before you can understand it you need to be specially trained in abstruse matters, but the contrast between understanding the subject and what most people *want* to see. Because of this the very things which are most obvious may become the hardest of all to understand. What has to be overcome is a difficulty having to do with the will, rather than with the intellect" (CV, 17).

43. Ellmann, *James Joyce*, 555. See James Conant, "Must We Show What We Cannot Say?," in *The Senses of Stanley Cavell*, ed. R. Fleming and M. Payne (Lewisburg, PA: Bucknell University Press, 1989), 242–83; and Michael Kremer, "The Purpose of Tractarian Nonsense," *NOÛS* 35, no. 1 (2001). Kremer writes, "The typical reader of the *Tractatus* . . . will begin by supposing herself to be

reading a book of philosophy, intended as a straightforward communication of intelligible thought. This thought may appear difficult and its expression highly compressed; the reader may struggle to come to an understanding of the author's point of view; but if the reader persists and makes it to the end of the book, it may surprise her to learn that she is to dismiss as nonsense what she had taken herself to understand. She may infer that she has understood nothing at all, and throw the book away—yet not in the way seemingly intended by Wittgenstein's image of the ladder which one throws away after climbing it—for this reader will not have been transformed in any interesting way by the experience, except perhaps in acquiring a distaste for certain kinds of philosophy" (39).

44. Virginia Woolf, "Modern Fiction," in *The Essays of Virginia Woolf*, vol. 4, *1925 to 1928*, ed. Andrew McNeillie (London: Hogarth, 1994), 163.

45. Eli Friedlander, *Signs of Sense: Reading Wittgenstein's* Tractatus (Cambridge, MA: Harvard University Press, 2001), 12.

46. Ludwig Wittgenstein, "A Lecture on Ethics," in *Philosophical Occasions, 1912–1951*, ed. James Klagge and Alfred Nordmann (Indianapolis: Hackett, 1993), 39–40. Henceforth cited parenthetically as LE.

47. See Bernard Benstock, *Narrative Con/Texts in* Ulysses (London: Macmillan, 1991), 134.

48. Wolfgang Iser, *The Implied Reader: Patterns of Communication in Prose Fiction from Bunyan to Beckett* (Baltimore: Johns Hopkins University Press, 1974), 219, 221.

49. See Friedlander, *Signs of Sense*, 12–17.

50. Cora Diamond, "Introduction to 'Having a Rough Story about What Moral Philosophy Is,'" in *The Literary Wittgenstein*, ed. John Gibson and Wolfgang Huemer (London: Routledge, 2004), 131; Iris Murdoch, "Vision and Choice in Morality," *Proceedings of the Aristotelian Society*, suppl. vol. 30 (1956): 32–58.

51. Ludwig Wittgenstein to Paul Engelmann, in Paul Engelmann, *Letters from Ludwig Wittgenstein with a Memoir* (New York: Horizon, 1968), 7.

52. Diamond "Introduction to 'Having a Rough Story,'" 130.

53. Ellmann, *James Joyce*, 501

54. Diamond, "Introduction to 'Having a Rough Story,'" 131.

55. Frank Budgen, *James Joyce and the Making of* Ulysses (Bloomington: Indiana University Press, 1960), 257.

56. Lawrence, "'Ithaca': The Order of Things," 55.

57. Quoted in Richard E. Madtes, *The "Ithaca" Chapter of Joyce's* Ulysses (Ann Arbor: UMI Research Press, 1983), 65.

58. DiBattista, "*Ulysses*'s Unanswered Questions," 268.

59. DiBattista, "*Ulysses*'s Unanswered Questions," 271.

60. Richard Ellmann, ed., *Selected Letters of James Joyce* (New York: Viking, 1975), 270.

61. Ludwig Wittgenstein, *Notebooks 1914–1916*, ed. G. H. von Wright and G. E. M. Anscombe, trans. G. E. M. Anscombe (Chicago: University of Chicago Press, 1961), 78. Hereafter cited as N.

62. Michael Fried, "Jeff Wall, Wittgenstein, and the Everyday," in *Why Photography Matters as Art as Never Before* (New Haven, CT: Yale University Press, 2008), 77.

63. Virginia Woolf, *A Sketch of the Past*, in *Moments of Being*, ed. Jeanne Schulkind (New York: Harcourt, 1985), 71, 67.

64. Eli Friedlander, "Wittgenstein, Benjamin and Pure Realism," in *Wittgenstein and Modernism*, ed. LeMahieu and Zumhagen-Yekplé, 119.

65. Lawrence, "'Ithaca': The Order of Things," 54.

66. Friedrich Waismann, "Notes on Talks with Wittgenstein," *Philosophical Review*, 74, no. 1:12–16.

67. Stanley Cavell, "Foreword," in *Must We Mean What We Say?* (Cambridge: Cambridge University Press, 1969), xxviii.

68. Derek Attridge, "Age of Bronze, State of Grace," in *J. M. Coetzee and the Ethics of Reading: Literature in the Event* (Chicago: University of Chicago Press, 2004), 180.

69. Toril Moi takes up accusations (Marcuse's and Gellner's in particular) of Wittgenstein's political quietism—attributed most often to what he says in *Philosophical Investigations* (4th ed., ed. P. M. S. Hacker and Joachim Schulte, trans. G. E. M. Anscombe, P. M. S. Hacker, and Joachim Schulte [Oxford: Blackwell, 2009]), §124: "Philosophy must not interfere in any way with the actual use of language, so it can in the end only describe it. For it cannot justify it either. It leaves everything as it is." Moi observes that "to change our language means to change our attitude, our way of dealing with others, our way of being in the world." See Toril Moi, *Revolution of the Ordinary: Literary Studies after Wittgenstein, Austin, and Cavell* (Chicago: University of Chicago Press, 2017), 155–58. See also Ben Ware, *The Dialectic of the Ladder: Wittgenstein, the "Tractatus" and Modernism* (London: Bloomsbury, 2015), 85–92.

70. See Friedrich Nietzsche, *The Gay Science*, trans. Walter Kaufmann (New York: Vintage, 1974), 125. Henceforth cited parenthetically as GS.

71. See Bernard Reginster, *The Affirmation of Life: Nietzsche on Overcoming of Nihilism* (Cambridge, MA: Harvard University Press, 206), esp. 229–30.

72. James Conant, "Putting Two and Two Together: Wittgenstein, Kierkegaard, and the Point of View for Their Work as Authors," in *Philosophy and the Grammar of Religious Belief*, ed. Timothy Tessin and Mario von der Ruhr (New York: St. Martin's, 1995), 302–3.

73. Cora Diamond, "Wittgenstein's 'Unbearable Conflict,'" (paper presented at the American Philosophical Association Eastern Division Meeting, New York, January 10, 2019), 15.

74. Kremer, "The Purpose of Tractarian Nonsense," 60.

75. Cora Diamond, "Criss-Cross Philosophy," in *Wittgenstein at Work: Method in the* Philosophical Investigations, ed. Erich Ammereller and Eugen Fischer (London: Routledge, 2004), 215.

76. See Diamond, *Realistic Spirit*, 8–22; Diamond, "Criss-Cross Philosophy"; James Conant and Cora Diamond, "On Reading the *Tractatus* Resolutely," in *Wittgenstein's Lasting Significance*, ed. Max Kolbel and Bernhard Weiss (London: Routledge, 2004), 80–87; James Conant, "Wittgenstein's Later Criticism of the *Tractatus*," in *Wittgenstein: The Philosopher and His Works*, ed. Alois Pichler and Simo Säätelä (Frankfurt am Main: Ontos Verlag, 2006); and James Conant, "Mild Mono-Wittgensteinianism," in *Wittgenstein and the Moral Life: Essays in Honor of Cora Diamond*, ed. Alice Crary (Cambridge MA:

MIT Press, 2007); Silver Bronzo, "The Resolute Reading and Its Critics: An Introduction to the Literature," *Wittgenstein-Studien* 3 (2012): 59.

77. Diamond, "Criss-Cross Philosophy," 207.

78. Diamond, "Criss-Cross Philosophy," 215.

79. Kevin Cahill, *The Fate of Wonder* (New York: Columbia University Press, 2011), 98.

80. See Diamond, "Criss-Cross Philosophy"; Conant, "Mild Mono-Wittgensteinianism," 140–42; James Conant, "A Development in Wittgenstein's Conception of Philosophy: From '*The* Method' to 'Methods,'" in *In Sprachspiele verstricht—oder: Wie man der Fliege den Ausweg zeigt*, ed. Stefan Tolksdorf and Holm Tetens (Berlin: De Gruyter, 2010), 55–80; and Conant, "Wittgenstein's Methods," in *The Oxford Handbook of Wittgenstein*, ed. Oskari Kuusela and Marie McGinn (Oxford: Oxford University Press, 2011), 620–45; Michael Kremer, "The Cardinal Problem of Philosophy," in *Wittgenstein and the Moral Life*, ed. Crary, 143–76; Oskari Kuusela, "Review of Barry Stocker: Post-analytic *Tractatus*, *European Journal of Philosophy* 16, no. 3 (2008): 120–32.

81. Terry Eagleton, *Wittgenstein: The Terry Eagleton Script, the Derek Jarman Film* (London: British Film Institute, 1933), 6–7.

82. For Moretti, "the great novelty of the stream of consciousness consists in its proceeding for pages and pages *without the slightest revelation.* . . . The view is determinedly earthbound, with nothing taking flight—as in the grand vision of the *Portrait*—towards a higher reality." Franco Moretti, *Modern Epic: The World-System from Goethe to García Márquez*, trans. Quintin Hoare (London: Verso, 1996), 152.

83. Conant, "Putting Two and Two Together," 303.

84. Wallace Stevens, "A Rabbit as King of the Ghosts," in *The Collected Poems of Wallace Stevens* (New York: Knopf, 1954), 209.

85. Sabina Lovibond, "Wittgenstein, Tolstoy, and the 'Apocalyptic View,'" *Philosophy of the Social Sciences* 46, no. 6 (2016): 568.

86. Lovibond, "Wittgenstein, Tolstoy, and the 'Apocalyptic View,'" 568; Caleb Thompson, "Wittgenstein, Tolstoy and the Meaning of Life," *Philosophical Investigations* 20, vol. 2 (1997): 110.

CHAPTER FIVE

1. J. M. Coetzee, *Elizabeth Costello* (New York: Penguin, 2003), 126–27. Henceforth cited parenthetically as EC.

2. J. M. Coetzee, *The Childhood of Jesus* (New York: Penguin, 2013), 141. Henceforth cited parenthetically as CJ.

3. Cora Diamond, "Wittgenstein on Religious Belief: The Gulfs between Us," in *Religion and Wittgenstein's Legacy*, ed. D. Z. Phillips and Mario van der Ruhr (Aldershot: Ashgate, 2005), 119.

4. Stanley Cavell, "Declining Decline: Wittgenstein as a Philosopher of Culture," in *This New Yet Unapproachable America: Lectures after Emerson after Wittgenstein* (Albuquerque, NM: Living Batch, 1989), 57.

5. Stephen Ross, "Introduction: The Missing Link," in Stephen Ross, ed., *Modernism and Theory: A Critical Debate* (London: Routledge, 2009), 382.

For an in-depth treatment of modernism's afterlife in contemporary fiction, see David James, *Modernist Futures: Innovation and Inheritance in the Contemporary Novel* (Cambridge: Cambridge University Press, 2012). See also the essays collected in David James, ed., *The Legacies of Modernism: Historicising Postwar and Contemporary Fiction* (Cambridge: Cambridge University Press, 2011), which examine a diverse group of Anglophone text in an exploration of the relationship between the innovations of early twentieth-century writing and those of fiction written since 1945.

6. See Douglas Mao and Rebecca Walkowitz, "The New Modernist Studies," *PMLA* 123, no. 3 (2008): 737–39. See also Walkowitz's own treatment of Coetzee in her "For Translation: Virginia Woolf, J. M. Coetzee and Transnational Comparison," in *The Legacies of Modernism*, ed. James, 243–63; and her *Born Translated: The Contemporary Novel in an Age of World Literature* (New York: Columbia University Press, 2015).

7. David James, "'Spare Prose and a Spare, Thrifty World': J. M. Coetzee's Politics of Minimalism," in *Modernist Futures*, 99.

8. Derek Attridge, "Modernist Form and the Ethics of Otherness: *Dusklands* and *In the Heart of the Country*," in *J. M. Coetzee and the Ethics of Reading: Literature in the Event* (Chicago: University of Chicago Press, 2004), 2, 7.

9. J. M. Coetzee, *Diary of a Bad Year* (New York: Random House, 2015), 192–93.

10. I am grateful to Reshef Agam-Segal for urging me to attend to this point.

11. J. M. Coetzee and Arabella Kurtz, *The Good Story: Exchanges on Truth, Fiction and Psychotherapy* (London: Harvill Seeker, 2015), 156.

12. Franz Kafka, "Von den Gleichnissen," in *Kritische Ausgabe: Nachgelassene Schriften und Fragmente II*, ed. Jost Schillemeit (Frankfurt am Main: Fischer Verlag, 2002), 531–32.

13. See Roger Bellin, "A Strange Allegory: J. M. Coetzee's *The Childhood of Jesus*, *Los Angeles Review of Books*, November 6, 2013, https://lareviewof books.org/article/magical-child-troubled-child-on-jm-coetzees-the-childhood -of-jesus/; Benjamin Markovitz's review in *Observer*, March 2, 2013, https:// www.theguardian.com/books/2013/mar/02/childhood-of-jesus-jm-coetzee -review; Joyce Carol Oates, "Saving Grace," *New York Times*, August 29, 2003.

14. Elizabeth Anker, "Why We Love Coetzee; or, *The Childhood of Jesus* and the Funhouse of Critique," in *Critique and Postcritique*, ed. Elizabeth Anker and Rita Felski (Durham, NC: Duke University Press, 2017), 186, 183. Henceforth cited parenthetically as Anker.

15. Elizabeth Anker and Rita Felski, "Introduction," in *Critique and Postcritique*, ed. Elizabeth Anker and Rita Felski (Durham, NC: Duke University Press, 2017), 24.

16. Toril Moi, *The Revolution of the Ordinary: Literary Studies after Wittgenstein, Austin, and Cavell* (Chicago: University of Chicago Press, 2017), 181. Hereafter cited parenthetically as RO.

17. Ludwig Wittgenstein, *Philosophical Investigations*, 4th ed., ed. P. M. S. Hacker and Joachim Schulte, trans. G. E. M. Anscombe, P. M. S. Hacker, and Joachim Schulte (Oxford: Blackwell, 2009). Hereafter cited as PI, followed by preface page or section number.

18. Stanley Cavell, "A Matter of Meaning It," in *Must We Mean What We Say?* (Cambridge: Cambridge University Press, 1969), 227. See Moi, RO, 180–95, 202–21.

19. Stanley Cavell, *The Claim of Reason: Wittgenstein, Skepticism, Morality, and Tragedy* (New York: Oxford University Press, 1979), 6.

20. Robert Pippin, "What Does J. M. Coetzee's *The Childhood of Jesus* Have to Do with the Childhood of Jesus?," in *J. M. Coetzee's* The Childhood of Jesus: *The Ethics of Ideas and Things*, ed. Jennifer Rutherford and Anthony Uhlmann (London: Bloomsbury, 2017), 9–34.

21. J. M. Coetzee and Arabella Kurtz, *The Good Story*, 156.

22. In the preface to the *Philosophical Investigations*, written in 1945, Wittgenstein remarks: "It is not impossible that it should fall to the lot of this work in its poverty and in the darkness of this time, to bring light into one brain or another—but, of course, it is not likely" (PI, xxxi). J. M. Coetzee, *Disgrace* (New York: Penguin, 1999), 216. Attridge discusses the relationship of Coetzee's literary endeavors to local and global political upheaval by attending to the repeated references he makes in *Disgrace* to the "these times." See the first section of his "Age of Bronze, State of Grace," in *J. M. Coetzee and the Ethics of Reading*.

23. Jennifer Rutherford, "Thinking about Shit in *The Childhood of Jesus*," in *J. M. Coetzee's* The Childhood of Jesus, ed. Rutherford and Uhlmann, 33–55. See also Willis Barnstone, ed., *The Other Bible* (New York: Harper Collins, 2005), 67. See also Jennifer Rutherford, "Washed Clean: The Forgotten Journeys of Future Maritime Arrivals in J. M. Coetzee's *Estralia*," in *Migration by Boat: Discourses of Trauma, Exclusion and Survival*, ed. Lynda Mannik (New York: Berghahn Books, 2016), 101–15.

24. For a more extended discussion of the irony and referentiality of Coetzee's "literary theme park" in *The Childhood of Jesus*, see Yoshiki Tajiri, "Beyond the Literary Theme Park: J. M. Coetzee's Late Style in *The Childhood of Jesus*," in *J. M. Coetzee's* The Childhood of Jesus, ed. Rutherford and Uhlmann, 187–211.

25. J. M. Coetzee, "Jerusalem Prize Acceptance Speech," in *Doubling the Point: Essays and Interviews*, ed. David Attwell (Cambridge, MA: Harvard University Press, 1992), 98.

26. Julika Griem, "'Good Paragraphing. Unusual Content': On the Making and Unmaking of Novelistic Worlds," in *Beyond the Ancient Quarrel: Literature, Philosophy, and J. M. Coetzee*, ed. Patrick Hayes and Jan Wilm (Oxford: Oxford University Press, 2017), 72.

27. Pippin, "What Does J. M. Coetzee's *The Childhood of Jesus* Have to Do with the Childhood of Jesus?," 25.

28. David James, "'Spare Prose and a Spare, Thrifty World,'" 110.

29. See Griem, "'Good Paragraphing. Unusual Content,'" 72–73, 84.

30. Rabaté points out that the story of Simón and David meeting during a search for his lost letter on the boat going to Belstar "comes straight out of Kafka, with Simón playing the role of the uncle who appears miraculously at the end of the first chapter of *Der Verschollene* or *Amerika*, an allegorical novel narrating the discovery of a new country, a novel with which *The Childhood of Jesus* has much in common." Jean-Michel Rabaté, "Pathos of the Future: Writing

and Hospitality in *The Childhood of Jesus*," in *J. M. Coetzee's* The Childhood of Jesus, ed. Rutherford and Uhlmann, 43.

31. Pippin, "What Does J. M. Coetzee's *The Childhood of Jesus* Have to Do with the Childhood of Jesus?," 16.

32. Friedrich Nietzsche, *Thus Spoke Zarathustra: A Book for All and None*, ed. Robert Pippin, trans. Adrian Del Caro (Cambridge: Cambridge University Press, 2006), 16.

33. Pippin "What Does J. M. Coetzee's *The Childhood of Jesus* Have to Do with the Childhood of Jesus?," 17, 26.

34. Derek Attridge, "Against Allegory," in *J. M. Coetzee and the Ethics of Reading*, 57. Henceforth cited parenthetically as AA.

35. Coetzee describes the scene of the strangely sexualized adoption ritual Simón intrudes on in the following way: "Diego's sister is kneeling on the bed with her back to them, straddling the boy—who lies flat on his back beneath her—her dress hoisted up to allow a glimpse of solid, rather heavy thighs. "Where is the spider, where is the spider . . . ?" she croons in a high, thin voice. Her fingers drift down his chest to his belt buckle; she tickles him, convulsing him in helpless laughter (CJ, 81). In *The Golden Bough*, Frazer writes of an adoption ritual in Bulgaria and among the Bosnian Turks, that "a woman will take a boy whom she intends to adopt and push or pull him through her clothes; ever afterwards he is regarded as her very son." Sir James Frazer, *The Golden Bough: A Study in Magic and Religion* (New York: Macmillan, 1922), 15. Wittgenstein's comment on this observation in his *Remarks on Frazer's "Golden Bough"* is as follows: "If the adoption of a child proceeds in such a way that the mother draws it from under her clothes, it is surely insane to believe that an error is present and that she believes she has given birth to the child." Ludwig Wittgenstein, *Remarks on Frazer's "Golden Bough,"* in *Philosophical Occasions, 1912–1951*, ed. James Klagge and Alfred Nordmann (Indianapolis: Hackett, 1993), 125.

36. Griem, "'Good Paragraphing. Unusual Content,'" 84.

37. See Joshua Landy, *How to Do Things with Fictions* (New York: Oxford University Press, 2012), 8–19.

38. Stephen Mulhall, "Health and Deviance, Irony and Incarnation: Embedding and Embodying Philosophy in Literature and Theology in *The Childhood of Jesus*," in *Beyond the Ancient Quarrel*, ed. Hayes and Wilm, 33. Henceforth cited parenthetically as "Health and Deviance."

39. Coetzee, "Jerusalem Prize Acceptance Speech," 98–99.

40. Pippin, "What Does J. M. Coetzee's *The Childhood of Jesus* Have to Do with the Childhood of Jesus?," 24.

41. Good Reads, "Community Reviews," https://www.goodreads.com/book/show/15799416-the-childhood-of-jesus.

42. Griem, "'Good Paragraphing. Unusual Content,'" 84–88; Tajiri, "Beyond the Literary Theme Park."

43. The growing fascination with Coetzee's fiction among a certain close network of philosophers, and those working on Wittgenstein and ethics under their influence, can be attributed to a number of overlapping factors: Coetzee's engagement with philosophical and ethical questions; his close long-term relationship

with members of the Department of Philosophy and the Committee on Social Thought at the University of Chicago and with Raimond Gaita in Australia; the influence of Cora Diamond's paper "The Difficulty of Reality and the Difficulty of Philosophy," in Cavell et al., *Philosophy and Animal Life* (New York: Columbia University Press, 2008); and philosophical engagement with Coetzee's Tanner Lectures more generally in that same volume, which features essays by Stanley Cavell, John McDowell, Ian Hacking, and Cary Wolfe alongside Diamond's. See also Stanley Cavell, "Companionable Thinking," in *Philosophy and Animal Life*, 91–126; Alice Crary, "Coetzee's Quest" and her "J. M. Coetzee, Moral Thinker," in *J. M. Coetzee and Ethics: Philosophical Perspectives on Literature*, ed. Anton Leist and Peter Singer (New York: Columbia University Press, 2010), 249–68; Raimond Gaita, *Good and Evil: An Absolute Conception*, 2nd ed. (London: Routledge, 2004); Raimond Gaita, *A Common Humanity: Thinking about Love and Truth and Justice* (London: Routledge, 2000); Raimond Gaita, *The Philosopher's Dog* (London: Routledge, 2003). Nora Hämäläinen discusses Gaita's references to *Disgrace* in her "Honor, Dignity and the Realm of Meaning," in *Language, Ethics and Animal Life: Wittgenstein and Beyond*, ed. Niklas Forsbert, Mikel Burley, and Nora Hämäläinen (London: Bloomsbury, 2012), 179–94. Stephen Mulhall, *The Wounded Animal: J. M. Coetzee and the Difficulty of Reality in Literature and Philosophy* (Princeton, NJ: Princeton University Press, 2009); Pippin, "What Does J. M. Coetzee's *The Childhood of Jesus* Have to Do with the Childhood of Jesus?," 9–32; Jonathan Lear, "The Ethical Thought of J. M. Coetzee," *Raritan* 28, no. 1 (Summer 2008): 68–97.

44. Wittgenstein's main attack on the idea of a private language can be found at PI, §§244–71. These sections, especially those from §256 onward, are commonly known as "the private language argument." The passages of the *Philosophical Investigations* that are referred to as the "rule-following sections" fall roughly between §143 and §202.

45. See Roger Bellin, "A Strange Allegory: J. M. Coetzee's *The Childhood of Jesus*; Theodor Adorno, "Notes on Kafka," in *Prisms* (Cambridge, MA: MIT Press, 1982), 96.

46. Griem, "'Good Paragraphing. Unusual Content,'" 86.

47. From prefatory remarks made at reading of an excerpt from his work in progress *The Childhood of Jesus* at the University of Capetown on December 21, 2012. Video available at https://www.youtube.com/watch?v=yXufoko-HgM.

48. See Pippin, "What Does J. M. Coetzee's *The Childhood of Jesus* Have to Do with the Childhood of Jesus?"; Rabaté, "Pathos of the Future"; and *The Infancy Gospels of James and Thomas*, ed. and trans. Ronald F. Hock (Santa Rosa, CA: Scholar's Bible, 1995), 111–35.

49. Rabaté, "Pathos of the Future," 55.

50. Fairy tales are another literary genre of interest to both Coetzee and Wittgenstein. The eerie Grimm-inspired fairy tale "Three Sons" that Inés tells David (and which the child then narrates to Simón) is thus also worth considering in relation to Wittgenstein's views about the ethically instructive power of fairy tales, as well as in relation to Diamond's frequent use of fairy tales in her own writing on Wittgenstein and moral philosophy. CJ, 146–47.

51. We saw one such example in Kafka's "On Parables" in chapter 2. Beckett is another writer whose works provide a wealth of examples of such jokes. One particularly fine example is to be found in *Endgame*:

> CLOV: Do you believe in the life to come?
> HAMM: Mine was always that. (Samuel Beckett, *Endgame*
> [New York: Grove, 1958], 49)

> See also Stanley Cavell's discussion of the terrible sadness of this deep joke, with its "knockout punchline," in his "Ending the Waiting Game," in *Must We Mean What We Say?* (Cambridge: Cambridge University Press, 1969), 121–22.

52. Adorno, "Notes on Kafka," 96.

53. Rita Felski, *The Limits of Critique* (Chicago: University of Chicago Press, 2015), 6.

54. See also James Conant, "Kierkegaard, Wittgenstein and Nonsense," in *Pursuits of Reason: Essays in Honor of Stanley Cavell*, ed. Ted Cohen, Paul Guyer, and Hilary Putnam (Lubbock: Texas Tech Press, 1993), 218.

55. Maria DiBattista, "*Ulysses*'s Unanswered Questions," *Modernism/modernity* 15, no. 2 (April 2008): 271.

56. A minor proviso: While I am on board with Moi's arguments about how our reading practices involve looking and thinking (and bringing our knowledge, curiosity, and thematic, formal, political, and ethical interests to bear on the texts we interpret), rather than any particular institutionally hardened critical method we may choose to employ over another, I am nonetheless at odds with her resistance to using words like "method" or "approach" when talking about what it is we do as literary critics or philosophers. Moi does not want to banish such words as they are commonly used (any more than she would reject words like "deep"), but only to steer us away from thinking of them scientistically (as Wittgenstein sought to do) as established scholarly critical methodologies or discrete spheres of theoretical inquiry, each competing for a place in the theoretical hierarchy. She instructively points to the announcement Cavell makes at the beginning of *The Claim of Reason* that he takes no rigid "approach" to the *Philosophical Investigations*, and to the fact that ordinary language philosophy proposes no method or laying down of requirements about how to read, but rather asks us to let the texts we read teach us how to consider them (just as Diamond suggests the *Tractatus* is a book that can teach us about ethical life even though there is nothing ethical said in it). While Moi's attention to the word "spirit" (which for her stands in opposition to "approach" or "method") brings Wittgenstein's (and Diamond's and Felski's) teachings to bear on literary criticism in thought-provoking ways, "approach" and "method" (unlike "theory," which ordinary language philosophy does actively oppose) are not necessarily always at odds with the "spirit," "tone," or "mood" that are the conveyors of ethics for Wittgenstein. "Method" is, after all, the word Wittgenstein himself uses to describe what it is he gives readers. And "method" is commonly used by Wittgenstein commentators like Diamond and Conant to describe it, and to distinguish

it from "theory" as well. In any case, throughout this book I frequently use the word "method" to describe Wittgenstein's way of engaging his readers in a way that remains otherwise consonant with Moi's arguments on this point.

57. Derek Attridge, "Age of Bronze, State of Grace," in *J. M. Coetzee and the Ethics of Reading*, 198.

58. See Cora Diamond, "Anything but Argument?," in *The Realistic Spirit: Wittgenstein, Philosophy, and the Mind* (Cambridge, MA: MIT Press, 1991), 291–309. Attridge discusses Diamond at some length in several recent essays on Coetzee. In particular, see his "Age of Bronze, State of Grace," 198, 202; and " 'A Yes without a No': Philosophical Reason and the Ethics of Conversion in Coetzee's Fiction," in *Beyond the Ancient Quarrel: Literature, Philosophy, and J. M. Coetzee*, ed. Patrick Hayes and Jan Wilm (Oxford: Oxford University Press, 2017), 96–97, 101, 106.

59. Attridge, "Modernist Form and the Ethics of Otherness," 7.

60. Coetzee and Kurtz, *Good Story*, 156. Lear, "Ethical Thought of J. M. Coetzee," 77; J. M. Coetzee, *Diary of a Bad Year* (London: Harvill Secker, 2007), 7.

61. Lear, "Ethical Thought of J. M. Coetzee," 77.

62. Ludwig Wittgenstein, *Wittgenstein's Lectures, Cambridge, 1932–1935: From the Notes of Alice Ambrose and Margaret MacDonald*, ed. Alice Ambrose (Chicago: Chicago University Press, 1979), 97.

63. Jan Wilm, *The Slow Philosophy of J. M. Coetzee* (London: Bloomsbury, 2016), 67.

64. Martin Woessner, "Coetzee's Critique of Reason," in *J. M. Coetzee and Ethics: Philosophical Perspectives on Literature* (New York: Columbia University Press, 2010), 241; Robert Pippin, *Henry James and Modern Moral Life* (Cambridge: Cambridge University Press, 2000), 240–41.

65. Lear, "Ethical Thought of J. M. Coetzee," 72.

66. Diamond, "Difficulty of Reality and the Difficulty of Philosophy," 56.

67. Walter Benjamin, "Franz Kafka: On the Tenth Anniversary of His Death," in *Illuminations: Essays and Reflections*, ed. Hannah Arendt, trans. Harry Zohn (New York: Schocken Books, 1968), 124.

68. In the context of this discussion of Wittgenstein's philosophical investment in conversion with reference to Kuhn's notion of the paradigm shift, it is worth pointing to the intimate relationship between the two. Kuhn's concept of the paradigm shift grew out of discussions with Cavell in the 1950s when they were colleagues at Berkeley and he had begun work on *The Structure of Scientific Revolution*. In *Revolution of the Ordinary*, Moi explores the communicative failures that lead to a mutual misunderstanding between ordinary language philosophers and critics working in a post-Saussurean tradition (as well as between ordinary language philosophers and positivists of the Anglo-American analytic tradition) in terms of the link between the figure of the duck-rabbit—emblem of Wittgenstein's investigations of aspect seeing—and Kuhnian paradigm shifts. Adherents to competing philosophical or critical paradigms, she argues, quoting Kuhn, "practice their trades in different worlds." Because the outlooks of members of these separate camps are so radically divergent, when they look on the same ideas, events, or texts, what they see are radically different things. What

seems intuitively obvious to one group appears utterly indemonstrable to the other. Where one sees only the duck, then, the other sees only the rabbit, resistant to the perceptive switching they would need to do to reach a shared understanding. See Thomas Kuhn, *The Structure of Scientific Revolution* (Chicago: University of Chicago Press, 1970), 150, quoted in Moi, RO, 10. The transformative aspects of Wittgenstein's philosophical revolution (legible in his commitment to getting readers to overcome nonsense, illusion, self-deception, or the wrong outlook or picture by adopting a different ethical attitude or way of seeing the world "rightly" or more perspicuously) is thus something worth exploring in a decidedly secular vein in relation to Kuhnian paradigm shifts (especially given Kuhn's connection to Cavell), even as we take seriously the decidedly spiritual aspects of the conversional aims of Wittgenstein's philosophy by attending to the lifelong interest in personal and scriptural religious conversion and the impact it made on his philosophical work.

69. Rabaté, "Pathos of the Future, 33–55. See also Barnstone, *The Other Bible*, 43.

70. For a fuller discussion of states of grace and disgrace in that novel, see Attridge, "Age of Bronze, State of Grace."

71. James Joyce, *Ulysses* (New York: Random House, 1934), 476.

72. Ludwig Wittgenstein, *Notebooks 1914–1916*, ed. G. H. von Wright and G. E. M. Anscombe, trans. G. E. M. Anscombe (Chicago: University of Chicago Press, 1961), 73.

73. Martin Woessner argues that Coetzee's recent fiction resonates with recent "post-secular" thought in that his devotion to the possibilities of the imagination opens up a space of possibility that the polar extremes of strict secularism and a strict religious fundamentalism foreclose. Woessner, "Beyond Realism: Coetzee's Post-Secular Imagination," in *Beyond the Ancient Quarrel: Literature, Philosophy, and J. M. Coetzee*, ed. Patrick Hayes and Jan Wilm (Oxford: Oxford University Press, 2017), 144–45).

74. Crary, "Coetzee's Quest," 135.

75. J. M. Coetzee, "Leo Tolstoy, *The Death of Ivan Ilyich*," in *Late Essays: 2006–2017* (New York: Viking, 2017), 156.

76. For a discussion of David's aberrant relation to mathematics in the novel, see Baylee Brits, "The Name of the Number: Transfinite Mathematics in *The Childhood of Jesus*," in *J. M. Coetzee's* The Childhood of Jesus, ed. Rutherford and Uhlmann, 129–48. See also Coetzee's "Confession and Double Thoughts: Tolstoy, Rousseau, Dostoevsky," *Comparative Literature* 37, no. 3 (1985): 193–232.

77. Crary, "Coetzee's Quest," 138.

78. Coetzee talks about reading as a conversion experience in his contribution to a roundtable discussion with Matthew Calarco, Harlan B. Miller, and Cary Wolfe, in John M. Coetzee, "Comments on Paola Cavalieri, 'A Dialogue on Perfectionism,'" in Paola Cavalieri, *The Death of the Animal: A Dialogue* (New York: Columbia University Press, 2008), 89.

79. Attridge, "'A Yes without a No," 100–101.

80. Coetzee, "Leo Tolstoy, *The Death of Ivan Ilyich*," 158.

81. Adorno writes: "Through the power with which Kafka commands interpretation, he collapses aesthetic distance. He demands a desperate effort of the

allegedly 'disinterested' observer of an earlier time, overwhelms him, suggesting that far more than his intellectual equilibrium depends on whether he truly understands; life and death are at stake. Among Kafka's presuppositions, not the least is that the contemplative relation between text and reader is shaken to its very roots." Adorno, "Notes on Kafka," 96.

82. J. M. Coetzee, "Reading Gerald Murnane," in *Late Essays: 2006–2017* (New York: Viking, 2017), 260.

83. Crary, "Coetzee's Quest," 135.

84. See James Conant, "Putting Two and Two Together: Wittgenstein, Kierkegaard, and the Point of View for Their Work as Authors," in *Philosophy and the Grammar of Religious Belief*, ed. Timothy Tessin and Mario von der Ruhr (New York: St. Martin's, 1995), 302–3.

85. Virginia Woolf, "Modern Fiction," in *The Essays of Virginia Woolf*, vol. 4, *1925 to 1928*, ed. Andrew McNeillie (London: Hogarth, 1984), 159–60.

86. Felski, *Limits of Critique*, 2.

87. Ludwig Wittgenstein, *Tractatus Logico-Philosophicus*, trans. C. K. Ogden (London: Routledge and Kegan Paul, 1922), 6.54; Ludwig Wittgenstein, *Tractatus Logico-Philosophicus*, trans. D. F. Pears and B. F. McGuinness (London: Routledge and Kegan Paul, 1961), 6.54. Henceforth cited parenthetically as TLP, followed by proposition number (or page number from Pears McGuinness's 1961 edition for passages from Russell's introduction and Wittgenstein's preface).

88. Ludwig Wittgenstein, *Culture and Value*, ed. G. H. von Wright, with Heikki. Nyman, trans. Peter Winch (Chicago: University of Chicago Press), 7. Henceforth cited as CV.

89. Ludwig Wittgenstein, "A Lecture on Ethics," in *Philosophical Occasions, 1912–1951*, ed. Klagge and Nordmann, 44. Henceforth cited parenthetically as LE.

90. For a fuller account of Coetzee's intertextual engagement with Plato's *Republic* in *The Childhood of Jesus*, see Lynda Ng and Paul Sheehan, "Coetzee's Republic: Plato, Borges and Migrant Memory in *The Childhood of* Jesus," in *J. M. Coetzee's* The Childhood of Jesus, ed. Rutherford and Uhlmann, 83–106. See also Mulhall, "Health and Deviance," 18–21.

91. See R. Lanier Anderson, "Nietzsche on Redemption and Transfiguration," in *The Re-enchantment of the World*, ed. Joshua Landy and Michael Saler (Stanford CA: Stanford University Press, 2009), 225–58.

92. Ben Ware, "Ethics," in *Understanding Wittgenstein, Understanding Modernism*, ed. Anat Matar (London: Bloomsbury, 2017), 255. See also Ben Ware, *The Dialectic of the Ladder: Wittgenstein, the "Tractatus" and Modernism* (London: Bloomsbury, 2015), 17–20.

93. Theodor Adorno, *Notes to Literature*, vol. 2, ed. Rolf Tiedmann, trans. Shierry Weber Nicholsen (New York: Columbia University Press, 1992), 93. Quoted in Ware, *Dialectic of the Ladder*, 20.

94. Cora Diamond, "Introduction to 'Having a Rough Story about What Moral Philosophy Is,'" in *The Literary Wittgenstein*, ed. John Gibson and Wolfgang Huemer (London: Routledge, 2004), 131. For further discussion of Wittgenstein's openness to Keatsian negative capability, see Michael LeMahieu,

Fictions of Fact and Value: The Erasure of Logical Positivism in American Literature, 1945–1975 (New York: Oxford University Press, 2013), 49; and Marjorie Perloff, *The Edge of Irony: Modernism in the Shadow of the Habsburg Empire* (Chicago: University of Chicago Press, 2016), 167.

95. Diamond, "Difficulty of Reality and the Difficulty of Philosophy," 48, 53.

96. Diamond, "Difficulty of Reality and the Difficulty of Philosophy," 69. For Cavell on deflection, see Stanley Cavell, "Knowing and Acknowledging," in *Must We Mean What We Say?* (Cambridge: Cambridge University Press, 1969), 238–66; and Cavell, "Declining Decline," 29–76. See also Virginia Woolf, "The Novels of George Meredith" (1928), reprinted in *Collected Essays*, ed. Leonard Woolf, 4 vols. (London Chatto and Windus, 1966–67), 1:230; and Virginia Woolf, "Philosophy in Fiction" (1918), in *The Essays of Virginia Woolf*, vol. 2, *1912–1918*, ed. Andrew McNeillie (New York: Harcourt Brace Jovanovich, 1987), 208–12.

97. Griem, "'Good Paragraphing. Unusual Content,'" 88.

98. J. M. Coetzee, "The Novel Today," *Upstream* 6, no. 1 (1988): 4. Quoted in Attridge, "Against Allegory," 37.

99. Norman Malcolm, *Wittgenstein: A Religious Point of View?*, ed. Peter Winch (Ithaca, NY: Cornell University Press, 1994), 97.

100. Northrop Frye, *Anatomy of Criticism* (New York: Atheneum, 1969), 89; Fredric Jameson, *Political Unconscious: Narrative as a Social Symbolic Act* (Ithaca, NY: Cornell University Press, 1981), 10.

101. See Susan Sontag, "Against Interpretation," in *Against Interpretation and Other Essays* (New York: Farrar, Straus and Giroux, 1966), 3–14; and Donald Davidson, "What Metaphors Mean," in *On Metaphor*, ed. Sheldon Sacks (Chicago: University of Chicago Press, 1979), 29–45.

102. Crary, "Coetzee's Quest," 138.

103. Benjamin, "Franz Kafka: On the Tenth Anniversary of His Death," 122.

104. Benjamin, "Franz Kafka: On the Tenth Anniversary of His Death," 122.

105. Frank Kermode, "Hoti's Business: Why Are Narratives Obscure?," in *The Genesis of Secrecy* (Cambridge, MA: Harvard University Press, 1980), 23.

106. Kermode, "Hoti's Business," 45.

107. Kermode, "Hoti's Business," 32.

108. See Conant, "Putting Two and Two Together," 248–331.

109. See Cora Diamond, "Throwing Away the Ladder: How to Read the *Tractatus*," in *The Realistic Spirit: Wittgenstein, Philosophy, and the Mind* (Cambridge, MA: MIT Press, 1991), 179–204.

Index

Cook, Eleanor, 289n56
counteradaptation, 207, 209, 245, 248, 260, 261, 266
Crary, Alice, 60, 231, 249, 250, 252, 271, 273
creativity, 41, 62, 64, 104, 194, 197, 208
curiosity, 112, 166, 200, 246, 257; death of, 226, 264

daily life, 63–64, 76, 79, 87–88, 97, 146, 198, 220. *See also* domesticity; everyday life/the everyday
Davidson, Donald, 270
death, 136–37, 144–45, 150, 154; in Coetzee, 227, 262–63; in Joyce, 176–77, 180, 189, 201, 209; in Kafka, 101, 104; and/in Wittgenstein, 41, 126, 194; in Woolf, 125, 127, 131, 134, 137, 138–39, 142, 154–58
Defoe, Daniel, 225, 230
deictics, 120, 133, 135–36
despair, 104, 111, 117, 124, 147, 185, 197
Detloff, Madelyn, 107
Diamond, Cora, 3, 14, 17–18, 28, 49–51, 57, 62–63, 76, 78, 83, 92, 94–95, 98, 108–10, 115–17, 121–22, 135, 171–72, 177–79, 181–82, 187, 191–92, 195, 198–200, 204, 207, 210–11, 231, 239, 241–42, 246, 251, 254, 267–68, 284n22; "The Difficulty of Reality and the Difficulty of Philosophy," 23, 37, 109–10, 116, 125, 128, 142–46, 149–53, 156, 160–61, 243, 268; "Ethics and Imagination and the Method of Wittgenstein's *Tractatus*," 50, 58, 62–63, 140–42, 152–53
DiBattista, Maria, 176–77, 190, 191–92, 240
Dickinson, Emily, 100
Diepeveen, Leonard, 25
difficulty: contingent, 29, 184; different order of, 6, 8–9, 28–29, 35–37,

109, 142, 160, 166, 180, 184–85, 220, 223; different orders/modes of, 5, 7, 25, 29, 35–36, 50, 65–66, 175; modal, 29; ontological, 29, 33–34, 100; of reality, 37, 109–10, 121, 126, 142–46, 148–62, 200, 243, 246, 254; tactical, 6, 9, 29–33, 50, 67–68, 71, 100, 220, 222
dignity, 158, 195, 197
discovery, 12, 120–21, 148, 197, 213, 221, 257
disenchantment, 18, 118, 204, 254
dissatisfaction, 140, 170–72, 199, 257, 259, 265
doctrine, 44, 86–87, 187, 191; philosophical/metaphysical, 3–4, 21, 47, 50–51, 59–60, 184, 261; religious/moral, 113, 179, 268, 273, 275. *See also* pseudo/mock/faux doctrine
dogma, 18, 38, 87, 118, 166, 191, 204, 210, 212; antidogmatic spirit, 87
domesticity, 133, 189, 227
Dostoevsky, Fyodor, 34, 112, 119, 121, 126, 150, 230

Eagleton, Terry, 213
Eldridge, Richard, 111, 120
elegy, 110, 161, 305n20
Eliot, T. S., 25, 26–27, 45, 165, 174, 216, 236, 315n20
elitism, 14–15, 27, 30–32
Emerson, Ralph Waldo, 16
emotion, 94, 111, 112, 188, 189
Empson, William, 25
endings: in Chekhov, 112; in Coetzee, 220, 229; in Joyce, 165, 167–68, 182, 185, 190, 193, 209; in Kafka, 104; in Wittgenstein, 185, 193; in Woolf, 161
Engelmann, Paul, 69, 114, 196, 198, 292n25, 307n37; Wittgenstein to, 187
enlightenment, 8, 12, 32, 72, 175, 180, 202, 264
epiphany, 5, 38, 105, 124, 126, 145, 162, 165, 168–70, 174, 192, 202–

Barré, Mallarmé + the Art of
Being Difficult, 1978